George Cross Heroes

George Cross Heroes

MICHAEL ASHCROFT

FOREWORD BY
CHRISTINA SCHMID

headline
review

First published in 2010
by HEADLINE REVIEW

An imprint of Headline Publishing Group

1

Cataloguing in Publication Data is available from the British Library

ISBN 978 0 7553 6082 6

Picture research: Jane Sherwood

Typeset in GaramondThree by Avon DataSet Ltd,
Bidford-on-Avon, Warwickshire

Printed and bound in Great Britain by
Clays Ltd, St Ives plc

Headline's policy is to use papers that are natural, renewable and
recyclable products and made from wood grown in sustainable forests.
The logging and manufacturing processes are expected to conform
to the environmental regulations of the country of origin.

HEADLINE PUBLISHING GROUP
An Hachette UK Company
338 Euston Road
London NW1 3BH

www.headline.co.uk
www.hachette.co.uk

This book is dedicated to all the brave men and women who risked and, in some cases, gave their lives in gallant actions that led to them being awarded the George Cross.

CONTENTS

ACKNOWLEDGEMENTS

I am indebted to the Victoria Cross and George Cross Association for its assistance in enabling me to research this book. Didy Grahame, the association's secretary, could not have been more helpful and I thank her for her time and patience. I have long been an admirer – and supporter – of the association's work in looking after the welfare of the holders of the Victoria Cross (VC) and George Cross (GC). In recognition of all its splendid work, I am donating all my author's royalties from this book to the association.

Furthermore, I am grateful to many of the living recipients of the GC for providing interviews for this book, and for enabling me to learn more about their backgrounds and the circumstances that led to them being awarded the decoration. In some cases, my gratitude extends to the families of the recipients of the GC.

My thanks go to Angela Entwistle, my corporate communications director. Angela and her team not only helped get this project off the ground but worked hard to assist me in the preparation and promotion of this book.

I am grateful to Michael Naxton, my medals' consultant, for allowing me to benefit from his expertise and his enthusiasm for gallantry awards. Michael was an invaluable sounding board and, like Didy Grahame, was kind enough to read and suggest corrections to the first draft of this book.

For the third time in five years, I am grateful to Headline for publishing a book of mine on bravery. It is always a delight dealing with Emma Tait and her team. I thank Headline and

Emma for, once again, enabling me to bring my passion for gallantry to a wider audience.

I am grateful to the Ministry of Defence for allowing me to interview Warrant Officer Class 2 (WO2) Kim Hughes, who is still serving in the Royal Logistic Corps, for this book.

My thanks go to Richard Bird, the former Secretary of the Ministry of Defence's Armed Forces Operational Awards Committee (AFOAC), who was kind enough to give me succinct guidance on the process relating to the award of a military GC.

I am not the first, and will not be the last, person to write about the GC. I cannot name everyone who has gone there before me but it would be wrong not to highlight the devotion and commitment of Marion Hebblethwaite to the award. She, along with her late husband Roger, accumulated enough information and anecdotes to write no fewer than nine volumes on the recipients of the GC. I am more than happy to acknowledge that her diligently amassed material provided biographical and other information used in this book. I also commend the books of John Frayn Turner and the late Brigadier The Rt Hon. Sir John 'Jackie' Smyth Bt, VC, MC, who have both written knowledgeably and passionately about the GC.

Last, but certainly not least, my gratitude goes to Christina Schmid, the widow of Staff Sergeant Olaf 'Oz' Schmid, who was awarded a posthumous GC as recently as March 2010. By all accounts, Schmid was a quite remarkable character and I am sure that Lieutenant Colonel Robert Thomson, the Commanding Officer of 2 Rifles Battle Group, chose his words carefully when he described his comrade as 'simply the bravest and most courageous man I have ever met'. I have been hugely impressed with Christina Schmid's commitment to ensuring that her husband's bravery should be widely recognised and to improving working conditions for his comrades. I thank her for doing me the honour of writing the foreword to my book.

FOREWORD

by Christina Schmid, the widow of Staff Sergeant Olaf 'Oz' Schmid GC

The George Cross is a wonderful subject for a book. Behind each of the 161 awards of the decoration is a remarkable story of gallantry. Often such courage also involves other human qualities too – including loyalty, duty, self-sacrifice, citizenship and humility.

When my husband, Staff Sergeant Olaf 'Oz' Schmid, was awarded a posthumous George Cross in March 2010, it meant a huge amount to me and to all his family. Oz was a unique maverick and I feel the award captured the essence of him and everything he represented. I had always known that Oz had been consistently brave in all areas of his life, particularly his bomb disposal work in Afghanistan. However, after I learnt about the exact circumstances in which Oz had died, I decorated him in my own mind with a gallantry medal because I was convinced that he deserved one. When it was announced much later that he had been awarded the George Cross, I felt an overwhelming sense of pride. When I read the citation, I had an enormous sense of satisfaction that Oz's bravery had been so carefully recorded for posterity. I also felt a sense of justice that Oz's relentless bravery had, finally, been publicly recognised. I know that if Oz was still alive, he would have been 'wowed' by what has been said about him. At the same time, he would have considered that his George Cross was for all his bomb disposal team. Yet I have spoken to his team and they have insisted that he was the 'superstar' – he was the person whose gallantry needed to be recognised.

I am a great believer in the concept of bravery awards. I admire the egalitarian aspect of most gallantry medals – the fact they can be awarded to people of all military ranks or from civilian life irrespective of their gender, religion and creed in order to recognise an act, or several acts, of particular gallantry. The award of a George Cross and other decorations sends a clear message to every individual that if he, or she, steps up to the plate and risks his, or her, life, then that exceptional bravery will be acclaimed.

Seventy years ago Europe was in the grip of war and turmoil. As the bombs fell on Britain's major cities and towns during the Blitz, the horror of global conflict was brought home to civilians from all walks of life. The Second World War witnessed not just great courage by our servicemen on foreign soil, in the skies and at sea, but also great gallantry by those at home. Up and down the United Kingdom, acts of outstanding bravery were regularly taking place for which the terms of existing military and civilian decorations were not deemed appropriate. Hence, the King and his ministers entered into a debate which, in turn, led to the creation of the George Cross.

Today, in places such as Afghanistan and Iraq, we are witnessing a new kind of warfare but the George Cross is as relevant today as it was when its creation was announced by George VI on 23 September 1940. Those who have been awarded the George Cross over the past seventy years represent a wide spectrum of different personalities and yet they all have a common strand: an overwhelming sense of humanity.

Lord Ashcroft has written a remarkable and uplifting book that gives an insight into the very best of human nature. I commend him for his diligence in recording so carefully the gallantry of so many in such frightening and difficult circumstances. Furthermore, I commend him for his decision to donate all his author's royalties from this book to the Victoria Cross and George Cross Association and for his incredible generosity in donating £5 million to build the Lord Ashcroft Gallery at the Imperial War Museum. I am certain that over the coming years the new gallery will enable hundreds of thousands of visitors to appreciate the outstanding qualities of the recipients of both the George Cross and Victoria Cross – those who are deserving of their place in history as the 'bravest of the brave'.

I share Lord Ashcroft's conviction that we must never forget those who have risked or even, like my courageous husband and others, given their lives to help others. And I am sure that everyone who reads this book will join me in thanking Lord Ashcroft for doing so much to highlight the merits of a quite exceptional British creation: the George Cross.

PREFACE

My half-century-long fascination with bravery stems partly from the fact that I do not – and never will – fully understand it. As someone who was born the year after the Second World War ended, I have never lived through a conflict that engulfed our entire nation and I have never had to fight for my country. However, in the early days of researching this book, I quickly realised that even those who have displayed supreme gallantry and who have read countless books on the subject find it equally difficult to measure bravery or fully to comprehend it.

The late Brigadier Sir John Smyth, the author of masterly books on gallantry, once wrote that 'any sort' of man could be awarded the Victoria Cross (VC) or George Cross (GC), adding: 'There is no rhyme or reason about it.' He felt, however, that courage was expendable: 'Most people only have a limited amount of it – and if the pitcher is taken too often to the well, then the well will run dry.' He felt that some physical torture or mental brain-washing might present greater tests of courage than bravery in battle but he added with refreshing honesty: 'I can't attempt to answer the unanswerable. Who can say whether it takes more courage to attack an angry bull elephant with a spear, than to disarm a very sensitive mine, or to have your toenails pulled out and still disclose nothing, or to dive into a burning aircraft to try to pull out members of the crew when the rescuer was well aware that the plane was carrying bombs which might explode at any moment.'

Sir John, Jackie to his friends, was also the founder, first Chairman and, after Sir Winston Churchill, the President, of the Victoria Cross and George Cross Association. If someone as brave and as knowledgeable as him could not understand bravery, then who am I – an international businessman – to answer such a riddle. So, instead of trying to comprehend gallantry, I have decided simply to cherish it and to pay tribute to those who have displayed it in abundance.

George Cross Heroes is my third book on the subject of bravery. My two previous titles, *Victoria Cross Heroes* and *Special Forces Heroes*, opened new doors for me and allowed me to meet some incredible characters who had risked their lives for their comrades and their country. Invariably, the gallantry of these individuals was matched only by their modesty.

As someone who has built up the largest collection of VCs in the world – well over a tenth of those in existence – I decided some time ago that I wanted to do something unique to bring the merits of the award and its recipients to a wider audience. It was for this reason that I announced in 2008 that I was donating £5 million so that a new gallery could be built at the Imperial War Museum in London. Not only will the new Lord Ashcroft Gallery, due to open in November 2010, house the collection of more than 160 VCs that I started assembling in 1986, but it will also show the VCs and GCs owned by, or in the care of, the museum.

George Cross Heroes tells the stories behind the award of 161 decorations earned in very differing circumstances. Yet each award has one thing in common – it was made for gallant deeds above and beyond the call of duty. This book deals only with the direct awards of the GC made in and after 1940. This is not, I stress, to belittle in any way the considerable achievements of those who received the GC after one of three awards – the Albert, Edward and Empire Gallantry Medals – were converted to GCs. I took the decision to concentrate on the direct awards for two reasons. First, 161 decorations is a far more manageable number than the total number of direct and converted decorations. Furthermore, information about many of the early

Albert, Edward and Empire Gallantry Medals is, sometimes, decidedly sketchy whereas, in general, there was more readily available material on the direct winners from the last seventy years.

The majority of the GCs that have been awarded were for gallantry linked to bomb disposal work, most for actions during the Second World War. This role was as important and dangerous during the Blitz of 1940 as it is today in Afghanistan. In the spring of 2010, I was privileged to be able to spend a full day observing and participating in the 'continuation training' of British servicemen at Merville Barracks, near Colchester, Essex. My generous hosts for the day were 621 EOD (Explosive Ordnance Disposal) Squadron, part of 11 EOD Regiment. The day provided me with a fascinating insight into the work that bomb disposal personnel undertake. Initially, in the morning, I learnt about conventional munitions disposal (CMD) work: how to dispose of a potentially deadly device, whether it is a rusting Second World War bomb or a sophisticated new hand grenade. Then, in the afternoon, I moved on to the even more high-risk improvised explosive device disposal (IEDD) work: how to deal with devices such as roadside bombs. During the morning, I saw live explosives detonated on a demolitions range only to be told that in Afghanistan the common IEDs are forty times larger than the ones I saw being exploded. This provided plenty of food for thought for my afternoon session when I was carrying out fingertip searches on a lifelike 'device' similar to those routinely encountered by our servicemen abroad. In the words of my host, Warrant Officer Class 2 (Staff Quarter Master Sergeant) Justin Bell, I was assessing and touching something that was 'very, very violent'. My host, a veteran ammunition technician who had been awarded the Queen's Gallantry Medal, contrasted the type of scenario regularly encountered by servicemen in Afghanistan with the situation they have faced in Northern Ireland. Both countries, he said, 'have equally devious terrorists'.

I participated in the Afghanistan scenario where the 'heat' meant I was only able to wear body armour and a helmet. I was briefed that a patrol had come across an area of suspicious ground and had identified the small corner of an IED: explosives wrapped in plastic with a wire coming off them. After the briefing, I was sent in to 'neutralise' the device. I had a close-protection bodyguard with me as I made my approach, oblivious of the fact that a 'secondary device' had been planted close to the first IED. I was talked through detailed procedures – which I will not repeat for security reasons. As I lay on the ground with my arms extended, I was able to 'neutralise' the initial device with a wire cutter. I then excavated the switch and was looking for the main charge – only to come across another firing system, which I also 'neutralised'. As I removed the main charge, I found a tertiary device: another IED underneath the original one designed to catch out the operator. The initial device weighed twenty kilograms and was two feet square; the tertiary device was shoebox size. I learnt that the 'Rolls-Royce' – or ideal – solution is rarely possible and it is then down to an individual's assessment of the situation as to what he, or she, does next. The operator bases his, or her, decision on training, experience and judgement, always knowing that one error will result in him, or her, being killed. I later learnt the IEDs I had dealt with had 'only' – my host's word not mine – been a 'mid-range' device in its complexity. My day had been exciting and terrifying in equal measure. One thing is certain: my experiences left me with an overwhelming feeling of admiration and respect for the absolutely astonishing courage of our bomb disposal teams.

I am delighted to say that in the summer of 2010, I bought my first GC. I negotiated the private purchase of the decoration and four other medals awarded to Special Constable Brandon Moss, of Coventry Police. The GC was awarded for his 'superhuman efforts and utter disregard for personal injury' in saving four lives during the bombing blitz on his home city on the night of 14/15 November 1940. This was a famous raid during which much of the city centre, including Coventry's historic cathedral, was destroyed. Moss's GC is the only decoration awarded to one of the 'Specials', as the old-time Special Constables were affectionately known. Moss's family is thrilled that the group is going to be on public display for the first time at the Lord Ashcroft Gallery. I feel it is appropriate that the initial GC that I have bought should be one of the first awarded to a civilian and for one of the most iconic incidents of the entire Second World War on the Home Front.

Although I have already conceded that I will never truly understand gallantry, I do know that great courage should be widely acclaimed and must never be forgotten. I hope the brave deeds detailed in these pages will inspire you as much as they have me.

'The bravest are surely those who have the clearest vision of what is before them, glory and danger alike, and yet notwithstanding, go out to meet it.'

Thucydides, Greek historian (c. 460–c. 395 BC)

1

A SHORT HISTORY
OF THE GEORGE CROSS

On 23 September 1940, King George VI addressed the nation to announce the institution of a new decoration for gallantry: the George Cross (GC). He said: 'In order that they should be worthily and promptly recognised, I have decided to create, at once, a new mark of honour for men and women in all walks of civilian life. I propose to give my name to this new distinction, which will consist of the George Cross, which will rank next to the Victoria Cross, and the George Medal for wider distribution.'

From the outset, the GC was intended to be a highly prestigious decoration and it would only be awarded to men and women who had shown quite outstanding bravery. The VC had been instituted by Queen Victoria in 1856 to recognise supreme gallantry in the face of the enemy – most notably for courage displayed by British servicemen during the Crimean War. Although the award was a resounding success, it was eventually realised that a separate award or decoration was needed to acknowledge supreme courage that did not actually take place in the heat of battle.

The King had adopted a painstaking approach towards planning the decoration and took enormous pride in getting it right. It was his wife, Queen Elizabeth (the Queen Mother), who later summarised the King's desire to respond to the unique circumstances of the Blitz early in the Second World War. As President of the Victoria Cross and George Cross Association, she wrote: 'In the early days of the war The King was impressed by some very heroic deeds in mine and bomb disposal: deeds performed far from any human enemy but requiring the peak of courage for a considerable time. He felt that no existing award for gallantry reflected such an impersonal bravery. In the following months there were more deeds of great courage when no enemy was present: more bombs and mines made safe, rescues after bombing, accident and disaster in truly terrifying circumstances.'

In short, the King had wanted to respond to the fact that the 'total' nature of the Second World War had brought the horror of conflict into civilian life as never before. This, in turn, had led to a number of incidents when astonishing bravery had been displayed by individuals who were not eligible for the VC owing to the fact that their bravery took place away from the battlefield. From early on, the new award was often referred to as 'the civilian VC', but this quickly proved to be somewhat inaccurate since a large number of the early GCs – no fewer than 76 of the first 100 awards – were, in fact, made to members of the Armed Forces.

George VI felt strongly that the terms of the existing non-military awards – notably the Albert, Edward and Empire Gallantry Medals – were not appropriate and he wanted to elevate the importance of acts of supreme gallantry that were not in the face of the enemy. He decided that in place of these decorations there should be two new awards: the GC and the George Medal. The GC was to be awarded for 'acts of the greatest heroism or of the most conspicuous courage in circumstances of great danger'. It was decided that the George Medal should be awarded for acts of great bravery that were not so outstanding as to merit the GC.

Although the latter was to be awarded more freely than the former, there was still a strong feeling that the standard of courage had to be high. The King decided that the GC, like the VC, could be awarded posthumously but that the George Medal could only be awarded to living men and women (this rule changed in 1978 when a new warrant meant the George Medal could also be awarded posthumously). To date, eighty-six awards – just over half of the total of GCs – have been posthumous.

The King ruled that his subjects in the British Commonwealth and Empire should likewise be eligible for the GC. He decided that it should be silver – a plain cross with four equal 'limbs'. In the centre, the cross would bear a circular medallion portraying St George slaying a dragon. The inscription around the central medallion would read simply: 'For Gallantry' – once again in common with the VC. George VI decided that in the angle of each limb of the cross, the royal cipher 'G VI' should form a circle concentric – sharing the same centre – with the medallion. The cross was to be worn suspended from a dark blue ribbon, which was to be 'garter blue'. It was stated that when the ribbon alone was worn it should have a miniature replica of the cross affixed to its centre – yet again another similarity to the VC. Originally, the cross was to be one and a quarter inches wide but this was increased to one and a half inches by a Royal Warrant of 8 May 1941.

The GC is worn on the left breast before all other decorations, with the exception of the VC. Women not in uniform wear the cross suspended from a wide bow of blue ribbon, below the left shoulder. The cross was designed by Percy Metcalfe and made by the Royal Mint. Engraved on the reverse is the name of the recipient and the date it was 'gazetted', i.e. the date the award was announced in the *London Gazette*, the Government's journal of record.

The King and others were aware that the terms of the new decoration might, in some cases, clash with existing awards: notably the Albert, Edward and Empire Gallantry Medals. The Albert Medal was named after Queen Victoria's husband and consort, Prince Albert, who had died on 14 December 1861. It was instituted on 7 March 1866 to be awarded for those who had risked their lives in trying to save others at sea. A Royal

Warrant issued in 1867 created two classes of Albert Medal: 1st and 2nd class. Ten years later, in 1877, the warrant was altered to allow the saving of life on land to be recognised by the award of the Albert Medal. On 13 July 1907, a Royal Warrant introduced the Edward Medal. This award was to recognise the bravery of miners and quarrymen who had risked their lives to rescue their fellow workers. On 1 December 1909, the original warrant was amended to broaden the category of recipients to include all industrial workers and this modification resulted in two versions of the Edward Medal: Mines and Industry. The Empire Gallantry Medal (officially called the Medal of the Order of the British Empire for Gallantry) was introduced on 29 December 1922. It had been instituted by George V and it was intended to recognise specific acts of gallantry.

The Empire Gallantry Medal was revoked by the Royal Warrant of 24 September 1940. Surviving holders, together with the next-of-kin of those who had been awarded the decoration posthumously, were required to have their decorations exchanged for the GC. Awards of the Albert and Edward Medals continued, but by the early 1970s it was acknowledged that there was little public appreciation of their importance. On 21 October 1971, it was announced that surviving holders of these decorations would have their awards translated to the GC and that no more Albert and Edward Medals would be awarded. Holders of the decorations were offered the opportunity to exchange their awards for the GC.

Early in the Second World War, Winston (later Sir Winston) Churchill, the great war-time Prime Minister, shared the King's enthusiasm for the new decoration. He realised that the Blitz would place a great strain on the residents of London and other cities and he believed that awards of the GC would be a significant morale booster for British citizens. It was Churchill who therefore personally issued firm instructions that recommendations for gallantry, particularly in the fields of rescue work or bomb disposal, should be delivered to him quickly in order to ensure deserving recipients had the minimum wait for their awards.

It was acknowledged early on that there would be times when, after supreme gallantry, it would be difficult to determine whether the GC or the VC was the appropriate decoration to be awarded. As I have stated, in the end 76 of the first 100 awards went to servicemen. Furthermore, this trend has continued. Of the 161 direct awards, only 50 have gone to civilians. The small number of civilians to receive the GC may be put down to both the demanding standards required for the award of the decoration and the fact that many members of the public remain unaware of the channels that must be followed in order to recommend someone for the award.

The rules relating to the GC allow that, as with the VC, a 'bar' – or second award – may be granted. However, whereas three men have received bars to their VCs, nobody has ever been honoured with a bar, or second, GC. No individual has ever been awarded the VC and the GC. Yet, the Seagrim family does have the honour of having members who were awarded the VC and the GC. Major (Temporary Lieutenant Colonel) Derek Anthony Seagrim and his brother, Temporary Major Hugh Paul Seagrim, received a posthumous VC and GC respectively for bravery during the final years of the Second World War. Eight people have been awarded both the GC and George Medal. Of this group of eight, two have received the George Medal twice. One civilian recipient from the group of eight has been awarded both the GC and George Medal. No brothers have ever been directly awarded the GC. However, two brothers, Samuel and David Booker, were originally awarded Edward Medals for rescue work in Littleton Colliery, South Staffordshire, on 14 May 1937. Their decorations were translated into GCs in 1971.

The youngest individual to be awarded the GC is John (better known as Jack) Bamford, who was fifteen years and seven months old when he saved the lives of two of his brothers, aged six and four, from a house fire at their home in Newthorpe, Nottinghamshire, in October 1952. His burns to his upper body were so severe that he required several skin grafts and months in hospital.

As with the VC, women are eligible for the GC. However, whereas no woman has ever been awarded the VC, four women have received the direct award of the GC. Furthermore, four women had their Empire Gallantry Medals translated to GCs in 1940 and another five had their Albert Medals translated to GCs in 1971.

There was no provision for the payment of any annuity contained in the original Royal Warrant. However, from 4 February 1965 living holders of the GC were granted a tax-free annual allowance of £100. This was all down to campaigning from Brigadier Sir John 'Jackie' Smyth, the founder and the former Chairman and President of the Victoria Cross and George Cross Association, which had come into existence in 1956 to mark the centenary of the VC. As a Conservative MP from 1950, he successfully raised the issue in the House of Commons. The annuity remained at £100 – and terribly behind the times, given inflation – until 15 August 1995 when it was raised to £1,300. In 2002, the annuity paid by the British Government was set at £1,495: the same amount as to VC holders. Since then, this amount has been increased at the same rate as service pensions.

Like all recommendations for gallantry in the military, one for a GC is initiated by the individual's commanding officer and passes up the chain of command for endorsement before being considered by the Ministry of Defence's Armed Forces Operational Awards Committee (AFOAC). AFOAC considers all awards for operations, be they for gallantry or meritorious service. It comprises 'two-star' officers from all three services, all of whom have had operational experience, and so is able to judge the relative merits of each case. Recommendations may be upgraded or downgraded at any stage of the process.

Recommendations for GCs are then forwarded to the Honours and Appointments Secretariat in the Cabinet Office for consideration by the George Cross (Military) Committee. This is, in turn, a sub-committee of the Honours and Decorations Committee. Once a GC recommendation is endorsed by the George Cross (Military) Committee it is forwarded alongside all other recommendations to the Queen for her approval through the Secretary of State for Defence. Recommendations for GCs are then cited in full in the *London Gazette*. Technically it is only at this stage that a recommendation becomes a citation: sometimes for reasons of security a citation may not be an exact match of the original recommendation. Recommendations for GCs for civilians go through a similar process. Various organisations – such as the Police, the Fire Service, Lord Lieutenants, High Sheriffs and corporations – submit their recommendations to the relevant Government department. The department, in turn, passes the recommendation on to the Honours and Appointments Secretariat in the Cabinet Office, before it follows a similar route to a military GC.

The following pages essentially tell the stories behind the direct award of the GC to 159 individuals, along with the two collective awards that have been made to groups of people: the island of Malta in 1942 and the Royal Ulster Constabulary (RUC) in 1999.

Shortly before completing this book, there were two new awards of the GC for gallantry in Afghanistan. The awards went to Staff Sergeant (now Warrant Officer Class 2) Kim Hughes and, posthumously, to Staff Sergeant Olaf 'Oz' Schmid.

At the time of writing, fourteen recipients who were directly awarded the GC are still alive. All of them keep in touch regularly through the Victoria Cross and George Cross Association.

2

THE AWARDS OF 1940

THOMAS HOPPER ALDERSON

Rank/title: **Mr**
Unit/occupation: Detachment Leader, Air Raid Precautions
DATE OF BRAVERY: SEPTEMBER 1940
GAZETTED: 30 SEPTEMBER 1940

Thomas Alderson was the first person to be awarded the George Cross (GC) – an announcement that followed a series of heroic and dangerous rescue operations in his home town of Bridlington, Yorkshire, during the Blitz. The public recognition of his gallantry – as a civilian – typified why George VI had introduced the award less than a year into the Second World War. His GC was announced in a radio broadcast during which the rescue parties in his home town were also praised for their efforts.

Alderson was born in Sunderland, Co. Durham, on 15 September 1903 and was the fifth of six children. He was brought up in nearby West Hartlepool. He attended the local primary school before going to Elwick Road Senior Boys' School, where he was head boy. As a schoolboy, he witnessed the bombardment of West Hartlepool by the German High Seas Fleet on 16 December 1914, an act that left 86 civilians dead and 424 injured. After leaving school at fifteen, he worked as an office boy and a draughtsman, before undertaking an engineering apprenticeship. He then joined the Merchant Navy in 1925, becoming a first engineer and eventually served for nine years. He married and, shortly after the birth of the couple's only child, a daughter, in 1935, he became an engineer for West

Hartlepool Council. He moved to Bridlington in 1938, where he got a job as a works supervisor for the local corporation. After the outbreak of war, local authorities were given responsibility for air raid precautions and they trained their own workforces in rescue work. Alderson attended a course on the subject and became an instructor.

The small seaside town of Bridlington was bombed several times by the Luftwaffe and, on at least three separate occasions during September 1940, Alderson showed outstanding bravery in attempting to save others. During an early air raid on the town on 15 September, a pair of semi-detached houses was destroyed. Alderson and his party were quickly on the scene and learnt that a woman was trapped in her demolished home. Alderson soon tunnelled under the unsafe wreckage to pull the woman to safety.

Some days later, two five-storey buildings were demolished and eleven people were trapped beneath the debris. Those trapped included six people in one cellar, which had completely given way. Alderson reached the cellar by tunnelling thirteen to fourteen feet under the main heap of unsafe wreckage. For three and a half hours, he worked tirelessly in cramped conditions despite the risk of flooding from fractured water pipes. This was not the only danger: enemy aircraft remained overhead and there was also a risk of gas leaks. However, he succeeded in releasing all the trapped people even though he received heavy bruising himself.

On a third occasion, some four-storey buildings were demolished by bombing, trapping five people in a cellar. Alderson again led the rescue work and excavated a tunnel from the pavement through to the foundations to the cellar. Then he tunnelled under the wreckage and rescued alive two people – one of whom subsequently died – from beneath a huge commercial refrigerator. During this difficult work, a three-storey wall swayed precariously in the wind directly over the position where the rescue party was working. During the rescue operation, Alderson worked almost continuously under the wreckage for five hours, during which time further air raid warnings were received and enemy aircraft were heard overhead.

Alderson's GC was announced in the *London Gazette* on 30 September 1940 for what his citation described as 'sustained gallantry, enterprise and devotion to duty during enemy air raids'. His citation ended: 'By his courage and devotion to duty without the slightest regard for his own safety, he set a fine example to the members of his Rescue Party, and their teamwork is worthy of the highest praise.'

Alderson survived the war and afterwards joined the East Riding of Yorkshire County Council as an assistant highways' surveyor. Later he joined the rescue section of the new Civil Defence Corps, which was designed to protect the civilian population from the threat of nuclear warfare as opposed to conventional bombing. Alderson died after a long illness at Northfield hospital in Driffield, Yorkshire, on 28 October 1965, aged sixty-two. He was cremated at Scarborough Crematorium and, after the death of his widow, Irene, in 1991, her ashes were scattered near his. His GC is on display at the Imperial War Museum, alongside the Silver Medal that he, and three other men, received from the RSPCA for rescuing two horses from a burning stable.

ROBERT JOHN DAVIES
Rank/title: Temporary Lieutenant
Unit/occupation: Corps of Royal Engineers
DATE OF BRAVERY: 12 SEPTEMBER 1940
GAZETTED: 30 SEPTEMBER 1940

GEORGE CAMERON WYLLIE

Rank/title: Sapper (later Corporal)
Unit/occupation: Corps of Royal Engineers
DATE OF BRAVERY: 12 SEPTEMBER 1940
GAZETTED: 30 SEPTEMBER 1940

Robert Davies was a Cornishman who was born in the fishing village of Newlyn on 3 October 1900. One of three children, he was educated in his home village before emigrating to Canada during the First World War. He joined the Canadian Army on 11 January 1918. He married a Scot in 1920 and the couple later had four children. George Wyllie was a Scot – the son of a coal miner – who was born in Hurlford, Fife, on 23 December 1908. Before the Second World War, he had worked in the Avro aircraft factory in Manchester. He married on Christmas Day 1940 and the couple later had one son.

The two men, both serving in the Corps of Royal Engineers, were called to deal with an unexploded bomb that had fallen close to St Paul's Cathedral in London during a day of heavy bombing on 12 September 1940. Temporary Lieutenant Davies was in charge of the bomb disposal section and Sapper 'Jock' Wyllie was a member of his team. The location made an already hazardous job even more difficult. If the bomb had exploded the cathedral would almost certainly have been badly damaged. This, in turn, would have been dangerous to those in or close to the building – and any damage to St Paul's Cathedral would have greatly harmed the morale of the British people at the height of the Blitz.

On a dark night, Davies and his team first had to spend quite some time locating the exact position where the bomb had fallen. Eventually, it was Wyllie who found the device, which had embedded itself deep into the pavement in front of the cathedral. This made their work extremely difficult and the men knew they would be killed instantly if the bomb exploded. Eventually, they managed to ease the bomb from the pavement at the same time as they withdrew its potentially lethal 'fangs'.

Davies was desperately worried for the safety of his team so he personally chose to drive the Army vehicle in which the bomb was placed. After driving some distance away from the scene, Davies safely disposed of the bomb. On 30 September 1940, just eighteen days after the incident, the two men's GCs were announced in the *London Gazette*. Davies' citation said: 'So conscious was this officer of the imminent danger to the Cathedral that regardless of personal risk he spared neither himself nor his men in their efforts to locate the bomb.' Wyllie (whose name was misspelt 'Wylie' in the citation) was singled out for discovering and removing the bomb. He was praised for his 'untiring energy, courage and disregard for danger' which 'were an outstanding example to his comrades'.

In an interview long after the incident, Wyllie said of the bomb:

Once we had located it, Davies went down himself for a look and then we got down to getting it out. I went down again and put a steel cable around the bomb to bring it out. Twice it broke. It should never have come out. It should have been blown up there because it had a special fuse in it, which we called a seventeenth fuse. The word from the War Office was 'blow them up' because there were booby traps in them. But the crater was just down the main steps from the Cathedral and there would have been a great deal of damage . . . The area was cordoned off and nobody was allowed in the vicinity . . . There was an additional danger as it was only about thirty yards from St Paul's underground station. It was just too dangerous to blow it up where it was. Davies inspired his men all the time. He was a great leader. He was at the top of it all the time giving instructions to me as I slung the half-inch thick cable around it and the lorry started to drag it away. Just after putting the wire on, I would climb back up and as it broke I went back down again. It broke twice because all sorts of cables and telephone wires were tangled up underneath the bomb. You

13

really didn't know what you were going to hit, whether it was a live cable or not. When we finally got it on to the lorry, it was estimated to weigh about 1,000 lbs, about five feet long and two feet across.

As the bomb was driven away to Hackney Marshes to be disposed of, Wyllie sat across the device, with one leg either side, to steady it. Later in the war, while working at a battery factory in Stamford Hill, Wyllie heard a 'doodle bug' heading straight for the building. He shouted for the manager to duck and threw the 'governor' behind a wall. The manager was killed and the factory was destroyed, but Wyllie and his boss survived.

Davies, who ran a building business well after the war, died in Sydney, Australia, on 27 September 1975, six days short of his seventy-fifth birthday. Wyllie, who after the war worked for twenty-four years at Ford's Dagenham factory, died at his home in Bow, east London, on 1 February 1987, aged seventy-eight. His GC is now on display at St Paul's Cathedral.

ARTHUR DOUGLAS MERRIMAN
Rank/title: Dr
Unit/occupation: Part-time Experimental Officer
DATE OF BRAVERY: 11 SEPTEMBER 1940
GAZETTED: 3 DECEMBER 1940

Arthur Merriman was born in south Manchester on 25 November 1892. He was the son of a warehouseman working in the cotton industry. He was a bright student and attended Central High School in Manchester, and the Universities of Cambridge, Durham and Lille. During the First World War, he served in the Royal Army Ordnance Corps (RAOC), entering France on 3 April 1918. After the war, he worked as teacher and academic.

Early in the Second World War, Dr Merriman began working

– along with Lord Suffolk – as one of just two Experimental Officers in the Directorate of Scientific Research. Although his duties were intended to be restricted to the office, he volunteered to deal with some of the early unexploded bombs that fell on Britain in the summer of 1940. Many of the duties that he undertook for the War Office and Air Ministry were fraught with danger.

On 11 September 1940 – four days into the Blitz – Merriman and Dr Gough, the Director General of Scientific Research, tackled a bomb that had fallen on Regent Street, a major shopping area in central London. Merriman took the lead in dealing with the bomb even though both men could hear it ticking. Knowing their lives were in considerable peril, the two men decided to take a calculated risk due to the fact that the bomb had fallen in such a busy, built-up area. Instead of trying to defuse the bomb, they removed as much of its explosive as possible and as quickly as possible. They hoped to be able to ensure the bomb was relatively harmless before it detonated.

The men, who had considerable scientific knowledge, worked calmly and swiftly. As soon as they calculated that they had removed sufficient explosive to make the device fairly safe, they retreated from the ticking bomb. Their timing was immaculate: no sooner had they left the scene than the bomb went off. Instead of bringing carnage to the centre of London, the explosion caused no more damage than some broken windows. Nobody was injured.

Merriman's GC was announced on 3 December 1940 when he was praised for 'conspicuous bravery in connection with bomb disposal'. He survived the war, being honoured with an OBE in January 1944. Merriman served from 1941 to 1944 as the Scientific Advisor to the Commander in Chief, Middle East, and for the final year of the war worked on a special intelligence assignment in Russia and Germany.

After the war, Merriman left the service with the honorary rank of colonel, and became the Principal Scientific Officer

(Technical Intelligence) at the Armaments Design Department, Ministry of Supply. A distinguished career followed in the research industry and he published sixteen books. Merriman, who was a married man, died in Streatham, south London, on 4 November 1972, three weeks short of his eightieth birthday.

BRANDON MOSS
Rank/title: Special Constable
Unit/occupation: Coventry Constabulary
DATE OF BRAVERY: 14–15 NOVEMBER 1940
GAZETTED: 13 DECEMBER 1940

Brandon Moss was born in Badingham, Suffolk, on 5 June 1909. He was the son of a poultry farmer, who later worked in a sugar refinery. Moss, who had five brothers and sisters, was educated at Coventry Elementary and Stratford-upon-Avon grammar schools. He worked in the building trade prior to the Second World War but he then worked as a fitter at Coventry's Armstrong Siddeley (later Hawker Siddeley) plant. Married with two daughters, he had been a Special Constable from 1932.

On 14 November 1940, the city of Coventry came under sustained attack from the Luftwaffe. At 8.15 p.m., the first incendiary devices were dropped as markers for following aircraft. A total of 437 aircraft dropped 394 tons of high explosives and 127 parachute mines. Under a full moon, the city's 250,000-strong population then endured no less than eleven hours of sustained attack which cost 380 lives. Hundreds of homes and more than twenty factories were damaged while Coventry's cathedral was destroyed.

No individual did more that night for Coventry than Special Constable Moss, who was on duty on 14 November. He initially stood defiantly as the bombs dropped on his home city and surveyed the devastation all around him. Amid the chaos and carnage, a bomb had dropped directly on one house, completely demolishing it and burying its three occupants beneath the rubble. With collapsing debris and leaking gas, the situation looked as hopeless as it was dangerous.

However, Moss, working on his own, managed to clear a tiny space through the ruins and crawled into an area where the three occupants had managed, against all the odds, to survive. One by one, he led the residents to safety. No sooner had he finished than he discovered that more people had been buried in the neighbouring property. Once again, he took charge of the rescue operation. Despite dodging falling beams and debris, he managed to pull another person out alive, while four dead bodies were also recovered from the house.

In all, Moss had worked for more than seven hours – from 11 p.m. to 6.30 a.m. the next day – without a break to save four lives. During the rescue operations, bombs fell continuously. Furthermore, Moss had all the time known that there was a delayed action bomb in the doorway of a pub some twenty yards away from where he was working. Moss's GC was announced on 13 December 1940 when the citation praised his 'superhuman efforts and utter disregard for personal injury'.

In fact, Moss was initially recommended for a George Medal but his award was elevated to the GC. After the war, Moss retired from work as a Special Constable in 1948 and returned to work in the building trade. He died in his beloved Coventry on 9 August 1999, aged ninety.

ERIC LAWRENCE MOXEY
Rank/title: Acting Squadron Leader
Unit/occupation: Royal Air Force Volunteer Reserve
DATE OF BRAVERY: 27 AUGUST 1940
GAZETTED: 17 DECEMBER 1940

Eric Moxey was the first person to be awarded the GC posthumously. He was born in São Paulo, Brazil, on 14 April 1894. His father was working in Brazil as the founder and Secretary of the São Paulo Railways. Moxey, who had a brother and two sisters, was educated at Malvern College in Worcester-shire and Sheffield University, where he read engineering. As a talented teenage motorbike rider, he won the gold medal in the Isle of Man TT race as the leading amateur. During the First World War, he served with the York and Lancashire Regiment and the Royal Flying Corps. He married on 10 January 1917 and the couple went on to have four sons. After being demobbed in 1918, he went back to a career in engineering.

Moxey was forty-five at the outbreak of the Second World War. At the height of the Battle of Britain, he was acting squadron leader with the Royal Air Force Volunteer Reserve. As a technical intelligence officer at the Air Ministry, he had joined the Special Branch which dealt with defusing unexploded bombs. He is credited with inventing a device for extracting fuses from German bombs called a 'Freddie'.

On 27 August 1940, two unexploded bombs were reported to be embedded at Biggin Hill RAF station in Kent, which had constantly come under attack from the Luftwaffe. At this point, the RAF was responsible for dealing with unexploded bombs which fell on its airfields and other sites. Without hesitation, Moxey volunteered to travel down from London to tackle them. By this time, he had already risked his life several times to deal with that particular menace.

On arrival at Biggin Hill, Moxey knew his task: to make safe the bombs so they could be removed from the scene. Knowing the dangers, Moxey tackled the first one, which must have been in a more unstable state than usual. As he set about his selfless task, the bomb went off with its full force, killing him. Moxey was forty-six. His Commanding Officer in the RAF recommended him for the GC saying: 'In my opinion Squadron Leader E. L. Moxey was the bravest man I ever met. His enthusiasm for his extremely dangerous task was supreme, and I consider that he is a fit recipient for the George Cross which, I understand, like the Victoria Cross, can be awarded posthumously.'

His GC was announced on 17 December 1940 when the

citation referred to the bomb that claimed his life, adding: 'On many occasions Squadron Leader Moxey had exhibited similar complete disregard for his personal safety.' Moxey's four sons all served in the Second World War, two in the RAF and two in the Fleet Air Arm. His second son was killed serving with the RAF in Egypt in 1942.

ROY THOMAS HARRIS
Rank/title: Mr
Unit/occupation: Air Raid Precautions Engineers Service, Croydon
DATE OF BRAVERY: 18 SEPTEMBER 1940
GAZETTED: 17 DECEMBER 1940

Roy Harris was born in Cardiff on 1 August 1902. At one point, he worked for the Powell-Duffryn Steam Coal Company in South Wales. He later moved from Bolton, Lancashire, to Croydon, Surrey, in 1937. A single man, he joined the staff of Croydon Borough Council and volunteered for bomb disposal training. After the outbreak of the Second World War, he had the unusual title of Chief Combustion Officer for Croydon Corporation. He was also a member of Croydon's Air Raid Precautions Engineers Service.

On 18 September 1940, a number of unexploded bombs fell behind Langdale Road School in Thornton Heath, Surrey. Despite being inexperienced in dealing with such devices, Harris showed remarkable courage in dismantling more than one of the exceptionally dangerous bombs. His GC was announced on 17 December when his citation praised his 'conspicuous bravery in carrying out dangerous duties'. Harris appears to have been inspired by his brave deeds to embark on a military career. He later joined the Corps of Royal Engineers and rose to the rank of lieutenant colonel. He died in Wolverhampton in the Midlands on 18 August 1973, aged seventy-one.

JOHN MACMILLAN STEVENSON PATTON
Rank/title: Lieutenant
Unit/occupation: 1st Battalion, Corps of the Royal Canadian Engineers
DATE OF BRAVERY: 21 SEPTEMBER 1940
GAZETTED: 17 DECEMBER 1940

John Patton was born in Warwick, Bermuda, on 29 August 1915. Despite being raised in Canada, he had both British and Bermudian citizenship – though he became a Canadian national as a result of his war service. After the start of the Second World War, Patton was posted to England where he was based with A Company, 1 Canadian Pioneer Battalion, of the Corps of the Royal Canadian Engineers. The unit's primary job was to build defences, although a few men – but not Patton – had received bomb disposal training.

On 21 September 1940, and with no Army bomb disposal personnel on hand, Lieutenant Patton, then twenty-five, was called to help deal with a large unexploded bomb that had fallen on the Vickers aircraft factory at Weybridge, Surrey. Both the location and the size of the bomb meant it was essential that it was tackled quickly. Realising that he did not have the expertise to dismantle the bomb, Patton loaded it on to a trailer. Then he got a lorry and towed the trailer to a recently formed bomb crater a long distance from the factory. The bomb, which could have gone off at any time, eventually exploded in the crater without causing damage to any person or property.

Patton's GC was announced on 17 December 1940 'for most conspicuous gallantry in carrying out very hazardous work'. Later in the war, Patton became an expert on weaponry, particularly flame-throwers. After the war, he returned to Canada, taking a law degree at Dalhousie University, Nova Scotia. He then returned to Bermuda, where he embarked on a career first in law, then in politics. He had four children by his first marriage and two stepchildren by his second marriage. Patton, who was also awarded the CBE, died in Bermuda on 13 May 1996, aged eighty.

PETER VICTOR DANCKWERTS

Rank/title: Sub-Lieutenant
Unit/occupation: Royal Naval Volunteer Reserve
DATE OF BRAVERY: AUTUMN 1940
GAZETTED: 20 DECEMBER 1940

Peter Danckwerts was born in Emsworth, near Southsea, Hampshire, on 14 October 1916. He was the son of a rear admiral and the eldest of five children. Educated at Winchester College and Balliol College, Oxford, he obtained a first-class honours degree in chemistry in 1939 – the year the Second World War broke out.

Sub-Lieutenant Danckwerts had served in the Royal Naval Volunteer Reserve (RNVR) for less than six weeks when he was presented with a challenge that would have been daunting even to bomb disposal veterans. Without orders and with the burden of incomplete equipment, he was dispatched to deal with landmines that were endangering an area of south-east London. It was the fact that they were landmines – rather than bombs – which made them the responsibility of the RNVR. Terrifying as it may seem, Danckwerts had never even touched a mine – except under instruction.

Yet, now he was to work without rest for nearly forty-eight hours, dealing successfully with sixteen enemy mines. In one incident, he and a chief petty officer had discovered two mines hanging from a parachute with their noses on a warehouse floor. Their gentle footsteps as they approached the devices had started up the clock inside one, but when they retreated it stopped ticking again. As they dealt with the timer, they knew its clock was highly sensitive and could only have a few seconds to run. However, Danckwerts and his colleague remained calm and withdrew the fuse from this mine, before doing the same

21

with the other device. His GC was announced on 20 December 1940 when the citation praised his 'great gallantry and undaunted devotion to duty'.

Later in the war, Danckwerts took part in the invasion of Sicily, when he was wounded. He was awarded the MBE in 1942. Danckwerts, who married in 1960 but did not have children, was as academically gifted as he was practical and courageous. He enjoyed a distinguished career, largely in the department of chemical engineering at Cambridge University. As well as being a Fellow of the Royal Society, he was a Fellow of Pembroke College, Cambridge, from 1959 to 1977. He died in his beloved Cambridge on 25 October 1984, eleven days after his sixty-eighth birthday.

REGINALD VINCENT ELLINGWORTH
Rank/title: Chief Petty Officer
Unit/occupation: Royal Navy
DATE OF BRAVERY: 21 SEPTEMBER 1940
GAZETTED: 20 DECEMBER 1940

RICHARD JOHN HAMMERSLEY RYAN
Rank/title: Lieutenant Commander
Unit/occupation: Royal Navy
DATE OF BRAVERY: 21 SEPTEMBER 1940
GAZETTED: 20 DECEMBER 1940

Reginald Ellingworth was born in Wolverhampton in the Midlands on 28 January 1898. Richard Ryan, the son of an admiral, was born in Kensington, west London, on 23 July 1903. Ryan followed his father into the Royal Navy, becoming a cadet in January 1917 and a midshipman in 1921 on HMS *Dunedin*. He quickly worked his way up through the ranks.

Early in the Second World War, Lieutenant Commander Ryan and Chief Petty Officer Ellingworth, who were stationed in HMS *Vernon*, were involved in the work of the Enemy Mining

Section. During this time, they had to familiarise themselves with the new magnetic mines that the Germans had been using in an attempt to sink British ships and to disrupt the shipping lanes. Indeed, when an enemy plane crashed at Clacton, Essex, Ryan successfully took apart one of the new type of mine, which was parachuted in by enemy aircraft, simply to study its mechanisms.

Their work with the Rendering Mines Safe (RMS) section from 1939 to 1940 meant they had to deal with two sorts of magnetic mine: C and D. Each device contained 1,500 lb of an explosive called hexanite and the bomb disposal team had to deal with a bomb fuse built into the side of the casing that was kept in position by a 'keep ring'. To neutralise the mine, the ring had to be unscrewed, the fuse withdrawn and the 'gaine' removed: the gaine was a small charge of explosive that fired the primers which, in turn, fired the main charge.

The main danger of these magnetic mines, which were being dropped indiscriminately in and around London, was the clock of the bomb fuse – its timing device. This was usually timed to detonate about twenty-two seconds after the fall, but it was when it failed to explode that it often produced an even greater hazard for the person, or persons, who had to deal with it. The bomb's failure to detonate was usually caused by the fact that the drop had damaged or broken the arming clock. However, if damaged rather than broken completely, a small movement of the bomb could start up the clock again. If those dealing with the bomb realised that the clock had been reactivated, they knew they barely had sufficient time to dash to safety.

Ryan and Ellingworth were a particularly effective partnership and, on one occasion, dealt with some half a dozen magnetic mines, one of which had fallen into a canal. Ryan, who always led from the front, waded into the deep, thick mud to deal with it, knowing he would have been unable to walk, let alone run, if the bomb had been reactivated. Despite being restricted by mud that came higher than his waist, he reached down into the muddy water to locate the fuse of the device and neutralise it. On another occasion, Ryan, once again aided by his trusted comrade and friend, successfully dealt with a mine that fell close to the RAF airfield at Hornchurch, Essex.

On 21 September 1940, the two bomb disposal veterans were called to deal with a device which was tricky even by their experienced standards. They found a magnetic mine in a warehouse that was still hanging precariously by its parachute. Never ones to duck a challenge, they attempted to neutralise the device but it went off, killing them both instantly. It is likely that the bomb, when it reactivated, would have started whirring so the two men would probably have known their fate for the seconds before they were killed. Their posthumous GCs were announced on 20 December 1940 when the citation praised their 'great gallantry and undaunted devotion to duty'.

Ryan, who left a widow, was thirty-seven when he died. He was later commemorated at the Haslar Royal Naval Cemetery in Gosport, Hampshire. Ellingworth, who left a widow as well as a son, was forty-two when he died. He is commemorated at the Milton Cemetery in Portsmouth, Hampshire, close to Fratton Park, the home of Portsmouth Football Club. It was only when his widow, Jessie, died that the family learnt she had sold his GC and other decorations after becoming short of money. However, his son later had a pools win and was able to buy his father's medals back and donated them to the Imperial War Museum in London.

WILLIAM MARSDEN EASTMAN
Rank/title: Lieutenant (later Brigadier)
Unit/occupation: Royal Army Ordnance Corps
DATE OF BRAVERY: JUNE–NOVEMBER 1940
GAZETTED: 24 DECEMBER 1940

ROBERT LLEWELLYN JEPHSON JONES

Rank/title: Captain (later Brigadier)
Unit/occupation: Royal Army Ordnance Corps
DATE OF BRAVERY: JUNE–NOVEMBER 1940
GAZETTED: 24 DECEMBER 1940

From June 1940, Malta came under sustained air attack from the German and Italian forces. The island was ill prepared to deal with such a relentless bombardment: there were no specialist Royal Engineer bomb disposal units. This meant that the task of dealing with unexploded bombs and mines was divided between the three Armed Forces. Devices dropped in the dockyard area were dealt with by the Royal Navy, while those that fell on airfields were handled by the Royal Air Force.

The vast majority of the bombs and mines that fell on Malta, however, became the responsibility of the Royal Army Ordnance Corps (RAOC), in general, and two men, in particular. One was Lieutenant William 'Bill' Eastman, who was born on 26 October 1911 in Brentford, Essex, and attended Uppingham School in Leicestershire. After working for a short time in a dry cleaning business, he went to Cambridge University but, after the outbreak of the Second World War, volunteered after attending just a single term. The second man was Captain Robert Jephson Jones, who was born in Bicester, Oxfordshire, on 7 April 1905. He was the son of a clergyman whose family had long connections with the Indian Army.

In Malta, Eastman and Jephson Jones were given the bulk of the responsibility for dealing with device after device that fell on the island. Eastman was given a short course in ammunition duties after the outbreak of hostilities. He had only been on Malta for three months when the bombs started to fall. Jephson Jones shared the task of dealing with the devices around the clock. They had no specialist training, no trained staff and little knowledge of the devices the enemy were using. In effect, they learnt as they went along, knowing that one mistake would cost them their own lives and might result in the loss of other lives, too. Yet between June and November 1940, the two men tackled a remarkable 275 bombs between them – an average of around a bomb a day per man. Against all the odds, they survived uninjured – and eventually handed over their responsibilities to a properly trained Royal Engineers' bomb disposal unit. Their GCs were announced on Christmas Eve 1940 'for most conspicuous gallantry in carrying out very hazardous work'. They were given the choice of receiving their decorations from the Governor of Malta or, all being well, the King when they returned to Britain. Both chose the latter which meant they had to wait until December 1944 before they were invested together by George VI at Buckingham Palace.

After the war ended, both men were destined to rise to the rank of brigadier. Eastman, who was married with two daughters, was Commandant of RAOC Training Centre in Blackdown, Hampshire, until 1966. He retired to Malta and, after he had suffered a number of strokes, he died on the island on 8 April 1980, aged sixty-eight. Jephson Jones was Deputy Director of Ordnance Services, Scottish Command, from 1954 to 1957 and then Commandant, Central Ordnance Depot, Branston, Staffordshire, from 1957 to 1960. He died in Ferndown, Dorset, on 27 October 1985, aged eighty. His ashes were interred with those of his wife, Pansy, who had died six months earlier.

RICHARD VALENTINE MOORE

Rank/title: Temporary Sub-Lieutenant (later Lieutenant Commander)
Unit/occupation: Royal Naval Volunteer Reserve
DATE OF BRAVERY: SEPTEMBER 1940
GAZETTED: 27 DECEMBER 1940

Richard 'Dick' Moore was born in London on St Valentine's Day 1916. He was educated at the Strand School in London and London University, where he took a degree in mechanical engineering. Moore worked for an electricity company from 1936 until the outbreak of the Second World War in 1939, when he was commissioned into the Royal Naval Volunteer Reserve (RNVR).

On the night of 16 September 1940, twenty-five parachute mines were dropped on London by the Luftwaffe. Although he had no practical training, Moore and a colleague volunteered to deal with the seventeen mines that had not exploded. On 20 September in Dagenham, Essex, four more parachute mines were dropped. Moore and the same colleague helped deal with the first three mines. His colleague and another man then went to deal with the fourth mine, which was hanging from its parachute in a warehouse some 200 yards away. As they were examining the mine, it exploded without warning, killing both men.

Moore's GC was announced on 27 December 1940 for 'great gallantry and undaunted devotion to duty'. Later in the war, Moore, who was married with three sons, reached the rank of lieutenant commander in the RNVR. After the war, he pursued a distinguished career in engineering and design, specialising in atomic energy and pioneering the gas-cooled reactor system. Moore, who was also awarded the CBE, died in Warrington, Cheshire, on 25 April 2003, aged eighty-seven.

JOHN HERBERT BABINGTON

Rank/title: Temporary Sub-Lieutenant (later Lieutenant Commander)
Unit/occupation: Royal Naval Volunteer Reserve
DATE OF BRAVERY: AUTUMN 1940
GAZETTED: 27 DECEMBER 1940

John Babington was born in Tai Chow Foo, China – where his parents had been working as medical missionaries – on 6 February 1911. After attending Wyggeston School in Leicester, he was educated at St Catharine's College, Cambridge. When the Second World War broke out, he was a teacher at

King's College School, Wimbledon, south-west London. After he was turned down for the submarine service, he joined the Royal Naval Volunteer Reserve (RNVR) to work in bomb disposal.

Sub-Lieutenant Babington tackled the sort of tasks that meant he was highly likely to lose his life carrying out his work. He experimented with the dismantling of a huge variety of German bombs at a time when the enemy was doing its best to come up with not just effective bombs, but also devices that were specifically intended to kill those trying to make them safe.

Royal Navy personnel tended to tackle mines and Army personnel usually tackled more traditional bombs. This meant that Babington worked on the first suspended parachute magnetic mines. These were particularly dangerous devices and one had already claimed the life of an RAF disposal officer. Shortly after that fatal incident, Babington was called to a particularly difficult incident in which a similar bomb had been dropped on the Royal Navy dockyard at Chatham, Kent. The bomb had lodged itself in a hole sixteen feet deep. Furthermore, the bomb was feared to be fitted with a new 'anti-stripping' or 'anti-withdrawal' device similar to the one that had apparently killed the RAF officer. The thinking behind the device was to prevent the bomb being defused or 'stripped', in the case of delayed action or failure to explode.

Babington volunteered to be lowered by colleagues into the hole where he carefully tied a line to the head of the fuse. However, the line broke twice during these delicate manoeuvres. Babington was then lowered into the pit for a third time and on this occasion his attempt to remove the fuse was successful. The bomb was then lifted out of the hole, taken away and destroyed. His GC was announced on 27 December 1940 for 'great gallantry and undaunted devotion to duty'.

Babington continued to deal with many more devices, particularly seaborne mines, later in the war. Despite his constant contact with some of the most fiendish mines and bombs around, Babington survived the war. Afterwards, Babington, who was married with three children, went on to pursue a successful career in education, becoming headmaster of Ashlyns School in Berkhamsted, Hertfordshire. He died in Oxfordshire on 25 March 1992, aged eighty-one.

ROBERT SELBY ARMITAGE
Rank/title: Temporary Lieutenant (later Lieutenant Commander)
Unit/occupation: Royal Naval Volunteer Reserve
DATE OF BRAVERY: SEPTEMBER/OCTOBER 1940
GAZETTED: 27 DECEMBER 1940

Vicar's son Robert Armitage was born in Birling, Kent, on 28 March 1905. He was educated at Rugby School before attending Trinity College, Cambridge. A talented hockey player and yachtsman, he was called to the Bar only to see his legal career interrupted by the Second World War. His ease with the sea came in useful when he took part in the Dunkirk evacuations in the spring of 1940. Captaining his own vessel, *Fidget*, he and his four sister ships rescued some 4,000 servicemen from the beaches.

Time and again during September and October 1940, Temporary Lieutenant Robert Armitage, then aged thirty-five, risked his life to disable landmines. His most dangerous work took place just weeks after six lives had been lost when a mine detonated which had been returned to HMS *Vernon* so that it could be stripped and useful knowledge could be gained about its contents. Experts recovered the remains of the mine and, eventually, perfected equipment to tackle the enemy's 'anti-stripping' devices.

He tackled some of his most dangerous tasks in his role for the Royal Naval Volunteer Reserve (RNVR). On one occasion, he was called to deal with a mine hanging from a tree in Orpington, Kent. The device could only be reached from a ladder and, while he delicately worked on the bomb, he knew that there was no chance of escape if the fuse activated.

On another occasion while dealing with a bomb, Armitage heard the clock start ticking and he began to run for his life. He was only thirty yards away when the device went off. His colleague, who had only narrowly escaped too, said: 'When it was all over I got up and looked for Armitage. I couldn't see him anywhere. Then from the far corner of the garden something stirred. Armitage got up from a compost heap and walked towards me. Actually, it was pretty bad. He was only thirty yards off when it fired – too close for comfort.' Armitage was made of stern stuff: the next day he simply turned up for work as if nothing had happened.

Armitage's GC was announced on 27 December 1940 for 'undaunted bravery'. On 1 February 1944, he was awarded the George Medal for further gallantry. Armitage often used his middle name of Selby as his surname so some knew him as 'Robert Selby'. Married without children, he died in Nettlebed, Oxfordshire, on 26 May 1982, aged seventy-seven.

3

THE AWARDS OF 1941

JOHN NOEL DOWLAND
Rank/title: Flight Lieutenant (later Wing Commander)
Unit/occupation: RAF
DATE OF BRAVERY: 11 FEBRUARY 1940
GAZETTED: 7 JANUARY 1941

LEONARD HENRY HARRISON
Rank/title: Mr
Unit/occupation: Civilian Armament Instructor
DATE OF BRAVERY: 11 FEBRUARY 1940
GAZETTED: 3 JANUARY 1941

Although Thomas Alderson's was the first GC to be publicly announced in the *London Gazette*, the first action for which GCs were awarded was carried out by Flight Lieutenant John Dowland and Leonard Harrison.

Dowland was born early in the First World War on 6 November 1914, possibly in Lewisham, south London. The son of a reverend and one of three children, he was educated at St John's School, Leatherhead, Surrey. He attended the RAF College at Cranwell, Lincolnshire, from 1934. During the Second World War, Dowland served with the RAF as a flight lieutenant. Harrison was born in Devonport, Devon, on 6 June 1906. During the First World War, his father worked as a recruiting officer. In January 1922, while still only fifteen, he enlisted into the RAF as a boy entrant aircraft apprentice at RAF Halton in Buckinghamshire. When he left the service in

1934, he had reached the rank of sergeant. Next he was employed by the Air Ministry as a Civilian Armament Instructor and became an expert in bomb disposal.

The two men were honoured for their bravery when, on 11 February 1940, the steamship *Kildare*, a grain carrier, was hit by two enemy bombs. One exploded in the grain, which shifted and caused the vessel to list heavily. The other bomb lodged in the aft deck cabin, but did not explode. The ship limped into Immingham Dock, north Lincolnshire, where Dowland and Harrison calmly set about the task of dealing with the situation. After entering the ship's cabin, the two men found that the crew had helped their cause by placing mattresses under the bomb to stop it moving around. They could see the fuses of the bomb facing upwards and they followed the procedures known to Harrison on what should be done. It was tense and dangerous work but they used a voltmeter to wear down the bomb's electric charge. Next they delicately removed the locking and locating rings, thereby ensuring the bomb was harmless. Their courage and skill meant the unexploded bomb could then be lowered over the side of the ship and into an RAF vehicle so that it could be taken away to be examined. A month later, Dowland and Harrison also dealt with another incident when they were called to Grimsby. On this occasion, they successfully dealt with an enemy projectile which had fallen on to the deck of a small fishing boat in the Humber.

The bravery of the two men was recognised with the announcement of their GCs in the *London Gazette* on 3 and 7 January 1941. The citations praised their 'conspicuous courage and devotion to duty in circumstances of exceptional danger'.

One year and nine days after the citation, on 14 January 1942, was published, Dowland was killed in action in Malta. He was twenty-seven. Later in 1941, Harrison rejoined the RAF, reaching the rank of wing commander. When he stopped flying, he remained at the Air Ministry until 1970 when he retired nearly half a century after first joining the RAF. He later served as Treasurer of the Victoria Cross and George Cross Association. Harrison, who was married twice and who had two sons and a daughter by his first wife, died on 15 July 1989 in Bexleyheath, Kent, aged eighty-three.

JOHN BRYAN PETER MILLER (LATER DUPPA-MILLER)

Rank/title: Temporary Sub-Lieutenant
Unit/occupation: Royal Naval Volunteer Reserve
DATE OF BRAVERY: LATE 1940
GAZETTED: 14 JANUARY 1941

JOHN STEPHEN TUCKWELL

Rank/title: Able Seaman
Unit/occupation: Royal Navy
DATE OF BRAVERY: LATE 1940
GAZETTED: 14 JANUARY 1941

Temporary Sub-Lieutenant John 'Jack' Duppa-Miller and Able Seaman Stephen Tuckwell had worked together on mine disposal since early in the Blitz. Duppa-Miller (then known only as Miller) was born in Stechford, Birmingham, on 22 May 1903. He was the son of an in-house lawyer for Birmingham City Council and was educated at Rugby School. After marrying in 1926, Duppa-Miller and his wife moved to Lagos, Nigeria, but returned to Britain after he contracted malaria. The couple had three sons before divorcing and he remarried in 1944. Tuckwell was born in Guildford, Surrey, on 16 April 1897. The son of a labourer, he had three sisters and a brother. After working as a milkman, he joined the Royal Navy for a twelve-year stint on 16 April 1915. He joined the Royal Naval Volunteer Reserve in 1927 and was called up in 1939.

The two men had successfully disposed of some ten mines, when a particular incident late in 1940 brought them to the nation's attention for their courage and skill. They were called to deal with a mine which had landed in soft mud in Roding River, which runs into Barking Creek in Essex. Having assessed the situation, Duppa-Miller borrowed a canoe and put it on a Fire Service fire-float. He and Tuckwell then set about finding the mine. Once they had located the device, they transferred from the fire-float to the canoe.

Working under difficult conditions, the two men managed to remove one fuse but they were unable to reach the other. At this point, they appealed for help to several crane drivers on a nearby wharf who had come to see what was going on. The workmen were keen to assist so Duppa-Miller and Tuckwell got back into the water and put ropes around the mine. With the crane drivers' help, the huge, slippery cylinder was carefully lifted out of the creek, over the muddy bank and up on to the wharf. There they made the mine safe. The two men were awarded the GC on 14 January 1941 'for great gallantry and undaunted devotion to duty'.

Duppa-Miller (still known as Miller when he was awarded the GC) later described the role of Tuckwell after reaching the mine. 'At this point I regained, with an effort, an official manner and asked Tucker to withdraw. I said he had better take cover on the bank opposite the mine and make the usual notes. He said . . . it would take him at least two hours to reach the place. Besides, I should have to work under about a foot of water, and would need someone to hand me the tools. In short, if my number was up, he would like to be with me.'

Duppa-Miller was later recommended by the First Lord of the Admiralty for a bar (a second GC) to his GC for dealing with a mine 'which was not only of the greatest importance to render safe but called for the strongest nerve and a nearly super-human devotion to duty'. However, no bar was awarded on this occasion – indeed no bar has ever been awarded to a GC.

After the war, Duppa-Miller moved to Africa with his second wife. He worked as Inspector-General at the Ministry of Education in Addis Ababa, Ethiopia, from 1945 to 1947 before working at the Education Department in Kenya for a decade until 1957. Duppa-Miller, who after the death of his second wife married for a third time, died in Somerset West, South Africa, on 15 December 1994, aged ninety-one. Tuckwell died in Sompting, Lancing, Sussex, on 2 October 1966, aged sixty-nine.

WILLIAM HORACE TAYLOR

Rank/title: Sub-Lieutenant (later Lieutenant Commander)
Unit/occupation: Royal Naval Volunteer Reserve
DATE OF BRAVERY: SEPTEMBER AND OCTOBER 1940
GAZETTED: 14 JANUARY 1941

Printer's son William Taylor was born in Salford, Lancashire, on 23 October 1908. He was educated at Manchester Grammar School. Before the Second World War, he was a partner and, later, managing director of an advertising company in the city.

Taylor had received his training on bomb disposal during the early days of the Blitz while serving in the Royal Naval Volunteer Reserve (RNVR). Sub-Lieutenant Taylor disposed of a number of mines while serving in HMS *Vernon*. He became widely known for his fondness for building 'funkholes' – intended as a protective bunker to leap into if the bomb he was tackling started to tick. Taylor told the late Sir John 'Jackie' Smyth, the VC recipient and author: 'I had it [the funkhole] dug; not very deep but fairly wide, as I should be coming over the top at some speed. My colleagues used to think that my funkholes were too close to the job, but I reckoned they were better too close than just out of reach!'

When he was operating in a built-up area where such digging was impossible, Taylor instead chose a nearby building to run to in the event of the bomb starting to tick. Despite taking such precautions, Taylor had a couple of close shaves, including one occasion when a parachute mine could not be immediately rendered safe at a cross-roads in a built-up area of Birmingham.

However, as he was deciding what to do next, he learnt that a colleague, Lieutenant Rowson, had decided to tackle it. Initially, Rowson had started the bomb fuse ticking and had run for his life. But when nothing happened he, accompanied this time by Taylor, went to have another go, armed with spanners and other tools. When Rowson added to their problems by dislocating his thumb, the two men opted to blow up the bomb where it lay.

Taylor told Smyth: 'We thought that if we set fire to it, a considerable portion of the charge would be burnt before the fire reached the detonators and would thus reduce the force of the explosion. But of course the bomb fuse might operate before that. Which happened first we shall never know because, after an enormous flare-up of fire, which ignited all the surrounding houses, the thing went off with an enormous explosion which blew us both reeling down the street, bruised, filthy, shaken – but still alive.'

Taylor's GC was announced on 14 January 1941 when the citation praised his 'great gallantry and undaunted devotion to duty'. Taylor, who was a devout Christian, later described how he was never afraid doing his work. 'It was prayer that kept me going. Every morning at breakfast time I'd ask God to hold my hand steady and deal with the treacherous little fuse. Each time my arm was taken in a firm grip and I was in safe-keeping.'

Later in the war, in 1944, Taylor became a diver and a pioneer of 'human minesweepers', which paved the way for the Royal Navy Minewarfare & Clearance Diving Branch. After the war, he married a Wren officer in 1946 and the couple later had four children. His career remained linked to the military: he worked for the RNVR and was responsible for training work, including diving instruction. In 1975, he was awarded the MBE for services to Scouting, his great passion before and after the war. Taylor died on 16 January 1999 in Banchory, Aberdeenshire, aged ninety.

ALBERT GEORGE DOLPHIN

Rank/title: **Mr**
Unit/occupation: Hospital porter
DATE OF BRAVERY: 7 SEPTEMBER 1940
GAZETTED: 17 JANUARY 1941

On 7 September 1940 – the start of the Blitz – Germany switched tactics. It halted its successful blanket bombing of Britain's RAF bases and instead targeted, first, London and, later, other British cities. Wave after wave of planes swept over London in the late afternoon, dropping their bombs predominantly in the east of the capital. As night fell, the bombing raids intensified and hard-pressed firefighters were tackling more than sixty major blazes and about 1,000 smaller ones.

Some 430 people died that night amid terrible scenes of carnage and chaos. Among the dead were four nurses who had been killed when a high-explosive bomb landed on the South Eastern Hospital in New Cross, south London. The victims had been standing on the ground floor of the kitchens of Ward Block 1. The explosion also badly injured others in the adjoining ward, including the ward sister and some of the patients. However, even more seriously injured was a nurse who had been in the ward kitchen on the first floor. She had been thrown through the collapsing floor and had ended up in the passage of the ground floor. As well as suffering from serious injuries, her legs had been trapped by some of the falling masonry.

Those who rushed to help the stricken nurse included Albert Dolphin, a hospital porter who, having been born in Bermondsey, south-east London, in 1896, was forty-four at the time. Having enlisted in 1915, he had fought during the First World War at the battles of the Somme in 1916 and Passchendaele in 1917. Dolphin, a married man, had worked as a porter at the hospital for more than twenty years – since the end of the First World War. As Dolphin and others worked to free the nurse, one of the surrounding walls gave a loud crack. The would-be rescuers had time to move away from the scene and all of them, except Dolphin, retreated. The porter, however, flung himself over the nurse's body as the wall collapsed in a frantic attempt to save her life. In doing so, Dolphin took the full weight of the falling masonry and was killed.

Dolphin's selfless act of bravery was not in vain: the nurse was later pulled from the rubble alive, though seriously injured. Dolphin's posthumous GC was announced on 17 January 1941, when his citation ended: 'There is no doubt that Dolphin, although aware the wall was about to collapse, deliberately remained where he was and threw himself across the nurse's body in an endeavour to protect her. This he succeeded in doing at the cost of his own life.'

LEONARD JOHN MILES
Rank/title: Mr
Unit/occupation: Air Raid Precautions warden
DATE OF BRAVERY: 21–22 SEPTEMBER 1940
GAZETTED: 17 JANUARY 1941

Leonard Miles was born in West Ham, east London, on 27 September 1904. The son of a gas meter maker, he worked as a painter and decorator until the outbreak of the Second World War when he volunteered as an air raid precautions (ARP) warden. At the height of the Blitz, he was on duty on the night of 21–22 September 1940. A bomb had fallen in a built-up area of Ilford, Essex, and experts could see it was highly likely to explode at any moment. Miles ignored his own safety as he raced around warning residents to evacuate the area. He had succeeded in ushering several people to safety when the bomb went off without warning. Miles received serious injuries in the blast but refused to allow ARP staff to treat him, instead directing them to deal with a fire caused by a fractured gas main. Miles's injuries were so serious that he died later that day, five days before his thirty-sixth birthday. He left a widow and son.

Miles was awarded a posthumous GC on 17 January 1941 when his citation (which incorrectly gave his middle name as 'John' in the *London Gazette*) ended with a description of his bravery immediately after the bomb went off: 'Whilst lying awaiting the ambulance to remove him to hospital, he was conscious and obviously suffering; this did not reduce his sense of duty and when a fellow warden approached him to render whatever aid he could, Miles instructed him to attend first to the fire which had been caused by a fractured gas main. Warden Miles showed magnificent courage and devotion to duty.'

VIVIAN HOLLOWDAY
Rank/title: Aircraftsman (later Corporal)
Unit/occupation: RAF
DATE OF BRAVERY: JULY AND AUGUST 1940
GAZETTED: 21 JANUARY 1941

Vivian 'Bob' Hollowday was born in Ulceby, Lincolnshire, on 13 October 1916 – even though he sometimes gave his birthplace as Barton-on-Humber in various application forms. The son of an engineer, he attended Caistor Grammar School in Lincolnshire and Worksop College in Nottinghamshire before joining a firm in Nottingham. He joined the RAF Volunteer Reserve on 5 September 1939 and by 6 June the following year was at RAF Cranfield, Bedfordshire, undergoing training.

While serving in the RAF during the Second World War, he displayed great courage on two occasions – in July and August 1940. In both incidents, he attempted to rescue injured airmen from their burning aircraft. In the first incident, when returning to RAF Cranfield, Hollowday saw an aircraft crash and burst into flames. He ran to the wreckage and made his way through the burning debris, which was scattered over a wide area by the force of the impact. He found the pilot, whose clothing was on fire, and put out the flames with his bare hands. Had the pilot not been killed instantly in the crash, this action would probably have saved his life. During August 1940, Hollowday was again returning to his camp when an aircraft suddenly spun to the ground and exploded. He immediately went to the crash site where a second explosion occurred. Ammunition was exploding all the time but, despite this, he borrowed a gas mask, wrapped two sacks over himself and spent some time in the flames, making four attempts before he succeeded in releasing the first occupant. He then re-entered the burning wreckage and successfully removed the second. However, the two rescued men and the airman who remained trapped all died from their injuries. Hollowday's GC was announced on 21 January 1941 when his citation ended: 'Aircraftsman Hollowday displayed amazing courage and initiative on both occasions.'

Hollowday, who was married without children, left the RAF in March 1946. He was an active member of the Victoria Cross and George Cross Association from 1958 to 1977. He was also a member of the Legion of Frontiersmen and a committee member of the Royal Society of St George. He died in his home town of Bedford on 15 April 1977, aged sixty.

LAURENCE FRANK SINCLAIR (LATER SIR LAURENCE)

Rank/title: Wing Commander (later Air Vice-Marshal Sir Laurence Sinclair)
Unit/occupation: 110 Squadron, RAF
DATE OF BRAVERY: 30 SEPTEMBER 1940
GAZETTED: 21 JANUARY 1941

Laurence Sinclair has the distinction of being both the most senior and the most decorated holder of the GC. Born on 13 June 1908 in Frinton-on-Sea, Essex, he came from a military family. He was the second son of an Army captain. He entered the RAF College, Cranwell, Lincolnshire, in 1926 and was commissioned in 1928. His first posting was to No. 4 Squadron at Farnborough, Hampshire, and he was later posted to Iraq and India.

In 1937, he returned to India and it was here, in 1938, that he contracted a stomach problem, which led to the discovery that he had been born with only one kidney. This seemed to put an end to his flying career. However, his fortunes changed when war broke out in 1939. Indeed, on the same day that the Germans began their attack against France and the Low Countries, he was given command of No. 110 Squadron at RAF Wattisham, Suffolk, and was almost immediately sent to France. He led the squadron in attacks against German lines of communications, and after the evacuation the squadron returned to Wattisham. From here, the squadron continued its attacks but now targeted the Channel ports and the assembling invasion barges.

On 30 September 1940, Wing Commander Sinclair – Laurie to his family and friends – was on duty at RAF Wattisham when an aircraft burst into flames while taking off. When it became clear that the crew were trapped, Sinclair raced to the scene from the Officers' Mess. Even before he reached the airmen, two of the four 250-lb bombs in the plane exploded. There was a significant danger that the other two would go off, but Sinclair ran into the flames and dragged the air gunner clear of the burning aircraft. Unfortunately, the serviceman died from his injuries. Sinclair was awarded the GC on 21 January 1941 when his citation read: 'In this act this officer displayed the most complete disregard for his own safety.' At his investiture on 24 May 1941, he became the first RAF officer to have his GC presented to him by the King.

Sinclair went on to enjoy a distinguished career both during and after the war. As well as serving as an aide-de-camp (ADC) to George VI, he was Senior Air Staff Officer to the Balkan Force and he commanded No. 2 Light Bomber Group (Germany). After the war, Sinclair continued his brilliant military career, eventually serving with distinction in the Ministry of Aviation and the Ministry of Defence.

Sinclair was repeatedly honoured for his war and peacetime activities. He was decorated with the KCB, the CBE, and the DSO (Distinguished Service Order) and bar. He was also decorated by foreign countries: he received the Legion of Merit from the USA, the Légion d'honneur from the French and the Partisan Star from Yugoslavia. He served as Treasurer of the Victoria Cross and George Cross Association from 1957 for two years and he was a committee member until his death. A keen fisherman, he landed his last salmon at the age of ninety.

Sinclair, who was married with two children, spent his retirement in Great Brickhill, Buckinghamshire, although he moved to Oxfordshire after the death of his wife. He died on 14 May 2002, aged ninety-three. The gallantry and service medals of this remarkable man are on display at the Imperial War Museum in London.

HERBERT JOHN LESLIE BAREFOOT
Rank/title: Acting Major
Unit/occupation: Corps of Royal Engineers
DATE OF BRAVERY: SEPTEMBER AND OCTOBER 1940
GAZETTED: 22 JANUARY 1941

Timber merchant's son Herbert Barefoot was born in Dulwich, south-east London, on 15 May 1887. He attended Dulwich College and then the Architectural Association School of Architecture in London before working as an architect before the First World War. Indeed, the family house that he designed appeared in *Ideal Home* in 1926. During the Great War, he served in the Royal Naval Volunteer Reserve (RNVR) and the Royal Army Medical Corps (RAMC). He was mentioned in dispatches for bravery in the Middle East and, later, helped man the searchlights used during the Zeppelin raids on London. By the time the Blitz started in the Second World War, he was fifty-three, married with three sons and a veteran of war and of bomb disposal.

Acting Major Barefoot was a pioneer in bomb disposal work which, by definition, meant he was undertaking highly dangerous tasks. He worked on the first suspended parachute magnetic mine and it was this action that largely earned him the GC. By surviving this daunting challenge, he was able to provide invaluable information for other bomb disposal teams. Barefoot's bravery and devotion to duty were said to have inspired those working under him. His GC was announced on 22 January 1941 for 'conspicuous gallantry in carrying out hazardous work in a very brave manner'. He was the first Army officer to be awarded the GC.

After the war, Barefoot successfully resumed his career as an architect. He was also a talented artist and pianist. He died on 23 December 1958 in Ipswich, Suffolk, aged seventy-one.

ALEXANDER FRASER CAMPBELL
Rank/title: Second Lieutenant
Unit/occupation: Corps of Royal Engineers
DATE OF BRAVERY: 17 AND 18 OCTOBER 1940
GAZETTED: 22 JANUARY 1941

MICHAEL GIBSON
Rank/title: Sergeant
Unit/occupation: Corps of Royal Engineers
DATE OF BRAVERY: 17 AND 18 OCTOBER 1940
GAZETTED: 22 JANUARY 1941

Just two days after its heavy attack on Birmingham, the Luftwaffe switched its attention to Coventry, which manufactured armaments, aeroplanes, engines and vehicles. The attacks on 17 and 18 October 1940 caused massive damage to the city. Bombs fell on two of the Triumph Engineering Company's factories, which were both carrying out war work. The incident caused work at the two factories, which employed around 1,000 people, to stop and some nearby residents were evacuated.

Lieutenant Alexander 'Sandy' Campbell and Sergeant Michael Gibson, both from the Corps of Royal Engineers, were called to deal with an unexploded bomb at the site. Campbell had been born in Dalmellington, Ayrshire, on 2 May 1898 and Gibson, a coal miner's son, had been born in Chopwell, Co. Durham, on 21 June 1906. They were confronted with a perilous situation. Campbell discovered that the bomb was fitted with a delayed action fuse. He assessed that it would be foolish to tackle the bomb where it lay because of the risk to people and property. Instead, he called in a lorry to transport the bomb to a safer location a mile away.

The bomb was carefully lifted on to the vehicle. Campbell was so worried that the bomb would detonate en route that he lay down next to it so that he could hear, above the noise of the moving lorry, the bomb starting to tick. He planned that if he heard the bomb tick, he would shout to the driver and they could both run for cover. Fortunately, the timer was not activated and, once they were away from people and property, Campbell and Gibson disposed of it safely at Whitley Common.

As the bombs continued to fall on Coventry the next day, the two men were called to deal with another bomb. This time they were not so lucky: the bomb exploded, killing them both. Campbell, aged forty-two, was married to a school teacher and they did not have children, while Gibson, aged thirty-four, was married with two sons.

Their posthumous GCs were announced on 22 January 1941 for 'most conspicuous gallantry in carrying out hazardous work in a very brave manner'. It is believed that after Agnes Campbell's death, Sandy Campbell's GC and other medals were passed to his sister-in-law, who, in turn, presented them in 1994 to the Royal Engineers Museum in Gillingham, Kent.

JACK MAYNARD CHOLMONDELEY EASTON
Rank/title: Temporary Sub-Lieutenant (later Lieutenant)
Unit/occupation: Royal Naval Volunteer Reserve
DATE OF BRAVERY: 17 OCTOBER 1940
GAZETTED: 23 JANUARY 1941

BENNETT SOUTHWELL
Rank/Title: Able Seaman
Unit/occupation: Royal Navy
DATE OF BRAVERY: 17 OCTOBER 1940
GAZETTED: 23 JANUARY 1941

At the height of the Blitz, and as bombs were falling on Coventry, the Germans continued to pound London. A large number of bombs and landmines fell on the East End, among which was a huge unexploded bomb in Hoxton. Amid fears the device would explode, a vast number of local residents were evacuated.

Sub-Lieutenant Jack Easton, who was born in Maidenhead, Berkshire, on 28 May 1906, and Able Seaman Bennett Southwell, who was born in Rotherham, South Yorkshire, on 21 March 1913, were called to deal with the Hoxton bomb. They walked through empty, slate-strewn streets to the place where the bomb had crashed through the roof of a house and was hanging suspended through a hole in the ceiling. It was in a precarious position with the nose of the bomb only some six inches off the floor. Having assessed the situation, Easton, who before the war had qualified as a solicitor, realised it was too risky to try to move the device and instead decided to tackle the bomb where it was. He asked Southwell, the son of a railway porter, to stay in the passage outside and hand him the necessary tools.

However, Easton had only been working on the bomb for a minute when it slipped and there was the sound of falling brickwork. Easton then heard the whirring of the bomb mechanism

45

starting up and he knew he only had some twelve seconds to get away. He shouted for Southwell to run and both men fled in different directions.

Southwell reached the apparent safety of a nearby road and Easton just managed to reach a surface air raid shelter when the bomb detonated with a quite incredible force. Easton was knocked unconscious and, when he came to, he was buried beneath rubble. Rescuers dug him out of the debris and took him to hospital, where he was treated for a fractured back, skull, pelvis and two broken legs. Southwell, who had worked as a gardener before the war, was killed in the blast. Aged twenty-seven, he was married with a young son when he died.

Easton later wrote vividly about the incident in an article for a publication called *Wavy Navy*. He captured the sense of loneliness and anticipation as all bomb disposal personnel were forced to walk down evacuated streets to deal with a bomb:

> The tenant of the house, a bit excited and self-important, described what he believed to be the position and size of the mine. Then, supplied with all available information, the rating and I set off down the drab street. Those solitary walks towards the location of a mine always reminded me of the last scenes in the pictures of Charlie Chaplin. I had the feeling that a vast audience was watching the way I walked. It has been the last scene for several men I knew, though such morbid thoughts were absent that day. I was looking for the house described.

Easton also described the minute or so that was so nearly the final moment of his life as he struggled to defuse the bomb, and he provided a brilliant description of how it felt to be buried alive:

> The fuse was clear of obstructions, but when I attempted to fit the misnamed safety horns I discovered that the fuse had been damaged, probably as the bomb crashed through the house. The

horns would not go into their place. I handed the attachment back to the rating as useless and took the tools for unscrewing the keep ring. The damage to this had jammed it, and, although I exerted as much effort as I could, it would not turn. I had been working to detach the ring for perhaps a minute when the bomb slipped in front of me. There was a sound of falling brickwork as the chimney pot overhead collapsed, and I heard the whirr of the bomb mechanism. Unless I got clear, I had exactly twelve seconds to live.

On such work one had to plan ahead. When I discovered that the door could not be opened without disturbing the mine I had decided on a sequence of movements if the mechanism did become active. Now, to the stimulant of the whirring sound, I grasped and pulled open the door against the weight of the planks, for now it no longer mattered if the mine were disturbed and I ran. I was through the hall in two leaps. As I emerged from the doorway I saw my rating running down the street to what he, poor devil, thought was safety. I had no time to use distance for safety, and ran across the roadway to a surface air raid shelter opposite where I was. It was a red brick and concrete-roofed structure. I reached it and flung myself on its far side, its bulk between me and the house I had just left. I flung myself tight against it, face down to the ground.

I heard no explosion. It has since been explained to me that if you are near enough to an explosion of such force unconsciousness is upon you before any sound it makes reaches you, which is a merciful thing. I was not blinded by the flash that comes split seconds before the explosion, but that was all I experienced. I do not know what time passed before I became conscious. When I did I knew I was buried deep beneath bricks and mortar and was being suffocated. My head was between my legs, and I guessed my back was broken, but could not move an inch. I was held, imbedded.

Men dug me out eventually. To this day I do not know how long I spent in my grave. Most of the time I was unconscious. The conscious moments are of horror and utter helplessness. Being buried alive is certainly a good example of a living hell, and in the war years to come after 1940 the brave men, women and children of London and all of the other cities and towns, and villages of Britain not only have my sympathies but some – those who had been buried alive – had my prayers. I really knew the physical and mental torture they endured.

My rating was killed. He was beheaded by the blast. The mine destroyed six streets of working-class homes, and it was six weeks before his body was found among the rubble. He was a brave man and left behind a brave widow. I saw her receive her husband's decoration from His Majesty the King.

On 23 January 1941, while lying in hospital recovering from his injuries, the nurses told Easton that they should all listen to the 6 p.m. news. Easton's GC and Southwell's posthumous award were announced for 'great gallantry and undaunted devotion to duty'. Hospital staff then proceeded to produce two cases of champagne that they had stored under his bed – and the celebrations went on long into the evening. Easton spent a year with his back in plaster but he eventually made a good recovery.

In another incident, Easton successfully defused a parachute mine that had fallen through the roof of the Russell Hotel in central London. The owner was so thrilled that his business had been saved that he wrote Easton a cheque for £140 – a huge amount at that time – and said he and his family could have Sunday lunch at the hotel for life. But Easton repeated the story to his Commanding Officer, who tore up the cheque and refused to allow him to take up the lunch offer. 'We do this for honour not for money', Easton was told firmly.

By the latter stages of the war, Easton, now a lieutenant, skippered minesweepers and armed trawlers. During the D-Day landings, he was leading a minesweeping flotilla when a seaborne mine exploded under his ship. However, once again he survived the explosion and went on to lead a long and full life after the war. He returned to work as a solicitor in his grandfather's law firm of William Easton & Sons. Together with his second wife Joan, he lived for many years in Hampshire. Easton died on 29 November 1994 in Chichester, West Sussex, aged eighty-eight.

Southwell's posthumous GC, which his son Michael occasionally wore in honour of his father, was stolen in 1945. After his widow Marion reported the theft, the family was granted a duplicate award. Many years later, however, the original came up for auction and it was deemed that the then owner of the GC had bought it in good faith and was therefore entitled to sell it. Michael Southwell, by now grown up, bought the medal at auction. He is believed to be the only owner of an original and official duplicate GC awarded to the same recipient.

WILSON HODGSON CHARLTON
Rank/title: Acting Flight Lieutenant (later Squadron Leader)
Unit/occupation: RAF
DATE OF BRAVERY: SEPTEMBER AND OCTOBER 1940
GAZETTED: 21 JANUARY 1941

Chemist's son Wilson Charlton was born in Lanchester, Co. Durham, on 9 April 1907. One of four children, he joined the RAF long before the start of the Second World War. He married in 1932, while stationed at RAF Worthy Down in Hampshire, and he and his wife went on to have a daughter. Acting Flight Lieutenant Charlton continued to serve in the RAF during the war and was working on special duty for bomb disposal. He was prolific in dealing with more than 200 unexploded bombs in September and October 1940. The lack of major incidents during his role bears testimony to his cool bravery and his successful technique.

His GC was announced on 21 January 1941 when the citation praised his 'undaunted and unfailing courage'. He was held as a Japanese prisoner of war in Java from 1942 to 1945. At one point Charlton and twelve others escaped into the jungle, but they were recaptured. When Charlton regained his freedom, he was finally able to receive his GC in 1945.

Charlton, who was known affectionately as 'Bombs', was soon back doing what he was best at: he commanded Bomb Disposal 5134 Squadron from 1946 to 1948. Next he worked as a group armament officer from 1948 to 1950. He retired as a squadron leader in 1953 after more than twenty-seven years' service in the RAF. Charlton died on 12 May 1953 in Roehampton, Surrey, aged forty-six.

NORMAN TUNNA
Rank/title: Mr
Unit/occupation: Railway shunter
DATE OF BRAVERY: 26–27 SEPTEMBER 1940
GAZETTED: 24 JANUARY 1941

Norman Tunna was born in Birkenhead, Cheshire, on 29 April 1908. He was a thirty-two-year-old railway shunter when the Luftwaffe carried out its first major bombing raids on Merseyside. The blitz started at 7.30 on the evening of 26 September 1940 and, for the next twelve hours, 140 men of the Great Western Railway battled with the carnage. At first, they worked alone but later they were aided by the Fire Service as they fought to save docks, ships, cotton, food, armaments and, ultimately, lives.

The Morpeth dock area of Birkenhead and the scores of railway lines crowded with trains bore the brunt of the attack. The German planes flew in low and fast on their targets, some of which had been 'stabled' for the night. These included wagons loaded with bombs and shells of various sizes which were due to be loaded on to barges and ships the next morning. Other wagons contained drums of high-grade spirit, flares, daylight bombs and cordite fuses, while beneath tarpaulins lay depth charges, a particularly lethal and unstable load.

The situation was chaotic. As the sound of sirens, anti-aircraft fire and enemy planes echoed through the still, clear night, the order was given to reverse the train with the ammunition wagons away from the main shed and on to the main line where it would be further away from people and property. As the train was moved, scores of incendiary bombs fell from the sky.

From his work that day, Tunna, who was the son of a goods' checker on the railway, knew there were six wagons containing high explosives: various devices up to 500-lb bombs. He went to examine the wagons to see the extent of damage and found that burning debris was dropping from one of them. Furthermore, two incendiary bombs were burning inside the wagon. Tunna ran back to the engine where he collected a bucket of water. Racing back to the scene of the fire, he threw the water on the flames, which put the fire out under the wagon. But Tunna could now see that there appeared to be a fire inside the wagon. Climbing on top of the wagon, he saw that there was an incendiary wedged between two of the bombs which were, in turn, becoming dangerously hot. Staying calm, Tunna grabbed a shunting pole and prised the two bombs apart so that the incendiary fell on to the line. Despite his efforts, the woodwork of the wagon was still burning so that the bombs remained in danger of exploding.

At this point, he ran to get a stirrup pump and sprayed the bombs with water until the fire on the wagon was extinguished. Just to ensure there was no danger, Tunna got the driver of the train to position it under the water column so that all the wagons were given a thorough soaking. For his cool courage and determination to tackle repeated hazards, Tunna was awarded the GC. His award was announced on 24 January 1941 when the citation ended: 'Tunna's action displayed courage in very high degree and eliminated the risk of serious explosions, the results of which it would be difficult to measure.'

Tunna's courage was also recognised in one other way: a British Rail engine was named after him – one that served on the London Midland Region for many years. Tunna, who was married with two children, continued to work for the Great Western Railway and to live in Birkenhead, where he died on 4 December 1970, aged sixty-two.

HAROLD REGINALD NEWGASS
Rank/title: Temporary Lieutenant (later Lieutenant Commander)
Unit/occupation: Royal Naval Volunteer Reserve
DATE OF BRAVERY: 28 NOVEMBER 1940
GAZETTED: 4 MARCH 1941

It would be almost impossible to exaggerate the dangers that Temporary Lieutenant Harold Newgass faced in November 1940. For it was, without any doubt, one of the most hazardous challenges any bomb disposal expert has ever been presented with. On 28 November a German landmine fell on the Garston Gas Works on Merseyside. Over a wide area, industry was halted and no fewer than 6,000 people removed from the vicinity. Railway and dock sidings were closed and the gas supply to the south and east of Liverpool was shut off.

The mine had fallen through a large gasometer and the parachute had become entangled in the hole in the roof. The gaping hole had allowed some of the gas to escape and some of the roof to sink – the mine had been left resting precariously on the floor nearly upright, nose down in some seven feet of foul, oily water. It was also leaning on one of the six-foot-high brick piers on which, in turn, the iron pillars that supported the roof were fixed. As if this was not enough of a challenge, the bomb fuse was directly against the pillar, meaning that the mine had to be turned before it could be defused.

A senior engineer had pumped away some of the water and then cut a hole into the side of the gasometer, but after that one man, at his own insistence, was left to tackle the situation alone.

Newgass, who had been born into a wealthy family in central London on 3 August 1899, had served in the Territorial Army from 1918 to 1934. Now he found he was only able to breathe inside the highly inflammable space with the aid of oxygen supplied in cylinders. Six cylinders supplied by the Fire Service, each with a life of about thirty minutes, were needed for the operation. If Newgass, who was married with two daughters, had stayed for too long, he would have been rendered unconscious – while the mine would have remained alive and ticking. So he tried to make significant progress during each half-hour 'bite', before leaving the scene to switch cylinders. As he got more and more tired, each cylinder lasted for less and less of the supposed thirty minutes. 'Working in an oxygen mask is a bit of a strain,' he said with masterly understatement.

On his first cylinder, he assessed the situation and made his plan. On the second, he took down the tools and a ladder. The third sortie was used to put sandbags around the nose of the mine, before climbing on top of the brick pier and lashing the top of the mine to the iron roof support. On the fourth, he turned the mine, then removed the bomb fuse along with the unit primer and detonator. The fifth cylinder was used to turn the mine further, then he undid the clock-keep ring. On his sixth and final cylinder, he withdrew the clock, rendering the mine safe.

Brigadier Sir John 'Jackie' Smyth, the VC recipient and author, captured the tense mood and seriousness of the situation when he wrote: 'During these two days in November the world of Bomb Disposal held its breath, and waited for news of his progress – or for the almost inevitable bang that would signal his demise.'

Unsurprisingly, given his courage and skill, Newgass, who had successfully defused other bombs earlier in his career, was awarded the GC on 4 March 1941 for 'great gallantry and undaunted devotion to duty'. On 28 November 1940, the odds had been high that Newgass would die aged forty-one. In fact, he lived more than twice that long, eventually dying in Dorchester, Dorset, on 17 November 1984, aged eighty-five.

RAYMOND MAYHEW LEWIN
Rank/title: Sergeant (later Pilot Officer)
Unit/occupation: 148 Squadron, Royal Air Force Volunteer Reserve
DATE OF BRAVERY: 3 NOVEMBER 1940
GAZETTED: 11 MARCH 1941

Raymond Lewin was born in Kettering, Northamptonshire, on 14 January 1915. The son of a successful and wealthy business-man, he attended Kimbolton School in Cambridgeshire from 1927 to 1933 and was a member of the Air Training Corps. At Northamptonshire Air Club on 19 July 1934, he made his first solo flight in a De Havilland Moth. After training as a pharmacist, he and his brothers were about to try to make their fortunes from lemonade manufacture when the Second World War broke out. By this time, he was already serving with the Royal Air Force Volunteer Reserve and had logged 103 flying hours.

Sergeant Lewin was the pilot of an aircraft that took off on a night-bombing raid from the beleaguered island of Malta on 3 November 1940. Disaster struck shortly after take-off when the plane began to lose height. It then crashed into a hillside and burst into flames. Lewin scrambled free from the burning wreckage. Three of his crew of four also managed to climb out of the escape hatch. Despite being dazed and badly injured, Lewin's thoughts were only for his co-pilot who was trapped inside the aircraft.

He ran around the blazing wing, where the full fuel tanks were burning and could have exploded at any moment. Then he crawled under the wing, located the injured airman and dragged him from the plane. Lewin then half carried and half dragged the co-pilot forty yards from the burning aircraft to a hole in the ground. He covered the co-pilot's body with his own just as the bombs on the plane exploded. The entire crew survived, although Lewin was treated for a cracked kneecap and severe contusions to his face and legs. His GC was announced on 11 March 1941 when his citation ended: 'This superbly gallant deed was performed in the dark under most difficult conditions and in the certain knowledge that the bombs and petrol tanks would explode.'

Lewin's reprieve was, however, short-lived. While serving as a pilot officer, his bomber took off from Luqa airfield on Malta on 3 November 1941 and, after failing to gain height, crashed into a hillside. Comrades on the ground fought through heavy gunfire from enemy planes overhead to reach Lewin and his co-pilot in their Wellington bomber. Both men were seriously injured and badly burned. The co-pilot died soon after the rescue and Lewin died, while still receiving medical care, nearly three weeks later, on 21 November 1941 in Oakington, Cambridgeshire. He was twenty-six.

WILLIAM RADENHURST MOSEDALE
Rank/title: Mr
Unit/occupation: Station Officer and Rescue Officer, Birmingham Fire Brigade
DATE OF BRAVERY: 11–12 DECEMBER 1940
GAZETTED: 28 MARCH 1941

William 'Bill' Mosedale was born in Birmingham on 28 March 1894. One of six children and the son of a railway porter at Birmingham New Street station, he was educated in his home city and left school at fourteen. He started work as a tinsmith, but later joined the 5th Battalion, Royal Warwickshire Regiment, as a private. In 1910, Mosedale joined the 5th Irish Lancers and, after three years, reached the rank of corporal. Then, due to the early death of his parents, he was released from military duties to look after his younger siblings and his widowed grandmother. Following in his father's footsteps, he became a railway porter. Mosedale, who was married with two children, was also Station Officer and Rescue Officer at an auxiliary fire station of Birmingham Fire Brigade.

On the night of 11–12 December 1940, an enemy bomb had demolished the fire station where Mosedale worked, along with an adjoining house. As hundreds of tons of debris covered the site, it emerged that a number of firemen were trapped in the station along with a number of civilians in the house. Mosedale tunnelled into the control room but, once he was there, realised he could not reach his trapped colleagues. Undaunted, he then burrowed in from another direction where he found five men: one dead and four injured. He gave the injured men oxygen before leading them back through the tunnel he had just dug.

Having done all he could for his comrades, Mosedale turned his attention to those trapped in the demolished house. He directed operations to remove debris from the cellar of the property, but then discovered that the cellar itself had collapsed. Once again, he persevered and, using a different route, eventually tunnelled in to find the trapped residents. This time he discovered that three had been killed when the bomb struck, but four more had survived with injuries. He gave them oxygen before leading them to safety. It now became apparent that four more people had been trapped in the cellar below the fire station. Yet again, Mosedale directed the tunnelling operation and the badly injured victims were eventually found and he guided them to safety. Just as the last of the victims was led away, the entire cellar collapsed.

In all, the rescue operation had lasted twelve hours and had taken place during an intense enemy bombardment. Mosedale's bravery and dedication had led to twelve injured survivors being rescued – as well as four dead bodies being recovered. His GC was announced in the *London Gazette* on 28 March 1941 – by chance his forty-seventh birthday. His citation ended: 'In effecting the rescues he repeatedly risked his own life.'

In September 1944, Mosedale retired from the Fire Brigade after thirty years' service to become a fire prevention consultant.

A keen fisherman, he also bred bull terriers. His courage was legendary in his home city and in 1968 he was interviewed about his remarkable life for his local paper, the *Evening Mail*. 'Don't for God's sake write about me as a hero. I wasn't. Just a fireman doing his duty. Damn it, I was in the rescue department, wasn't I?' He died on 27 March 1971, a day before his seventy-seventh birthday.

MICHAEL FLOOD BLANEY

Rank/title: Acting Captain
Unit/occupation: Corps of Royal Engineers
DATE OF BRAVERY: SEPTEMBER–DECEMBER 1940
GAZETTED: 15 APRIL 1941

Michael 'Max' Blaney was born on 14 November 1910, almost certainly in Newry, Co. Down. He was the son of a GP from Newry. One of five children, he attended the Christian Brothers' Schools in the city. Later he attended University College, Dublin, where, as well as taking an engineering degree, he also won the bantam and lightweight boxing titles in 1929 and 1930 respectively. In 1931, his bravery was highlighted in the *Newry Reporter* after he rescued a twelve-year-old boy from drowning in Sandycove Bay, Co. Dublin. After university, he worked as a roads engineer for Newry Borough Council. Following the outbreak of the Second World War, he was granted an emergency commission as a lieutenant in March 1940. After being wounded in France, he returned to Britain and, in December 1940, joined the Royal Engineers' bomb disposal team.

Time and again Acting Captain Blaney risked his life to help residents of London's East End during the Blitz. On at least three occasions, the circumstances he encountered when arriving at the scene of an unexploded bomb were particularly hazardous. Wherever possible, Blaney preferred to tackle any device entirely alone so that no other life was put at risk. Early in the morning of 18 September 1940, an unexploded bomb fell in the centre of Manor Way, close to the junction with the East Ham and Barking by-pass. Blaney arrived at the scene and successfully dealt with the bomb, thereby enabling thousands of war workers to reach their places of employment. On 20 October 1940, an unexploded bomb fell in Park Avenue, East Ham. It was one of the few bombs to have two time fuses fitted to it and it presented a terrible danger to those chosen to tackle the device. Yet Blaney, as usual working alone in the most difficult of circumstances, successfully defused the bomb.

On 13 December, Blaney was called to deal with another unexploded bomb off Romford Road and Manor Road. The bomb had fallen on 5 December and, for more than a week, had caused serious disruption to an important traffic route in the area. By the end of 1940, the devices faced by bomb disposal men were often highly sophisticated. The bomb Blaney encountered that day was fitted with a Type-17 delayed action clockwork fuse together with a Type-50 fuse, which was specifically designed to delay any explosion until the bomb was moved or tapped.

On this day, Blaney had been accompanied to the scene by a colleague, Lieutenant James, where they found the bomb embedded some twelve feet below ground level. They had telephoned for steam sterilising equipment to deal with the device but, due to the breakdown of the vehicle bringing it, the equipment never arrived. This left them with only two gadgets with which to tackle the sophisticated bomb that they found: a new magnetic clock stopper (or Q-coil) and an electric stethoscope (an electric amplifier fitted with headphones). The purpose of the first piece of equipment was to stop the movement of the clock inside the fuse; the purpose of the second was to listen for any ticking in the bomb which was a sign it was about to explode.

Blaney assessed the difficult situation and hoped that, after more than a week, the Type-50 fuse would be inert. He decided to place the Q-coil on the bomb before the device was lifted and taken to an open space where it could be dealt with more easily and safely. A sling was positioned around the bomb in order to hoist it clear but the Q-coil presented a problem because it was getting in the way of the lifting tackle. He decided that the only solution was to lift the bomb without the Q-coil but that it should be re-fitted once the bomb was at ground level. As the bomb was lifted a couple of feet above its 'nest', it started to swing and so Blaney steadied it. Just as he stepped forward, the bomb exploded with maximum force.

Blaney, who was thirty, was not the only man to lose his life. Nine others perished with him: his colleague Lieutenant James, a staff sergeant, a lance corporal and five sappers were also killed, along with a police superintendent who had been watching the operation. Blaney's posthumous GC was announced on 15 April 1941 for 'most conspicuous gallantry in carrying out hazardous work in a very brave manner'.

Blaney's CO, Colonel H. J. S King, wrote to Blaney's parents to commiserate. He said: 'Your son's keenness, charm of manner, and unfailing gallantry endeared him to everyone with whom he came in contact, and I had the utmost confidence in his judgement and common sense . . . qualities which led me to single him out for such rapid promotion from Second Lieutenant to Captain . . .'

GEORGE WALTER INWOOD

Rank/title: Section Commander
Unit/occupation: 30th Warwickshire (Birmingham) Battalion, Home Guard
DATE OF BRAVERY: 15–16 OCTOBER 1940
GAZETTED: 27 MAY 1941

The Germans delivered a heavy attack on the industrial city of Birmingham on the night of 15–16 October 1940. Section Commander George Inwood, who was in charge of men from the 30th Warwickshire (Birmingham) Battalion of the Home

Guard, went to assist as the Luftwaffe bombs fell.

Police summoned Inwood, who had been born in the city on 14 September 1906, and his six men. They discovered that several people were trapped in a cellar beneath a house that had received a direct hit. The situation was made all the more hazardous by the fact that the cellar was full of gas which had left all those in it unconscious. Leading his men from the front, Inwood was lowered down into the cellar by a rope. Somehow he managed to drag and lift two of the trapped men to safety even though their state of unconsciousness made them dead weights. Despite being overcome himself by the gas, he insisted on being lowered down again in order to try to save more lives. However, his condition deteriorated after he was lowered down for the second time and he collapsed. Inwood was dragged out by a fellow member of the Home Guard, but died from the effects of gas inhalation, aged thirty-four.

Inwood, who was married with a son, was awarded a post-humous GC on 27 May 1941. The citation praised his 'most conspicuous gallantry in carrying out hazardous work in a very brave manner'. His widow, Lily, received his decoration at an investiture on 10 October 1941. His GC is in the Birmingham Museum and Art Gallery.

GEOFFREY GLEDHILL TURNER
Rank/title: Sub-Lieutenant (later Commander)
Unit/occupation: Royal Naval Volunteer Reserve
DATE OF BRAVERY: DECEMBER 1940
GAZETTED: 27 JUNE 1941

Chartered accountant's son Geoffrey Turner was born in Sheffield, Yorkshire, on 10 September 1903. He was educated at King Edward VII School in Sheffield before joining the family firm. He joined the Army on the outbreak of the Second World War, but was discharged on medical grounds and joined the Royal Naval Volunteer Reserve (RNVR).

By December 1940, Sub-Lieutenant Turner had some experience in handling explosive devices and had dealt with some fifteen unexploded mines in total. Turner had to handle a particularly difficult device in his home city when a landmine fell on the London, Midland & Scottish railway station, closing it and leaving its parachute draped over a railway carriage.

The landmine that fell on a wool factory in Great Howard Street, Liverpool, on 21 December 1940 was even more precarious. The one-ton device was partly suspended by its parachute, with its nose on the floor and its fuse hidden. However, Turner again dealt with it successfully.

Yet another landmine fell in the yard of a house in Cambridge Street, Seaforth, some 150 yards from the main Liverpool–Southport railway line. It was clear that the mine had been badly damaged and it was therefore essential to remove it as quickly as possible. Turner rigged a wire and moved the mine so as to expose the fuse and enable him to fit the safety device. However, only the top half of the fuse came away, leaving the clockwork and operating mechanism still in the mine. Turner elected to try to pick out the remains of the fuse with his bare fingers. Just as he was finishing his dangerous task, the clock started and he hurriedly retreated. After waiting five minutes, he decided it was safe to return to the mine. The situation was perilous because Turner had no idea how long the fuse still had to run. As soon as he touched the fuse, the clock started a second time. Again, he tried to race clear but the mine detonated almost immediately. Miraculously, Turner survived, though he was badly injured and severely shocked.

His GC – which was so close to being a posthumous award – was announced on 27 June 1941 for 'great gallantry and undaunted devotion to duty'. The extent of Turner's recovery from his injuries was remarkable. He rose to the rank of commander in the RNVR later in the war and commanded a Marine Commando unit during the invasion of Normandy, took part in the capture of Brest and fought with commandos into

Germany. In 1943, he was awarded the George Medal for still further courage.

After the war, he worked for a firm of manufacturing chemists and he married in 1946. Turner died in Halstead, Essex, on 9 February 1959, aged fifty-five.

FRANCIS HAFFEY BROOKE-SMITH
Rank/title: Sub-Lieutenant (Lieutenant Commander)
Unit/occupation: Royal Naval Volunteer Reserve
DATE OF BRAVERY: DECEMBER 1940
GAZETTED: 27 JUNE 1941

Francis Brooke-Smith was born in Letwell, Yorkshire, on 21 September 1918. The son of a sea captain, he was one of eight children. Brooke-Smith was educated at Downside Prep School near Bath and King Alfred's School in Wantage, Oxfordshire.

Sub-Lieutenant Brooke-Smith was just twenty-two when he had to deal with a desperately difficult situation while working for the Royal Naval Volunteer Reserve when he was called to an unexploded bomb. The device had plunged inside the deck locker alongside the engine room of fire-float *Firefly* in the Manchester Ship Canal. On arrival, Brooke-Smith found the bomb was firmly wedged but, using a rope, he was able to pull the device slightly clear of the engine room. Next, lying on the sloping engine casing and almost upside down, he managed to put a 'safety gag' in the fuse of the bomb. Barely able to move, the worst thing imaginable happened – the fuse's clock started to tick. Realising he had no chance of getting clear, he continued dealing with the device and, miraculously, the clock stopped and he eventually made it safe.

Brooke-Smith's achievement was all the more remarkable because it was the first time he had used a safety gag. Furthermore, as well as working almost upside down, he had to work only by touch because he could not see the hidden fuse. In short, the chances of him surviving were extremely slender.

Brooke-Smith's GC was announced on 27 June 1941 for 'great gallantry and undaunted devotion to duty' in relation to the Manchester Ship Canal incident. However, Brigadier Sir John 'Jackie' Smyth, the VC recipient and author, recounts that, in January 1941, Brooke-Smith was involved in an equally memorable incident. In all, he defused some twenty mines, before being transferred to HMS *Broadwater*, a former US destroyer. The ship was torpedoed by a German U-boat off Ireland on 18 October 1941 but, although there were heavy casualties, Brooke-Smith survived this and many other scrapes.

After the war, Brooke-Smith returned to live in his home county. After all the dangers he encountered during the war, it was perhaps ironic that he should die in an accident while riding his bike in Woodbridge, Suffolk, on 3 December 1952. Brooke-Smith, who had married only the previous year in New York, was thirty-four when he died and his widow later gave birth to their son.

JAMES PATRICK SCULLY
Rank/title: Acting Corporal
Unit/occupation: Royal Pioneer Corps
DATE OF BRAVERY: 8 MARCH 1941
GAZETTED: 8 JULY 1941

James Scully was born in Dublin on 20 October 1909. One of eight children, he went to school in Dublin before moving to London in around 1925. He worked as a labourer before, like many other Irishmen, joining the Royal Pioneer Corps.

On 8 March 1941, the situation seemed hopeless when rescue teams arrived at a row of houses in Merseyside that had been destroyed during the Blitz. The search for survivors, led by Lieutenant Chittenden, looked as though it would fail. However, also on the scene was Acting Corporal Scully. Shortly after arriving, Scully heard the faint voices of a man and a woman beneath the rubble of one of the houses. Eventually, the rescue team managed to clear away enough debris to reach the point where the two survivors were trapped. The rubble surrounding the man and woman was so heavy that the rescue team decided they needed to use wooden props and planks to support the weight. But the position was precarious and it was touch and go whether the wood would give way under the strain. Hour after hour, Scully stayed beside the trapped couple encouraging them and telling them that their ordeal would soon be over.

As one plank began to bend, Scully positioned himself beneath it so that his back was supporting the weight above him. However, the props all around were slipping and it looked highly likely that Scully and the two trapped people would be buried alive. Yet both Scully and Chittenden refused to leave the scene and at one point both men were supporting each end of the main supporting plank. The plank dropped lower and lower down and forced Scully to lie across the trapped man, who was by now unconsciousness.

In an incredible feat of endurance and courage, Scully remained in his position throughout the night until back-up rescue workers were able to reach the casualties and take them to safety. The entire operation had taken seven hours.

Scully's GC was announced on 8 July 1941 when his citation ended: 'When they first entered the house, Lieutenant Chittenden and Corporal Scully knew there was a grave risk of injury or death as the high walls nearby appeared about to collapse at any moment. Had this collapse occurred, they would have been buried under many tons of debris. Corporal Scully risked his life to save the two people and, though the position looked hopeless, Lieutenant Chittenden stayed with him.' Chittenden was awarded the George Medal.

Scully, a married man with six children, worked as a painter and decorator after the war. He died in South Shields, Tyne and Wear, on 28 December 1974, aged sixty-five. Two months after his death, Scully's five grown-up daughters fulfilled their father's wish that his medals should be donated to his regiment, where they are now on display at the Royal Logistic Corps Museum in Camberley, Surrey.

CHARLES HENRY GEORGE HOWARD

Rank/Title: The Right Honourable the Earl of Suffolk and Berkshire
Unit/occupation: Bomb disposal expert
DATE OF BRAVERY: SPRING 1941
GAZETTED: 18 JULY 1941

The wartime record of Charles Howard (the Earl of Suffolk and Berkshire) made him anything but a typical hereditary peer. He was born in Malmesbury, Wiltshire, on 2 March 1906, the eldest son of the 19th Earl of Suffolk and 12th Earl of Berkshire. His father was killed near Baghdad, Iraq, on 21 April 1917 while serving with the 1st Wiltshire Battery, Royal Field Artillery, meaning that Jack, as he was known to his family, inherited the title and family seat aged just eleven.

Suffolk, as I shall refer to him, was educated at Radley College in Oxfordshire and, after finishing his schooling, took a 'gap year' – rare in those days – to sail around the world. Science was his passion and, in 1934, he went to Edinburgh University. He married in the same year and the couple went on to have three sons.

By early in the Second World War, Suffolk was in charge of a scientific experimental unit and was tasked with finding ways to deal with new types of unexploded bombs. In order to do his job properly, he often went to examine devices in a specially equipped van, accompanied by his driver/handyman and his secretary. Suffolk's speciality was to analyse how to overcome the effects of a booby trap and other hazards that the enemy had used in its devices.

By definition, it was hazardous work but time and again Suffolk proved the better of the anonymous German bomb-makers. One of his most ingenious achievements was to defeat a so-called ZUS 40 device. This was designed to grip the inside end of the bomb fuse and mechanically fire the main charge when the fuse was pulled out. Suffolk's solution to this challenge was to cut a hole through the casing of the bomb so that he could remove the ZUS 40 in one single unit, complete with the fuse. However, he also devised an entirely different method of dealing with the ZUS 40 whereby he removed the main charge by inserting a high-pressure steam jet.

The skilful method that Suffolk used was hailed as an important and life-saving development. Although it was slow and tedious, it meant that every type of bomb and mine could be handled with greater safety, with the exception of an acoustic device in which sound provided the weapon's firing system.

On 12 May 1941, Suffolk and his small team were called to deal with an old, rusty bomb recovered from a weapons' dump the previous day. Suffolk decided they should take the device to a place in the Erith Marshes in Kent to examine it. One of Suffolk's superior officers visited the three workers as they studied the bomb and expressed surprise that they were taking such precautions to deal with such an old, and apparently harmless, device. However, when the officer got back to his London office, he was told the bomb had detonated, killing Suffolk, aged thirty-five, and his two assistants.

Suffolk never knew that he had been awarded the GC for his earlier work on the ZUS 40 device. His posthumous honour was announced on 18 July 1941, two months after his death, for 'conspicuous bravery in connection with bomb disposal'. His courageous and dedicated work undoubtedly saved many more lives throughout the rest of the war.

Suffolk's mother erected a memorial to her eldest son at Radley College. Furthermore, Greville Howard later paid an affectionate tribute to his elder brother in an interview with *Reader's Digest*:

Many were puzzled by my brother. He never used his title if he could avoid it and he was utterly without class consciousness. Unimpressed by rank, he treated generals and privates with the same grave courtesy. Some people, deceived by the tall, stooping figure with the ironic wit and long, black cigarette holder, thought him a titled eccentric playing with danger. But beneath the casual, easygoing facade was the brain of a trained scientist, dexterity of a skilled mechanic . . . Jack was a big man, exceptionally strong. When a factory making fuses for one of his experiments was blitzed, I saw him pick up a machine weighing 200 pounds and carry it to safety over a collapsed floor. His zest for life matched his size. He loved people, and seemed to attract them wherever he went, thriving on good company and good talk.

HARRY ERRINGTON

Rank/title: Mr
Unit/occupation: Tailor/Fireman, Auxiliary Fire Service
DATE OF BRAVERY: 17 SEPTEMBER 1940
GAZETTED: 8 AUGUST 1941

Harry Errington was born in Soho, central London, on 20 August 1910. One of three children, he was the son of Polish immigrants called Ehrengot, who had come to Britain in 1908. The couple had anglicised their surname shortly after arriving in London. Errington was educated at Westminster Jewish Free School in central London and won a scholarship to train as an engraver. However, he switched career to that of a tailor. During the war, he combined his craft with working as a volunteer fireman with the Auxiliary Fire Service (AFS).

Shortly before midnight on 17 September 1940, a bomb landed with devastating effect on a building that had been taken over by the AFS. The three-storey building, formerly a garage, was severely damaged as much of it had collapsed under the force of the bomb. Some twenty people were killed, including six firemen. When the bomb struck, Errington was one of three men who were in the basement, an area which doubled up as a rest room and an air raid shelter. Errington was knocked out by the blast and when he regained consciousness he discovered a fierce fire was sweeping through the basement. Dazed and injured, he picked himself up and made a rush for the exit. As he did so, he heard anguished cries from one of his fellow firemen, John Hollingshead. Errington rushed to Hollingshead's side and found him lying face down with his legs trapped by fallen debris. Despite the intense heat and handicapped by his own burned hands, Errington struggled to free his colleague. At one point, he used a blanket to shield himself and Hollingshead from the heat. After several minutes, Errington managed to free his colleague and then led him up a narrow back staircase which was partially blocked by fallen masonry.

However, as the two men staggered up the staircase in the choking dust and scorching heat, Errington saw a second colleague lying unconscious beneath a radiator. First, he took Hollingshead into the ground-floor courtyard, before leading him through an adjoining building and into the relative safety of a street. Then he turned around and went back into the burning building to try to recover his second colleague, John Terry. Errington was able to lift up the radiator and pull Terry free, before carrying him up the stairs.

All three were taken by ambulance to the Middlesex Hospital where they were treated for serious burns and other injuries. By the end of the year, all three men had recovered and were back on duty. Hollingshead and Terry both testified to the calmness, bravery and quick thinking of Errington. His GC was announced on 8 August 1941, nearly a year after the incident, when his citation ended: 'He showed great bravery and endurance in effecting the rescues, at the risk of his own life.'

Errington, who was a great sportsman with a love of basketball, spent much of his remaining career as a tailor. After he retired, he went on to become the Treasurer of the Victoria

Cross and George Cross Association from 1981. He was always a welcome visitor to his local fire station in Soho, where he was given a ninetieth birthday party in 2000. He was especially proud that the Fire Services College at Moreton-in-the Marsh, Gloucestershire, named a road on its site after him. Errington died in London on 15 December 2004, aged ninety-four.

HENRY HERBERT REED
Rank/title: Bombadier
Unit/occupation: 1 Maritime Anti-Aircraft Regiment, Royal Artillery
DATE OF BRAVERY: 20–21 JUNE 1941
GAZETTED: 23 SEPTEMBER 1941

Herbert Reed was born in Sunderland, Co. Durham, in 1911 (his exact date of birth is not known). The son of a sea captain and the eldest of four children, he was educated at Bede Collegiate School – now Sunderland College of Education – in his home city. He worked as a shop assistant before joining up. Initially, in 1938, he enlisted into the Royal Engineers Territorial Army, before transferring to the Royal Artillery two years later.

On the night of 20–21 June 1941, Bombadier Reed was serving in the steamship *Cormount* when it came under attack in the North Sea from E-boats (fast motorboats armed with torpedoes and other weaponry) and aircraft. At the time, she was sailing in convoy from the port of Blyth, Northumberland, to London. *Cormount* received a direct hit under the navigating bridge, but nevertheless returned fire.

The enemy bombardment was heavy but, despite a hail of bullets and cannon shells, those on board the ship continued to return fire. In the initial enemy fire, Reed had been badly wounded, but he had refused to leave his anti-aircraft gun. As the fighting continued, Reed could see that his chief officer had also been badly wounded. He ran to his aid, then carried him from the bridge and down two ladders to the deck in order to put his comrade in a safer, more sheltered place.

No sooner had he completed his task than Reed, who was single, dropped dead, aged thirty. Although he had made light of his own injuries, his stomach had been ripped open by machine-gun bullets. He was the only fatality of the attack. His body was returned for burial at Bishopswearmouth Cemetery in Sunderland. Reed's posthumous GC was announced on 23 September 1941 when his citation ended: 'By his gallant and utterly selfless action Gunner Reed saved the life of the Chief Officer.' Reed was also posthumously awarded the Lloyd's [War] Medal for bravery at sea.

BERTRAM STUART TREVELYAN ARCHER

Rank/Title: Acting Lieutenant (later Lieutenant Colonel)
Unit/occupation: Corps of Royal Engineers
DATE OF BRAVERY: 2 SEPTEMBER 1940
GAZETTED: 30 SEPTEMBER 1941

Stuart 'Archie' Archer was born in Hampstead, north London, on 3 February 1915 – during the First World War. He attended Sheringham House School in Hampstead and the then Regent's Street Polytechnic. Aged twenty-one, he qualified at the youngest possible age as an associate of the Royal Institute of British Architects. He pursued a career as an architect all his working life – with the exception of his time in the Army. In 1937, he joined the Honourable Artillery Company, Territorial Army.

In January 1940, the year after getting married, he was commissioned as an officer into the Corps of Royal Engineers and was posted to 553 Field Company. Lieutenant Archer quickly became a veteran bomb disposal expert and, by the end of August 1940, he had already dealt with some 200 bombs. These incidents included difficult and dangerous work on 27 August 1940, when he had to tackle the first enemy bomb with a new type of delayed action fuse. At this time, enemy bomb-makers had been deliberately tasked with coming up with a fuse which would kill bomb disposal experts – and others within its range. The arrival of the delayed action fuse meant that eighty hours were meant to elapse between the bomb being dropped, or found, and the device being tackled – unless there were exceptional circumstances.

The events of 2 September 1940 were most certainly exceptional. To start with, they took place after four of the most sustained days of bombing of the entire war. The German bombings of Britain had started in June 1940, shortly after the Dunkirk evacuations. But 29 August marked the start of another sustained period of enemy bombing which resulted in there being 2,500 unexploded bombs waiting to be tackled within forty-eight hours. During this period of heavy bombing, Archer, plus a sergeant from the Royal Engineers and twelve sappers were based in Cardiff, the Welsh capital.

It was around 9 a.m. on 2 September that Archer was told that a large number of unexploded bombs were hampering attempts by firefighters to control a major blaze at the Anglo-Iranian Oil Company's refinery at Llandarcy, near Swansea. Time and again already that year, Archer had held his nerve and displayed great courage while dealing with unexploded bombs.

But the situation he found shortly after arriving at the oil refinery at around 10 a.m. was more hazardous than even he had encountered before. The officer with the local bomb disposal section led him to a storage area where some oil tanks were already burning fiercely and others were so hot they seemed as though they were ready to burst into flames at any moment. In a relatively small part of the storage area, there were four unexploded bombs, including one directly under an oil tank.

Archer chose to tackle this bomb first, judging this to be the best way to prevent further fires from breaking out. Although this oil tank was not alight, two others just fifty and eighty yards away were already in flames. These were generating such intense heat that it was feared the tank that Archer was working on might also burst into flames. Indeed temperatures became so high that steel melted and – in the words of the historian John Frayn Turner – 'the tanks flared like gigantic Roman candles'.

To add to their already considerable difficulties, the bomb that Archer and his team were tackling had embedded itself diagonally in the corner of the concrete plinth at the base of the oil tank. With the heat generated from the two nearby burning oil tanks bearing down on them relentlessly, Archer and his men had to work in short, sharp stints before retreating to gather themselves for the next inevitable onslaught. Archer figured out that fifteen-minute shifts were ideal because they reduced the chance of one of his men making a fatal mistake.

After two hours of the most tense and arduous work, and with flames and smoke spiralling hundreds of feet into the sky, one of the three other bombs – the one nearest to the device they were working on – went off. The midday explosion took place 150 yards from where the men were working, forcing them to throw themselves on the floor in case they were hit by debris, flames or boiling oil. By 2 p.m., just as Archer and his colleagues were uncovering the bomb case on their device, another of the two other bombs in their area exploded. Miraculously, yet again the bomb disposal team escaped injury.

The bomb that Archer and his team were tackling was a 250-kilogram device, the casing of which had been split on impact with the ground. This left the main explosive so exposed that it was clearly visible through the crack. The fuse box had also been ripped away and there was a tangle of wires visible, too. Perhaps the most remarkable aspect of the whole operation was that Archer spent most of the time that he was defusing the bomb hanging upside down and reaching deep into the device at full stretch. Initially, he took off the circular base plate. Then he saw that it was powder explosive, which he scooped out of the way. Next, he examined the fuse pocket. As he gripped the exposed wires with pliers, he pulled until the fuse came away. This exposed the clockwork delayed action apparatus at the rear. Then he unscrewed the 'gaine' mechanism and placed the clockwork components in his pocket. When he looked again into the tube and shook it gently, another mechanism with another gaine came into view. He realised he was looking at a sophisticated booby trap that had been intended to kill any bomb disposal expert who was seeking to make safe the device. Moments after Archer unscrewed this second gaine there was a crack and a flash – which he realised had been caused by the detonation of a small cap.

The worst of the bomb disposal team's ordeal was over by 2.50 p.m. By then, they had been working in the hottest, tensest and most dangerous of circumstances for more than four and a half hours. During the operation, the men must have been aware that they were more likely to die than live, yet at no time did they flinch from their task, or ask to withdraw.

A study of the device by experts at the War Office revealed that the mechanism Archer had discovered was fitted with an anti-withdrawal fixture. It worked on the basis that, if the first gaine was removed, the second would detonate, causing death and carnage. Archer had been fortunate in that his bomb, unlike two others that had dropped nearby, was not timed to explode until after the period when he was handling it. He emerged from the experience with the distinction of being the first man to pull out a fuse from an anti-withdrawal booby trap and live to tell the tale.

Archer's GC was announced on 30 September 1941 when his citation praised his 'most conspicuous gallantry in carrying out hazardous work in a very brave manner . . . He had enjoyed unbelievable immunity from death and showed sustained nerve and courage of the highest order.' On another occasion during the war, after defusing ten small bombs in Swansea, he crashed his car into a lorry because of the blackout and broke his leg. His wife reacted to the news by saying 'Thank God for that!', hoping it would mean his dangerous bomb disposal work was ended for a time. However, Archer was soon back defusing bombs.

Archer, who rose to the rank of lieutenant colonel, survived the war and later became closely involved with the Victoria Cross and George Cross Association. Indeed, when, in 1965, the association was given permission to lay a wreath at the Cenotaph on Remembrance Day, Archer was one of the five men chosen to carry out the task. The wreath that he and his former comrades laid was one of the six main wreaths laid during the service. Archer also served as chairman of the association from 1994 until 2006. Once again, while in his eighties, he was chosen to lay a wreath at the Cenotaph in his role as chairman of the association. Archer, who retired as an architect from his firm Archer & Son in 1995, represented the association at the funeral of Queen Elizabeth the Queen Mother in 2002.

Archer, who has also been awarded the OBE, lives in north London. His wife Kathleen, who was known to family and friends as Kit, died fifteen years ago. However, he has three grown-up children, ten grandchildren and seven great-grandchildren. At ninety-five, he is the oldest surviving recipient of the GC. In the summer of 2010, his health was too frail for him to be interviewed for this book. However, there are some five hours of his tapes at the Imperial War Museum in London in which he talks about bomb disposal work. Furthermore, his daughter kindly supplied me with two diagrams that her father had drawn some two decades ago to explain the work he carried out near Swansea on 2 September 1940 – more than seventy years ago. The first showed a close-up view of the device that he tackled and the initial seven steps that he took to make it safe. He wrote in capital letters:

1. Took off the circular base plate.
2. Saw that it was powder explosive.
3. Scooped out the powder explosive.
4. I could then see the fuse pocket.
5. The fixing of the fuse pocket had been badly damaged at this end.

6. I grabbed hold of the fuse pocket and wrenched and levered it free at this end.
7. With wrenching back and forth I managed to break the fuse pocket free of its welding at this end then took it out altogether complete with fuse etc.

The second diagram is even more revelatory for it shows Archer reaching, upside down and with his sleeves rolled up, deep down into the bomb, which was, in turn, embedded in concrete close to an oil tank. By way of explanation, he again wrote two short notes in capital letters. The first note read: 'We excavated out to get at the fuse but the fuse top had been broken off by passing through the concrete and I could not get the fuse out from this side.' The second note, which had an arrow pointing at his arm as it extended into the bomb, read: 'Could just get at the fuse pocket by reaching inside.'

Archer's daughter was also keen to point out that on numerous occasions her father, after making a bomb as safe as he could at the scene, had insisted on driving it on his own to a remote place to detonate it. This was so the men working with him were not put at risk. 'He was well known for the love and care of his men,' she said.

In March 2010, a month after his ninety-fifth birthday, Archer and Major Pete Norton were the two GC recipients invited to attend an event in London to mark the announcement of the award of the GC to Staff Sergeant (now Warrant Officer Class 2) Kim Hughes and a posthumous GC to Staff Sergeant Olaf 'Oz' Schmid to mark their recent gallantry in Afghanistan.

4

THE AWARDS OF 1942

THE ISLAND OF MALTA
Rank/title: N/A
Unit/occupation: N/A
DATE OF BRAVERY: JUNE 1940–APRIL 1942
GAZETTED: 15 APRIL 1942

The island of Malta received the first of only two collective awards of the GC on 15 April 1942. The award came not in the traditional way – an announcement in the *London Gazette* – but instead in a handwritten letter from George VI to the Governor of Malta. It read: 'To honour her brave people I award the George Cross to the Island Fortress of Malta to bear witness to a heroism and devotion that will long be famous in history.'

Sir William Dobbie, the Governor, replied: 'The people and garrison of Malta are deeply touched by Your Majesty's kind thought for them in conferring on the Fortress this signal honour. It has greatly encouraged everyone and all are determined that by God's help Malta will not weaken but will endure until victory is won. All in Malta desire to express once again their loyal devotion to Your Majesty and their resolve to prove worthy of the high honour conferred.'

As the letter suggests, there was still considerable work to be done in repelling the enemy when the award was made in the spring of 1942 but the honour was in recognition of the bravery of the island's people during the previous two years. During this period, Malta became the most heavily bombed location on earth. This was because the island was seen as a vitally important strategic location for Britain and the Allied powers. It provided a crucial defence route to North Africa and the Middle East and its splendid natural harbour provided a safe haven for ship repairs. Furthermore, it provided a much-needed springboard for Allied forces – notably by air and sea – seeking to attack the enemy forces of Germany and Italy. It was no exaggeration to say that if Malta had fallen between 1940 and 1942, the whole North African campaign could have been lost too.

Malta's battle for survival began on 10 June 1940 when Italy joined the war. In his book *Faith, Hope and Malta GC*, Tony Spooner writes: 'Until 10 June, 1940, the island of Malta, nestling quietly in the Mediterranean, had had a quiet and not unpleasant war. It was only on that day that the Italian Dictator, Benito Mussolini, brought his country into the war on the side of her so far victorious German ally and so began Malta's travail from the new Axis forces. The fall of Paris just four days later, followed by the total French collapse by the 17th, further added to Malta's plight.'

In fact, Italy's entry into the war had changed things overnight for the islanders. On 11 June 1940, Italian bombers made eight raids on Malta. At the time, the island, which is smaller than the Isle of Wight, had a civilian population of around 250,000 as well as some 18,000 troops. Sir Winston Churchill and the Chiefs of Staff were in no doubt of Malta's importance. It was what Admiral Sir Andrew Cunningham later called 'the lynchpin of fate'. However, with Allied resources already thinly spread across the globe, it was left to three Gloster Gladiator biplanes to take on the weight of the Italian air force that had been given responsibility for crushing the island. *Faith, Hope* and *Charity*, as the planes were named by Flying Officer John Walters, spent three weeks repelling the enemy. By the end of June, four Hurricanes arrived as aerial reinforcements. During July, they joined the Maltese aircraft in taking on up to 200 enemy planes operating out of Sicily. The raids took place almost every day but such was the ferocity of the defence that the Italians soon restricted the raids to night-time. Yet the

Allied losses during this time were only one Hurricane and one Gladiator.

The enemy soon grasped Malta's strategic importance, too. The number of raids was stepped up and the Allies realised that, unless they provided Malta with further reinforcements, the island would fall. On 2 August 1940, HMS *Argus* reached within 200 miles of Malta to fly off twelve Hurricanes and two Skuas, which all landed safely on the island. Lieutenant General Sir William Dobbie, who was also the island's Commander-in-Chief, was a tenacious, disciplined Scot. As well as pressuring Churchill for air and ground reinforcements, he introduced conscription, a move that was unpopular with some but which provided much-needed additional manpower for anti-aircraft artillery and battalions of infantry. Until August, the enemy had concentrated their attacks on the dockyards in and around Valetta, the Maltese capital. Then they began a heavy bombardment of the airfields in an attempt to wipe out the island's first line of defence. Throughout the autumn of 1940, the enemy stepped up its offensive. First, the Italians used German dive-bombers – Junkers 87s – and then the Luftwaffe arrived on airfields in Sicily. By November, further reinforcements were on their way to the island, again on board HMS *Argus*. However, with the Italian fleet approaching, twelve Hurricanes and two Skuas took off from their maximum flying distance. Only four Hurricanes and one Skua reached the besieged island – the rest ran out of fuel. Brave deeds from servicemen and islanders alike were commonplace and Christmas Eve 1940 saw the award of the first of eight GCs for individual bravery involving the defence of Malta.

Malta was lurching from one crisis to another as it saw in the New Year. The aircraft carrier HMS *Illustrious*, stricken by an earlier enemy attack, reached the island's Grand Harbour with a convoy. The inevitable enemy aircraft attack – involving more than seventy aircraft – soon followed on 16 January despite the fiercest anti-aircraft barrage of Malta's war. No fewer than 200 homes on the island were destroyed and a further 500 damaged.

Yet, despite this intense barrage from the skies, *Illustrious* slipped away safely towards Alexandria under cover of darkness on 23 January. The first six months of 1941 saw a relentless wave of attacks, sometimes involving more than 100 aircraft. Yet more Hurricanes were dispatched in an attempt to prevent the island from falling. However, there was a slight let-up at the end of June when Hitler sent his armies into Russia and he withdrew the Luftwaffe from Sicily in order to support them. Indeed, the Allies now went on the offensive, intensifying attacks on Italian shipping. Between July and September, British naval forces based on Malta sank 150,000 tons of Axis shipping and in October alone some 60 per cent of Mussolini's supply ships were sunk. But there were setbacks, too: after the fall of Crete in June 1941, Malta found itself 1,000 miles from her nearest help.

Early in 1942, Hitler became determined to end Malta's resistance once and for all and the Luftwaffe returned to the skies above the island, this time for the 'kill'. By March, with the onslaught at its height, fifteen Spitfires flew to Malta from the aircraft carrier HMS *Eagle*. April's onslaught was even more intense with 6,728 tons of bombs dropped on the island. In the same month, 300 people were killed on Malta and more than 10,000 buildings were destroyed. Each day typically saw three raids and 170 bombers so that during April the island spent a total of twelve days ten hours and twenty minutes under bombing alerts. However, with America now fighting with the Allied forces, Churchill persuaded President Franklin D. Roosevelt that Malta needed help and he allowed the fast aircraft carrier USS *Wasp* to sail between Gibraltar and Malta at night with up to fifty Spitfires. Although further Spitfires and Hurricanes arrived in Malta, they were always hugely out-numbered by enemy planes. On occasions, just a dozen Hurricanes took off to confront around 100 enemy aircraft. It was halfway through this month – April 1942 – that the King conferred the GC on Malta.

It was on 13 September 1942 that the GC, which had been awarded five months earlier by the King, was presented to the recipients. Field Marshal Lord Gort, who had succeeded Sir William Dobbie as Governor, presented the decoration to Sir George Borg, Chief Justice, who received it on behalf of the people of Malta in the ruins of the Palace Square. The GC was later taken all around the island so that its inhabitants could see their award. It was a much-needed morale booster for the island, which remained well and truly under siege.

It would easily be possible to devote an entire book to the bravery of Malta's people prior to 15 April 1942 and another to the island's heroism after that date. However, *George Cross Heroes* deals with the stories behind all 161 awards and the details of the battles to lift the siege of Malta must be left to other history books. Yet a few statistics tell their own story. Between June and November, the island had 3,215 air raid warnings – and an average of one every seven hours for two and a half years. During the same period, the Germans and Italians dropped 14,000 tons of bombs which killed 1,468 Maltese civilians and destroyed or damaged some 24,000 buildings. Yet the enemy also lost 1,129 aircraft, including almost 200 in April 1942 alone.

There were many remarkable moments. On 10 May 1942, HMS *Welshman*, a mine-laying cruiser, steamed into Grand Harbour loaded with ammunition. As the Germans launched the inevitable attack, Spitfires were scrambled while a regiment of British soldiers successfully unloaded the ship. Early in May, some 172 enemy aircraft were shot down for the loss of three Spitfires.

Yet, despite the mayhem, the 'normal' life of the island continued. Brigadier Sir John 'Jackie' Smyth, the VC recipient and author, wrote: 'The peasant farmers worked in the fields, the shopkeepers kept open – those of them who still had shops; the schools remained open most of the time; the priests celebrated Mass regularly; the Police Force could have good reason to be proud of the part it played; and the nurses and the nuns devoted themselves selflessly to the care of the wounded, the maimed and the sick. It was lack of food which so nearly brought the Maltese to their knees.'

By August 1942, with food and other supplies on the island at an all-time low, the Governor of Malta was close to capitulation. Operation Pedestal was mounted to save the day and get much-needed oil and kerosene supplies to the island. The *Ohio*, a 14,000-ton tanker owned by the Texas Oil Company and loaned to the British Ministry of War Transport, was chosen to transport the oil and kerosene. The battleships HMS *Nelson* and HMS *Rodney* were chosen to lead the main covering force. Force Z, as the escorting ships were known, also contained cruisers and cargo ships and, vitally, aircraft carriers, notably HMS *Indomitable* and HMS *Victorious*, which were capable of putting seventy aircraft into the air. The RAF ensured extra air protection from Malta and the US made a contribution of two fully-manned merchant ships to join the convoy. On 8 August 1942, the convoy sailed from the Strait of Gibraltar under cover of darkness. On 11 August, the first action saw the carrier HMS *Eagle* sunk by a U-boat and the next day brought heavy air attacks. One merchant ship and a destroyer were sunk and HMS *Indomitable* was badly damaged. Other heavy losses – seven merchant ships and two cruisers – took place overnight and *Ohio* was struck by a torpedo. By the evening of 13 August, three ships had somehow managed to reach Grand Harbour but the *Ohio* was still under relentless attack and, after a Stuka crashed on to her deck breaking her 'back', she was twice abandoned and twice reboarded. On 14 August, *Ohio* was hit twice more. However, as dawn broke on 15 August, *Ohio* was lifted between two destroyers into Valetta harbour amid joyous scenes. After the last of her fuel was pumped off, the stricken ship sank. Only five out of the original fourteen merchant ships also got through and there was a heavy loss of life: some 350 merchant seamen and servicemen. However, Malta had been resupplied and the island had survived to fight on.

By early October, the island was still facing a heavy bombardment but Rommel's defeat in late October and the advance of the Americans from the west saw the tide gradually turn in favour of the courageous islanders. In 1943, it was the Italians, rather than the Maltese, who felt the pressure until their eventual capitulation in September. On 11 September 1943, Admiral Cunningham signalled the Admiralty: 'Be pleased to inform their Lordships that the Italian battlefleet now lies at anchor under the guns of the fortress of Malta.'

Britain was not the only Allied power to recognise the heroism of the people of Malta. During his visit to the island, President Roosevelt read out a citation, dated 7 December 1942: 'In the name of the people of the United States of America I salute the Island of Malta, its people and defenders, who, in the cause of freedom and justice and decency throughout the world, have rendered valorous service far above and beyond the call of duty.

'Under repeated fire from the skies, Malta stood alone but unafraid in the center of the sea, one tiny bright flame in the darkness − a beacon of hope for the clearer days which have come. Malta's bright story of human fortitude and courage will be read by posterity with wonder and with gratitude through all the ages.

'What was done on this island maintains the highest traditions of gallant men and women who from the beginning of time have lived and died to preserve civilization for all mankind.'

Today there are numerous reminders of the courage of the Maltese people. They include a coastal monument which commemorates the award of the GC to Malta and honours some 7,000 service personnel and civilians who gave their lives during the Siege of Malta from 1940 to 1943. *Faith*, the sole surviving defending biplane, is on show at the National War Museum in Valetta along with the original letter from George VI which conferred the GC. While the rest of Valetta has been rebuilt, the Opera House has been left derelict as a reminder of the islanders' suffering. In 1992 a handsome silver £5 coin was struck to commemorate the fiftieth anniversary of Malta receiving the GC. In the same year, also to mark the anniversary, the Queen and the Duke of Edinburgh travelled to Malta along with twenty-two George Cross holders. Ten years later, in 2002, fifteen George Cross holders were invited by the Government of Malta to visit the island for a week of celebrations. Today the small silver cross – Malta's GC – has a special place of honour in the Governor's Palace: a fitting tribute to the world's only 'George Cross Island'.

ERNEST OLIVER GIDDEN

Rank/title: Temporary Lieutenant (later Lieutenant Commander)
Unit/occupation: Royal Naval Volunteer Reserve
DATE OF BRAVERY: 17 APRIL 1941
GAZETTED: 9 JUNE 1942

Ernest 'Mick' Gidden was born in Hampstead, north London, on 15 March 1910. He was educated at the University College School in Hampstead. In 1940, he joined the Royal Naval Volunteer Reserve – and he married in the same year.

In the spring of 1941, bombs were still falling on Britain before the pause as Hitler switched his resources to target Russia. On 17 April, an unexploded mine dropped on to Hungerford Bridge, central London, causing immediate chaos. The nearby Charing Cross Hotel was burning to the ground and sleepers on the railway track were also ablaze. Many buildings, including the War Office, were evacuated and the Underground trains were halted. This was the scene that greeted Temporary Lieutenant Gidden as he arrived at the scene shortly after dawn.

By April 1941, Gidden had already dealt with some twenty-five mines over the previous year. However, this one was in a different league of difficulty. The mine was lying across the live electric rail – partly fused on to the track – and the bomb fuse and primer release mechanism were facing downwards. This meant that the bomb had to be turned over before the fuse – one of the sensitive and dangerous clockwork variety – could be tackled.

As gently as he could, Gidden rolled over the mine and removed a large piece of melted metal from the fuse. However, the damage to the device meant he was unable to position a gag into the fuse to prevent the mine from detonating. Gidden eventually used a hammer and chisel to ease the mine away from the railway line and he was then able to make it safe. The operation had taken six hours. It was sixteen months later – on 5 June 1942 – that his GC was announced for 'gallantry and undaunted devotion to duty'.

Gidden, who had one son, also received the George Medal and the OBE for his courageous wartime work. After the war, he ran the family firm, Gidden's of Mayfair. He died in London five days before Christmas Day 1961, aged fifty-one.

KARL MANDER GRAVELL

Rank/title: Leading Aircraftsman
Unit/occupation: Royal Canadian Air Force
DATE OF BRAVERY: NOVEMBER 1941
GAZETTED: 11 JUNE 1942

Karl Gravell was born in Norrköping, Sweden, on 27 September 1922. He was initially educated in Sweden before attending King Edward High School in Vancouver for a year from 1939. He joined the Royal Canadian Air Force as soon as he could in the Second World War. During the autumn of 1941, Leading Aircraftsman Gravell, who had boyish good looks, was training at the Canadian Wireless School in Calgary.

In November 1941, he and his pilot were in their Tiger Moth training aircraft when the engine stalled and the plane crashed and burst into flames. Gravell crawled from the wreckage and clear of the scene, with his clothes still alight. He was in a pitiful state: blinded in one eye, with critical burns to his body and suffering from acute shock. Yet, as soon as he realised the pilot was still trapped in the burning wreckage, he staggered back to the aircraft in an attempt to pull Flying Officer James Robinson to safety. Before he was able to reach his comrade, Gravell was again engulfed in a mass of flames which forced him to retreat.

As he was being taken to hospital by ambulance, he told the medic: 'Please don't tell my mom, she would only worry.' Gravell subsequently died from his injuries on 10 November, 1941, aged nineteen. He is buried at Mountain View Cemetery in Vancouver. His posthumous GC was announced on 11 June 1942 when his citation ended: 'Had he not considered his pilot before his own safety and had he immediately proceeded to extinguish the flames on his own clothing, he would probably not have lost his life.'

WILLIAM EWART HISCOCK
Rank/title: Acting Lieutenant Commander
Unit/occupation: Royal Navy
DATE OF BRAVERY: SEPTEMBER 1941
GAZETTED: 16 JUNE 1942

William Hiscock was born in Dorchester, Dorset, on 13 January 1886. His father worked as a pattern-maker to an engineer. Hiscock joined the Royal Navy in 1904 on his eighteenth birthday and was commissioned at the start of the First World War. In 1934, Lieutenant Hiscock retired from the Royal Navy following a distinguished career that spanned thirty years. His retirement, however, lasted just five years. After the outbreak of the Second World War in 1939, he was recalled and sent to St Angelo, Malta, to take charge of the disposal of seaborne mines which were being laid by the enemy in the island's sea lanes and harbours.

In September 1941, Hiscock, by now fifty-five, was promoted to acting lieutenant commander. He was still responsible for dealing with seaborne mines and, in 1941, it was announced he had been awarded the Distinguished Service Cross (DSC) for 'courage, enterprise and devotion to duty in contact with the enemy'.

Hiscock was also given the task of dealing with a 'torpedo machine' – a specialist weapon favoured by the Italians. The deadly device had been dropped in fifteen feet of water in St George's Bay. It was an operation fraught with danger; apart from the possibility of booby traps, no information was available on the firing mechanism of the explosive head. In particular, its behaviour when parted from the device was not known.

Throughout his naval career, Hiscock had led from the front. As he and his assistant, a petty officer, tackled the device, the clock mechanism started ticking. There was no opportunity to make their escape and so they continued calmly to work on it. Mercifully, it failed to detonate and the pair eventually succeeded in disarming it. Hiscock also ensured he learnt more about its mechanism for future reference.

Five months later, on 15 February 1942, Hiscock was killed in Malta while attempting to defuse yet another bomb. He was fifty-six. He was unaware that he had received the GC, which was announced on 16 June 1942 for 'great gallantry and undaunted devotion to duty'. He is commemorated at Capuccini Naval Cemetery, Malta.

ALBERT MATTHEW OSBORNE
Rank/title: Leading Aircraftsman
Unit/occupation: Royal Air Force Volunteer Reserve
DATE OF BRAVERY: JUNE 1940–APRIL 1942
GAZETTED: 10 JULY 1942

Matt Osborne, as he was known to family and friends, was born in Grimsby, South Humberside, on 19 October 1906. He was the son of a fisherman, who, after a bad accident, had opened a business with his wife close to their home in Cleethorpes. Osborne is believed to have gone to boarding school in Blackpool before enlisting into the RAF in July 1940.

During the enemy air attacks on Malta, Osborne repeatedly showed astonishing courage. Indeed, the remarkable citation for his GC on 10 July 1942 lists no fewer than nine acts of gallantry. It said: 'During a period of fierce enemy air attacks on Malta, Leading Aircraftman Osborne has displayed unsurpassed courage and devotion to duty. In circumstances of the greatest danger he was always first at hand to deal with emergencies, whether in fire-fighting operations or in rescue work.'

The nine examples of his courage listed were that he:

- Rendered safe the torpedo of a burning torpedo aircraft, working three feet from the main petrol tank for ten minutes.
- Extinguished a burning aircraft during a heavy bombing attack.
- Attempted to save a burning aircraft and subsequently removed torpedoes from the vicinity.
- Assisted in saving the pilot of a burning aircraft and extinguishing the fire.
- Saved an aircraft from destruction by fire.
- Attempted for six hours to extricate airmen from a bombed shelter, despite continued heavy bombing and danger from falling stonework.
- Fought fires in two aircraft, saving one of them.
- Freed the parachute of a burning flare caught in an aircraft, enabling the pilot to taxi free.
- Halted the fire in a burning aircraft, thereby leaving most of it undamaged.

Yet more bravery followed. During a heavy air attack, Osborne led a party to extinguish the flames of a burning aircraft. During this incident, a petrol tank exploded and he was injured and affected by the fumes. Once he felt he had recovered sufficiently, he returned again to fight the fire. This time, while attempting to pour water over torpedoes that were in danger of exploding, he was killed by the explosion of an 'air vessel'. He died on 1 April 1942, aged thirty-five. Through his repeated firefighting and rescue operations, Osborne had undoubtedly saved many lives. The lengthy citation to his posthumous GC ends: 'This airman's fearless courage and great leadership on all occasions have been beyond praise. The Air Officer Commanding, Royal Air Force Mediterranean, has stated that he was "one of the bravest airmen it has been my privilege to meet".'

DUDLEY WILLIAM MASON
Rank/title: Captain
Unit/occupation: Merchant Navy
DATE OF BRAVERY: 12–15 AUGUST 1942
GAZETTED: 4 SEPTEMBER 1942

Dudley Mason was born in Surbiton, Surrey, on 7 October 1901. One of two brothers, his family moved to nearby Long Ditton, where Mason and his brother went to school. Aged nineteen, Mason joined the Eagle Oil Company as an apprentice.

By early in the Second World War, Captain Mason was an officer in the Merchant Navy. In August 1942, he was in command of the SS *Ohio*, a 14,000-ton American tanker belonging to the Texas Oil Company. However, she had been chartered by the Ministry of War Transport and was only under the nominal ownership of Mason's long-time employer, the Eagle Oil Company. By this point in the war, Winston Churchill, Britain's war leader, was acutely aware of the strategic importance of ensuring that Malta did not fall into enemy hands. He needed to keep resupplying the island and, in August 1942, fourteen merchant ships took part in such an operation code-named Operation Pedestal. The convoy was escorted by strong naval and air support. The *Ohio* was carrying some 1,000 tons of fuel while the other thirteen vessels were carrying food, medicine and additional fuel.

The Axis command, however, learnt of the convoy and on 11 August launched a fierce and sustained assault on the ships. During the early morning, an Italian torpedo struck the *Ohio* and for four days she came under relentless attack. The air attacks began on 12 August and it soon became clear that the *Ohio* was the focus of attention from U-boats and enemy planes. A second torpedo caused extensive damage while two sticks of bombs lifted her right out of the water when they struck. Another bomb damaged her boiler room, while a Stuka plane crashed and exploded on the deck of the *Ohio*, resulting in her 'back' being broken.

Yet, Mason, aided by Chief Officer Douglas Gray, who was at the helm and was steering by 'eye' without a compass, somehow kept the *Ohio* going. The ship struggled on towards Malta and the short-range Malta Spitfires were able to ward off some enemy attacks. Eventually, the *Ohio* and the *Dorset* were hit once again and the latter sank. For forty-eight hours from 11 a.m. on 13 August, the stricken *Ohio* had to be towed. With Mason and his crew suffering from exhaustion, she came to a halt some twenty miles from the Maltese capital of Valetta. As the towing wires snapped and the ship came under yet further punishment, the *Ohio* eventually needed four separate lines and had to be carried over the line, lashed between two destroyers. After two of the attacks, the damage had been so bad that the order was given to abandon ship and she was later reboarded. Mason and his crew were given a hero's welcome. It was only when the last of the fuel had been pumped out that the *Ohio* finally sank.

Mason, who had received burns to his hands, and his friend and comrade, Chief Engineer James Wyld, who had also performed heroically, were flown back to Britain. Wyld later became the first officer in the Merchant Navy to receive the

Distinguished Service Order (DSO). Five Distinguished Service Crosses (DSCs) and seven Distinguished Service Medals were awarded to other officers and crew. Mason's GC was announced on 4 September 1942 and ended with the words: 'The violence of the enemy could not deter the Master from his purpose. Throughout he showed skill and courage of the highest order and it was due to his determination that, in spite of the most persistent enemy opposition, the vessel, with her valuable cargo, eventually reached Malta and was safely berthed.'

Earl Mountbatten of Burma, whose nephew had been in the escort party that helped the *Ohio* into harbour and who had reported back on Mason's courage, wrote the captain a letter praising his 'courage and perseverance' resulting in the award of a gallantry medal. 'May I offer you my most sincere congratulations on one of the best earned George Crosses of the war,' Mountbatten said. Mason, however, considered the award was to his entire crew.

Mason, who was twice married, was the subject of a bronze bust now on show at the Imperial War Museum in London and a painting, picturing his ship under enemy attack, by Terence Cuneo. He died in Brockenhurst, near Lymington, Hampshire, on 26 April 1987, aged eighty-five.

GEORGE HERBERT GOODMAN

Rank/title: Temporary Lieutenant (later Lieutenant Commander)
Unit/occupation: Royal Naval Volunteer Reserve
DATE OF BRAVERY: 1941–2
GAZETTED: 15 SEPTEMBER 1942

George Goodman was born in Bromsgrove, Worcestershire, on 25 November 1900. He was the third child of a Birmingham solicitor and he was educated at West House School, Edgbaston, and Dauntsey's School, West Lavington, Wiltshire. After leaving school, Goodman, a talented pianist and figure skater, worked as a farming student for a land agent and, later, a chartered surveyor. Goodman joined the Royal Naval Volunteer Reserve on 6 October 1939, aged thirty-eight. He was a talented mine and torpedo disposal officer and was awarded the MBE on 29 August 1941. Shy, retiring and careful, he was affectionately known as 'Granny' by his comrades. On Christmas Eve 1941, he had rendered safe and stripped the first 'Sammy' mine recovered in the eastern Mediterranean.

It was with great trepidation that on 15 January 1942 Temporary Lieutenant Goodman and his small team approached an Italian self-destroying surface torpedo off the North African coast. Just days earlier, the torpedo officer of HMS *Medway* and his support team had been killed tackling a similar device. Goodman knew that he had the chance to become the first person to render safe an Italian example of this fiendish machine. Working under huge strain, he removed three detonating pistols from the device and also separated the 'strikers' from the detonators and primers. As well as saving his own life and that of others, he learnt valuable secrets about how the device was made, ones that could be used in future recovery operations.

Goodman's GC was announced on 15 September 1942 for 'great gallantry and undaunted devotion to duty'. He survived the war in Europe but died near Rotterdam, The Netherlands, on 31 May 1945, aged forty-four, apparently after entering a booby-trapped house. He is buried at Westduin General Cemetery in The Hague.

JOHN STUART MOULD

Rank/title: Lieutenant (later Lieutenant Commander)
Unit/occupation: Royal Australian Naval Volunteer Reserve
DATE OF BRAVERY: 14 NOVEMBER 1941–30 JUNE 1942
GAZETTED: 3 NOVEMBER 1942

Architect's son John Mould, 'Mouldy' to his friends, was born in Gosforth, Newcastle upon Tyne, Northumberland, on 21 March 1910. His family emigrated to Australia when he was two. Mould was educated at Sydney Grammar School before studying part-time at Sydney Technical College while working in his father's architect's practice from 1927 to 1932. He then spent two years in London, becoming an associate of the Royal Institute of British Architects, before returning to Australia to join his father's architect's business, which became Mould and Mould Architects. In April 1935, he married and the couple later had one child.

Mould always looked upon himself as Australian rather than British and on 14 June 1940 he enlisted in the Australian Imperial Force. He fell ill but, after recuperating, joined the Royal Australian Naval Volunteer Reserve on 14 September 1940 as a sub-lieutenant. He was sent to Britain where he joined HMS *Vernon* to work on enemy mines. He joined at about the same time as his fellow Australian Hugh Syme and, between them, they eventually successfully handled more than 100 mine disposals. The two men were physically courageous and technically skilled – a perfect combination for their line of work.

As Lieutenant Mould, he worked as part of the Rendering Mines Safe (RMS) section of the Royal Navy, which meant he specialised in mines dropped at sea or washed up on the shore. It was his work in tackling German G mines that resulted in him being decorated. Between 14 November 1941 and 30 June 1942, Mould took part in repeated mine disposal work. Time and again, he tackled mines fitted with 'anti-stripping' devices, which had claimed the lives of many other bomb disposal experts. He constantly devised ingenious and unique solutions to bomb disposal.

Mould's GC was announced on 3 November 1942 for 'great gallantry and undaunted devotion to duty'. His citation ended noting that 'he has carried out the most important recovery, rendering safe and investigation of the first German magnetic acoustic unit and moored magnetic mine'.

In January 1943, Mould was promoted to acting lieutenant

commander. He now trained 'P' parties, preparing for the invasion of Western Europe, in how to clear mines and other devices from newly captured harbours. It was vital work and, after the German surrender in May 1945, he was sent to Ceylon (now Sri Lanka) and Australia to prepare more 'P' parties in the Far East and the Pacific. Mould was an inspirational teacher and a popular figure who combined his highly dangerous, highly technical work with a hard-living, hard-drinking, devil-may-care lifestyle.

After the war, he worked on reconstruction programmes in Germany. He married for a second time in 1947 and went on to have another two sons and a daughter after returning to Australia in 1948. Once back in Sydney, he returned to his career as an architect. He worked for the Department of Public Works before being appointed Chief Architect to the Housing Commission of New South Wales in 1950. He designed Sydney apartment blocks which are still standing to this day. Mould died in Sydney on 9 August 1957, aged forty-seven.

DENNIS ARTHUR COPPERWHEAT

Rank/title: Lieutenant (later Lieutenant Commander)
Unit/occupation: Royal Navy
DATE OF BRAVERY: 22 MARCH 1942
GAZETTED: 17 NOVEMBER 1942

Dennis Copperwheat was born in Raunds, Northamptonshire, on 23 May 1914. He was the son of a worker in the shoe industry, which was centred on Northampton. After winning a scholarship to Kimbolton School in Cambridgeshire, he joined the Royal Navy as a boy sailor in 1930. In April 1939, Copperwheat, who was married with a daughter, was promoted to gunner before being commissioned as a lieutenant in 1941.

By late March 1942, the Allied leaders realised that the besieged island of Malta was in desperate need of resupplying. On 20 March 1942, one naval auxiliary and three merchantmen (supply ships) sailed from Alexandria unaware that the Germans had just decided to launch an immediate and all-out air attack on Malta from Sicily and Sardinia. The four ships were given substantial protection from four cruisers and sixteen destroyers, while a flotilla leader also sailed from Malta to join them.

When the four ships got to within twenty miles of Malta, one of the merchantmen, *Clan Campbell*, was sunk by German bombers. The naval supply ship, *Breconshire*, edged to within eight miles of the island before she too was hit and disabled, before being beached and destroyed by German bombers. Only a small part of her valuable cargo of oil was saved. A large part of the Maltese population lined the battlements of Valetta harbour to cheer in the two surviving merchantmen, *Pampas* and *Talabot*. However, when only a quarter of their food and ammunition had been unloaded, both ships were hit in yet another German bombing raid.

One of the ships – the one loaded with most ammunition – was only forty yards offshore when she burst into flames. Everyone present knew that if she was not scuttled quickly, the ship would explode, at the same time badly damaging Grand Harbour, which provided Malta's lifeline to the outside world.

Lieutenant Copperwheat, who was on board the cruiser *Penelope*, was sent with a party to sink the ship. As Copperwheat approached the inferno, he would have been in no doubt that his task was fraught with danger. As well as the fierce blaze on board, ammunition had started to explode all around the ship. On arriving at the scene, Copperwheat quickly assessed the situation. Because of the fires on board, it was impossible to place scuttling charges in the holds. Instead, they had to be slung over the side of the ship. Furthermore, the electric cables for firing the charges were only just able to reach the ship from the shore.

When everything was in place, Copperwheat sent the rest of his party to shelter away from the ship while he remained at the scene to detonate the charge. When the explosion detonated, he was lifted off his feet. But the situation was saved. His GC was announced on 17 November 1942 when the citation ended: 'But for his brave action the ship must have blown up, and grave damage would have been done to the harbour. Moreover, much of the ammunition was saved and some very heavy bombs, part of the cargo, were soon afterwards dropped in Italy.'

Shortly after receiving his gallantry award, Copperwheat told the BBC:

> While we were working, there was terrific heat and ammunition was exploding all over the place, but everything was ready in a very short time. When we started off for the jetty, we found that our electric cable was too short, so we had to junction a piece more on. Having finally got ashore, I looked around for a sheltered place from which to fire the charge and escape the blast. The cable was rather short but it just reached the corner of the building. Having sent the men to shelter, I touched the ends of the leads on to the battery but nothing happened. I got from under my shelter and checked up and found that I was not holding the end of the "earth" connection. So pleased was I to find this that I touched the correct leads on the battery without getting back in the shelter. However, I got there quickly enough because the force of the explosion threw me in it!

Copperwheat underwent training in HMS *Vernon* as a torpedo and explosives expert. Later in the war, he survived a second scare while serving as a torpedo officer on the carrier HMS *Indomitable*. A fuel leak on the vessel caused a sudden explosion which blew Copperwheat off his feet. He remained in the Navy after the war and retired in 1957 as lieutenant commander. He then embarked on a civilian career, working first for a firm of London insurance brokers and later as a specialist on the treatment of timber.

His personal life was not entirely conventional. After divorcing his first wife, Olive, he remarried and had two further children. He later remarried Olive and, after her death, married for the fourth time. He died on 8 September 1992 at Weekley, Kettering, Northamptonshire, aged seventy-eight.

WILLIAM GEORGE FOSTER
Rank/title: Lieutenant
Unit/occupation: 7th Wiltshire (Salisbury) Battalion, Home Guard
DATE OF BRAVERY: 13 SEPTEMBER 1942
GAZETTED: 27 NOVEMBER 1942

William Foster was born at sea, apparently while his family were travelling, on 12 December 1880. He is believed to have been the fifth of ten children living in the Royal Marine barracks at Alverstoke, Hampshire, where his father was based. After leaving school, he worked as a clerk before embarking on a full-time Army career.

Aged nineteen, he enlisted in 1900 to serve with the Royal Fusiliers during the Boer War. After being promoted to lance corporal, he sailed to South Africa with the 1st Volunteer Service Company. Being a fine horseman, he transferred in 1901 to the 2nd Imperial Light Horse. After breaking his leg in 1902, he was medically discharged and sent home, where he married and the couple later had a daughter.

After the outbreak of the First World War, he re-enlisted with the Royal Fusiliers and held the rank of regimental sergeant major, serving in the regiment's 4th Battalion as a company sergeant major. It was one of the first battalions to go to France, where Foster fought in the Battle of Mons. His battalion suffered 112 casualties – dead and wounded. During the famous 'retreat' that followed, the battalion again suffered such heavy casualties that by November it had lost 1,900 men and 50 officers. Foster, who had been wounded, was one of just 170 men on the battalion's depleted roll. Foster was awarded the Distinguished Conduct Medal (DCM) in 1915 and the Military Cross (MC) in 1916. Incredibly, given the action that he saw, he survived the First World War, ending it as a temporary major. After being promoted to company commander, he retired from the Army in 1920 with the rank of substantive captain.

He moved to Wiltshire and, during the General Strike of 1926, he worked as a special constable. Following the outbreak of the Second World War, Foster served as a lieutenant in the 7th Wiltshire (Salisbury) Battalion of the Home Guard. On 13 September 1942, Foster was instructing a group of recruits on how to throw hand grenades from a slit trench at Ashley Hill, Clarendon Park, near Salisbury, Wiltshire. Before the exercise using live grenades, he had said: 'If anything happens, leave everything to me.' One of the men threw a live Mills grenade, intending it to go over the top, but it hit the parapet and fell back into the trench. Typical of the man, Foster did not hesitate: he threw himself on to the grenade which just a second later exploded. Aged sixty-one, Foster was killed instantly, but his courageous action prevented thirty men with him from being killed or seriously injured.

Foster's posthumous GC was announced on 27 November 1942 'in recognition of most conspicuous gallantry in carrying out hazardous work in a very brave manner'. On 12 January 1947, Foster's widow and daughter were present when a memorial for him was unveiled at St Mary's Church, Alderbury, Wiltshire. The memorial ends with the words from John xv, 13: 'Greater love hath no man than this. That a man lay down his own life for his friends.'

5

THE AWARDS OF 1943

CYRIL ARTHUR JOSEPH MARTIN

Rank/title: Temporary Major
Unit/occupation: Corps of Royal Engineers
DATE OF BRAVERY: JANUARY/FEBRUARY 1943
GAZETTED: 11 MARCH 1943

Vicar's son Cyril Martin was born in Derby on 23 July 1897. One of four children, he attended Berkdale Preparatory School in Sheffield before going on to Trent College near Nottingham. In 1916, he joined the Territorial Army (TA) and he was commissioned into the Royal Garrison Artillery as a second lieutenant. On 22 June 1918, he was awarded the Military Cross (MC) after he and two other men extinguished a burning ammunition dump while under heavy enemy fire. After the end of the First World War, Martin attended Emmanuel College, Cambridge, in 1919, where he was awarded a BA in mechanical sciences in 1922. Later he worked as an electrical engineer, as well as marrying and having two children.

After the start of the Second World War, Martin was recommissioned on 17 August 1940 and joined the Royal Engineers. He was posted to the Ministry of Supply Directorate of Bomb Disposal in London. From the beginning of the Blitz, he dealt with countless numbers of unexploded bombs in 1940 and 1941. He was undoubtedly one of the most skilled and courageous bomb disposal experts in the country by the beginning of 1943, when he was called on the night of 17–18 January to deal with a large bomb that had fallen on the warehouse of the Victoria Haulage Company in Battersea, south

London. The warehouse was full of new, heavy and valuable tools from the USA and the bomb had come to rest on a lathe. Other unexploded bombs had fallen that night, but this one was seen as a priority.

It quickly emerged that the 500-kilogram bomb had been fitted with a deadly new fuse which was intended to be 'safe ' from any known disarming technique or equipment. Martin decided to remove the base plate of the bomb and extract the main explosive filling. Once he had done this, he found the bomb contained solid-cast TNT, which could only be removed by high-pressured steam. Normal methods were deemed too risky so Martin applied the steam nozzle by hand, only using it in small bursts so that the TNT could be softened and then scraped away in tiny quantities. It was difficult and highly dangerous work because Martin and a comrade, Lieutenant Deans, had to work in a cramped hole filled with steam and water. They tackled their task from the afternoon of Wednesday 20 January, to 8.30 a.m. the next day, by which time they had succeeded in removing most of the main filling of TNT from the bomb. In early February, Martin again had to deal with two similar bombs in the most difficult of circumstances. In the second incident, on 4 February, an officer working under Martin's orders found his clothing to be on fire from flames from the liquid oxygen being applied to the bomb. Martin and another officer put out the flames before helping the injured man to hospital. Martin then went down to the bottom of the shaft alone and worked on the bomb until it had been disarmed. His GC was announced on 11 March 1943 for 'conspicuous gallantry in carrying out hazardous work in a very brave manner'.

After the end of the war, Martin went back to work as an electrical engineer for Crompton Parkinson, whom he had first joined in 1929. He retired from the company in 1962 after thirty-three years' interrupted service. After moving to Somerset, Martin became a church warden, a member of the

Royal British Legion and kept a cider orchard. He was the first holder of the GC to become an officer of the Victoria Cross and George Cross Association, serving as honorary secretary from 1961 to 1970. He died on 29 November 1973 in South Cadbury, near Yeovil, Somerset, aged seventy-six.

JAMES HENDRY

Rank/title: Corporal
Unit/occupation: No. 1 Tunnelling Company, Corps of Royal Canadian Engineers
DATE OF BRAVERY: 13 JUNE 1941
GAZETTED: 2 APRIL 1943

James Hendry was born in Falkirk, Scotland, on 20 December 1911. When he was about two, Jim, as he was known to his parents, emigrated with his family to Quebec, Canada, where he was known as 'Scotty'. He worked as a miner after leaving school.

After the outbreak of the Second World War, Hendry wanted to join up in Toronto and was persuaded by an acquaintance to join the Royal Canadian Engineers. As an experienced miner, Corporal Hendry was well equipped for his wartime role at Loch Laggan, Inverness-shire, Scotland, during the Second World War. He was in charge of a working party constructing a tunnel at Loch Laggan in a munitions factory.

At around 4 p.m. on 13 June 1941, Hendry emerged from the tunnel to find a gunpowder store on fire. He sprang into action: raising the alarm at the top of his voice, he ran to warn the compressor men and steel sharpeners in the workshop of the dangers. Hendry knew that if the fire got out of control it was likely that the magazine would blow up. This, in turn, would cause extensive damage and halt the wartime tunnelling for some time. Hendry therefore tried to put the fire out himself. However, as he embarked on his dangerous task, the magazine exploded, killing him and another man, and injuring a number of others. Hendry's prompt actions had undoubtedly saved several lives.

Hendry died some six months short of his thirtieth birthday. Initially, his courage seems to have been overlooked in terms of his being recommended for a posthumous gallantry award. However, on 2 April 1943, nearly two years after the incident, his GC was announced for 'most conspicuous gallantry in carrying out hazardous work in a very brave manner'. His parents and youngest brother, Bill, were invited to Ottawa in the autumn of 1943 to receive Hendry's GC and his medals are now held at the Canadian War Museum in Ottawa.

GRAHAM LESLIE PARISH

Rank/title: Sergeant
Unit/occupation: Royal Air Force Volunteer Reserve
DATE OF BRAVERY: 16 SEPTEMBER 1942
GAZETTED: 2 APRIL 1943

Graham Parish was born in Ecclesall Bierlow, Sheffield, Yorkshire, on 29 August 1912. The second of three children, his father was a stores manager until he was called up as a private during the First World War. However, Parish's father died of malaria at the end of the war, aged thirty-six, while serving with the 10/11th Mechanical Transport Company, Army Service Corps. His mother was a skilled milliner. Parish was educated at Abbeydale School in Sheffield and Firth Park Grammar School in the same city. After leaving school at fifteen, Parish first got a job in a bookshop before joining Sheffield Central Library in 1929. In 1939, he was promoted to Borough Librarian at Lytham St Annes, Lancashire. He was one of the youngest senior librarians in the country.

Parish enrolled in the Royal Air Force Volunteer Reserve in February 1941 after receiving a white feather through the post – an anonymous method of accusing a man of cowardice for not joining up. After early training in Britain, he went to South

Africa. However, in 1942, Parish returned to Britain and joined a Bomber Squadron. He took part in the regular nightly bombing raids over Europe, including participating in Operation Millennium: the 1,000-bomber raid on Cologne and Essen. During this period, he was almost killed when a shell tore through the plane he was in and hit his thermos flask as he was bending over.

By the autumn of 1942, Sergeant Parish was a navigator on a delivery flight from Britain to the Middle East Command. On the morning of 16 September 1942, his Wellington aircraft took off from Khartoum airfield in the Sudan. Early in the flight, the port engine failed and the pilot attempted to return to the airfield to land. The ground was rough which meant he was unable to make full use of the plane's brakes on landing. The aircraft careered out of control, struck a building and burst into flames. All the crew escaped with the exception of one man, who sustained two broken legs in the crash-landing, and Parish, who chose to stay with him even though he could have made a quick escape. The injured man was at the emergency door in the floor of the fuselage. However, the door was unusable because the undercarriage had collapsed and the fuselage was resting on the ground.

The blaze was so fierce that no emergency workers were able to get to the plane. Inside the aircraft, Parish had lifted his comrade to the rear turret in the hope they could make good their escape. But they became overwhelmed by the fire and smoke and perished inside the bomber, which was completely destroyed. Parish was awarded a posthumous GC on 2 April 1943 when his citation ended:

When the blaze subsided Sergeant Parish's body was found leaning against the rear gun turret and the passenger was beside him with his arm over the airman's shoulder. As the passenger could not walk, owing to his broken legs, it is clear that Sergeant Parish had carried him from the emergency door to the rear turret, a distance of eight yards, in the hope that both could escape through the turret. Undoubtedly both were overcome and burned to death in the attempt. Sergeant Parish could have made his escape through the astro-hatch but his unselfish desire to assist the passenger cost him his life. He displayed gallantry of the highest order.

Parish, who was thirty and single when he died, is now buried at Khartoum War Cemetery, his third and final resting place.

DONALD OWEN CLARKE
Rank/title: Mr
Unit/occupation: Apprentice, Merchant Navy
DATE OF BRAVERY: 9 AUGUST 1942
GAZETTED: 20 JULY 1943

Donald Clarke was born in Chester-le-Street, Co. Durham, on 5 March 1923. He was one of two children. After attending Chester-le-Street Secondary School, he joined the Merchant Navy in 1939, aged sixteen. He had been bright at school, but he had always wanted to go to sea. During the Blitz, he saved a dock gateman from drowning during an incident in Liverpool in May 1941. For his courage, he received the Silver Medal of the Liverpool Shipwreck and Humane Society and a cash reward from the Mersey Docks and Harbour Board.

In the summer of 1942, Clarke was a member of the crew of the *San Emiliano*, a tanker which had sailed alone from Trinidad with a cargo of petrol. On 8 August 1942, when the ship was some forty-eight hours off the Caribbean island, it was hit by two torpedoes fired from a German U-boat. Fire tore through the ship. The first explosion had split the ship in two and most of the crew perished. Clarke, who was still an apprentice, was badly burned but managed to make his way to the deck. Along with some other crew, many of whom were also badly burned,

Clarke got into the only lifeboat that managed to get away from the ship.

Initially, the lifeboat stayed well clear of the *San Emiliano*, but it then started to drift towards the burning ship. Most men were too badly hurt to help, but Clarke grabbed an oar and for two hours – without a word of complaint – he frantically rowed in order to keep the lifeboat from danger. Only then did the crew realise how badly Clarke himself was injured – his hands had to be cut from the oar because his badly burned flesh was sticking to it. Clarke died from his injuries the next day, aged nineteen.

It is understood that only eight (including Clarke) of the forty-eight crew made it to the sole lifeboat launched. Four more had dived into the sea, but although they were picked up by the lifeboat they all died soon afterwards from their severe injuries. The ship's master, Captain James Tozer, had also shown great courage: despite being badly wounded by the explosion of the first torpedo, he had refused to allow the lifeboat to endanger itself by coming alongside the burning tanker to try to save him and others. Clarke received a posthumous GC on 20 July 1943 when his citation ended:

> He had pulled as well as anyone, although he was rowing with the bones of his hands. Later when lying at the bottom of the boat his thoughts were still with his shipmates and he sang to keep up their spirits. Next day he died, having shown the greatest fortitude. By his supreme effort, undertaken without thought of self and in spite of terrible agony, Apprentice Clarke ensured the safety of his comrades in the boat. His great heroism and selfless devotion were in keeping with the highest traditions of the Merchant Navy.

Clarke's courage was likened in the media to that of Jack Cornwell, the 'boy sailor', who was only sixteen when he was awarded the Victoria Cross for courage while serving in the

Royal Navy during the First World War. A headline in the *Daily Express* described Clarke as the 'Boy Cornwell of the Merchant Navy' after his GC was announced. A new launch for the sea cadets of Chester-le-Street was named in Clarke's memory and other memorials were erected. The owners of the ship put up a tablet at the Royal Victoria Infirmary in Newcastle upon Tyne which read: 'To the memory of Donald Owen Clarke GC, endowed by the owners of *MV San Emiliano*. Eagle Oil & Shipping Company.'

HUGH RANDALL SYME

Rank/title: Lieutenant
Unit/occupation: Royal Australian Naval Volunteer Reserve
DATE OF BRAVERY: NOVEMBER 1942
GAZETTED: 3 AUGUST 1943

Hugh Syme was born in Melbourne, Australia, on 28 February 1903. He was educated at Scotch College in Melbourne before attending Melbourne University. He worked at *The Age*, the family newspaper, before the outbreak of the Second World War. He had married in 1931 but he divorced in 1940 – the same year he volunteered for service in Britain with the Royal Australian Naval Volunteer Reserve. Syme, known as Hughie to his friends, arrived in Liverpool, aged thirty-seven, with twenty-three other Australians on SS *Strathnaver* on 27 October 1940. In March 1941, they were sent to HMS *Vernon* for Rendering Mines Safe duties and, after a rushed period of instruction, were quickly assigned to bomb disposal tasks. Syme's courage was matched by his skill. He was awarded the George Medal on 27 June 1941 and a bar (a second George Medal) a year later, on 9 June 1942.

During his twenty-one months in the Enemy Mining Section of HMS *Vernon*, Lieutenant Syme carried out nineteen mine disposal or recovery operations, including dealing with eight magnetic, five acoustic and two acoustic magnetic mines.

ght Lieutenant (later Wing Commander) John
wland was involved in the first action for which
GC was awarded. Dowland, along with Leonard
rrison, a civilian armament instructor, defused
omb on board a steamship in February 1940.
wland, who served in the RAF, was killed in
ion in Malta two years later.

Harry Errington GC was among the guests at the
Tower of London in August 1995 to mark the 50th
anniversary of VJ Day. Errington, a fireman, was
awarded his GC in August 1941 for gallantry the
previous year when he saved two colleagues from a
blaze caused by a bomb at their Auxiliary Fire Service
base in London.

e first presentation of a GC was made in May 1941 to Temporary Lieutenant (later Lieutenant Commander)
bert Armitage, who served in the Royal Naval Volunteer Reserve. He attended the investiture at Buckingham
ace with his wife and a friend after being awarded the decoration for repeatedly dealing with complex mines.

THE HEROIC BOMB-DISPOSAL SQUAD WHO SAVED ST. PAUL'S CATHEDRAL.

THREE DAYS' PERILOUS TOIL TRIUMPHANTLY REWARDED : LIEUT. R. DAVIES (CENTRE) WITH THE UNIT WHICH REMOVED THE TIME-BOMB FROM DEAN'S YARD. (G.P.U.)

LIEUT. R. DAVIES, COMMANDING THE BOMB-DISPOSAL UNIT WHICH SAVED ST. PAUL'S. HE DROVE THE LORRY BEARING THE TIME-BOMB TO HACKNEY MARSHES. (G.P.U.)

CLEARLY DEMONSTRATING THE MIRACULOUS ESCAPE OF WREN'S MASTERPIECE FROM TOTAL DESTRUCTION : THE POINT OF ENTRY OF THE BOMB, BURIED ONLY 26 FT. FROM THE CATHEDRAL WALL. (Keystone.)

WHAT MIGHT HAVE HAPPENED TO ST. PAUL'S : THE 100-FT. CRATER MADE WHEN THE BOMB WAS EXPLODED ON HACKNEY MARSHES AFTER REMOVAL. (I.B.)

THE HOLE FROM WHICH THE TIME-BOMB WAS REMOVED WITH GREAT DIFFICULTY AFTER THREE DAYS' UNREMITTING STRUGGLE. (G.P.U.)

The most stirring deed of heroism yet called forth by the Nazi raids on London was the removal of the huge time-bomb which dropped near St. Paul's Cathedral on September 15, by an Army bomb-disposal squad. It was a ton in weight and "looked like a vast hog," being about 8 ft. long and fitted with fuses which made it extremely dangerous to touch or move. It was apparently slipping further and further down in the black mud under St. Paul's, and in addition it was highly burnished by its passage through the earth, making it extremely difficult to get a purchase on it. After three days' heartbreaking toil it was hauled out of the hole by two lorries in tandem. The streets were then cleared from St. Paul's to Hackney Marshes, and it was driven on a fast lorry at high speed by Lieut. Davies himself and blown up by the Bomb-Disposal Section. Mr. Eden sent a special message to the bomb-disposal units expressing his "warmest appreciation of the courage and devotion to duty exhibited by all ranks "—the St. Paul's episode being only one instance of their heroism and efficiency.

A heroic bomb disposal squad saved St Paul's Cathedral in London from being destroyed by a massive unexploded device in September 1940. Later the same month, it was announced that Temporary Lieutenant Robert Davies and Sapper (later Corporal) George Wyllie, both of the Corps of Royal Engineers, had been awarded the GC.

MARY EVANS ARCHIVE

IWM HU055417

...ion Commander George Inwood, of the ...ne Guard, was awarded a posthumous GC in ...7 1941 after he was killed while attempting to ...ue six people from a gas-filled cellar beneath a ...se destroyed by the bombing of Birmingham ...October 1940. Inwood died from the effects of ...inhalation, aged thirty-four.

Lieutenant (later Lieutenant Commander) Stuart Mould, of the Royal Australian Naval Volunteer Reserve, was awarded the GC in November 1942 for repeatedly tackling mines, many of which were fitted with 'anti-stripping' devices. 'Mouldy', as he was widely known, is pictured next to a landmine jettisoned by a British plane in a wood in Hertfordshire.

IWM HU058436

...porary Lieutenant (later Lieutenant Commander) Harold Newgass, of the Royal Naval Volunteer ...erve, was awarded the GC in March 1941 for defusing a German landmine that fell on a Merseyside gas ...ks in November 1940. It was regarded by some as the most hazardous bomb disposal operation ever ...ied out. Newgass (*left*) is photographed sitting on a defused 'B' type mine in Milford Haven, Dyfed.

Leading Aircraftsman Matt Osborne, of the Royal Air Force Volunteer Reserve, was awarded a posthumous GC in July 1942 for nine separate acts of gallantry in Malta. He had been killed in April 1942, aged thirty-five, in an explosion while pouring water over torpedoes that were in danger of detonating.

Lieutenant William Foster, of the Home Guard, w awarded a posthumous GC in November 1942 for throwing himself on a live grenade to save thirty comrades during an accident on a training exercise Wiltshire two months earlier. He was aged sixty-o

Captain Dudley Mason, of the Merchant Navy, required bandages to his badly burned hands after the SS *Ohio*, which he was commanding, was bombed and hit as it took fuel supplies to the besieged island of Malta in August 1942. He was awarded the GC the following month.

Leading Aircraftsman Kenneth Spooner, of the Royal Canadian Air Force, was awarded a posthumous GC in January 1944 for taking over controls of a plane after the pilot fainted during instructional flight. He enabled three comrades t jump to safety in May 1943 but Spooner was kil aged twenty, along with the pilot as he attempte land the aircraft.

Captain Mateen Ansari, of the Indian Army, was awarded the GC in April 1946 for resistance to brutal torture at the hands of the Japanese during the Second World War. He was beheaded by his captors in October 1943, when still in his late twenties.

Flight Lieutenant Hector Gray, of the RAF, was awarded a posthumous GC in April 1946 for resistance to brutal torture at the hands of his Japanese captors years earlier. Dolly, as he was widely known, was executed in December 1943, aged thirty-two.

George VI, who gave his name to the GC after announcing its creation in September 1940, inspected RAF personnel in North Africa in June 1943. He is pictured (*left*), in uniform, at Hammamet airfield, Tunisia.

Flying Officer Roderick Gray, of the Royal Canadian Air Force, was awarded the GC in March 1945 for gallantry when his Wellington bomber was shot down over the Atlantic in August the previous year. Despite a serious injury, Gray, who was widely known as 'Cy', clung to the side of a dinghy for three hours before he perished, aged twenty-six.

Wing Commander Forest Yeo-Thomas, of the Royal Air Force Volunteer Force, was awarded the GC in February 1946 for undercover work and fortitude in prison camps after being captured by the Nazis in France. Yeo-Thomas, who had being carrying out work for the Special Operations Executive, later escaped and survived the Second World War.

Albert Heming (*left*), of the Civil Defence Rescue Service, is pictured being congratulated on his GC in October 1945 after his investiture at Buckingham Palace. The congratulations came from Canon Edmund Arbuthnott, who he had rescued earlier that year from the ruins of a Roman Catholic Church that had been bombed in Bermondsey, south-east London.

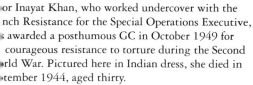

…or Inayat Khan, who worked undercover with the …nch Resistance for the Special Operations Executive, … awarded a posthumous GC in October 1949 for … courageous resistance to torture during the Second …rld War. Pictured here in Indian dress, she died in …tember 1944, aged thirty.

Violette Szabo worked for the Special Operations Executive – in conjunction with the French Resistance – partly to avenge the death of her husband. She was awarded a posthumous GC in December 1946 for her work and her resistance to torture. She had been shot dead in early 1945, aged thirty-three, leaving an orphaned daughter.

…GC was awarded to Odette Sansom (later Churchill and Hallowes) in August 1946 for her work for the …cial Operations Executive and her resistance to torture after her capture. Sansom, who had worked with the …ch Resistance, is pictured with Captain Peter Churchill, her former CO and second husband, and her three …ghters from her first marriage after receiving her GC at Buckingham Palace in November 1946.

Lieutenant (later Lieutenant Commander) George Gosse, of the Royal Australian Naval Volunteer Reserve, was awarded the GC in April 1946 for clearing deadly mines in Bremen, Germany, in May 1945, shortly after the defeat of the Nazis. He was said by a friend to have lived 'as though every day was his last'.

Squadron Leader (later Wing Commander) Herbert Dinwoodie (*left*), of the Royal Air Force Volunteer Reserve, was awarded the GC in February 1947 for bomb disposal work in 1946, including defusing eleven unexploded bombs in the Baltic port of Lübeck. He and his small German-based team had been called to the docks after a bomb was accidentally dropped, killing six people.

Furthermore, the tall, thin Australian was responsible for the recovery of the first and only Type T Sinker mine in November 1942 when he was tasked with removing it from the drifter *Noontide*. It was a particularly difficult assignment: removing the device from the ship, he had to insulate the detonator wires without 'earthing' the weapon. At the time he was working up to his knees in mud and the nature of his work meant he received a number of painful electric shocks. At a vital stage in his mission, Syme even had to hang upside down in a hole in the mud. If the mine had become unstable, there was no chance of his escaping. Yet he carried out the task successfully and gained valuable information from the mine when it was dismantled.

Syme needed to return to Australia early in 1943 on the death of his father. There he remarried and the couple went on to have three daughters. His GC was announced on 3 August 1943 for 'great bravery and undaunted devotion to duty'. He wanted to return to Britain to resume his work with HMS *Vernon* but his request was blocked by the Australian authorities. Syme died quietly in Melbourne on 7 November 1965, aged sixty-two. There is a memorial for him in Springvale Crematorium in his home city.

JOHN SAMUEL ROWLANDS (LATER SIR JOHN)
Rank/title: Wing Commander (later Air Marshal)
Unit/occupation: Royal Air Force Volunteer Reserve
DATE OF BRAVERY: 1941-3
GAZETTED: 10 AUGUST 1943

John Rowlands was born in Hawarden, near Chester, Cheshire, on 23 September 1915. He attended Hawarden School before obtaining a degree in physics at the University of Wales. Rowlands joined the Royal Air Force Volunteer Reserve (RAFVR) in 1939 and received armament engineering training at RAF Manby in Lincolnshire. He also received pilot training at Tern Hill, Shropshire.

Despite being a member of the RAFVR, he spent most of his time during the war on bomb disposal work. A quiet, modest man, Wing Commander Rowlands' work took him all over Britain and also to North Africa, Italy and Germany. He was awarded the GC for his bravery in dealing with hundreds of bombs and mines from 1941 to 1943. During this two-year period, he was tasked with rendering safe and dismantling new types of enemy bombs. He also dealt with Allied weapons in crashed aircraft.

In one incident in 1943, Rowlands was called to RAF Snaith in Yorkshire, where the accidental detonation of a bomb had set off a chain reaction, killing some eighteen people. Fierce fires threatened to set off more bombs and the working conditions could hardly have been more perilous. As always, Rowlands remained calm and collected as he dealt with bombs with delayed action fuses and anti-handling devices. Working with a team, he cleared the area of some bombs and made others safe on the spot. The exhaustive work took fully ten days, during which time his courage and patience were fully stretched.

Rowlands' GC was announced on 10 August 1943 when his citation read: 'For over 2 years, Wing Commander Rowlands has been employed on bomb disposal duties and has repeatedly displayed the most conspicuous courage and unselfish devotion to duty in circumstances of great personal danger.' The year before he received his gallantry award, Rowlands married and the couple later had two daughters. He was invested with the GC by George VI at Buckingham Palace on 20 July 1945.

Rowlands' bomb disposal work continued long after he received the GC and at the end of the Second World War he was posted to a permanent commission having attended Staff College in Haifa, Israel. For five years from 1947 he was based at RAF Aldermaston in Berkshire. He initially worked on research for the British atom bomb. After successful testing, he was put in charge of one of the first atomic weapons units in

Bomber Command. Later he worked on the hydrogen bomb. In 1961, he was appointed Special Attaché at the British Embassy in Washington before taking on a number of senior posts in Britain until 1973. After being knighted and having risen to the rank of air marshal, he returned to civilian life and became Assistant Principal at Sheffield Polytechnic (now Sheffield Hallam University). Rowlands was appointed an OBE in 1954 and a KBE in 1971. He died in Sheffield on 4 June 2006, aged ninety.

FREDERICK JOHN CRADOCK
Rank/title: Mr
Unit/occupation: Boilerman
DATE OF BRAVERY: 4 MAY 1943
GAZETTED: 10 SEPTEMBER 1943

Frederick Cradock was born in Hendon, north London, in the second half of 1886 – his exact date of birth is not known. He enlisted in late 1915, aged twenty-nine, and served in the Royal Field Artillery with the rank of driver. He served in France and Belgium and, having survived the First World War, was discharged in 1919.

On 4 May 1943, Cradock, by now aged fifty-six, was working as a boilerman in Glemsford, Suffolk. An explosion took place at a boiler house that led to it being filled with scalding steam and water. A colleague of Cradock's was trapped in a well between the wall and the furnace. Cradock, who had been working on top of the furnace, could have jumped to safety on the side away from the steam.

However, Cradock, who was in charge of the boiler house at the time, chose instead to try to rescue his workmate. Calling for a ladder, he turned into the steam in an attempt to reach the man and haul him to safety. Before he could reach his colleague, he was overcome by the steam and severely scalded. Cradock was forced to stagger away from the heat and, once again, could have made it to safety. Instead, he ignored his injuries and made a second attempt to get down into the well. This time he died trying to reach his colleague, who also perished.

Cradock's posthumous GC was announced on 10 September 1943 when his citation ended: 'Cradock showed outstanding heroism and gave his life in an endeavour to save his workmate.' This was the first GC that had no direct connection with the war or war work.

FRANCIS ANTHONY BLAIR FASSON
Rank/title: Lieutenant
Unit/occupation: Royal Navy
DATE OF BRAVERY: 30 OCTOBER 1942
GAZETTED: 14 SEPTEMBER 1943

COLIN GRAZIER
Rank/title: Able Seaman
Unit/occupation: Royal Navy
DATE OF BRAVERY: 30 OCTOBER 1942
GAZETTED: 14 SEPTEMBER 1943

Tony Fasson, as he was known, was born in Edinburgh on 17 July 1913. He was one of three children born to an Army captain, who played rugby for Scotland, and his wife. In 1927, aged just thirteen, Fasson attended Royal Naval College, Dartmouth, in Devon. After Dartmouth, he joined the Fleet Air Arm where he was almost killed when he was forced to ditch his Flying Swordfish aircraft into a field. The local ploughman saved him from being strangled by wires that had cut across his throat. After a spell in hospital, he returned to the Navy. Fasson, a keen sportsman like his father, was a hugely sociable and popular character. Colin Grazier was born in Tamworth, Staffordshire, on 7 May 1920. He joined the Royal Navy early in the Second World War.

Lieutenant Fasson had already been mentioned in dispatches

for bravery at the 1st Battle of Narvik before he was posted to HMS *Petard*. The crew also included Able Seaman Grazier who, aged twenty-two, had married his childhood sweetheart two days before the ship sailed for the Mediterranean. At one point, HMS *Petard* crossed with a ship carrying Fasson's elder brother James, known as Jim, to Singapore. Fasson was able to invite his elder brother aboard for breakfast before they said their farewells and went off to their different fates.

On 30 October 1942, a German U-boat, which had surfaced, was spotted by a British aircraft. The crew of the plane reported its whereabouts and the Royal Navy's Twelfth Destroyer Flotilla began an immediate search in an attempt to find and destroy the U-boat. After a lengthy search by four ships, contact was made with the submarine. Depth charges struck *U-559* and she was forced to surface, whereupon she was holed by gunfire from the destroyers. The submarine's crew abandoned ship and were taken as prisoners of war.

The Royal Navy, meanwhile, had been carefully briefed on the importance of recovering documents and code machines from any captured submarines or ships. The instructions were that no craft should be sunk if there was a chance of capturing it. The captain of HMS *Petard* instructed Sub-Lieutenant Connell to swim to the submarine but, before he could obey the order, Fasson, knowing his comrade was married, said that he would go instead. Grazier accompanied him, along with Tommy Brown, who was just sixteen.

After dropping down into the U-boat, Fasson and Grazier, who were well aware they were in a perilous situation, quickly bundled up all the documents they could find, including code books. By now, the U-boat was taking in water and had been plunged into darkness. Using a torch, Fasson also found a machine bolted to the bulkhead, which he managed to free so it could be hauled up by a line. Brown carried all the documents up a ladder and handed them to Connell who was in a whaler, a small sea boat. Then, without warning, *U-559* suddenly plummetted like a stone to the bottom of the ocean taking Fasson and Grazier to their deaths.

The crew of HMS *Petard* were distressed at the loss of the two brave men – and unhappy at the irony that the U-boat's crew had been saved. Fasson, in particular, was hugely liked by the men. Reg Crang, who witnessed the events, later said of Fasson: 'Jimmy, as we all knew him, was a real man's man, already a legend on the ship. Handsome but deadly efficient, he was admired by everyone . . . We cannot imagine there is a finer First Lieutenant in the Navy.'

Admiral John Hayes wrote a letter to Fasson's parents in which he paid an affectionate tribute to their son: 'Tony was always the tonic which you expect from someone who by nature was so full of zest and natural friendliness. I cannot think of him unless it was laughing . . . It would take more than a war to get Tony down. He will be missed by all whose luck it was to know him, and remembered as a character you could not help loving for the way he tackled things – no matter whether some mad-cap escapade of Dartmouth days, or the serious demands made on us today.'

There was a debate over whether Fasson and Grazier should receive the Victoria Cross or the GC. They were eventually awarded the latter on 14 September when their citations deliberately, for security reasons, made no reference to the circumstances of their bravery. Their citations simply paid tribute to their 'outstanding bravery and steadfast devotion to duty in the face of danger'. Young Brown was awarded the George Medal for his part in the action.

Yet it was only much later that the consequences of Fasson and Grazier's courage became known. It is no exaggeration to say that their action saved many lives and may even have brought the war to a quicker close. Indeed, a bench at the National Memorial Arboretum in Staffordshire carries the inscription: 'In memory of Colin Grazier, Tony Fasson & Tommy Brown of HMS *Petard*. The Enigma Codes they retrieved from a

German U-boat shortened World War II.'

For, in the aftermath of their finds in the autumn of 1942, HMS *Petard* had sailed to Haifa, Israel, under escort and the documents and machine were handed to intelligence officers. They were then taken on to London and Bletchley Park, the national codes and cipher centre. The two most crucial documents retrieved from the submarine were the *Short Signal Book* and the 1942 edition of the *Short Weather Cipher*. It was the information from the second book that enabled code-breakers to find the key to the four-rotor Enigma machine. It took them some six weeks to make the first decrypts, then only a matter of hours to reveal the positions of fifteen U-boats. The find is widely considered to have halved the number of losses in the Atlantic. In short, the lives of Fasson and Grazier were certainly not sacrificed in vain.

The courage of Grazier was championed in recent years by his local paper, the *Tamworth Herald*. He was described as 'one of the greatest and most unsung heroes of WWII'. A building in the town was named Grazier House and the town's former police station was turned into the £1 million Colin Grazier Hotel.

CHARLES ALFRED DUNCAN
Rank/title: Private
Unit/occupation: Parachute Regiment
DATE OF BRAVERY: 10 JULY 1943
GAZETTED: 9 NOVEMBER 1943

Charles Duncan was born in Bexhill-on-Sea, Sussex, on 13 April 1920. In July 1943, when aged twenty-three, he was a member of Signal Platoon, 4th Parachute Battalion – part of the 2nd Parachute Brigade – which was serving in North Africa.

On 10 July, Duncan was returning to his camp near M'Sakan after the postponement of an airborne operation against the enemy. He was removing primed grenades from his equipment when he saw one drop to the ground with its safety pin out. Duncan, who was surrounded by several colleagues at the time, threw himself over the grenade and waited until it exploded. He was killed but he had saved the lives of his comrades.

His posthumous GC was announced on 9 November 1943 when his citation said the gallantry award was 'in recognition of most conspicuous gallantry in carrying out hazardous work in a very brave manner'.

ANDRE GILBERT KEMPSTER (FORMERLY ANDRE GILBERTO COCCIOLETTI)

Rank/title: Temporary Major
Unit/occupation: Duke of Wellington's Regiment, Royal Armoured Corps
DATE OF BRAVERY: 21 AUGUST 1943
GAZETTED: 9 NOVEMBER 1943

André Kempster was born on 26 October 1916 in Westminster, central London. He attended Cheltenham College in Gloucestershire from 1925 to 1933. His birth name was André Gilberto Coccioletti. However, nine days after enlisting into the Green Jackets on 10 May 1939, he made an announcement in the *London Gazette* that he 'Andrew Gilberto Coccioletti, Hotel Manager, at the Stafford Hotel, St James's, London, was changing his name to Kempster'. He made the switch by deed poll, apparently to lose his Italian name during the Second World War.

On 21 August 1943, Temporary Major Kempster was serving with the Duke of Wellington's Regiment, attached Royal Armoured Corps. He was in a pit at Philippeville on the Algerian coast demonstrating grenade-throwing to two of his men. One of the grenades he threw hit the top of the parapet and rolled back into the pit. Kempster frantically tried to scoop it up but failed. Knowing there were only one or two seconds left before the grenade exploded, he threw himself on top of it.

114

Kempster, who was twenty-six, died when it exploded, but the lives of the other two men were saved.

Kempster's posthumous GC was announced on 9 November 1943 when his citation said the award was 'in recognition of most conspicuous gallantry in carrying out hazardous work in a very brave manner'.

GEORGE PRESTON STRONACH

Rank/title: Chief Officer
Unit/occupation: Merchant Navy
DATE OF BRAVERY: 19 MARCH 1943
GAZETTED: 23 NOVEMBER 1943

George Stronach was born in Port Gordon on the Moray coast of Scotland on 4 December 1914. One of seven children, his father was a blacksmith and his mother worked as a domestic servant. Stronach attended Balnacoul School in Banff and Milne's Institution (now Milne's Primary School). He became apprenticed to a chemist but, while convalescing from a bicycle accident, he told his local minister he wanted to go to sea and in 1932 he began at Gravesend Sea School in Kent. He first worked as a deckhand and held a number of jobs at sea before the Second World War broke out in 1939.

In the summer of 1942, the SS *Ocean Voyager*, on which Stronach worked as chief officer, was requisitioned in order to take a military cargo to the Middle East. Further military duties followed and, on 19 March 1943, she was anchored in Tripoli harbour when she was hit by enemy bombs and torpedoes. The vessel, which had a large supply of petrol and ammunition on board, caught fire. Despite attempts to fight the blaze, the crew had to abandon ship.

Because the master had been killed in the initial attack, Stronach, who had been knocked out, found himself in charge once he had regained consciousness. He went looking for survivors, rallied the crew and led many of them to a boat which had come alongside the *Ocean Voyager*. As his men were being led to safety, ammunition started exploding. Stronach feared other survivors were still on board. First, however, he lowered another boat and brought it alongside the ship.

The blaze on board was fierce but Stronach made his way to the officers' accommodation amidships. There he found a hose, with a trickle of water coming from it, which he held above his head to keep himself wet enough to give protection from the worst of the heat and the flames. With great difficulty, Stronach then climbed into the collapsed accommodation, where he found one of the deck officers, unconscious and badly burned. After pulling him clear, he dragged him along the deck and lowered him into the boat.

Stronach returned to the accommodation again and removed debris to free another officer who was also trapped. With what was later described as 'almost superhuman efforts', he dragged the injured man through a porthole and along the deck. He then tied a rope around the survivor's waist and lowered him over the side to the boat. Concerned that the burning ship would explode, he ordered another man to take the boat to safety.

Even now, Stronach's work was not done. He returned again midships where he found a third officer with severe injuries. Yet again, he dragged the survivor along the deck and this time lowered him by rope on to a raft that had returned in response to his calls for help. Stronach insisted on returning one final time to check there were no survivors and this time found a greaser who was unconscious. Yet again, he dragged the man along the deck. On this occasion, there was no boat or raft to lower him into and so he tied a lifebelt around the man and flung him overboard. Only now was Stronach satisfied there were no further survivors and so he jumped overboard himself and swam to a raft which, under his direction, successfully picked up the injured greaser from the water.

A detailed description of the rescue was published on 23

November 1943 when Stronach's GC was announced. The citation ended: 'In the full knowledge that she was likely to blow up at any moment, Chief Officer Stronach stayed on this burning vessel searching for survivors for an hour and twenty minutes. His inspiring leadership induced a number of the crew to get away and so saved their lives and by his gallant efforts, undertaken with utter disregard of his personal safety, he saved the lives of three officers and a greaser, all of whom were badly hurt. His action equals any in the annals of the Merchant Navy for great and unselfish heroism and determination in the face of overwhelming odds.'

Stronach, however, did not escape unscathed. He was hospitalised by a back injury sustained in the rescue. After the war, he worked for the Clyde Pilotage Authority. In 1968, he became pilot master, a post he held until he retired in 1979. Married with two children, Stronach had many interests, including being the Scout Master of his church Scout group, music, dance and bee-keeping. He died in Inverness, Scotland, on 12 December 1999, eight days after his eighty-fifth birthday.

6

THE AWARDS OF 1944

KENNETH GERALD SPOONER
Rank/title: Leading Aircraftsman
Unit/occupation: Royal Canadian Air Force
DATE OF BRAVERY: 14 MAY 1943
GAZETTED: 7 JANUARY 1944

Kenneth Spooner was born in Smith Falls, Ontario, Canada, on 24 May 1922. After attending local public schools and Smith Falls Collegiate Institute, he started work as a civil service clerk. This job lasted from 1940 to 1941 and was followed by another as a rodman with the Canadian Pacific Railway from 1941 to 1942.

On 31 July 1942, he enlisted in Montreal with the Royal Canadian Air Force. After initial training, Spooner, a student navigator, and three other young crew were on an instructional flight in an Avro Anson aircraft over Lake Erie when the pilot, Flight Sergeant Dana Nelson, aged twenty-four, fainted at the controls.

None of the four knew how to fly the plane but Spooner coolly took charge of the situation. He told the other three to leap out of the plane, which they did successfully, and then took control of the aircraft. He kept it at a safe height for about an hour but, with the pilot still unconscious, eventually had to land even though he had never attempted the manoeuvre before. However, he lost control of the aircraft and it crashed, killing both Spooner and the pilot. Spooner was ten days short of his twenty-first birthday when he perished.

Spooner's posthumous GC was announced on 7 January

1944. The citation paid tribute to his 'great courage, resolution and unselfishness'. It ended: 'This airman, with complete disregard for his personal safety and in conformity with the highest traditions of the service, sacrificed his life in order to save the lives of his comrades.' Five years after Spooner's death, a new elementary school in Ontario was named in his honour.

JOHN RENNIE
Rank/title: Acting Sergeant
Unit/occupation: The Argyll and Sutherland Highlanders of Canada
DATE OF BRAVERY: 29 OCTOBER 1943
GAZETTED: 26 MAY 1944

John Rennie was born in Aberdeen, Scotland, on 13 December 1920. One of five children, his parents moved to Kingston, Ontario, Canada, in 1924. Rennie, who was better known as Jock rather than John, and his brother George enlisted early in the Second World War. Rennie, a regular church-goer with a good voice, served in British Columbia and Jamaica before going overseas with the Argyll and Sutherland Highlanders of Canada.

On 29 October 1943, Acting Sergeant Rennie was supervising grenade-throwing by his unit at a Canadian training camp in Slough, then in Buckinghamshire. One grenade had been thrown successfully but a second failed to clear the protective embankment and rolled back to the throwing area. Rennie had time to get clear of the danger but, concerned for the safety of his men, he ran forward and tried to pick up the rolling grenade and throw it clear. However, the grenade exploded as he did so and he was fatally injured. Three other soldiers within some five yards of the sergeant escaped any serious injuries.

Rennie, who was twenty-two when he died, received a posthumous GC on 26 May 1944 in recognition of 'most conspicuous gallantry in carrying out hazardous work in a very brave manner'.

ANTHONY SMITH
Rank/title: **Mr**
Unit/occupation: Chimney sweep/Civil Defence Rescue Service, Chelsea
DATE OF BRAVERY: 23 FEBRUARY 1944
GAZETTED: 30 MAY 1944

Tony Smith was born in Christchurch, Hampshire, on 3 August 1894. At the turn of the century, his father worked in a shop and his mother worked as a charlady. One of seven children, Smith left school at fourteen and joined the chimney-sweeping business run by his father and brother, a business which included Buckingham Palace among its customers. He also made shoes as a sideline. Smith enlisted, aged twenty, in the Royal Marine Light Infantry. After the First World War ended, he worked as a night watchman at a central London hotel. However, by 1926 he was back working in the family chimney-sweeping business, again with shoe-making as a sideline.

During the Second World War, and by now in his mid- to late forties, Smith was a member of the Civil Defence Rescue Service, Chelsea, while also making his living as a sweep. On 23 February 1944, a string of bombs fell on the World's End, Chelsea, causing massive damage. A whole wing of the Guinness Buildings was destroyed, killing eighty-six people and injuring 111.

Nearby, a row of four-storey houses was also demolished, leaving behind only the partition walls which were in a perilous state. Gas and water mains had fractured and gas had ignited, setting fire to the wrecked building, which soon turned into a raging inferno. Two floors had 'pancaked' but Smith managed to burrow through the burning ruins to reach a casualty trapped in a front basement. Although he succeeded in releasing the victim, by this time the entire front of the building was a wall of flame. Furthermore, the upper floors were collapsing, thereby cutting off his escape route.

Smith carried the casualty towards the back of the house through the fire and smoke. There he found a six-inch hole in the wreckage, which he enlarged and forced his way through. He managed to pass the casualty to safety moments before the front of the house collapsed into the area where they had just been. Smith's eyebrows and hair were burned and he was close to being overcome by smoke and fumes. However, he then insisted on going to the aid of a comrade who was trying to rescue an injured woman from the basement of an adjoining building. The walls of this building were also close to collapsing but Smith, now working up to his waist in water, battled for a further hour before successfully freeing the woman. Even then, he managed to get a change of clothing and finished his shift until his squad was relieved.

Smith's GC was announced on 30 May 1944 when the lengthy citation ended: 'Smith displayed outstanding gallantry and devotion to duty in conditions of the utmost danger and difficulty.' When, much later, the buildings were reconstructed, Smith performed the opening ceremony.

After the Second World War ended, Smith lived in rented rooms but used to take his meals with one of his sisters and her six children, who lived nearby. A single man, he died in Chelsea on 20 October 1964, aged seventy.

JOSEPH HENRY SILK
Rank/title: Private
Unit/occupation: Somerset Light Infantry
DATE OF BRAVERY: 4 DECEMBER 1943
GAZETTED: 13 JUNE 1944

Harry Silk, as he was known, was born in London on 14 August 1916. The eldest of seven children, he was brought up by his maternal grandparents and adopted their surname of Silk in place of his own, Kibble. Silk was in the Territorial Army and originally joined the Devonshire Regiment at an unknown date. Some time after the Dunkirk evacuations, Silk joined the Somerset Light Infantry.

The conflict in Burma during the Second World War was sometimes known as the 'forgotten war'. An incident in the jungle three weeks before Christmas 1943 might have been forgotten too were it not for the incredible bravery of Private Silk. On 4 December 1943, Silk, then aged twenty-seven, was with other members of his platoon, apparently cleaning their weapons in a jungle clearing. Above and below him in the thick jungle were men going about similar tasks; Silk could hear their voices but he could only see the men sitting directly around him. For some unknown reason, one of the primed grenades belonging to Silk ignited and the fuse reportedly started to hiss. He shouted a warning and then rolled over, clutching the grenade to his stomach, with his body between the deadly weapon and most of the men.

When the grenade exploded, Silk was killed instantly but, contrary to initial reports that two comrades had been slightly injured, no one else was hurt. Silk's courage had almost certainly saved many lives. With only a second or two to assess the situation, he had apparently concluded that if he tossed the grenade away he might have killed his own men positioned above and below him. Instead, he chose to sacrifice his own life.

Silk was buried at the Taukkyan War Cemetery in Rangoon, Burma. His GC was announced on 13 June 1943 and the citation simply said that the posthumous award was 'in recognition of most conspicuous gallantry in carrying out hazardous work in a very brave manner'.

However, eyewitnesses provided a more vivid description of their fallen comrade's courage. One of them, Bill Witchell, cast doubt on some of the facts of the incident that had been reported in *The Times*. However, he was in no doubt about the thrust of the story – that Silk gave his own life to save his comrades from death or injury. 'There is no doubt in my mind that Pte Silk either saved my life or at least saved me from a peppering of shrapnel by the supreme act he took in sacrificing his own life. He was a member of my company. I was some half-dozen paces from him when the tragic accident happened. No one else was even scratched . . . It was an act of sublime heroism . . .'

JOHN BRIDGE

Rank/title: Temporary Lieutenant (later Lieutenant Commander)
Unit/occupation: Royal Naval Volunteer Reserve
DATE OF BRAVERY: AUGUST 1943
GAZETTED: 20 JUNE 1944

John Bridge was born in Culcheth, Warrington, Lancashire, on 5 February 1915. One of seven children, he attended Leigh Grammar School, in what is now part of Greater Manchester. After obtaining a 'special honours' degree in physics from King's College London in 1937, he was awarded a teaching diploma the following year. After sending out more than 100 job applications, he finally got a series of teaching jobs.

Early in the Second World War, he had to put his teaching career on hold to join the Royal Naval Volunteer Reserve. He became a member of an eight-man bomb disposal team – known as the 'First 8'. For most of the war, he was actively involved in bomb and mine disposal.

Lieutenant Bridge was a true war hero. He was the first recipient of the George Medal and bar (a second George Medal). He received his first gallantry medal for disarming a dangerous bomb with a delayed action fuse on 7 September 1940. He received the bar to his medal for raising and defusing a bomb that had fallen between two docks at Falmouth, Cornwall, on 17 May 1941. After this, he spent time in South Africa, Malta and Sicily. In South Africa, he taught others how to carry out mine and bomb disposal work. He and his students dealt with about twelve German mines that had washed up on beaches to the east and north of Cape Town.

In August 1943, he was given a particularly difficult and dangerous task: to clear Messina harbour, Sicily, of its depth charges. Indeed, all the previous members of a bomb disposal team had been killed (five of them) or wounded (two of them) by explosions when he took over the task. On 26 August, Bridge began a four-day reconnaissance of the dockyard and harbour. He and his team discovered that there were scores of depth charges scattered around the quays, in pump-houses and sub-stations. There were also forty in the harbour. Having located all of them, he was able to begin diving on 30 August. Intermittent shelling continued from enemy guns on the other side of the strait.

Bridge and his team made no fewer than twenty-eight dives to tackle the problem. Altogether 207 devices were dismantled or 'discredited' from on or below the surface. They had a variety of firing mechanisms, including two with previously unknown systems. Thanks to the enthusiasm, skill and ingenuity of Bridge and his men, Messina harbour was declared open on 2 September, the day before the main assault on Italy began.

'I was the only one diving,' Bridge said later. 'I had an assistant and several men working above water. My longest spell was one of twenty hours. I did not suffer any particular discomfort and never got tired. I left that to afterwards.' Bridge's GC was announced on 20 June 1944. His recommendation read: 'For the most conspicuous and prolonged bravery and contempt of death in clearing Messina Harbour of depth charges. The recommending officer stated that he had never before had the fortune to be associated with such cool and sustained bravery as Lieutenant Bridge displayed during the 10 days of the operation.'

In September 1944, Bridge displayed still more heroics when twelve crack German swimmers swam twelve miles upstream to place torpedo-shaped mines under the Nijmegen Bridge in Belgium. Some of the captured swimmers had revealed that the timing devices had been set for four hours but no one knew the precise time they had been triggered. The rail bridge had been destroyed but the road bridge could be saved – provided it was not further damaged. Bridge looked at the dirty water of the Waal River and, after stripping to his underpants, located a mine with his toes. With great dexterity, he threaded a piece of wire around his toe and slipped a loop around the mine. Waiting Royal Engineers lifted the mine up and placed it in a rowing boat. Once it had been taken well clear of the area, Bridge used a hammer and chisel to smash the locking ring and remove the firing mechanism.

In the final year of the war, Bridge considered he had landed a safer job – dismantling bombs closer to home rather than abroad. This was as a result of his being posted to Liverpool and being promoted to lieutenant commander. He married and the couple went on to have three daughters. Demobilised in 1946, he returned to education. He became Assistant Education Officer for Southport in 1947 and served as Director of Education for Sunderland Borough Council from 1963 to 1976. From 1952, he was involved in the reorganising of primary schools and, later, secondary education after the introduction of comprehensive schools.

In retirement, Bridge lived at Roker, in Sunderland, where his recreations were gardening, fell-walking, fishing, photography and travel. He also published a memoir, *Trip to Nijmegen*. Bridge died on 14 December 2006, aged ninety-one.

SUBRAMANIAN
Rank/title: Subedar
Unit/occupation: Queen Victoria's Own Madras Sappers and Miners
DATE OF BRAVERY: 24 FEBRUARY 1944
GAZETTED: 30 JUNE 1944

Subramanian was born in the village of Keezha Ottivakkam, near Kanchipuram, India, on 18 December 1912. A married man, he enlisted in Queen Victoria's Own Madras Sappers and Miners on 15 October 1932. He served with the 11 Field Park Company, 4th Indian Division, and on 13 February 1943 he was promoted to the rank of subedar.

On 24 February 1944, Subedar Subramanian was serving in Mignano, Italy, when, as he approached the crest of a hill with a mine-detector, he realised that a mine was about to explode beside a comrade who had become rooted to the spot in fear. Subramanian knocked the man out of the way and spreadeagled himself on the mine in order to try to save the lives of his comrades. He was killed when it exploded, aged forty-one. One other comrade, the man closest to the mine, was nevertheless killed and another received minor injuries. Subramanian was cremated and his ashes were interred at Sangro River Cremation Memorial, in northern Italy.

Subramanian was awarded a posthumous GC on 30 June 1944 for 'conspicuous gallantry in carrying out hazardous work in a very brave manner'.

BENJAMIN GIMBERT
Rank/title: Mr
Unit/occupation: Engine driver, London & North Eastern Railway
DATE OF BRAVERY: 2 JUNE 1944
GAZETTED: 25 JULY 1944

JAMES WILLIAM NIGHTALL
Rank/title: Mr
Unit/occupation: Engine fireman, London & North Eastern Railway
DATE OF BRAVERY: 2 JUNE 1944
GAZETTED: 25 JULY 1944

Ben Gimbert was born in Ely, Cambridgeshire, on 6 February 1903. The sixth of sixteen children, he lived on the family farm until, in 1918, aged fifteen, he went to Peterborough to work on the Great Eastern Railway. Initially a cleaner, he was promoted several times until he achieved his ambition of becoming an engine driver in 1942. He was married with three children, although his third child, a baby son, died. By 1944, he was working for the London & North Eastern Railway (LNER), which had absorbed the Great Eastern Railway in the 1920s.

James Nightall was born in Littleport, Cambridgeshire, on 20 May 1922. He was an only child. His father, a farm worker, found him a job, aged fourteen, on a chicken farm after he left the local secondary school. However, he quickly joined the LNER, also as a cleaner. He was later, at the age of twenty-two, promoted to fireman.

By the summer of 1944, Gimbert and Nightall were firm friends and colleagues. On 2 June 1944 – four days before D-Day – they were taking an ammunition train of fifty-one trucks, filled with unfused bombs destined for an American Air Force base in East Anglia.

The train was approaching Soham station in Cambridgeshire at 1.25 a.m. with Gimbert the engine driver and Nightall as fireman. There was no moon and it was pitch dark when Gimbert noticed that the wagon next to the engine was on fire. He knew the unfused bombs would not withstand a fierce fire and that, in turn, the detonation of the bombs would have caused massive destruction. The driver realised the burning truck had to be separated from the rest of the train as quickly as possible.

Knowing that to slam on the steam brakes would almost certainly lead to an explosion, Gimbert applied them very slowly so that the train came to a halt over a distance of half a mile. As the train was slowing down, he gave two blasts on the engine whistle to ensure that the guard and nearby signalman knew there was an emergency. When the train finally stopped just outside Soham station, Nightall jumped from the cab, raced to the burning wagon and attacked the coupling with a hammer. It took him a minute to uncouple the blazing truck and he then ran back to join Gimbert.

Gimbert started to draw the engine away from danger but, after 100 yards, he decided to stop at the signal box to ensure that the signalman did not allow any other train to enter the danger zone. In fact, a mail train was due shortly on the opposite line. At that moment, the forty-four 500-lb HE bombs in the blazing wagon exploded with an astonishing force. As well as causing a crater twenty feet deep and sixty feet wide in the middle of the railway track, the explosion obliterated almost all the buildings at Soham station. The station hotel was destroyed and 600 other buildings were badly damaged.

Nightall, aged twenty-two, was killed and the signalman, Frank Bridge, later died from his injuries. Gimbert was blown high into the air but, remarkably, was not killed, even though his engine was blown on to its side, belching smoke. Thirty-two pieces of metal were later removed from his body in hospital. The guard, Herbert Clarke, also survived the blast.

However, Gimbert and Nightall's bravery had saved the town and preserved the much-needed ammunition for D-Day. Nightall's posthumous GC and Gimbert's own GC were announced on 25 July 1944, less than two months after the incident. The citation ended:

> Gimbert and Nightall were fully aware of the contents of the wagon which was on fire and displayed outstanding courage and resource in endeavouring to isolate it. When they discovered that the wagon was on fire they could easily have left the train and sought shelter, but realising that if they did not remove the burning vehicle the whole of the train, which consisted of 51 wagons of explosives, would have blown up, they risked their lives in order to minimise the effect of the fire. There is no doubt that if the whole train had been involved, as it would have been but for the gallant action of the men concerned, there would have been serious loss of life and property.

Both men were also awarded the LNER Silver Medal for Courage and Resource and the Order of Industrial Heroism. Nightall's mother, Alice, never recovered from her only child's death and wore black every day until she died. Gimbert reluctantly became a national celebrity. He retired as an engine driver in 1966 and died in March, Cambridgeshire, on 6 May 1976, aged seventy-three.

On 28 September 1981, at March station, two locomotives were named in honour of the courageous railwaymen: *Benjamin Gimbert GC* and *James Nightall GC*. Nightall Road in Soham was also named in honour of the fireman.

LEONARD VERDI GOLDSWORTHY
Rank/title: Lieutenant (later Lieutenant Commander)
Unit/occupation: Royal Australian Naval Volunteer Reserve
DATE OF BRAVERY: JUNE 1943–APRIL 1944
GAZETTED: 19 SEPTEMBER 1944

Leon, or 'Ficky', Goldsworthy, as he was known to friends, was born in Broken Hill, New South Wales, Australia, on 19 January 1909. He attended Kapunda High School, South Australia, followed by the Adelaide School of Mines and the University of Adelaide. He moved to Perth after graduating and worked for the Rainbow Neon Sign Company. He married on 4 November 1939 and the couple later had a daughter.

After the outbreak of the Second World War, Goldsworthy was recruited to the Royal Australian Naval Volunteer Reserve. He arrived in Britain two months after his wedding, where he became a member of the Rendering Mines Safe section at HMS *Vernon*.

His education in physics and electricity stood him in good stead for his work, as did his slim but muscular physique. Along with two other future GC holders – John Mould and Hugh Syme – Lieutenant Goldsworthy invented a new diving suit that enabled bomb disposal experts to dive deeper without experiencing decompression problems. His combination of skill and courage meant that he was brilliant at his job.

Goldsworthy was awarded the George Medal on 18 April 1944 for various bomb disposal exploits, including making safe a German ground mine off Sheerness. It was only the second time ever that such a deadly weapon had been rendered safe underwater. Later the same year, he was awarded the GC for further bravery in dealing with dangerous acoustic-type mines. One of these, at Milford Haven in Wales, had been in place for two and a half years because no one had dared tackle it. Goldsworthy said of the device: 'like an old soldier an acoustic mine never quite dies: although the batteries run down they don't run out'. As always, Goldsworthy rose to the challenge, removing first the fuse and primer and, later, the intact mine. Other mines he tackled during this period were at locations ranging from Dorset to West Hartlepool. The citation for his GC on 19 September 1944 said that the award was for 'great gallantry and undaunted devotion to duty'.

Late in 1944, Goldsworthy and other bomb disposal experts were seconded to the US Navy in the Pacific. In January 1945, Goldsworthy was awarded his third gallantry medal, this time a Distinguished Service Cross (DSC) for stripping, in fifty feet of water, a German 'K' mine in Cherbourg harbour. At the time, the harbour had to be hurriedly cleared to assist with the Allied invasion of Normandy. When the war ended, Goldsworthy was the most decorated Australian naval officer of the conflict.

Goldsworthy retired as a lieutenant commander in 1946 and moved back to Perth where he returned to the Rainbow Neon Sign Company, working for the firm, in all, for forty-six years. After his first wife died, he remarried. Goldsworthy himself died in Perth on 7 August 1994, aged eighty-five.

RICHARD ARTHUR SAMUEL BYWATER

Rank/title: Mr

Unit/occupation: Factory development officer, Ministry of Supply

DATE OF BRAVERY: 22 FEBRUARY 1944

GAZETTED: 26 SEPTEMBER 1944

Arthur Bywater, as he was better known, was born in Birmingham on 3 November 1913. The youngest of six children and the son of the chief clerk in charge of stores at the Austin Motor Company, he was educated at King's Norton Grammar School in the city, where he had won a scholarship. Later he attended Birmingham University, where he obtained a first in chemistry and then a master's degree. He was working at the Royal Filling Factory at Woolwich Arsenal in London when the Second World War broke out. He later moved to the Ministry of Supply Factory at Kirkby, near Liverpool, which had been built in 1941 at a cost of £8 million. Altogether 10,000 operatives worked at the factory turning out 150,000 anti-tank mine fuses a week.

On 22 February 1944, nineteen staff, mainly women, were at work in one area of the factory. Their role was the last stage of filling ammunition fuses and each operative had on a bench in front of her, or him, a tray with twenty-five fuses. The fuses were stacked on tables each holding forty trays, or 1,000 fuses. Altogether, there were more than 12,000 fuses in the building that day.

At 8.30 a.m., one of the fuses detonated which, in turn, detonated the whole tray. The girl working on the tray was killed outright, while two others were injured, one fatally. Furthermore, the factory itself was badly damaged. The superintendent on duty on the morning of 22 February was Arthur Bywater, the factory development officer. He surveyed the scene of devastation at the factory: the roof of the building had been torn off and electrical fittings were hanging precariously. Fuses are always sensitive but Bywater realised that the same problem

– already identified as a defective striker that had led to the carnage – might exist in other fuses, resulting in a massive explosion. He concluded that the only thing to do was to try to remove all the fuses to a place of safety where they could subsequently be dealt with.

Then thirty, Bywater, who had volunteered to take charge of the task, was aided by three others. They began the job at once and worked at it solidly for three days, until 5 p.m. on 24 February. By then, they had removed 12,724 fuses from the badly damaged building. Of these, 4,000 were identified as possibly being defective. They were taken to a burning ground a mile away and Bywater destroyed them in a series of controlled explosions beneath sandbags.

During the course of removing the fuses from the factory, Bywater identified twenty-three of them as definitely being defective. With each discovery, he made the other staff take cover while he removed the fuse personally. One of these fuses was so defective that it would have detonated with the slightest movement. Because of his experience, Bywater knew of two men who had previously tried to handle such sensitive fuses; both had been blown to pieces. If, however, the fuse had been destroyed in the factory, it could have caused even more damage. Bywater therefore arranged for a safe to be positioned a short distance away with sandbags surrounding it. Knowing his chances of survival were slim, he picked up the fuse and tiptoed up to the safe – where, after withdrawing, he successfully detonated it. As a precaution, the other fuses were destroyed under supervision, a task which took Bywater and his assistants five hours a day, seven days a week for a month.

Bywater's GC was announced on 26 September 1944 'for outstanding heroism and devotion to duty when an explosion occurred in a factory'. After dealing with another explosion at the same factory, he was awarded the George Medal on 18 September 1945. He therefore became the only civilian to be awarded the GC and George Medal.

Bywater married in 1947 and went on to have a son and a daughter. After getting a job as a works manager for a company in Nailsea, Bristol, he retired in 1954 and emigrated to Australia. An inactive retirement, however, did not suit him: he set up an ordnance factory and later joined the Reserve Bank of Australia in Melbourne as general manager. He then became involved in Australia's decimalisation programme in 1966. After retiring a second time in 1976, he and his wife ran a 240-acre farm on the banks of the Murray River where they grew wheat and fattened lambs. Bywater died in Scone, New South Wales, on 5 April 2005, aged ninety-one.

ARTHUR DWIGHT ROSS
Rank/title: Air Commodore
Unit/occupation: Royal Canadian Air Force
DATE OF BRAVERY: JUNE 1944
GAZETTED: 27 OCTOBER 1944

Dwight Ross, as he was better known, was born in Winnipeg, Manitoba, Canada, on 18 March 1907. An only child, his paternal grandfather had been an MP involved in the early development of the Canadian railways. His only uncle went down with the *Titanic*, while his father was an engineering architect. The young Ross went to public school in Winnipeg followed by Upper Canada College in Toronto and the Royal Military College (RMC) in Kingston, Ontario. He graduated from the RMC in 1928 and received a permanent commission to the Royal Canadian Air Force (RCAF). After being awarded his pilot's 'wings', he attended a flying boat and seaplane conversion course at Jericho Beach Station, Vancouver. Ross married in June 1935 and went on to have two daughters.

After the outbreak of the Second World War, by which time he was a wing commander, he held senior positions in the RCAF before being transferred overseas to RAF Bomber Command. He was put in charge of the RAF station at Middleton St George in Yorkshire. On 1 March 1944, he was appointed air commodore in command of RAF Tholthorpe in North Yorkshire. It was here, one night in June 1944, that a Halifax bomber was attempting to land when it crashed into another Halifax parked in the dispersal area which was loaded with bombs. The landing Halifax had broken into three parts and was burning fiercely. Air Commodore Ross and a corporal, who was in charge of the ground crew, raced to the scene and helped to extricate the pilot, who had received serious injuries.

However, just as they were rescuing the pilot, ten 500-lb bombs in the second Halifax, some thirty yards away, exploded, hurling the officer and airman to the ground. Once the hail of debris had subsided, cries could be heard from the rear of the crashed plane. Despite exploding bombs and petrol tanks, Ross and the corporal returned to the plane and tried to rescue the rear gunner. Even though the port tail area was burning furiously, Ross hacked at the Perspex with an axe in a frantic attempt to get to the rear gunner. Another 500-lb bomb now exploded, almost severing Ross's right arm. He calmly walked to the ambulance and an emergency amputation was performed when he arrived at the station's 'sick quarters'.

Ross's GC was announced on 27 October 1944. The citation praised the actions of four other men and said of the officer: 'Air Commodore Ross showed fine leadership and great heroism in an action which resulted in the saving of the lives of the pilot and rear gunner.' After a spell in hospital, Ross was appointed to RCAF Overseas Headquarters in London.

After the war ended, he continued to pursue a successful military career in Canada and the UK. He retired from the RCAF in February 1961 after more than thirty years in the service. Ross then went into the insurance business, eventually retiring from his civilian career in 1966. A keen sportsman, despite the loss of an arm, he enjoyed swimming, yachting and curling. Ross, who was also awarded the CBE and Canadian gallantry awards, died in Kingston, Ontario, on 27 September 1981, aged seventy-four.

7

THE AWARDS OF 1945

JENKIN ROBERT OSWALD THOMPSON

Rank/title: Captain
Unit/occupation: Royal Army Medical Corps
DATE OF BRAVERY: MAY 1940, 10–14 JULY 1943,
10–15 SEPTEMBER 1943, 23–24 JANUARY 1944
GAZETTED: 2 FEBRUARY 1945

The GC that Captain Jenkin Thompson received is a unique award in that it cited bravery in four separate episodes during the Second World War. He spent most of the war aboard hospital ships where he was devoted to the patients on board. Thompson was born in Fulham, south-west London, on 13 July 1911. He was the son of a doctor and, after leaving school, he too qualified as a doctor, becoming registered on 7 February 1939. JRO, as he was often known, was married with two children. After the outbreak of the Second World War, he was commissioned as a lieutenant in the Royal Army Medical Corps – a fact announced in the *London Gazette* of 13 February 1940. Later he was promoted to captain.

The episodes during which Thompson had shown great gallantry were: in the HM hospital ship *Paris* at Dunkirk in May 1940; in the *Sicily*, 10–14 July 1943; at Salerno, 10–15 September 1943; and at Anzio, 23–24 January 1944. During this time he showed indifference to danger and physical exhaustion despite repeated dive-bombing attacks on the ships and shellfire during the battles.

In his book *Hospital Ships and Ambulance Trains*, John Plumridge painted a vivid picture of the scene during the chaotic Dunkirk evacuation when *Paris* was sent to help with the removal of the sick and wounded.

> At that time the most unpleasant place to be this side of hell was the foreshore and the sea that lay off the little strip of coast between La Panne and Dunkirk for the area, thick with weary soldiers and ships of all sizes, was under constant artillery and air attack whilst, later on, German heavy machine guns added their contribution to the general beastliness as their bullets spattered the water with an effect like showers of pebbles thrown from the shore . . . Conditions in the carrier [*Paris*] were far from pleasant but there was a job to be done and the crew, doctors and nursing staff went on with it quietly, doing their best to turn deaf ears to the roar of battle going on around them. Their only defence lay in their somewhat inadequate tin hats, slightly hysterical little jokes when something dropped particularly close, and occasional tots of rum and brandy from the hospital store . . . In conditions such as these it seems surprising that the conduct of any one man should have earned particular notice. The complete disregard of all danger that was displayed by Captain Thompson was, however, noticed by many people and, in particular, by his superiors. They also noticed that, in addition to having nerves of steel, he also seemed to be tireless and, when there were patients to be treated, he simply went on and on without a break for sleep or meals.

Nearly four years later, nothing had changed: Thompson was as fearless and as committed as ever. In Anzio Bay, the *St David* had wounded British and US servicemen on board in order to transport them to Naples. The hospital ship was accompanied by the *St Andrew* and the *Leinster*. The dive-bombing and dropping of flares by enemy planes were relentless and eventually the *St David* was hit. As the ship went down, Thompson calmly supervised the removal of patients, including seriously wounded men, to rescue boats. He succeeded in saving all those from his ward and others besides. However, still on board was one seriously ill patient who had been unable to move and was lying trapped below decks. Unable to move the man, Thompson stayed with him as the ship slipped beneath the waves.

Thompson was thirty-two when he died. His posthumous GC was announced on 2 February 1945 in recognition of 'most conspicuous gallantry in carrying out hazardous work in a very brave manner'.

LESLIE OWEN FOX
Rank/title: Mr
Unit/occupation: Deputy Party Leader, London County Council Heavy Rescue Service
DATE OF BRAVERY: 20 FEBRUARY 1944
GAZETTED: 20 FEBRUARY 1945

Leslie Fox was born in Fulham, south-west London, on 4 December 1904. The son of a bus driver who lived with his wife above a police station, the young Fox attended the local school and then trained to be a carpenter. He plied his trade working at the Regent Palace Hotel in Piccadilly.

During the Second World War, Fox worked for the London County Council Heavy Rescue Service, a section of the Civil Defence programme that was designed to deal with buildings damaged by German bombing. The service was employed to stabilise damaged buildings and to lift heavy debris to enable rescuers to reach trapped victims of the bombing. Fox had the title of Deputy Party Leader with the group.

On 20 February 1944, the Heavy Rescue Service was called to an incident in Fulham where some houses had been demolished by high explosive and incendiary bombs. The wreckage was ablaze and the walls of some of the houses were poised to collapse at any moment. When cries were heard from beneath the rubble, Fox immediately began tunnelling through the blazing ruins. Debris that he passed back was too hot to handle and his men had continuously to spray him with water to try to keep down the intolerable heat from the flames.

Fox, aged forty, managed to shore up the entrance to his makeshift tunnel, although adjoining it was a crumbling party wall. After two hours of tireless and dangerous work, Fox eventually reached the injured man. He ignored pleas from others for them to take over and instead stayed on the scene to supervise the rescue. As Fox waited, the dangerous wall collapsed, blocking the way through to the injured man and causing the tunnel he had dug to subside. Fox started retunnelling from a different access point. Now desperately weary from his exertions, he eventually spent another two hours tunnelling fifteen feet into the rubble. This time he was able to clear the debris from over the head of the casualty and cover him with makeshift protection. Eventually, Fox was joined by a medical officer and they brought the injured man to safety.

Fox's GC was announced on 20 February 1945 and the citation ended: 'Fox performed his duty in a most gallant and determined manner and, by his courage and tenacity, saved a man from what appeared to be almost certain death.'

After the war, Fox returned to his job as a carpenter at the Regent Palace Hotel, where he stayed for thirty years. He married and acquired a stepson who, in turn, had three children. Fox enjoyed a pint at his local Fulham pub, the Golden Lion, and a bet on the horses. He died in Fareham, Hampshire, on Boxing Day 1982, aged seventy-eight.

RODERICK BORDEN GRAY
Rank/title: Flying Officer
Unit/occupation: Royal Canadian Air Force
DATE OF BRAVERY: 27 AUGUST 1944
GAZETTED: 13 MARCH 1945

Roderick Gray was born in Sault Ste Marie, Ontario, Canada, on 2 October 1917. He was educated in his home town until June 1937 when, aged nineteen, he went to work as a freight handler on the Canadian Pacific Railway. A married man, Gray joined the Canadian Army on 13 July 1940, but he transferred to the Royal Canadian Air Force on 12 October 1941.

An internal military report in early 1942 assessed Gray, who was often known as 'Cy', as 'cool, calm and conscientious, confident and dependable'. In August 1944, when Flying Officer Gray was the navigator in a Wellington bomber shot down by a German U-boat over the Atlantic, he proved to have all these qualities and more. Gray, who received a severe wound to one of his legs in the crash-landing, managed to escape from the bomber, as did the three other members of his crew.

Despite his injury, Gray succeeded in inflating his dinghy and assisting his captain, who had also been wounded, into it. Shortly afterwards, cries were heard from another crew member, who had broken his arm, and Gray assisted him into the small dinghy. Knowing that the dinghy could hold no more than two people, he refused to try to get in as well. Instead, in severe pain after apparently having the lower part of his left leg shot off, he clung to the side of the dinghy for three hours. He eventually lost consciousness and died. His body was never recovered. Gray was twenty-six when he perished.

His posthumous GC was announced on 13 March 1945 when the citation ended with a description of his final moments: 'When it became light, his companions realised that he was dead and they were forced to let his body sink. The survivors were rescued later. Flying Officer Gray displayed magnificent courage and unselfish heroism, thus enabling the lives of his comrades to be saved.'

Warrant Officer Bulley, one of the surviving crew, wrote a letter to Gray's widow paying tribute to her husband's actions: 'Never so long as I live will I forget Cy Gray's courage. I definitely owe my life to him. In my opinion he was just about the biggest hero that ever lived.'

KENNETH HORSFIELD
Rank/title: Corporal
Unit/occupation: Manchester Regiment, attached Special Air Service
DATE OF BRAVERY: 18 AUGUST 1944
GAZETTED: 23 MARCH 1945

Kenneth Horsfield was born in Stockport, near Manchester, on 29 September 1920. The elder of two sons, he attended the local Leigh Street School, but left at fourteen to become a butcher. He joined the 9th Territorial Battalion, Manchester Regiment, in 1939. Later in his Army career, he trained abroad with the SAS but he never discussed this with his family. It is known, however, that Corporal Horsfield served in North Africa, the Middle East and, finally, in Brindisi, southern Italy. He married in June 1942 while on fourteen days' embarkation leave.

On 18 August 1944, an explosion occurred at about 1.45 p.m. during the demolition of a military establishment in Bari, north of Brindisi. Three people were killed and three more injured in the incident. Horsfield, who had been working nearby, was one of the first on the scene. Peering through a window, he saw a man lying injured and trapped by rubble. By now a fire was raging and he raced to try to release the man, but was unable to do so. Horsfield then got a thirty-two-gallon fire extinguisher which, standing at the doorway, he aimed at the fire to try to prevent it reaching the trapped man. Knowing a second explosion was likely, he ordered everyone away from the scene as he tackled the blaze single-handed. Eventually, a second explosion took place, seriously injuring Horsfield. He later died from his injuries, aged twenty-three.

His posthumous GC was announced on 23 March 1945 in recognition of 'the most conspicuous gallantry in carrying out hazardous work in a very brave manner'.

ALBERT EDWARD HEMING

Rank/title: Mr
Unit/occupation: Section leader, Civil Defence Rescue Service, Bermondsey
DATE OF BRAVERY: 2 MARCH 1945
GAZETTED: 17 JULY 1945

Albert Heming was born on 13 June 1910 in Wood Green, near Edmonton, Middlesex. One of eight children, his father was a sergeant major in the East Yorkshire Regiment and his mother was a seamstress. After attending school in Forest Hill, south-east London, he entered the building trade. Heming married on 23 September 1930, when he was working as a baker's roundsman, and the couple went on to have six children. Heming, known to his friends as Ted, pursued a variety of occupations including those of mosaic tiler, carpenter and milkman. He joined the Civil Defence Rescue Service in 1939 after the outbreak of the Second World War.

In March 1945, just two months before the end of the war in Europe, London was still under serious threat from the air. One of those dealing with the damage was Heming, the section leader of the Civil Defence Rescue Service in Bermondsey, south-east London. On 2 March 1945, V2 rockets fell and several people were trapped in the wreckage of the Roman Catholic church and adjacent buildings in Bermondsey. It soon became apparent that four priests and two female house-keepers were missing and that the chances of them still being alive were slim. Heming, who was quickly on the scene, and his men began searching for survivors, particularly in a house where the four walls had 'pancaked'. After some time, cries were heard coming from the crypt of the church. Heming burrowed into the debris, taking a saw with him, and found a V-shaped void in the rubble. He had to dig his way through a mass of beams, masonry and plaster. He eventually found the survivor, a priest, pinned down by a support timber that was fixed to the floor. They exchanged names but the situation was desperate.

To add to their difficulties, coal gas was escaping from a damaged pipe. The regional commander suggested the rescue attempt was too dangerous and ought to be abandoned but Heming was having none of it. He said he was not willing to abandon someone that he had spoken with, even though others had given the priest the last rites from a distance.

Heming, then aged thirty-four, continued to remove debris and rubble for three hours. For much of the time, he was upside down as he burrowed but, eventually, the priest was freed. When they reached the surface, both men were taken to hospital by ambulance. Within minutes of the rescue, the main wall fell down and all hope of finding further survivors was thus ended. The trapped man, Canon Edmund Arbuthnott, recovered after a long spell in hospital. Heming was back at work the next day, but he endured lung and stomach problems for the rest of his life as a result of the gas he had inhaled.

Heming's GC was announced on 17 July 1945 when the citation ended: 'Although from the outset, it appeared impossible to effect a rescue, Heming refused to abandon the victim and, with great gallantry and determination, successfully accomplished a task seemingly beyond human endurance.'

Heming and the priest remained good friends and the canon gave his rescuer the silver crucifix that he had been wearing when he was pulled to safety. The inscription on it read simply: 'In gratitude for 2.3.45'. In 1959, when Father Arbuthnott was the subject of a *This Is Your Life* television programme, his rescuer from fourteen years earlier was a surprise guest. Father Arbuthnott wrote about his wartime experiences in his autobiography, *A Priest's Life*. He recalled that he had lapsed into unconsciousness as he lay in the rubble of the church. He could see nothing and could hear only water dripping and bells ringing. He spent much of the time praying until he saw a light and called out.

Father Arbuthnott, who had been the youngest of twelve children, continued working in the church until his retirement. He moved to Worthing, West Sussex, where he lived until his death in 1998, aged eighty-nine.

Despite Heming's poor health, which sometimes prevented him from working full-time, he enjoyed a long and eventful life. After the war, he was employed by the Ministry of Works before opening his own toy manufacturing business. Towards the end of his career, he worked in the photographic department of the Imperial War Museum until his retirement on 13 June 1975. He struggled for money and came close to being forced to sell his GC to settle his debts. Heming died in Forest Hill, on 3 January 1987, aged seventy-six.

ST JOHN GRAHAM YOUNG

Rank/title: Lieutenant
Unit/occupation: Royal Tank Regiment, attached the Central Indian Horse (21st King George V's Own Horse), Indian Armoured Corps
DATE OF BRAVERY: 23–24 JULY 1944
GAZETTED: 20 JULY 1945

DITTO RAM

Rank/Title: Sowar
Unit/occupation: Central Indian Horse (21st King George V's Own Horse), Indian Armoured Corps
DATE OF BRAVERY: 23–24 JULY 1944
GAZETTED: 13 DECEMBER 1945

St John Young was born in Esher, Surrey, on 16 June 1921. He received a Regular Army Emergency Commission into the Royal Armoured Corps on 3 January 1942. He served in the Middle East in 1942 and by the summer of 1944, having transferred to the Royal Tank Regiment, was attached to the Indian Armoured Corps. Ditto Ram is believed to have been born in 1915 or 1916 in India. He joined the Army in 1941 or

1942. By the summer of 1944, he too was serving with the Indian Armoured Corps.

On 23 July 1944, men from the Central Indian Horse (21st King George V's Own Horse), including Lieutenant Young and Sowar Ram, were on night patrol in a remote area of Italy. As the patrol neared the hill it had been advancing on, explosions could be heard. Young, who was in command, withdrew but then, without warning, the patrol found itself in the middle of a minefield. Three more explosions could be heard from their midst and Young ordered the men to remain where they were until first light in the hope that they would fare better then than in the darkness.

Two hours later, and when it was still dark, Sowar Niru, a member of the patrol, could be heard calling out in great pain, having been earlier wounded by an exploding mine. Crawling towards the casualty, Young felt for, located and rendered harmless three Schu mines. However, as he carefully approached the injured man, he knelt on another Schu mine which exploded, blowing off his right leg. Undeterred but in great pain, Young crawled to Sowar Niru. He found him unconscious but administered a field dressing to the wounded soldier.

It was now about 1 a.m. on 24 July. For the next five hours, Young encouraged his men as he lay horribly injured in the darkness. He assured them that once it was light they would be able to reach safety. At first light, Jemadar Hosenak Singh reached Young and carried him to safety. However, he quickly lost consciousness and died that evening. He was twenty-three. Sowar Niru also died from his injuries.

Elsewhere in the minefield, Ram had been injured by a mine which blew off his left leg below the knee. He applied a field dressing and then, having heard calls for help from another sowar, crawled towards his comrade. On reaching him, Ram learnt that the man's thigh had been shattered. His comrade was in terrible pain but Ram applied a field dressing to his wound, too. In Ram's own distressed state, this was a difficult manoeuvre. Having completed this task, Ram lost consciousness within a few minutes and died. He is believed to have been about twenty-nine years old.

St John was initially considered for a VC but instead his GC was announced on 20 July 1945 in recognition of 'most conspicuous gallantry in carrying out hazardous work in a very brave manner'. Ram's GC was announced later – on 13 December 1945. His fuller citation ended: 'Sowar Ditto Ram was a very young soldier with only two years' service, nevertheless, besides showing the greatest personal courage and disregard for pain, by crawling through a minefield to help a wounded companion he set the finest example of soldierly comradeship and self-sacrifice. He maintained consciousness only long enough to finish the bandaging of his comrade before he died without a murmur of complaint.'

ISLAM-ud-DIN

Rank/title: Lance Naik
Unit/occupation: 6th Battalion, 9th Jat Regiment, Indian Army
DATE OF BRAVERY: 12 APRIL 1945
GAZETTED: 5 OCTOBER 1945

Islam-ud-Din, a married man born in India in either 1925 or 1926, was serving with the 6th Battalion, 9th Jat Regiment, of the Indian Army at Khanda, Burma, fighting against the Japanese at the end of the Second World War.

The leadership qualities and steadfast courage of Lance Naik Islam-ud-Din had been noticed by his superiors in early 1945. Then, on 12 April 1945, he and his comrades were at Pyawbwe, central Burma, when a stray live grenade threatened to cause widespread casualties. Unhesitatingly, Islam-ud-Din threw himself on the grenade: he was killed, aged nineteen or twenty, but he saved the lives of his companions.

His posthumous GC was announced on 6 October 1945 in

recognition of 'most conspicuous bravery in carrying out hazardous work in a very brave manner'. His name is inscribed on the Rangoon Memorial in Burma.

KENNETH SMITH
Rank/title: Signalman
Unit/occupation: Royal Corps of Signals
DATE OF BRAVERY: 10 JANUARY 1945
GAZETTED: 19 OCTOBER 1945

Kenneth Smith was born on 7 December 1920 in Market Rasen, Lincolnshire. The son of a farm labourer, he was one of at least five children. He enlisted into the Royal Corps of Signals on 23 January 1939. In 1941, he joined the Long Range Desert Group (LRDG), a band of tough, brave men who operated behind enemy lines in inhospitable territory and were effectively the forerunners of the SAS Regiment. At the beginning of 1945, Smith was billeted, along with some of his detachment, on the Adriatic island of Ist with local civilians, including children. Enemy saboteurs, who had landed on the north of the island, were trying to disrupt the Allied activities on Ist.

On 10 January 1945, after hearing shots, Smith ran to the wireless room in his billet where he found a ticking bomb on the table. There were other partisans in the room and children upstairs so he picked up the bomb in order to place it behind a wall. However, he was only a few yards outside the house when the bomb went off, blowing him to pieces. Smith was twenty-four.

Smith's posthumous GC was announced on 19 October 1945 in recognition of 'most conspicuous gallantry in carrying out hazardous work in a very brave manner'. One of Smith's brothers, Michael, was only three when the signalman died. He later wanted to find out more about his brother's death and visited Ist. He discovered that his brother's decoration had been sold and tried to trace its whereabouts via the internet.

The GC eventually went up for auction and was bought by the Royal Corps of Signals, with Michael Smith being present at the time. He was thrilled at the outcome: 'I am delighted that the medal has finally found a safe place where it will be respected and treasured,' he said. 'I am a very happy man. It will now be on show as a permanent reminder to the nation of those who gave their lives so freely that we may live on in freedom.'

8

THE AWARDS OF 1946

FREDERICK DAVIES

Rank/title: Mr
Unit/occupation: Fireman, National Fire Service
DATE OF BRAVERY: 22 AUGUST 1945
GAZETTED: 5 FEBRUARY 1946

Frederick Davies was born in Shepherd's Bush, west London, on 17 February 1913. He left school at fourteen. In 1935, aged twenty-two, he married. The previous year he had started working as a fireman at Willesden Fire Station in north-west London and served there throughout the Second World War. The men of No. 34 (London) Area celebrated VJ-Day along with the rest of the nation.

A week later, at 11 a.m. on 22 August 1945, a fire broke out at a flat above a shop in Harlesden, also in north-west London. Davies was one of the first on the scene and was told that two children were in the front room on the second floor of the house. Fierce flames from the ground floor prevented any hope of a rescue by the stairs. An escape ladder was raised to the middle room of the second floor.

Even before the ladder was properly in place, Davies was swiftly climbing up the rungs even though flames were already coming from the windows of the second floor and licking the outside of the building. The intense fire initially blocked his entrance, but he eventually entered the room with his back turned to the flames. A colleague could see him trying to take off his tunic – apparently to wrap around one of the children inside – but his hands were already too badly burned for him to do this successfully. After a quick circuit of the flame- and smoke-filled room, he emerged with one child, a girl, and handed her through a window to a fellow fireman.

Davies refused an order to come down and instead returned for the other child, also a girl. He was next seen flinging himself out of the window and on to the escape ladder. The child was almost certainly already dead when she was brought down. When Davies reached the foot of the ladder, he was a human torch and he died the next day from his horrific injuries. The first girl to be rescued also died from her injuries. The dead sisters were aged eleven and eight.

Davies, who was a keen footballer, was thirty-two when he died. He already had a son and his daughter was born after he perished. His GC was announced on 5 February 1946 when the lengthy citation ended: 'The gallantry and outstanding devotion to duty displayed by Fireman Davies was of the highest order. He knew the danger he was facing, but with a complete disregard of his own safety he made a most heroic attempt to rescue the two children. In doing so he lost his life.' His GC was later donated by his daughter, Doreen, to the Fire Brigade Museum in London.

FOREST FREDERICK EDWARD YEO-THOMAS
Rank/title: Wing Commander
Unit/occupation: Royal Air Force Volunteer Reserve
DATE OF BRAVERY: FEBRUARY 1943–APRIL 1945
GAZETTED: 15 FEBRUARY 1946

Forest Yeo-Thomas, who was widely known simply as Tommy, was born in Holborn, central London, on 17 June 1902. The eldest of three sons, he lived with his family in France and had a mixed English and French education. Yeo-Thomas had found himself too young to fight in the British and French armies in the First World War so instead he joined the US Army, apparently from around 1918 to 1922. Brigadier Sir John

'Jackie' Smyth, the VC recipient and author, wrote: 'He campaigned with the Poles against the Russians, was captured by the Bolsheviks and for the first of many times in his turbulent and adventurous life, just escaped being shot.'

Yeo-Thomas then trained as an accountant and worked in banking, but he ended up as the manager of a fashion house, while also having a part-share in a gym because of his love of boxing. He married in September 1925 and the couple later had two daughters. When his marriage ended, he entered a long-term relationship with another woman at the start of the Second World War but they did not marry.

In 1939, he joined the RAF as an aircraftsman 2nd class. He had anything but a straightforward flying career. Instead, he underwent radar training and left France on one of the last boats out before the Germans invaded. Speaking fluent French and familiar with the country, he was determined to return to France. After he was commissioned, he went as an intelligence officer to 308 Polish Squadron at Baginton in the West Midlands. In February 1942, he joined the secretive Special Operations Executive (SOE), which had been formed in the summer of 1940 after the fall of France.

Rapidly reaching the rank of wing commander, Yeo-Thomas was a fine organiser and coordinator. On 25 February 1943, he and Andrew Dewavrin were parachuted into France to join Pierre Brossolette of the Free French Secret Service. The next two years were to be truly eventful and he was to show the most amazing courage time and time again. His first mission was a success: he enabled a French officer, who was being followed by the Gestapo in Paris, to reach safety and to resume his secret activities in another area. He also took charge of a US Army Air Corps officer who had been shot down. Because the officer spoke no French, he was in danger of capture but he came back to Britain in the same aircraft that picked up Yeo-Thomas on 15 April 1943, after nearly two months behind enemy lines.

On 17 September 1943, Yeo-Thomas, who was known as the

'White Rabbit', returned to France for a second mission. Soon after his arrival, many French patriots were arrested and the situation had become tense and dangerous. However, he continued with his clandestine activities. On no fewer than six occasions, he narrowly avoided arrest himself. On 15 November 1943, once again after nearly two months in France, he returned to Britain with intelligence documents obtained from a house the Gestapo had been watching.

In February 1944, Yeo-Thomas was again parachuted into France. However, this time he was betrayed to the Gestapo and seized on 21 March. While being taken by car to Gestapo headquarters, he was brutally beaten up. He then underwent four days of interrogation, interspersed with torture. He suffered regular 'immersions': his head held down, with his arms and legs in chains, in ice-cold water. For the next two months, he underwent regular interrogation and he was told that he would be freed in return for information about the head of a Resistance Secretariat. Because one of his wrists had been cut by chains, he suffered blood poisoning and nearly lost his left arm. Incredibly, he even made two daring, but unsuccessful, attempts to escape. His punishment was four months in solitary confinement at Fresnes prison, including three weeks in a darkened cell with little food. The torture continued for all of four months, but he refused to divulge anything of use to his captors.

On 17 July 1944, Yeo-Thomas was sent with a party to Compiègne prison, from where he tried to escape twice more. He and thirty-six other prisoners were then transferred to Buchenwald concentration camp, near Weimar, Germany. En route, they stopped for three days at Saärbrücken where they were kept in a tiny hut and beaten. They arrived at Buchenwald on 16 August, where sixteen of them were executed and, later, on 10 September, cremated. Undaunted, Yeo-Thomas continued to organise resistance within the camp despite the threat of a similar fate. At this stage, he accepted the opportunity to change his identity with that of a dead French prisoner – but only after a guarantee that others would be given the same opportunity. This switch of identity enabled him to save the lives of two other officers.

The Germans now transferred him to a work camp for Jews. He managed to escape from the camp but was picked up nearby. Claiming French nationality, he was transferred to a camp near Marienburg, Poland, for French prisoners of war. As the war appeared to be drawing to a close, Yeo-Thomas led an escape by twenty prisoners from the camp in broad daylight. Ten were killed by gunfire from guards and the rest split up into small groups. After three days without food, Yeo-Thomas became separated from his companions. He kept going for another week but was recaptured when he was only 800 yards short of American lines. Amazingly, he escaped yet again soon afterwards and he then led a party of ten French PoWs through German patrols to American lines.

It was not until 15 February 1946 that Yeo-Thomas was awarded the GC. His lengthy citation ended: 'Wing Commander Yeo-Thomas thus turned his final mission into a success by his determined opposition to the enemy, his strenuous efforts to maintain the morale of his fellow prisoners and his brilliant escape activities. He endured brutal treatment and torture without flinching and showed the most amazing fortitude and devotion to duty throughout his service abroad, during which he was under the constant threat of death.'

For his earlier bravery, Yeo-Thomas had been awarded the MC and bar (a second MC), in March and May 1944 respectively. His other medals and decorations included the Légion d'honneur and Croix de Guerre and the Polish Cross of Merit. He died in Paris on 26 February 1964, aged sixty-one. Six years later, Barbara Dean, his long-term partner, donated his gallantry and service medals to the Imperial War Museum, London.

ARTHUR FREDERICK CRANE NICHOLLS
Rank/title: Brigadier
Unit/occupation: Coldstream Guards
DATE OF BRAVERY: JANUARY/FEBRUARY 1944
GAZETTED: 1 MARCH 1946

Arthur Nicholls was born in Hampstead, north London, on 6 February 1911. He was the son of a stockbroker and one of three children. Nicholls was educated at Shardlow Hall School, Derby, from 1917 to 1924, and Marlborough College, Wiltshire, from 1924 to 1929. He spent seven months at the Sorbonne in Paris and a year in Germany, as a consequence of which he spoke fluent French and German. Between 1931 and 1933, he read law at Pembroke College, Cambridge. After leaving university, Nicholls became a stockbroker until the outbreak of the Second World War in 1939. He married the following year and the couple later had a daughter.

In October 1943 Acting Brigadier Nicholls parachuted into Albania while serving with the Coldstream Guards. He also held the title of General Staff Officer to the Allied Military Mission, which was organising resistance activities against the Germans in Albania. The mission was heavily attacked on three sides by German troops and Albanian collaborators in December 1943. At the time, there were four feet of snow on the ground. After escaping the attack, Nicholls and others were forced to live in the mountains as fugitives. The weather was bitterly cold and they survived in the harshest of conditions.

Just before Christmas Day, the group had to move from their temporary shelter because they believed it had been discovered by the enemy. Their route took them up a mountain stream in which their boots became saturated. Nicholls' feet froze and he refused to remove his boots in case he could not get them on again. One day in early January, the Germans ambushed the party and they had to retreat up a sheer slope of bare snow that offered them no cover from fire.

Another officer, Brigadier Davies, ordered everyone to climb and anyone who was hit – and was either wounded or dying – was left behind. The group included five British soldiers, two Italians and three Albanians. When three of the party, including Brigadier Davies himself, were wounded and captured, Nicholls took command of the group. With Alan Hare, an interpreter, and two partisans, the men continued their journey for a further sixteen hours: their aim was to reach the next British Mission further north. After stopping for rest at a sheepfold, Nicholls could no longer stand – poison had set into both his feet. It is understood that, eventually, Nicholls suffered such severe frostbite and poison to his legs that he had to ask a man, who was not a surgeon, to amputate them without an anaesthetic, although this claim is disputed. For fifteen more days, he was dragged on his greatcoat, first by two men, then later by a mule. Nicholls eventually reached the British Mission, near starvation and very close to death.

From 26 January, Nicholls faced a journey of five more days and nights down the mountain to Tirana, the capital of Albania. There he was taken to a house and it was noted by Major George Seymour that 'his fighting spirit was unimpaired. He was full of fight and determined to carry on with his work. He began at once to discuss the re-organisation of the Mission and to plan for future operations.' Nicholls also wrote up his report on the experiences that he and his men had been through. However, he had pushed his body too far and he died of gangrene and heart failure on 11 February 1944, five days after his thirty-third birthday. Because of the political situation, a headstone could not be erected where he was buried. Instead, he and thirty-seven others were later given one at a cemetery in Athens, Greece.

An announcement appeared in the *London Gazette* on 1 June 1944 stating that Nicholls had 'died of wounds' and praising his 'gallant and distinguished service in the field'. His post-humous GC was not, however, announced until 1 March 1946. Even then, it only said that the award was in recognition of 'most conspicuous gallantry in carrying out hazardous work in a very brave manner'.

Nevertheless the at-the-time unpublished recommendation for the award from General Stawell told the full story of his courage. It ended: 'Brigadier Nicholls, despite his terrible sufferings, realised throughout the supreme importance of getting in touch with his headquarters. He set an example of heroism, fortitude, courage, leadership, the will to win, and devotion to duty which has seldom been equalled and never surpassed. He carried on far longer than could normally be considered humanly possible, and this undoubtedly caused his death.'

KIRPA RAM
Rank/title: Naik
Unit/occupation: 13th Frontier Force Rifles, Indian Army
DATE OF BRAVERY: 12 SEPTEMBER 1945
GAZETTED: 15 MARCH 1946

Kirpa Ram was born in Bhupral, Bilaspur, India, some time in 1916. His father and three uncles had served in the British Army during the First World War. Ram, an only son, was working by the age of twelve because his family, who lived on a farm, were impoverished. On 9 January 1935, aged eighteen, he joined the Indian Army serving in the 8th Battalion, 13th Frontier Force Rifles.

During the Second World War, he served mainly in Waziristan and Burma, earning a number of medals for field service. While on leave at the end of the Second World War in 1945, he married. On 12 September 1945, Naik Ram was commanding a section on a field-firing exercise at Thondebhavi, India. He was lying near a sepoy, who was firing grenades from a discharge cup. The remainder of the section were positioned behind the two men when the third grenade that was fired fell short, only some eight yards in front of the section. Ram realised that many of the men would be killed or wounded if the grenade exploded so he ran forward and shouted: 'Get back and take cover.' He picked up the grenade but, before he could throw it to a safe spot, it exploded. His body took the main impact of the blast and he later died, aged twenty-eight or twenty-nine. Two other men were slightly injured.

His posthumous GC was announced on 15 March 1946 in recognition of 'most conspicuous gallantry in carrying out hazardous work in a very brave manner'. However, his War Office recommendation was more fulsome and ended: 'Naik Kirpa Ram knowing full well the possible consequences, risked his life in order to save those of the men under his command. His fine spirit of sacrifice and devotion to duty will ever be remembered in his regiment and will be a constant source of inspiration to all ranks.'

MATEEN AHMED ANSARI
Rank/title: Captain
Unit/occupation: 7th Rajput Rifles, Indian Army
DATE OF BRAVERY: DECEMBER 1941–OCTOBER 1943
GAZETTED: 18 APRIL 1946

Mateen Ansari was born in 1915 or 1916, the second son of a professional Indian family, many members of whom had worked for the Raj and served in the Indian Army. A tall, good-looking man, Ansari survived plague and cholera as a youngster. He trained at the Indian Military Academy, Dehra Dun, before taking the King's Commission. He was a solitary figure and he did not fit in easily with military life. However, one night in the Officers' Mess he got into a fight and he knocked down an aggressive fellow officer, who had previously worked as a tea planter. He went from outcast to hero overnight.

Captain Ansari, of the 7th Rajput Rifles, Indian Army, became a prisoner of war of the Japanese when they invaded Hong Kong in December 1941. Immediately after his capture, he was treated relatively well as a PoW. However, once the Japanese realised that he was closely related to the ruler of a great Indian state, they tried to persuade him to renounce his allegiance to the British and spread subversion among the ranks in the prison camps. Ansari steadfastly resisted such approaches and remained loyal to his roots and to his principles.

In May 1942, after warnings and repeated beatings failed to turn his allegiance, he was thrown into Stanley Jail. He remained there until September of the same year having been brutally tortured and starved. Unable to walk, he was released into a camp hospital at Matauchung. Once he recovered, he returned to an Indian 'other ranks' camp where he organised a system of help for would-be escapers. In May 1943, Ansari was betrayed and again thrown into Stanley Jail. He was inhumanely treated for five more months at the jail where his courage and defiance were admired by fellow prisoners. In October 1943, he was sentenced to death with thirty other British, Indian and Chinese prisoners. In a final act of defiance, he chose to be beheaded rather than shot to show how much he despised his captors. He is believed to have been killed on 19 or 29 October 1943, when he was aged twenty-seven or twenty-eight.

Ansari and two officers from the British Army were awarded posthumous GCs on 18 April 1946 in recognition of 'most conspicuous gallantry in carrying out hazardous work in a very brave manner'. Ansari's name became a byword for deliberate and cold-blooded heroism among other PoWs. In a letter from George VI to his family, the King offered his 'heartfelt sympathy in your great sorrow' and added: 'We pray that your country's gratitude for a life so nobly given in its service may bring you some measure of consolation.' Ansari is commemorated on the Stanley Military Memorial in Hong Kong.

DOUGLAS FORD

Rank/title: Captain
Unit/occupation: Royal Scots
DATE OF BRAVERY: DECEMBER 1941–DECEMBER 1943
GAZETTED: 18 APRIL 1946

LANCERAY ARTHUR NEWNHAM

Rank/title: Temporary Colonel
Unit/occupation: Middlesex Regiment
DATE OF BRAVERY: DECEMBER 1941–DECEMBER 1943
GAZETTED: 18 APRIL 1946

Douglas Ford was born in Galashiels, Scotland, on 18 September 1918. He was one of four children in a close-knit family. His father was a factory manager and, like his two brothers, he was educated at the Royal High School, Edinburgh. The young Ford was a keen scholar and sportsman. Jim Ford, his brother, later recalled: 'His school and his family imbued him with a sense of loyalty, compassion, independence of spirit and pride in traditional Scottish values. These self-same characteristics commanded respect from all those who knew him . . .' After leaving school, he trained as an accountant but, after the outbreak of the Second World War, he took a commission in the Royal Scots in September 1939. In January the following year, he was posted to the 2nd Battalion, Royal Scots, at Murray Barracks, Hong Kong. After being sent for a course in signalling in Poona, India, Ford was promoted to captain.

Lanceray Newnham, often known as Lance or Lan, was born in India on 3 August 1889. His father was a lieutenant colonel in the Army and he was born while his parents, and elder brother, were on an extended visit to India – his father was then the Military Attaché to the Russian court of Tsar Nicholas. He attended Bedales School in Hampshire, and was a brilliant sportsman, playing on Centre Court at Wimbledon in 1914, aged twenty-four. In the same year, he joined the Middlesex

Regiment as a career officer. He was awarded the Military Cross (MC) for bravery during the Great War. By the time the Second World War broke out, Newnham, who was married with a son, was nearly fifty years old.

Colonel Newnham and Captain Ford were both serving in Hong Kong when the Japanese invaded in December 1941. Both became prisoners of war. Ford was held at Sham Sui Po prison camp, often known by its initials SSP, while Newnham was initially held at Argyle Street, a prison mainly for officers. While in captivity, the two men managed to make contact with British agents. They were plotting a mass breakout from SSP and Argyle Street when they were betrayed and arrested, along with two other men, on 10 July 1943. Letters between the two men fell into Japanese hands and were used as evidence against them. They were interrogated, starved, beaten, tortured and eventually sentenced to death. Throughout a thirty-nine-day torture ordeal both men refused to implicate fellow prisoners. They were both executed on 18 December 1943.

After the war, James Allan Ford MC (no relation), who had been a fellow inmate, recounted the bravery of Douglas Ford during his brutal interrogation:

> There was one small thing that Ford did to alleviate the torment, the solitary confinement and the hideous conditions. He made contact with Dr Bunje in the cell beneath his by tapping on the wall. This, Dr Bunje later said, saved his own sanity as he 'listened' to the story of Douglas' life. On 18th August the six British men [some arrested over other activities] were put into new cells on remand there for 91 days. It was here that Ford met and became friends with [Mateen] Ansari (one of the 42 other prisoners who were interrogated and tortured) who was to be executed on 29th October 1943. There are reports of Douglas' fortitude and cheerfulness as they all awaited their fate at this terrible time. On 1st December the six were brought before a Court Martial, charged with espionage, and Ford, Newnham and [Hector] Gray

sentenced to death, while the other three were sentenced to 15 years hard labour. There followed 17 days of waiting during which Ford cared for his two fellows both of whom were ill and this incredible compassion finally led him to supporting them on their last walk and to digging their graves down by the sea-shore. Respectful of Ford's courage, the Japanese moved him to the right, the place of honour though the youngest of the three and there on the beach the three men were shot.

Ford was twenty-five when he died, while Newnham was fifty-four. Newnham knew before his death that his son had qualified as a doctor. Rex Young, a fellow PoW, described Newnham's final days: 'We met in Stanley Jail in October 1943. We were all on starvation rations. N was very mentally alert though suffering from the ill-effects of his treatment. I think he fully realised what might happen to him . . . At the time of the court-martial he had a temperature of 103 [degrees Fahrenheit]. No defence was allowed although he had prepared one. After the trial we were not allowed to be in contact with him though we saw him daily. During the whole of the remaining time he and Gray were sick men and they received no treatment at all.' Newnham even wrote a diary from 25 December 1941 to 21 August 1942. It was written on rice paper and hidden in his shaving tin and both exist to this day at the Imperial War Museum thanks to the generosity of his son, Dr Claude Newnham.

Ford and Newnham were awarded their posthumous GCs on 18 April 1946 in recognition of 'most conspicuous gallantry in carrying out hazardous work in a very brave manner'. Both are commemorated on the Stanley Military Memorial in Hong Kong.

HECTOR BERTRAM GRAY

Rank/title: Flight Lieutenant
Unit/occupation: Royal Air Force
DATE OF BRAVERY: DECEMBER 1941–DECEMBER 1943
GAZETTED: 19 APRIL 1946

Hector Gray, who was known as 'Dolly' to his comrades, was born in Gillingham, Kent, on 6 June 1911. He was one of eight children in a close but unconventional family. Gray joined the RAF in January 1927, while still only fifteen, as an apprentice at RAF Halton, Buckinghamshire. His initial training was as a wireless operator mechanic and he served for a time in the Fleet Air Arm. In 1936, Gray was promoted sergeant pilot, flying with 48 and 148 Squadrons before being posted to the Long Range Development Unit. He had previously been the wireless operator for a successful attempt by the unit to set a world record for the longest non-stop flight – 7,158 nautical miles from Ismailia, Egypt, to Darwin, Australia, in two Wellesley aircraft. George VI sent the unit a telegram to congratulate them on their achievement over forty-eight hours in November 1938.

Like Captain Douglas Ford and Colonel Lanceray Newnham, Gray – by now a flight lieutenant – was taken prisoner of war after the fall of Hong Kong in December 1941. Despite his ordeal, he remained cheerful and displayed great leadership qualities. During his time in captivity, he was held at Sham Shui Po and Argyle Street prisons. He arranged for medical supplies – desperately needed by sick prisoners – to be smuggled into the camps. Gray also ran a clandestine news service so that information gathered from outside the camps was circulated to the PoWs. However, the Japanese got to hear of his activities and he was brutally tortured in an attempt to force him to reveal the names of his informants.

At his court martial, Gray was charged with espionage and found guilty along with Ford and Newnham. His health was already failing as a result of his inhumane treatment and he was executed, with Ford and Newnham, on 18 December 1943, aged thirty-two. Gray's posthumous GC was announced on 19 April 1946 in recognition of 'most conspicuous gallantry in carrying out hazardous work in a very brave manner'. He is commemorated on the Stanley Military Memorial in Hong Kong.

GEORGE GOSSE

Rank/title: Lieutenant (later Lieutenant Commander)
Unit/occupation: Royal Australian Naval Volunteer Reserve
DATE OF BRAVERY: 8 MAY 1945
GAZETTED: 30 APRIL 1946

George Gosse was born in Harvey, Western Australia, on 16 February 1912. His father was apparently killed in action with a British regiment in the First World War. Gosse, who had at least one sibling, attended St Peter's Preparatory School in Adelaide from 1920 to 1925. He did not attend secondary school but instead joined the Royal Australian Navy aged just thirteen. In late 1925, he passed the entrance exam to the Royal Australian Naval College in Jervis Bay, graduating in 1930. In August 1931, he was 'loaned' to the Royal Navy for training. During this time, he was promoted to acting sub-lieutenant in September 1932. However, when he failed his final exam, the 'loan' was ended on 25 August 1933 and Gosse returned to Australia where his service with the Royal Australian Navy was also terminated on 30 October 1933.

Gosse married on 1 October 1938 and the couple later had two daughters. On 1 September 1939 – the day of the German invasion of Poland – Gosse, still only twenty-seven, offered his services to the Navy, but they were declined. Bizarrely, given his experience, he was eventually selected for service as an ordinary seaman in October 1940. He entered the Royal Australian Naval Volunteer Reserve (RANVR), once again going to England for training. His first appointments were to HMS *Collingwood* and HMS *King Alfred*. Gosse was later promoted to sub-lieutenant in April 1941 and posted to HMS *President* for duties with the Director of Torpedoes and Mines. Gosse was a late developer. In 1940, he was regarded by his superiors as 'below average, for whom it was doubtful a niche could be found'. Yet, by 1942, he was described as 'a reliable officer who shows great keenness and ingenuity . . . has a daring character and a good knowledge of mines in which he is very interested'. Gosse initially joined HMS *Lanka* in July 1942 for mine disposal duties in the Bombay area, but returned to England in 1944 having already risked his life many times.

It was on 8 May 1945 – ironically, VE-Day – that Lieutenant Gosse was presented with his greatest challenge while clearing the docks and waterways of Bremen, Germany. Divers found a new and deadly mine which they did not know how to tackle. Gosse went down and recognised it as a GD pressure, or 'oyster', mine and he decided to try to recover the mine intact. Gosse opted to tackle the mine underwater, where it lay, the next day. Using what were described as 'improvised tools', he removed the primer, an action which was followed by a loud and sinister metallic crash. The mine was lifted to the quayside where it was established that the detonator had fired as soon as the primer had been removed. Over the next ten days, Goose rendered safe two more 'oyster' mines found near the first one – and, each time, the detonator fired before the mine reached the surface.

Gosse, who always sported a beard, was a true character. His GC was announced on 26 April 1946 and the citation ended:

This form of operation called for exceptionally high standards of personal courage and also a high degree of skill. The conditions were always arduous and were combined with the presence of known mines in the docks and with all forms of underwater obstruction – human corpses – which together with lack of visibility produced a set of conditions which would deter the boldest. This officer displayed courage and zeal far in excess of the usual course of duty and contributed greatly to the success of a most difficult and important operation.

Gosse was demobilised in March 1946. He was appointed Lieutenant Commander (Special Branch) to the Citizen Naval Forces (RANVR) in 1955, a post he held for three years. Gosse joined the Victoria Cross and George Cross Association in 1964 when he came to Britain for a reunion. Typically, he was the life and soul of the party. Brigadier Sir John 'Jackie' Smyth, the VC recipient and author, wrote of him that 'he always lived right on top of the world, as though every day was his last'. He died in Adelaide on 31 December 1965, aged fifty-three.

MAHMOOD KHAN DURRANI

Rank/title: Captain (later Lieutenant Colonel)
Unit/occupation: 1st Bahawalpur Infantry, Indian State Forces
DATE OF BRAVERY: 1942–5
GAZETTED: 23 MAY 1946

Captain (later Lieutenant Colonel) Mahmood Durrani was the only Japanese prisoner of war to be awarded a George Cross and to survive his brutal ordeal. Born in Multan City, Western Punjab, on 1 July 1914, by the Second World War he was serving in the 1st Bahawalpur Infantry of the Indian State Forces.

After Malaya was overrun by the Japanese in 1942, Durrani and a small party were cut off from their colleagues. They remained in hiding for three months before they were betrayed by the enemy-sponsored Indian Nationalist Army (INA). Durrani was sent to a PoW camp where he refused to become a member of INA, led by the Cambridge-educated Subha Chandra Bose and which eventually totalled 25,000 men. Not only did Durrani refuse to join INA, but he did all he could to gather intelligence on this subversive organisation and, in particular, its attempts to infiltrate members into India.

At one point, he acted as a double agent, setting up a school, the Sandicraft School, to send men back to India 'to champion the Nationalist ideology of the Indian National Congress'. It was a dangerous game: on the face of it he was training agents to land from submarines and engage in sabotage in India. In fact, these men had been hand-picked by Durrani to spy for Britain. However, the Japanese became suspicious of his activities and they arrested him in May 1944. From around D-Day, they started to torture him brutally to try to identify his accomplices. Burning cigarettes were stubbed out on his legs, but Durrani told his captors nothing. He was then handed over to INA, who tortured him and condemned him to death. However, Bose, the INA leader, wanted to extract a confession from Durrani under torture before executing him. Durrani's life was only saved when the Japanese surrendered.

Durrani returned to Multan City, which became part of Pakistan after partition. He was in poor health for some time but eventually recovered. Durrani was awarded the GC on 23 May 1946 in recognition of 'most conspicuous gallantry in carrying out hazardous work in a very brave manner'. The official recommendation for the decoration concluded: 'His outstanding example of deliberate cold-blooded bravery is most fully deserving of the highest award.' He received his GC from Field Marshal Lord Wavell, the Viceroy, in India.

His autobiography, *The Sixth Column*, in which he graphically describes his suffering, was published in 1955. In a chilling chapter called 'Arrest and Torture', he described how, already weak from dysentery and starvation, he was given no food or water for two days and was then interrogated by a Japanese captain, through an interpreter, for about three hours. He wrote:

> The Jap Captain wielded his sword over my head every now and then, particularly when my mental energy failed and I sat dumbfounded like a piece of stone. In order to wake me up from such a state of mental deterioration and make me speak, all three

Japs applied their smouldering red-hot cigarette ends to my legs and kept them there until they were extinguished. But my body proved to be almost dead to this torture to start with, and I felt the intensity of the pain only when I gained full consciousness later. This physical unconsciousness was probably due to my over-consciousness about and determination not to make any mistake in answering the tricky questions shot at me by the Jap Captain . . . After about three hours of interrogation every night, I was ordered to move from the chair. But each time I could not, my whole body being paralysed; there appeared to be hardly any blood circulating in my veins. In order to remedy this inertia, red-hot cigarette ends were tapped on my legs by all the Japs present, causing burns, the acute pain of which brought me back to consciousness. Some massage of my legs was also done by them. Then two Japs supported me under the armpits and dragged me along, with my face covered, and hurled me back into my cell. At the end of these three days and nights, I was left a heap of lifeless bone and flesh, remaining all the time in a fainting condition.

At his next destination, the INA concentration camp, he was sentenced to death and a firing squad was lined up to dispose of him. However, Bose's determination to force a confession from his Muslim prisoner saved Durrani's live. 'You have got to confess eventually and meet your fate, so why undergo tortures unnecessarily,' Durrani was told by Bose. He was later brutally whipped and his fingers were crushed in specially designed finger presses, but still he refused to confess. Next he was subjected to the 'water treatment', almost drowning under a stream of running water.

Durrani wrote:

It may interest the reader to know how I felt when I stood before the firing squad or when I underwent the tortures and what I did at those particular moments.

On that fateful evening of my trial, even prior to it, I was determined to die honourably and contentedly; for I had undertaken the hazardous task voluntarily and with full realization of the consequences that could be nothing short of capital punishment. Arguing thus, I made up my mind that I should not be sorry for dying at all. But when I was facing the firing squad, a strange and most grievous feeling crept over me; I felt it a great pity that I was dying while nobody in the whole wide world, except my enemies, knew how and why I was dying. Yet that was the only human weakness which I could not overcome at what appeared to be the last minutes of my life.

As to my feelings whenever I underwent tortures at the hands of the INA people, I was fired with a righteous wrath – a wrath more intense than that when I was tortured by the Japs – and my mind strengthened beyond imagination. I scorned my torturers as the scum of the Indian people, who, I thought, might go ahead this time with their mean mentality and blackest butchery, but who would eventually have to pay for it. And so every time they tortured me grievously, I said to myself: 'Let them go ahead with their tortures and do anything with me, but by the grace of God they will not be able to subdue my spirit and make me do anything like making a confession, which would be no less mean an act than the acts of those butchers.'

When not under any torture, I had moments of fear and hopelessness. I brooded over the next torture that might be in store. And when I thought of this, I realized at once that my heart was so weak that if a slight stroke were given on the body I would succumb to it immediately; but it surprises me to remember that such a heart as I had in those days would soon turn into an unconquerable fortress once the tortures began. And on occasions, as I underwent the torture tests, I laughed contemptuously in my mind at the futile attempts of my torturers to defeat me in keeping my sacred resolve.

Durrani served in the Pakistani army until retiring in 1971. He married and had three sons and a daughter. He was one of the first members of the George Cross Committee of the Victoria Cross and George Cross Association. He and his wife attended a garden party hosted by the Queen for association members in July 1962. Brigadier Sir John 'Jackie' Smyth, the VC recipient and author, wrote in 1968: 'The British Commonwealth holds no more loyal and enthusiastic supporter than Colonel Mahmood Durrani.' Durrani died in Pakistan on 20 August 1995, aged eighty-one.

ODETTE MARIE CELINE SANSOM (LATER CHURCHILL, LATER HALLOWES)
Rank/title: Mrs
Unit/occupation: Women's Transport Service ('FANY')
DATE OF BRAVERY: APRIL 1943–MAY 1945
GAZETTED: 20 AUGUST 1946

Odette Sansom was the first woman to be awarded the GC and few recipients can have done more to earn the decoration. After the Second World War, she became a national heroine and, for many, the symbol of defiance against the Nazi regime. Furthermore, she was the only one of the three female Resistance workers awarded the GC to survive her ordeal at the hands of the Germans.

Odette Brailly – her maiden name – was born in Amiens, France, on 28 April 1912. Her father was killed during the First World War at the Battle of Verdun in 1916, when his daughter was four. As a child, she suffered from temporary blindness and rheumatic fever, both of which she overcame and, in 1926, her family moved from Saint-Saens to Boulogne. She married an Englishman, Roy Sansom, in 1931 and the couple had three daughters, two of whom were born in Britain, to where the couple had moved in 1932–3.

Early in 1942, and nearly three years into the Second World War, Sansom heard a broadcast which appealed for photographs of France. She wrote to the War Office explaining that she was

French and where she had lived. Sansom ended up going for an interview and, on 28 June 1942, she was asked back to meet Captain Selwyn Jepson, the author and, at the time, the senior recruiting officer for the Special Operations Executive (SOE), which had been formed in the summer of 1940 after the fall of France.

Jepson later told how he preferred recruiting women rather than men. When interviewed by the Imperial War Museum long after the Second World War, he said:

> I was responsible for recruiting women for the work, in the face of a good deal of opposition, I may say, from the powers that be. In my view, women were very much better than men for the work. Women, as you must know, have a far greater capacity for cool and lonely courage than men. Men usually want a mate with them. Men don't work alone, their lives tend to be always in company with other men. There was opposition from most quarters until it went up to Churchill, whom I had met before the war. He growled at me, 'What are you doing?' I told him and he said, 'I see you are using women to do this,' and I said, 'Yes, don't you think it is a very sensible thing to do?' and he said, 'Yes, good luck to you.' That was my authority!

Jepson's style was to tell potential recruits: 'I have to decide whether I can risk your life and you have to decide whether you're willing to risk it.' After much soul-searching, Sansom agreed to work for the SOE. As a cover, she was enrolled in the Women's Transport Service ('FANY'), while her three young daughters went to live in a convent.

What made Sansom willing to give up her children and risk her life as an undercover agent? She had a deep love of both her French homeland and her adopted country, Britain. She wanted to help the Allied cause and, because she spoke fluent French and knew France well, she concluded that her most valuable role would be with the Resistance. She was single-minded so that, once she had made her decision to join the SOE, she was determined to see her role through to the end, come what may.

During her training, Sansom received an early setback. She had a bad fall during her parachute instruction and her injuries delayed her drop into France. After three abortive attempts to land her in France by air, she sailed to Gibraltar in a troopship. From there, in October 1942, she and six other agents were landed in France from a fishing boat. Her code name was 'Lise'. On 2 November, she joined up in Cannes with Peter Churchill – code name 'Raoul' and the leader of the so-called Spindle circuit. The intention had been for her to proceed to Auxerre but Churchill, realising her value to him as a courier, got permission from the Baker Street headquarters of the SOE for her to remain in Cannes.

After the Germans and Italians overran southern France, Churchill and Sansom were forced to move on. Accompanied by their wireless operator, Adolphe Rabinovich, they transferred to St Jorioz, near Annecy, in the French Alps. When Churchill returned to London for instructions, Sansom was tricked into revealing her sympathies. She was approached by a 'Colonel Henri', who claimed to be a German officer who wanted to defect to the Allies. In fact, the man was Sergeant Bleicher of the Abwehr – German military intelligence. Although Sansom was suspicious of the 'officer', her cover was blown and she and, later, Churchill – who was by then back in France from the UK – were arrested.

As they were being moved, Churchill and Sansom secretly agreed that their cover story was to be that he was related to the British Prime Minister and that they were married. This story may well have saved their lives. Sansom was taken to Paris and to the notorious Fresnes prison outside the city. There she endured terrible torture and deprivation. During fourteen brutal interrogations, she stuck to the cover story and even repeated that Churchill – in fact, her Commanding Officer –

had only come to France at her insistence. She took full responsibility for her actions and insisted that she, not Churchill, should be shot. Her story was believed and her Commanding Officer only had to endure two interrogations. The Gestapo were also desperate to trace a wireless officer and a British officer working with the Resistance. They repeatedly tortured Sansom in an attempt to extract the information: her back was burned with a hot iron and her toenails were pulled out but she gave nothing away. This meant she not only saved the officers' lives but their valuable secret work was able to continue.

In June 1943, Sansom was sentenced to death but instead she was reprieved and taken to Ravensbrück concentration camp, in northern Germany. There she was kept in solitary confinement for two years. At one stage she spent three months and eleven days in a darkened room – her personal punishment for the Allied landings in the South of France. As the war neared its end, Fritz Suhren, the German camp commandant, decided that handing over Sansom might guarantee him lenient treatment from the Allies. He took her to an American unit and handed her over. He was wrong: Sansom returned to his car and found photograph albums which were used against him at the war crimes trials.

Her physical and mental health was frail for some time after the war. Her doctor's report prepared at the end of 1945 concluded:

Mrs O. Sansom of 75 Harcourt Terrace, S.W.10 has been under my care since June 1945. At that time she was in a state of high nervous tension due to maltreatment received in German captivity. Some nails on her toes were missing; there was on her back a rounded scar of about half an inch in diameter, the result of a burn deliberately inflicted in the concentration camp. Since last July she has had numerous injections of calcium, artificial sunlight and intense general medicinal treatment. Her nails have grown again but some of them are still deformed. The scar on her back is still evident. She is still receiving treatment for her general nervous condition, and anaemia.

Sansom's GC was announced on 20 August 1946. Her lengthy citation ended: 'During the period of over two years in which she was in enemy hands, she displayed courage, endurance and self-sacrifice of the highest possible order.' Sansom was reunited with her children after the war, but her marriage did not survive. In 1946, she was a witness at the trial in Hamburg of sixteen members of Ravensbrück's staff. In 1947, she married Peter Churchill, with whom she had endured so much. However, the couple divorced in 1953 and she married Geoffrey Hallowes, another former Resistance fighter, in 1956. Hallowes had already been awarded the Croix de Guerre for his 'cloak and dagger' actions, while Sansom had received the Légion d'honneur.

In 1949, Jerrard Tickell published his book *Odette: The Story of a British Agent* after Sansom told him her story. A biographical film, *Odette*, starring Anna Neagle, was released in 1950. Sansom died in Walton-on-Thames, Surrey, on 13 March 1995, aged eighty-two. After her death, a plaque in her honour was placed underneath the FANY Memorial in Wilton Place, Knightsbridge, London.

SIMMON LATUTIN

Rank/title: Captain
Unit/occupation: Somerset Light Infantry, attached Somalia Gendarmerie
DATE OF BRAVERY: 29 DECEMBER 1944
GAZETTED: 10 SEPTEMBER 1946

Simmon Latutin, the son of Latvian parents, was born in St Pancras, central London, on 25 July 1916. He grew up in London and attended the London Polytechnic School before winning a scholarship to the Royal Academy of Music. He was a talented musician and played the violin and, later, the viola.

In 1940, he married a Polish woman whom he had met at the academy. He initially became a member of the Pioneer Corps but was commissioned into the Somerset Light Infantry on 21 August 1942. After serving in Northern Ireland, he was posted to East Africa.

Captain Latutin commanded an Infantry Training School of Swahili troops from Kenya and taught infantry skills to the Somali troops. He displayed great physical and mental stamina in his work. Four days after Christmas Day 1944, a fire broke out at the training school of the Somalia Gendarmerie in Mogadishu. The blaze had somehow started when some Italian rockets were being taken out of the store to give to another unit as part of their New Year's entertainment. Latutin was present with another officer, a company sergeant major, and a young boy helper. Within no time there was a raging inferno. There were 170 ammunition cases in the store and a large number of rockets had already exploded and burned. Latutin ignored the exploding rockets, the fierce flames, the intense heat and the choking smoke and raced into the store room. He managed to drag clear the officer, who was almost unconscious as a result of his serious injuries. By now, Latutin's uniform was alight but he ignored his own distress and ran into the store again, this time emerging with the company sergeant major, whose clothes had all been burned off him. The situation for the boy was hopeless and his charred, unrecognisable remains were found later. Despite prompt medical treatment, Latutin died from his own serious injuries the next day, aged twenty-eight, and at a time when his wife was pregnant with their second child.

His posthumous GC was not announced for more than eighteen months. However, on 10 September 1946, the lengthy citation paid tribute to his incredible courage, part of which read: 'The heroism of Captain Latutin was superb as he fully realized the acute danger he must incur in entering the building, ablaze with explosives and flames; his unquenchable determination to succour the injured is evinced by his second entry into the store, though himself and his clothes [were] already alight. His action was illustrative of the finest degree of British courage and a magnificent example of undaunted selflessness.'

Latutin was initially buried in Mogadishu but later, without the consultation of his widow, his remains were moved to the Nairobi War Cemetery, which lies to the south-west of the Kenyan capital. His parent regiment was not told of Latutin's GC for many years because it had been assumed, wrongly, that he was a member of the Somalia Gendarmerie. There are now, however, memorials to Latutin at the Somerset Military Museum, Taunton Castle, and the Royal Academy of Music in London.

ABDUL RAHMAN
Rank/title: Acting Havildar
Unit/occupation: 9th Jat Regiment, Indian Army
DATE OF BRAVERY: 22 FEBRUARY 1945
GAZETTED: 10 SEPTEMBER 1946

Adbul Rahman – his surname is also sometimes spelled Rehman – is believed to have been born in 1921 in the village of Talad, Rhotak District, India. He married a woman from an area of India which later became part of Pakistan and, aged about eighteen, he enlisted in the Indian Army. Rahman was awarded the Military Medal (MM) for an act of bravery in July 1944 during a fierce firefight in which his platoon commander was wounded.

In early 1945, Acting Havildar Rahman was serving with the 3rd Battalion, 9th Jat Regiment, in the Dutch East Indies. On 22 February 1945, Rahman and five other soldiers were travelling in a jeep in Kletek, Java. The vehicle hit a mine and was hurled into a ditch where it burst into flames. Although Rahman was thrown clear, three of his comrades were trapped under the burning jeep. As if the situation was not dangerous enough, some of the ammunition in the jeep started to explode. Ignoring the flames, Rahman managed to drag one man from the wreckage. He then returned to the blazing vehicle and pulled a second man clear. By now a water truck and an ambulance were on the scene.

As Rahman returned to the blazing vehicle a third time, he shouted to the ambulance driver, who had parked some fifty yards away: 'Come on quickly, one man still remains. I have got the rest out.' Rahman then raced to the vehicle again to try to rescue the trapped driver. He was pulling at the man's arm in an attempt to free him when the fuel tank exploded, killing both men. Rahman is believed to have been twenty-three when he died.

Rahman's GC was announced on 10 September 1946 in recognition of 'most conspicuous gallantry in carrying out hazardous work in a very brave manner'. His name is commemorated on the Rangoon War Memorial in Burma and also on the Memorial Gates at Constitution Hill in London.

HUGH PAUL SEAGRIM

Rank/title: Temporary Major
Unit/occupation: 19th Hyderabad Regiment, attached Force 136
DATE OF BRAVERY: FEBRUARY 1943–SEPTEMBER 1944
GAZETTED: 12 SEPTEMBER 1946

Major Hugh Seagrim and Lieutenant Colonel Derek Seagrim, who were brothers, represent the only time a GC and Victoria Cross have been awarded to members of the same family. The latter was awarded his posthumously for gallantry in Tunisia, North Africa, in March 1943.

Hugh Seagrim, the fifth son of the Reverend Charles Seagrim, was born on 24 March 1909 at the vicarage in Ashmansworth, Hampshire, but the family later moved to Whissonsett, Norfolk. Seagrim attended Norwich Grammar School as a boarder, followed by King Edward VI School in nearby Bury St Edmunds, Suffolk. Like his four older brothers, Seagrim was sporty rather than academic. Indeed, he was such a talented goalkeeper that he played for Norwich City reserves. He attended the Royal Military Academy, Sandhurst, and was commissioned on 31 January 1929. Seagrim became a lieutenant on 30 April 1931 and was appointed to the 5th/6th Rajputana Rifles in August 1931. After being promoted to captain, he was attached to the Burma Rifles from 1940 to 1941 and later served with the 19th Hyderabad Regiment (now the Kumaon Regiment).

Seagrim knew Burma so well that he was selected for an elite special group that was fighting the Japanese in the Karen Hills. From February 1943, the group carried out a number of ambushes on the enemy but, by the end of the year, the Japanese intensified their efforts to track down the group code-named Force 136. They coerced and tortured locals in order to try to intercept and catch the group. In February 1944, after a year of effective activities behind enemy lines in Burma, the group was ambushed. The two British officers with Seagrim were killed but he escaped along with the officer from the Karen area. The Japanese were incensed that Seagrim had evaded them and they now arrested 270 Karens, including village elders. Many were killed, others brutally tortured but still those sheltering Seagrim refused to give him up.

However, in March, the Japanese got a message to Seagrim informing him that the campaign of reprisals and fear would end if he gave himself up. On learning of this assurance, Seagrim walked out of the village where he was hiding and surrendered to the enemy on 15 March 1944 – even though he was well aware of the horrors that awaited him in Japanese hands.

The Japanese moved him to Rangoon where he was court-martialled, along with eight other men from his patrol who had been captured earlier, on 2 September 1944 and condemned to death. As soon as the sentences were read out, Seagrim stepped forward and addressed the president of the court. He said that the other men had simply followed orders – therefore only he should die and the others should be spared. His pleas for clemency were ignored and the group was returned to prison where he comforted his men and prepared them for their fate. Such was his inspiration that every one of the eight concluded that they did not want any more attempts to be made for their lives to be spared: if their commander was going to die, they wanted to die with him.

Every evening in Burma, Seagrim had conducted prayers around a campfire and read passages from the Bible to the men in Burmese. He confided to one man that during his thirteen months in the Karen Hills he had read the Bible from cover to cover twelve times. He encouraged the men to take strength from prayer. On the night before his execution, he told one of those due to die with him: 'Don't worry, Ta Roe, we are Christians and must have faith in God. Pray to God, Ta Roe, and trust Him. Christ came down to earth and suffered on a cross. We must suffer like Him.' Seagrim also showed his comrade a passage from the Bible that read: 'If we die with Him, we shall also live with Him.'

Seagrim went bravely to his death on 14 September 1944, aged thirty-five. He had wanted to be a missionary after the Second World War and no one doubted that he would have suited that role perfectly.

The citation for his posthumous GC published on 12 September 1946 – shortly before the second anniversary of his death – said simply that the award was in recognition of 'most conspicuous gallantry in carrying out hazardous work in a very brave manner'. Lieutenant Colonel J. R. Gardiner, who made the recommendation, concluded: 'I count it as a privilege to recommend this very gallant officer for the George Cross.'

As Supreme Allied Commander in South East Asia, Lord Mountbatten personally approved Seagrim's GC and said he had saved many Allied lives in Burma. However, Seagrim was also awarded a posthumous MBE and a posthumous Distinguished Service Order (DSO). His recommendations for these two awards also give an indication of this remarkable man's astonishing courage deep behind enemy lines.

The recommendation for the MBE read:

> It was to this officer's faith in the Karen that the formation of the Karen Levies was largely due. For weeks he sat several days' march behind the Japanese forward positions and trained Karen irregulars. His presence and training maintained Karen morale and friendship to us long after the civil administration had ceased to exist and our armies had retreated north. His actions in thus living behind the enemy will prove of great benefit to us when we counter-attack, for he built up a useful number of guerrillas who on several occasions resisted incursions by pro-Jap Burmese rebel bands.

The recommendation for the DSO, prepared when Seagrim was still alive, read:

> This officer has remained 380 miles within enemy-held territory ever since its occupation by the Japanese forces in April 1942. During this period he has sustained the loyalty of the local inhabitants for a very wide area and thereby has provided the foundation of a pro-British force whenever occupying forces arrive in that area. This officer has now been contacted by Major Nimmo, ABRO, and is passing valuable military intelligence by wireless. The fact that he has remained alone in constant danger and has maintained pro-British sympathies in such adverse circumstances, has proved his determination, courage and devotion to be of the highest order.

After the war, Seagrim's mother, Annabel, on one occasion wore his GC and her son Derek's VC at a War Memorial Parade in

Eastbourne, East Sussex. It is believed to be the only time that anyone has worn both prestigious gallantry awards in public.

KENNETH ALFRED BIGGS
Rank/title: Major
Unit/occupation: Royal Army Ordnance Corps
DATE OF BRAVERY: 2–3 JANUARY 1946
GAZETTED: 11 OCTOBER 1946

SYDNEY GEORGE ROGERSON
Rank/title: Acting Staff Sergeant
Unit/occupation: Royal Army Ordnance Corps
DATE OF BRAVERY: 2–3 JANUARY 1946
GAZETTED: 11 OCTOBER 1946

Kenneth Biggs was born in Greenway, Totteridge, Hertfordshire, on 26 February 1911. In May 1928, three months after his seventeenth birthday, he started work at the Oxford Street branch of the Midland Bank and, in 1936, he transferred to the Knightsbridge branch. He joined the Royal Army Ordnance Corps (RAOC) in July 1940 and was commissioned five months later. Biggs had married in 1938 and the couple later had a son.

Sydney Rogerson was born in Mitcham, Surrey, on 14 May 1915. The middle child of three, he attended Gorringe Park School in Mitcham. As a youngster, he was a Boy Scout and later a Scout Master. Before the Second World War, Rogerson worked for Horne Brothers in Hackney, north London, a company that made greatcoats for the Army. He married in 1937 and the couple later had two daughters. He joined the RAOC in 1941.

Major Biggs and Acting Staff Sergeant Rogerson both survived the Second World War. Less than six months after the end of hostilities and two days after seeing in the new year, they were completing the loading of a train with surplus American and German ammunition in Savernake Forest, close to the market town of Marlborough, Wiltshire. Present were men from the RAOC, the Pioneer Corps and the Royal Army Service Corps and in the same siding was a train loaded with British ammunition. In total, there were ninety-six ammunition wagons outside Marlborough on that bitterly cold afternoon.

Without warning, at 2.50 p.m. there was a blinding flash and a loud explosion as two railway wagons and a three-ton lorry were blown to pieces. The detonation claimed eight lives and seriously injured six more men. Fierce flames swept through the area and more wagons were soon ablaze. It was feared the fire would spread to other wagons and such huge explosions would take place that the 5,000 residents of nearby Marlborough would be endangered – quite apart from the servicemen in the immediate vicinity.

The situation was spiralling quickly out of control. Soon twenty-seven of the ninety-six wagons had blown up, along with two lorries carrying shells, mines and other ammunition. At the time, Biggs, aged thirty-four, was commanding the Sub-Depot and Rogerson, aged thirty, was his acting staff sergeant. Rogerson was one of the first on the scene and, as the most senior non commissioned officer (NCO), he began to direct operations. Rogerson climbed under a burning truck to rescue two badly injured men and directed the other rescuers in small groups. Soon afterwards Biggs arrived and he took over command. Together the two men uncoupled one of the burning wagons and put out the flames. As well as trying to extinguish the fire, Biggs organised the removal of some empty wagons to create 'fire breaks'. At about 4.30 p.m., Biggs was knocked to the ground by an explosion from one of the nearby wagons. However, he picked himself up and organised the fire-fighting operation all through the afternoon, evening and the night. Remarkably, the servicemen, aided by a team of firemen, had prevented any more ammunition wagons catching fire.

It was not until daylight that the full scale of the devastation could be seen. Brigadier Sir John 'Jackie' Smyth, the VC recipient and author, wrote: 'In the cold light of dawn the area presented an amazing sight, with two huge craters and the remains of wagons, lorries, shells, mines, detonators, packages and telegraph poles strewn all over the countryside. But sixty-nine of the wagons had been saved from exploding. It was 11 am before the last of the fires was extinguished.'

One local newspaper said the power of the explosions was 'like an atomic bomb', while a fireman added: 'Trucks disappeared as if by magic. It was like two or three veritable volcanoes all in one.' The calmness, leadership and gallantry of Biggs and Rogerson were recognised on 11 October 1946 when they were awarded GCs for 'most conspicuous gallantry in carrying out hazardous work in a very brave manner'. For the same action, two George Medals, one MBE and five British Empire Medals were also awarded.

By the time of the announcement of his GC, Kenneth Biggs had been demobilised and had been back behind a bank desk for six months. Along with Rogerson, he was invested by King George VI at Buckingham Palace on 10 December 1946. Biggs subsequently managed three London branches before retiring in February 1971 after forty-three years with Midland Bank (including the war years). A quiet, private man, he died on 11 January 1998, aged eighty-six. He was cremated at Guildford Crematorium in Surrey.

Sydney Rogerson was demobbed in June 1946 and became a bus conductor with London Transport. He later joined the East Kent Road Car Co., where he rose to chief inspector. His other jobs were at Ramsgate Hospital, Kent, and at Lanthorne School for Handicapped Children in Thanet, Kent, from which he was forced to retire because of poor health. A gentle, kind man, he died on 23 September 1993, in Ramsgate, aged seventy-eight.

ERIC GEORGE BAILEY

Rank/title: Sergeant
Unit/occupation: New South Wales Police
DATE OF BRAVERY: 12 JANUARY 1945
GAZETTED: 29 OCTOBER 1946

Eric Bailey was born in Tenterfield, New South Wales, Australia, on 14 October 1906. The son of a compositor, he was his parents' ninth child. At the age of sixteen, he began work for the Postmaster General's Department but left to become a police constable. He officially joined the New South Wales Police on 16 March 1927 and was attached to No. 4 Station in Sydney. He married, aged twenty-two, on 24 November 1928 and the couple later had a son and daughter. After various posts, he was transferred to Moruya in April 1939. During the Second World War, he was highly commended for going to the aid of a fishing trawler, *Dureenbee*, which had been attacked by a Japanese submarine on 3 August 1942.

Towards the end of the war, after being based at Blayney, New South Wales, for just eight days, Bailey was involved in a dramatic incident while on duty. It was 8.30 p.m. on 12 January 1945 when Bailey stopped a man who was acting suspiciously in Adelaide Street, Blayney. During the questioning, the suspect pulled a revolver from his pocket and shot the officer in the stomach at point-blank range. Bailey tussled with his assailant and refused to let go. The suspect then fired two more shots that left Bailey bleeding heavily and in a state of shock. Even now the officer would not let go and he pinned the man to the ground until help arrived. Bailey died soon afterwards from his severe injuries, aged thirty-eight.

On 29 October 1946, Bailey's posthumous GC was announced. His lengthy citation ended: 'The fortitude and courage manifested by this Police Officer, in spite of the mortal injuries sustained by him at the outset of the encounter, constitute bravery and devotion to duty of the highest order.' By this time, the New South Wales' Police Commissioner had made history by promoting Bailey posthumously to sergeant in recognition of his bravery during the robbery and two other incidents when he had been highly commended on both occasions. In the second incident, Bailey and another officer had been wounded when they tackled a lone gunman who had robbed a bank – the gunman then committed suicide. Bailey's killer was jailed for life for murder and, at the end of the trial, the judge also commended the victim's bravery and devotion to duty.

Bailey loved his job and so it was fitting that his son, John, followed him into the police force. For a time, before Bailey Snr was killed, the two men served together at Woolongong. After Bailey's death, his grandson Stephen, the son of his daughter Doreen, also followed the family tradition and became a police officer.

JOHN ALEXANDER FRASER
Rank/title: Mr
Unit/occupation: Assistant Attorney General, Colonial Service, Hong Kong, serving with the British Army Aid Group
DATE OF BRAVERY: 1942–3
GAZETTED: 29 OCTOBER 1946

John Fraser was born in Edinburgh, Scotland, on 12 February 1896. One of two children, he is believed to have been the son of a mercantile clerk. Fraser attended Trinity Academy, Leith, where he was head boy, and Edinburgh University. Fraser joined the Royal Scots Fusiliers, serving as an officer during the First World War. During the Great War, he was awarded the Military Cross (MC) and bar (a second MC) in 1916 and 1918 respectively. After the war, he joined the Colonial Service and was posted to Hong Kong, which was to become his home for the rest of his life. He married, but was widowed after just two years. He later remarried and his second wife bore him two sons. After studying to become a barrister, he was appointed Assistant Attorney

General of Hong Kong. Prior to the Second World War, it was widely believed that he was working with British intelligence.

When the Japanese invaded Hong Kong in December 1941, Fraser was imprisoned in the Civil Internment Camp in Stanley. Conditions were harsh but Fraser wasted no time in organising escape plans and a clandestine wireless service for his fellow prisoners. Despite being aware of the ill treatment that would come his way if he was caught, he not only received news from outside but also relayed important information to others outside the camp. Eventually, however, he was arrested and subjected to severe and prolonged torture by the Japanese. The enemy wanted to extract information from him and to learn the identities of those who were working with him. Fraser refused to utter a single word of useful information or give away anything that might bring retribution upon others. Frustrated and angered by his resistance, the Japanese beheaded him on 29 October 1943. He was forty-seven.

It was only much later – after an assessment of the bravery of those held in Hong Kong – that Fraser was awarded a posthumous GC. The gallantry award was made exactly three years to the day after his death. The lengthy citation ended: 'His fortitude under the most severe torture was such that it was commented upon by the Japanese prison guards. Unable to break his spirit the Japanese finally executed him. His devotion to duty, outstanding courage and endurance were the source of very real inspiration to others and there can be no doubt the lives of those whom the Japanese were trying to implicate were saved by his magnificent conduct.'

After the war, Fraser's widow received a bundle of clothes belonging to her late husband – together with a last, private message from him. Some of those who knew Fraser remain angry and frustrated that his story of immense courage and self-sacrifice has received less publicity that those of the military prisoners of war who were held in Hong Kong during the war.

ARTHUR BANKS

Rank/title: Sergeant
Unit/occupation: 112 Squadron (Desert Air Force), Royal Air Force Volunteer Reserve
DATE OF BRAVERY: 27 AUGUST–20 DECEMBER 1944
GAZETTED: 5 NOVEMBER 1946

Arthur Banks was born in Llanddulas, Abergele, North Wales, on 6 October 1923. He was the only son of a distinguished former officer who had been awarded the Military Cross (MC) during the First World War. Banks attended the school – Arnold House in Llanddulas – run by his father before attending St Edward's School, Oxford, where he was head of house.

Banks enlisted in the Royal Air Force Volunteer Reserve (RAFVR) in June 1942, aged eighteen. He underwent training at Mevagissey in Cornwall and, in August 1944, he was posted to 'Shark Squadron': 112 Squadron, Desert Air Force, RAFVR. He had been with the squadron less than three weeks when he found himself one of the crew on a Mustang which was carrying out an armed reconnaissance of the Ravenna and Ferrara areas of northern Italy. During the sortie, the aircraft was so badly damaged by anti-aircraft fire that the crew were forced to land behind enemy lines. After destroying the plane, Sergeant Banks and the others tried to reach Allied lines.

After making contact with a group of Italian partisans, Banks remained behind enemy lines. Over a period of several months, he became a heroic figure among them, advising and encouraging them how to attack the enemy. It was early in December 1944 that a risky crossing into Allied territory by boat was attempted. However, the whole party was surrounded and captured. Banks was handed over to the German commander of the district who personally supervised his brutal torture. Remarkably, at one point during his interrogation he managed to get hold of a light machine gun and was preparing to attack several of his captors. One of the partisans, however, fearing terrible reprisals if they were subsequently caught alive, jumped on Banks and pinned his arms to his side. Banks was then 'badly knocked about' by his captors.

On 8 December 1944, Banks, together with other partisans, was taken to a prison at Adria. There, on 19 December 1944, he was handed to the commander of a detachment of the notorious 'Black Brigade'. Next he was taken to another prison at Ariano Polesine, where he was stripped and tortured yet again. After being bound, he was thrown into the River Po, where it was thought he would drown. Undaunted by his injuries and his restrictions, he managed to struggle free and made it to the riverbank. The Fascists then took him back to his prison where they shot him in the back of the head. It was five days before Christmas 1944: Banks was twenty-one.

The circumstances of Banks' death only emerged after a post-war investigation and a subsequent war crimes trial. Almost every aspect of Banks' treatment at the hands of the enemy broke the Geneva Convention. Those deemed responsible were charged with murder and other offences. Their trial took place in Naples from 29 August to 25 September 1946. Two former guards were sentenced to twenty years' imprisonment, another received eight years and two others were each sentenced to five years. Six others were acquitted.

Banks was awarded a posthumous GC on 5 November 1946. His lengthy citation ended: 'At the time of his capture, Sergeant Banks was endeavouring to return to the Allied lines, so that he might arrange for further supplies to the partisans. He endured much suffering with stoicism, withholding information which would have been of vital interest to the enemy. His courage and endurance were such that they impressed even his captors. Sergeant Banks' conduct was, at all times, in keeping with the highest traditions of the Service, even in the face of most brutal and inhuman treatment.'

Banks' name is listed on the Memorial Board in the chapel at St Edward's School, Oxford. A school prize for bravery was endowed by his father, Charles, while his gallantry award was received on 3 December 1946 from King George VI at Buckingham Palace by his half-sister, Margaret.

ALBERT-MARIE EDMOND GUERISSE (LATER PATRICK ALBERT O'LEARY)

Rank/title: Lieutenant Commander (later Major General)
Unit/occupation: Royal Navy
DATE OF BRAVERY: 1941–5
GAZETTED: 5 NOVEMBER 1946

Albert Guérisse was born in Brussels, Belgium, on 5 April 1911. He read medicine at Brussels University before joining a Belgian cavalry regiment as a 'Medical Captain' in 1940, just a few months into the Second World War. He took part in the eighteen-day campaign in May 1940 that resulted in the German occupation of his homeland. Guérisse's resourcefulness matched his bravery and he managed to escape to England via Dunkirk. He was soon commissioned into the Royal Navy under a pseudonym: Lieutenant Commander Patrick Albert O'Leary. The aim was that he would operate in France as a secret agent using a French Canadian identity.

Guérisse readily embraced his new and dangerous role and was initially tasked with landing agents in the South of France. He served in HMS *Fidelity*, a converted French trawler, which was responsible for a series of clandestine operations in the Mediterranean. In April 1941, Guérisse was involved in an abortive mission to save Polish officers trapped in France. As he tried to make his own way back to his ship, he was captured by Vichy French police. Guérisse escaped en route to a French prison and one of his first stop-offs was a hospice, where he was aided by nuns. After that, he devoted his time to remaining in France and helping to organise an escape route for Allied prisoners of war and others. Such a group already existed and Guérisse met with Captain Ian Garrow, who had already been tasked with operating the escape line. Guérisse changed his name to 'Joseph Cartier' and threw himself into his new role. A network of safe houses and escape routes was set up and the entire operation expanded hugely under his guidance. When Garrow was arrested, Guérisse took over the leadership of the operation and the escape route became known as the 'Pat' or the 'O'Leary' Line.

To inspire the confidence of the group and to keep up the pressure for everyone to work at full capacity, Guérisse made frequent trips between the Dutch border and the South of France. He personally escorted many of those escaping and, whenever a mission was particularly dangerous, he would insist on undertaking it himself. To many, Guérisse was 'the Scarlet Pimpernel' of the Second World War. However, the expansion of operations brought an increased risk of betrayal. In March 1943, the 'line' was betrayed by a double agent and Guérisse and many others were arrested. He was subjected to brutal torture in an effort to force him to reveal the names, whereabouts and duties of other members of the organisation. He was even subjected to 'ferocious experiments' by the Germans, but still he refused to give away any information to the enemy. Next he was sent to a concentration camp, where he was again tortured. Guérisse was eventually held at four camps: Mauthausen, Natzweiler, Neubremm and Dachau. He nearly died when he was beaten senseless while working in the Neubremm quarries. Incredibly, he survived all these horrors and was freed from Dachau – where he had been sentenced to death – along with all the other inmates at the end of the war.

Guérisse was awarded the GC under his pseudonym O'Leary on 5 November 1946. The final words to his lengthy citation provided a telling insight into the selfless nature of this fearless and remarkable man:

Throughout his time in prison, Lieutenant-Commander O'Leary's courage never faltered. Numbers of prisoners have given evidence that his moral and physical influence and support saved their lives. On his liberation from Dachau, Lieutenant-Commander O'Leary refused to leave the Camp, where he had been made 'President' of all the prisoners (including some thousands of Russians), until he had ensured that all possible steps had been taken to ease the lot of his fellows. He was then given the opportunity to return to his family, but he insisted on proceeding to France, to trace the surviving members of his organisation, and to help them in any way he could. From the time of inception to the end of the war, Lieutenant-Commander O'Leary's group was responsible for the rescue and successful return of over 600 British and American officers and men. It is now known that over 250 owe their safety directly to Lieutenant-Commander O'Leary, whose fortitude and determination matched every task and risk.

Brigadier Sir John 'Jackie' Smyth, the VC recipient and author, described Guérisse as 'a most fabulous character, who was in turn soldier, doctor and secret agent. Just as truth is said to be stranger than fiction so the exploits which won him the George Cross are more hair-raising than any of the Scarlet Pimpernel.'

Awards were bestowed on Guérisse thick and fast. As well as holding the GC and Distinguished Service Order (DSO) from Britain, he was awarded the Légion d'honneur and the Croix de Guerre from France, the War Cross from Poland, the Medal of Freedom from America, the Distinguished Service Cross (DSC) from Korea and the Order of Leopold from his native Belgium.

Guérisse rejoined the Belgian army under his own name in 1946 and, the following year, married a British woman who, after bearing him a son, predeceased him. In April 1951, he turned up in Korea as medical officer of the British 29th Brigade, then part of the American Third Division. Typically, he was decorated for saving the life of a Belgian soldier. Later he was in charge of medical services for the Belgian Armed Forces and for NATO personnel in Belgium. His remarkable military career came to an end in 1970 when he retired with the rank of major general.

Guérisse died in Waterloo, Belgium, on 26 March 1989, aged seventy-seven. By then, he is believed to have amassed a total of about thirty-five decorations. Before his death, his numerous gallantry awards had earned him the unofficial title of the 'most decorated man alive'.

VIOLETTE REINE ELIZABETH SZABO
Rank/title: Ensign
Unit/occupation: Women's Transport Service ('FANY')
DATE OF BRAVERY: APRIL 1944–JANUARY/FEBRUARY 1945
GAZETTED: 17 DECEMBER 1946

Violette Bushell was born in Paris on 26 June 1921. Her father was English, her mother French; the couple met when he was serving in France during the First World War. The young Violette – her married name was to be Szabo – had an older brother and three younger brothers but, being so sporty, she often competed against the four boys on equal terms. As well as being beautiful, with dark hair and olive skin, Bushell had an inner strength that was to remain a vital part of her character for all her life. After criss-crossing England and France, the family finally settled in Stockwell, south London, from 1932. After leaving school in 1935 aged fourteen, Bushell got a job in a branch of Woolworth's but she switched to the Bon Marché store in Brixton, south London, in 1939, the year the Second World War broke out.

From early in the war, Bushell was determined to make her mark and she and a friend, Winnie Wilson, joined the Land Army. On 14 July 1940, to mark Bastille Day Bushell's mother urged her to go to the Cenotaph in central London and invite a French soldier home for a meal. Bushell accomplished the task when, accompanied by Winnie, she got talking to a French soldier and asked him back. The man, Sergeant Major Etienne Szabo, a member of the French Foreign Legion, fell in love with Bushell and six weeks later – on 21 August 1940 – they were married in Aldershot, Hampshire. Inevitably, their time together was short for Szabo's husband had to go to fight in North Africa and they did not see each other for a year. They were briefly reunited in Liverpool in the summer of 1941 before Etienne Szabo had to return to duty. They never saw each other again. She was pregnant when he departed, and he was killed at El Alamein in October 1942, four months after the birth of their daughter, Tania.

In October 1941, a year before her husband's death, Szabo, ever keen to 'do her bit' for the war effort, had joined the Auxiliary Territorial Service (ATS), serving with 481 (M) Heavy Anti-Aircraft Battery. Szabo had to leave the battery for several months for the birth of her daughter, but she then left the baby girl with a friend in Havant, Hampshire, because London was so dangerous during the war. After her maternity leave, Szabo took a job at the Rotax aircraft factory, where her father also worked. It was while working here that she learnt that she had been widowed, aged just twenty-two.

Early in 1943, Szabo received a letter from a 'Mr E. Potter' asking her to attend an interview. In fact, the letter was from Selwyn Jepson, the author and, at the time, the senior recruiting officer for the Special Operations Executive (SOE), which had been formed in the summer of 1940 after the fall of France. Jepson had got to know about Szabo's fluent French and her half-British/half-French background. Szabo was eager to work for the SOE and joined in June 1943, when her daughter was exactly a year old, and she soon underwent training as a secret agent.

Brigadier Sir John 'Jackie' Smyth, the VC recipient and author, wrote: 'Violette was a "natural" for this type of work. She had fluent French, was a born athlete, a very good shot and had the self-confidence of a healthy, adventurous, beautiful and life-loving young woman. In the ATS she had learnt self-discipline and, owing to the death of her much-loved husband, she had grown mature beyond her years. She went through her strenuous training with ease and an enthusiasm sharpened by her bitter bereavement and a love of the two countries she had volunteered to serve.'

Her first mission took place in April 1944, two months before D-Day. She was dropped into France on a high-risk operation at a dangerous time. Her job was to act as a courier to a French Resistance leader whose group, based in Rouen, had been broken up. Because it was not safe for him to be seen in Rouen, this role fell to Szabo. She had to travel alone from Paris to Rouen and make contact with those the Resistance leader thought had been 'unmolested' by the disbandment of the group. At the time, Rouen was in Occupied France and was in the specially restricted area of the Channel ports.

Szabo carried out her first mission calmly and competently. She made her contacts and prepared a comprehensive report on what she found. Furthermore, she brought back a German 'Wanted' poster, taken from a street in Rouen, which bore a photograph of her chief and his wireless operator based on their false identity papers. This was valuable information because it showed that at that time the Gestapo had not been able to establish their true identities. Szabo's mission was so successful that after only six weeks in France, she, along with her chief and his wireless operator, were picked up in a Lysander aircraft and brought back to Britain. Szabo was reunited with her parents, who were by now caring for her daughter. The family's relaxation time was, however, all too short.

Szabo's superiors soon had another mission for her – this one even more dangerous than the last. She was left under no illusions that she might well not return from it so she made her will – leaving everything she possessed to her daughter – and told her parents that if they did not hear from her they must not inquire into her whereabouts. Her farewell to her daughter at around the time of Tania's second birthday was deeply emotional because she realised she might never see her again and that, if this happened, Tania would be orphaned.

On 7 June 1944, some twenty-four hours after D-Day, Szabo was back on French soil with new orders to assist the Resistance. She was to act as a courier for the same chief and wireless operator whom she had worked for in Rouen. Her code name for the mission was 'Corinne', while she was given the fake identity of 'Madame Villeret'. After parachuting from a Liberator aircraft, she headed for an established Maquis – a guerrilla group – in central France, south of Châteauroux. Its role was to orchestrate attacks on German troops who were moving up to reinforce units opposing the Allied landings in the Normandy area. The Maquis was spread in small groups over a wide area: Szabo's role was to carry instructions and money to the groups north of the main Maquis. Szabo had a guide/driver, a young Frenchman called Jacques Dufour. Code-named 'Anastasie', he knew the terrain well. On 10 June 1944, after just three days back in the country, Szabo was being driven by Dufour from Sussac to Salon-la-Tour. On the way, they stopped to pick up a friend of Dufour's, Jean Bariaud. They had a Sten gun concealed in the car in case they encountered trouble.

As the group headed into the village of Salon-la-Tour, they saw a German roadblock at a crossroads. They decided to stop the car and make a run for it. Bariaud escaped, while Szabo and Dufour, who had the Sten gun, fired at the Germans, killing or wounding at least one soldier. As they retreated towards a wood, Szabo was wounded. Aware that she was slowing down Dufour and determined he should escape, she ordered him to flee while she continued engaging the enemy. When she eventually ran out of ammunition, she surrendered. Bariaud raised the alarm when he returned to Sussac, while Dufour also escaped, apparently by hiding in a haystack or a wood pile.

Despite her injuries, Szabo was taken to the military prison in Limoges where she was brutally interrogated. Eyewitnesses saw her limping across the courtyard to the Gestapo offices for her twice-daily interrogations. A plan was made by the Resistance to spring her from prison but on the day of the escape bid she was transferred to Fresnes prison, near Paris. After further torture at the Gestapo headquarters in Avenue Foch, she went back to Fresnes where she spent her twenty-third, and final, birthday wracked with pain. In August, she was moved to Ravensbrück concentration camp in Germany. Those moved with her included Denise Bloch and Lilian Rolfe, fellow prisoners of war. The train came under heavy bombing from the RAF and the German guards, fearing for their own lives, jumped off it. On board were thirty-seven male PoWs crammed into two compartments. Szabo, who was shackled to another woman prisoner, managed to fill a jug of water in the train's toilet and crawled back to give it to the desperately thirsty and undernourished PoWs. One of them, Wing Commander Forest Yeo-Thomas (the so-called 'White Rabbit' and himself later awarded the GC) always remembered the incident and Szabo's kindness, and he later reported it back to London.

The conditions in which Szabo was kept for the next five months went from bad to worse. After a short stay in Saärbrücken concentration camp, she went to Ravensbrück on or about 25 August 1944. After a mutiny at Ravensbrück, she was transferred to Torgau, then to Königsberg, some 300 miles north-east of Ravensbrück. In the sub-zero winter temperatures, the women PoWs worked in thin clothes chopping wood and clearing the land. For nourishment, they received only weak soup and tiny amounts of bread. In January 1945, the three women were transferred back to Ravensbrück. By now Szabo was in a desperately weak physical condition and she was convinced she was going to die. Some time between 25 January and 5 February, the three women were taken to the crematorium where their death sentences were read to them. Finally, they were put against a wall and shot in the back of the neck, one after the other, before their bodies were incinerated.

It was only on 13 April 1946 that the fate of the three women became known, from the second-in-command at Ravensbrück. At the time, he was being questioned in Hamburg by Vera Atkins of the SOE, who was determined to learn of the women's fate. Szabo's GC was announced on 17 December 1946 when the citation ended: 'She was arrested and had to undergo solitary confinement. She was then continuously and atrociously tortured but never by word or deed gave away any of her acquaintances or told the enemy anything of any value. She was ultimately executed. Madame Szabo gave a magnificent example of courage and steadfastness.'

Szabo's parents, Charles and Reine Bushell, had received a postcard – sent from Leipzig – from their daughter in January 1945. Ironically, the card indicating that she was still alive arrived just as she was about to be executed. In 1949, the Bushells emigrated to Australia to begin a new life, taking little Tania with them.

The memorials to Szabo include a plaque at Lambeth Town Hall, in the south London borough where she spent much of her childhood. Szabo's remarkable story was turned into a film, *Carve Her Name with Pride*, starring Virginia McKenna. The 1958 film helped perpetuate the moving – though possibly mythical – story of the 'Code Poem', written by Leo Marks, that Szabo was meant to have used as part of her work as a secret agent. The poem reads:

> The life that I have is all that I have,
> And the life that I have is yours.
> The love that I have of the life that I have,
> Is yours and yours and yours.
>
> A sleep I shall have, a rest I shall have,
> Yet death will be but a pause,

For the peace of my years, in the long green grass,
Will be yours and yours and yours.

Virginia McKenna was among many who supported an appeal launched in 1998 to open a museum in Szabo's honour in the grounds of the home of one of the secret agent's greatest admirers, Rosemary Rigby. The museum eventually opened in Herefordshire on 24 June 2000 – the closest Saturday to what would have been Szabo's seventy-ninth birthday.

9

THE AWARDS OF 1947–9

HUBERT DINWOODIE

Rank/title: Squadron Leader (later Wing Commander)
Unit/occupation: Royal Air Force Volunteer Reserve
DATE OF BRAVERY: 20–24 AUGUST 1946
GAZETTED: 4 FEBRUARY 1947

Hubert Dinwoodie was born in Bournemouth, Dorset, on 24 March 1896. The son of a master draper, Dinwoodie served as an officer during the First World War. He became involved in munitions and bomb disposal work fairly early on in his career. During the Great War, Dinwoodie received the Military Cross (MC) for bravery in battle. Little is known about Dinwoodie's life between the wars. However, he appears to have been a civilian from 1920 to 1939 while also being in the Royal Air Force Volunteer Reserve (RAFVR) for some of this time. He resumed his military career after the outbreak of the Second World War, when he was aged forty-three.

On 20 August 1946, a year after the war ended, German high-explosive bombs were being loaded into barges at Lübeck, an important Baltic port that had been heavily bombed during the war. The intention was to dispose of the bombs at sea and two trainloads of bombs, weighing about 1,100 tons in total, had pulled into the quayside. Everything was going to plan until a 50-kilogram bomb, which everyone thought was harmless, was dropped some four feet by the German loading party. The device, one of a batch of twelve, immediately detonated killing six people and injuring another twelve. Immediately, there were fears that the other eleven bombs could detonate or, even worse, the entire trainload might go off. It was decided to call in the experts and an RAF bomb disposal squadron based in Germany was called to deal with the problem.

Squadron Leader Hubert Dinwoodie quickly assessed the situation. On beginning his hazardous work, he discovered that the eleven remaining bombs were an experimental type with a special shock-sensitive, electrically operated fuse. Dinwoodie, working with Corporal Garred, was tasked with defusing one of the bombs in order to identify the cause of the explosion. They soon learnt that the accident had happened as a result of defective German workmanship, or design: it appeared that in several of the devices the fusing device had already moved, rendering the bombs dangerous.

The work on these delicate fuses, which had already been damaged by the earlier explosion, took place in an atmosphere of enormous tension. The lack of understanding of the precise cause of the initial blast and the fear that defusing the bombs would cause further detonations made the situation precarious. The docks at Lübeck are in the middle of the town meaning that any large explosion would have caused heavy casualties and huge damage. One by one, Dinwoodie and Garred made the eleven bombs safe. The entire operation took four days during which time Dinwoodie was also ably assisted by Leading Aircraftsman Hatton. At one point, it was necessary to move a damaged rail wagon, still laden with bombs, which Hatton achieved calmly and courageously.

Garred received the George Medal and Hatton the British Empire Medal. Dinwoodie's GC was announced on 4 February 1947. The lengthy citation, which also praised Hatton's gallantry, concluded:

Throughout the operation, Squadron Leader Dinwoodie displayed cold blooded heroism and initiative in extremely critical circumstances. He was ably assisted by Corporal Garred who showed courage and devotion to duty of a very high order. Although both were aware that they were in great personal danger, they completed a task which probably averted a serious disaster to the port of Lübeck . . . During the past year, Squadron Leader Dinwoodie and Corporal Garred have frequently shown outstanding gallantry in handling and defusing dangerous bombs. Squadron Leader Dinwoodie has been responsible for clearing and organising the demolition of very large dump of German bombs, many of which were in a very unsafe condition.

Dinwoodie, who later rose to the rank of wing commander and who also received the MBE, died in Ringwood, Hampshire, on 28 August 1968, aged seventy-two. He was cremated at Bournemouth Crematorium, a short distance from his birthplace.

HERBERT CECIL PUGH

Rank/title: The Reverend/Squadron Leader
Unit/occupation: Royal Air Force Volunteer Reserve
DATE OF BRAVERY: 5 JULY 1941
GAZETTED: 1 APRIL 1947

Herbert Pugh was born in Johannesburg, South Africa, on 2 November 1898. He was the son of a builders' merchant and the second of seven children. He was educated at Jeppe High School for Boys in his home city.

As a young private, he had served with the South African Field Ambulance from 1917 to 1919 and spent a great deal of time in France. A devoted Christian, he had long wanted to enter the Church. Indeed, when a visiting chaplain was killed on the front line, he took up his role. After the Great War, he attended Mansfield College, Oxford, and he was later ordained into the Congregational Church in 1924. Pugh joined the Chaplains' branch of the Royal Air Force Volunteer Reserve shortly after the outbreak of the Second World War.

By then, he was a family man, aged forty.

At the end of June 1941, the Rev. Pugh, who had the rank of squadron leader, left Britain, along with more than 1,300 service personnel, on the troop carrier *Anselm* for Takoradi, West Africa. In the early hours of 5 July 1941, when the ship was in the middle of the Atlantic, *Anselm* was torpedoed by a German U-boat. It soon became clear that the ship was sinking – and rapidly. The situation was desperate: one torpedo had hit a hold on C deck, blocking the means of escape from below. Pugh, the ship's padre, emerged on deck in his dressing gown and did his best to comfort the injured and those in shock. He helped some into lifeboats and then went to other parts of the ship to help. In the words of one eyewitness, 'he seemed to be everywhere at once'.

When Pugh learnt that some injured airmen were trapped in the damaged hold, he insisted on going to their aid. Indeed, he was lowered by rope below the waterline which, with the ship already taking in water, was, at best, extremely hazardous, and, at worst, suicidal. Once he arrived, he knelt and prayed with the men and continued to comfort them even when the water had reached his shoulders. Time and again, he was offered the chance to leave the ship and save his own life. But he would have none of it and, as the ship plunged to the depths, he went with it. Only one of the officers who was with him in the hold escaped to safety – and he, along with others, was able to provide a vivid description of Pugh's courage.

Pugh was forty-two when he died along with 253 others as the ship went down. Yet his bravery was overlooked for an embarrassingly long time. However, on 1 April 1947, nearly six years after the event and two years after the end of the war, his posthumous GC was announced in the *London Gazette*. His citation ended with the words: 'He had every opportunity of saving his own life but, without regard to his own safety and in the best tradition of the Service and of a Christian minister, he gave up his life for others.' It is believed that a series of letters to a national newspaper prompted the belated award of the GC to Pugh. His courage is also remembered in several memorials including Runnymede Memorial in Surrey; Mansfield College, Oxford; and Jeppe High School in Johannesburg. One later eyewitness account claimed that Pugh's last words were: 'My love of God is greater than my fear of death. I must be where the men are.'

JOSEPH HUGHES

Rank/title: Driver
Unit/occupation: Royal Army Service Corps
DATE OF BRAVERY: 21 MARCH 1946
GAZETTED: 26 JUNE 1947

Joe Hughes was born in Glasgow, Scotland, on 1 September 1926. Brought up in the tough Gorbals district of the city, he was the son of a carter and one of four children. Hughes attended St John's School in the Gorbals and, while still a teenager, he was a driver with the Royal Army Service Corps, serving in the Far East. On 21 March 1946, he was driving a three-ton lorry carrying ammunition and explosives into the magazine at Lyemun Barracks, Hong Kong. Suddenly, as the vehicle was entering the compound, the sensitive cargo started smouldering, then caught fire. Hughes knew that the lorry was likely to blow up at any time yet he had plenty of time to run for cover. Instead, he first raised the alarm so that others could escape the area and then did all he could to put out the fire. Despite small explosions, he tried to remove the burning camouflage net. Next he used fire extinguishers, but they proved ineffective. Moments later, his lorry blew up, fatally injuring him. He died on 23 March 1946, two days after the explosion, aged nineteen. A statement from the War Office concluded: 'Driver Hughes' courage in remaining at his task, thereby attempting to minimise the danger to others when he could have run to safety, was an outstanding example of devotion to duty.'

His GC was not announced for more than fifteen months – on 26 June 1947 – when it said simply that the decoration was in recognition of 'most conspicuous gallantry in carrying out hazardous work in a very brave manner'.

By coincidence, Hughes's sister, Sarah, later married another GC holder (originally an Albert Medal), William Goad. Hughes's bravery was not forgotten by his colleagues. There is a brass bell and plaque, which was originally placed at the Gun Club Hill Barracks in Hong Kong, but which is now at the Lyemun Barracks where the incident happened. A verse on it reads:

> Joseph Hughes GC
> (For a hero he was)
>
> His body lies cold
> Far away, in the earth
> But let's bring his soul home
> To the place of his birth.
>
> So let's always remember
> With a thought and a prayer
> Joseph Hughes from the Gorbals
> And his courage so rare.

LIONEL COLIN MATTHEWS

Rank/title: Captain
Unit/occupation: Corps of Signals, Australian Military Forces
DATE OF BRAVERY: 15 FEBRUARY 1942
GAZETTED: 28 NOVEMBER 1947

Lionel Matthews was born in Stepney, South Australia, on 15 August 1912. The son of a plumber, he was the third child in the family. Matthews attended East Adelaide Public School followed by Norwood High School in Adelaide. After leaving school, he became a shop salesman. Matthews, who was a fine swimmer, married on Boxing Day 1935 in Kensington, South Australia, and the couple later had a son. He trained as a signalman in the Citizen Naval Forces and then enlisted in the Australian Army on 11 April 1939.

Matthews was commissioned in the Australian Army School of Signals in January 1940. On 10 July 1940, he was transferred to the 8th Division Signals, of the then Australian Imperial Force. Matthews left for Singapore in February 1941 and was promoted to captain in January 1942. For the next month, he was involved in operations against the Japanese. After the fall of Singapore on 15 February 1942, Matthews – who was known affectionately by comrades as 'The Duke' – was reported as missing in action the next day. More than a year later, on 29 March 1943, he was reported to be a prisoner of war in Borneo.

It later emerged he had been held as a PoW by the Japanese at Sandakan, Borneo, from August 1942 to the beginning of March 1944. His courage in battle was more than matched by his bravery in captivity. During his time in the PoW camp, Matthews undoubtedly considered himself to be still at war with the enemy – not simply a helpless prisoner. He directed an underground intelligence organisation that used local contacts to deliver medical supplies, food and money. This boosted morale in the camp and saved many lives. Matthews was also instrumental in arranging a secret radio link with the outside world – and he even arranged the delivery of firearms, intended for future use, to a secret rendezvous. Despite being a PoW, he also held the formal position of commanding officer to the North Borneo Armed Constabulary and prepared for the group – and locals in Sandakan – to rise against the Japanese. By contacting guerrilla forces in the Philippines, he arranged escape parties. However, the Japanese eventually learnt about his activities – through the torture of a Chinese captive – and arrested him in July 1943. Matthews was then brutally tortured, but refused to reveal any secrets or to give up the identities of those working with him. At his trial, he was accused of insurrection, endeavouring to possess arms and other offences. His fellow Australians were forced by their captives to dig his grave long before the inevitable guilty verdict. He was executed on 2 March 1944 in Kuching, Borneo, but not before telling his comrades: 'Keep your chins up, boys. What the Japs do to me doesn't matter. They can't win.' Matthews was thirty-one when he died. In recognition of his courage, he was given a full military funeral with Australian officers and troops present, as well as Japanese officers in full dress and wearing their decorations.

Many of those in the camp suffered an even worse fate after Matthews' death. Over the next year, conditions at the camp worsened and PoWs were beaten, starved and overworked. By February 1945, the Japanese anticipated Allied landings in Borneo and more than 1,000 PoWs were forced to participate in the 'Death Marches' to Ranau. The final destination was actually 160 miles from Ranau and only 260 out of an estimated 2,700 PoWs survived. Of these, just six lived to see the end of the Second World War, having managed to escape and live with local tribesmen in the jungle.

Matthews received two posthumous awards after the end of the war. On 8 January 1946, he was awarded the Military Cross (MC) for courage in Malaya in 1942. On 28 November 1947, he was awarded the GC in recognition of 'gallant and distinguished services whilst a prisoner-of-war in Japanese hands (prior to September, 1945)'.

Matthews' remains were later moved from his original grave in Kuching to the Labuan War Cemetery situated on a small island in Brunei Bay, off the coast of north-west Borneo. The bravery of this fearless and inspirational soldier has never been forgotten. The Lionel Matthews Merit Award was established on New Year's Day 1966 for achievement on the Schools of Signals' courses. Furthermore, in Gowrie, Canberra, a road – Matthews Place – has been named in his honour.

JOHN ARCHIBALD BECKETT

Rank/title: Sergeant
Unit/occupation: Royal Air Force
DATE OF BRAVERY: 28 MARCH 1947
GAZETTED: 16 DECEMBER 1947

John Beckett was born in Lurgan, Co. Armagh, on 14 March 1906. His parents had lost two of their other sons in the Second World War, killed while serving in the Merchant Navy and the RAF respectively. Beckett attended St Enoch's Public Element-ary School in Belfast and then worked as a fitter. He enlisted in July 1935 and initially worked as a rigger's mate – part of the ground crew – in the RAF. After apparently being evacuated from France in 1940, he worked in Canada for two years from March 1942 as a fitter. He did the same job after the war, working this time in the Middle East.

On 28 March 1947, a major blaze broke out during the refuelling of a Lancaster aircraft of No. 38 Squadron. The incident took place at an RAF base at Ein Shemer Air Head-quarters, Levant, Israel. Beckett was the driver of the refuelling vehicle. The flames raged out of control, engulfing not just the fuselage of the aircraft but also Sergeant Beckett himself. He sustained severe burns to his face and hands before a fellow airman could beat out the flames.

Beckett then realised there was a great danger that the main tank of the refuelling vehicle, containing more than 2,000 gallons of fuel, would explode, thereby undoubtedly destroying the twenty aircraft at the base. Such an explosion would almost certainly also have killed or injured many RAF staff. Despite being in severe pain from his serious burns, Beckett leapt into the driver's seat and drove the vehicle some 400 yards to a safe position outside the aircraft park. He managed to get out of the vehicle, but then collapsed. He was taken by ambulance to receive urgent medical treatment, but died from his injuries fifteen days later on 12 April 1947. He was forty-one.

Beckett had sacrificed his own life for his comrades and for the greater good of the RAF. His posthumous GC – the RAF's first since the end of the war – was announced on 16 December 1947. The lengthy citation ended: 'The fires in the Lancaster aircraft and in the vehicle were eventually brought under control, and extinguished with no further damage to persons or property. There is no doubt that, by his prompt and gallant action, Sergeant Beckett saved a number of valuable aircraft from almost certain destruction and his comrades, who were working in the vicinity, from risk of serious injury.'

THOMAS RAYMOND KELLY
Rank/title: Able Seaman
Unit/occupation: Merchant Navy
DATE OF BRAVERY: 18 MARCH 1947
GAZETTED: 10 FEBRUARY 1948

Thomas Kelly was born on 19 March 1928 in Newry, Co. Down. The eldest of six children, he attended the Christian Brothers School but ended his education aged fourteen. Brought up in a seaport, he was a strong swimmer and well known for his endurance. Despite his mother's worries (she had been widowed when her husband died aged thirty-seven), Thomas opted for a career at sea and joined the Merchant Navy.

On 18 March 1947, the SS *Famagusta* of London got into trouble in heavy seas in the Bay of Biscay while on a voyage to Cyprus. The steamer developed a list to port and, as the sea got rougher and the winds reached near gale force, this list worsened. The ship put out an SOS message and the SS *Empire Plover*, also of London, came to her assistance. The *Famagusta* launched a lifeboat, which headed for the *Empire Plover*. However, the lifeboat capsized, spilling its ten occupants into the raging sea. *Empire Plover* manoeuvred into position and the crew lowered ropes, ladders and scrambling nets. Three of her crew stripped off and dived or jumped into the water. Two of them remained beside the nets and ladders ready to help survivors up towards safety.

Able Seaman Kelly, one of the sailors aboard *Empire Plover*, swam off with a line towards some of the lifeboat occupants who were struggling in the rough sea. He first returned with an officer who had been badly injured. Kelly then swam off a second time and returned with a second member of the crew. By now exhausted, he swam off a third time towards a woman who was struggling in the sea some fifty yards away. He succeeded in reaching her but both were struck by a giant wave and disappeared. The body of Kelly, who would have been nineteen the next day, was never recovered. Five of the ten occupants of the capsized lifeboat also drowned.

Bridget Kelly, the teenager's mother, was heartbroken to receive a telegram saying that her son had died in a 'gallant attempt' to save a member of the *Famagusta*'s crew. Her eldest child was the family breadwinner and so the Kelly Relief Fund Appeal was launched to raise much-needed money for the family. The captain of *Empire Plover* said: 'Kelly was a gallant, brave Irish boy whose courage will never be excelled in this world. Our ship is a sad one and no one talks because of his death. In a full gale – unasked – he stripped and dived overboard into the Atlantic with the ships steadily approaching each other.'

Kelly's GC was announced on 10 February 1948 when the lengthy citation ended: 'Kelly showed a very high order of bravery and it was due to his determined and gallant action that two lives were saved. Each time he left the *Empire Plover* he risked his life. To leave his ship on the third occasion, with the full knowledge which his first two rescues must have given him of the risk and difficulty of his undertaking and in the face of the bodily fatigue which those rescues must have entailed, was an act of supreme gallantry.'

A housing estate in Newry was later named in honour of Kelly. Bridget Kelly always kept her eldest child in her prayers.

She remained convinced that a large dark bruise, like a hand print, on her thigh, which she discovered the day after his death, had been somehow caused by her son as he drowned.

STANLEY JAMES WOODBRIDGE
Rank/title: Flight Sergeant
Unit/occupation: Royal Air Force Volunteer Reserve
DATE OF BRAVERY: FEBRUARY 1945
GAZETTED: 28 SEPTEMBER 1948

Stan Woodbridge was born in Chelsea, south-west London, on 29 August 1921. The middle one of three children, his father was a pawnbroker. The family later moved to Walthamstow, east London, where his father bought and ran a business selling second-hand and antique furniture. Woodbridge went to the Thomas Gamuel Primary School in Walthamstow and later to nearby Markhouse Road School. After leaving school at fourteen, he attended Clarke's College where he took business studies. His first job was as an office boy in the City of London. Woodbridge, who was already a member of the Home Guard, volunteered for the RAF in 1941. However, as he was not immediately accepted, he worked for his father for six months. By now, the family lived in Chingford, north-east London. Once in the RAF, Woodhouse was trained in Blackpool as a wireless operator. By the time he joined 159 Squadron, Royal Air Force Volunteer Reserve, he had been promoted to flight sergeant. In February 1944, the squadron was posted to Air Command in South East Asia.

On 31 January 1945, as the Second World War entered its final year, Flight Sergeant Woodbridge was a wireless operator on a four-engined US Liberator bomber. The aircraft was on a top-secret mission to Burma to try to discover, using specialist equipment, the whereabouts of Japanese radar establishments in the Far East. This would have led to Allied bombers targeting them. However, the plane crashed in the jungle and six crew members, including Woodbridge, were captured by the Japanese. The enemy set about torturing them to obtain information useful to the Japanese Intelligence Service. The four non commissioned officers (NCOs) were separated, taken to a forest area and beheaded.

Woodbridge, however, was singled out for the most horrific torture because the Japanese were convinced that, as a wireless officer, he knew technical information that would be useful to them about wireless equipment, secret codes, wavelengths and such like. A Japanese officer, assisted by two interpreters, was given the task of extracting the information. Woodbridge was kicked and beaten with a belt and sword, but revealed nothing. His final interrogation took place at the site of his execution, when it was clear he was about to die. He again said nothing other than if the Japanese were going to kill him, they should do it quickly. Woodhouse was beheaded at a prisoner-of-war camp in Burma on 7 February 1945, aged twenty-three.

His father, James, who was close to his middle child, later travelled to Rangoon and placed a wreath on his son's grave with the words: 'From Stanley's dad. Boy, I'm proud of you!' Although not a rich man, James Woodbridge had insisted on going to Burma to hear the three-month trial of his son's torturers. Three officers and three non commissioned officers from the Japanese Imperial Army faced a military court. They were found guilty of the torture and murder of the initial four airmen who had been executed. Three were hanged and three given lengthy prison terms. It was from their trial that details of Woodbridge's abhorrent treatment emerged.

Woodbridge's GC was announced on 28 September 1948. The lengthy citation ended: 'Flight Sergeant Woodbridge behaved throughout [his captivity] with supreme courage. His fortitude, loyalty to his country and his complete disregard for his own safety, even unto death, constitute one of the highest examples of valour in the annals of the Royal Air Force.'

Woodbridge was eventually buried three times and his third and final grave is at the Rangoon War Cemetery in Burma. Woodbridge's father was for a long time aggrieved that his son had not received the Victoria Cross (VC), feeling the GC was an inferior award. It had to be explained to him by Brigadier Sir John 'Jackie' Smyth, the VC recipient and author, that the GC was not in any way an inferior award, just that it was awarded for gallantry not in the face of the enemy. Indeed, Sir John told the grieving father that 'the George Cross heroes often had to suffer tortures which would have made some of their VC comrades shudder'.

DAVID RUSSELL

Rank/title: Lance Corporal
Unit/occupation: 22nd Battalion, 2nd New Zealand Expeditionary Force
DATE OF BRAVERY: JULY 1942–FEBRUARY 1945
GAZETTED: 24 DECEMBER 1948

David Russell was born in Ayrshire, Scotland, on 30 March 1911. The son of a byreman (a man who tends cows), he was one of three children and his mother died when he was six. Aged about sixteen, he followed his elder brother to Australia but, with work scarce, soon moved on to New Zealand. Russell found work as an orderly in Napier Hospital, Hawke's Bay. After the outbreak of the Second World War, he joined up, serving in the 2nd Battalion, 2nd New Zealand Expeditionary Force. He took part in the 22nd's bayonet charge in the battle for Crete, before moving on to Egypt.

On 14 July 1942, soon after writing to his sister that all was well with him, Lance Corporal Russell was taken prisoner of war in Italy. He was imprisoned there and managed to escape several times, only to be recaptured on each occasion. He wrote postcards home which indicated that he was held at both camps 57 and 107 in Italy at various times.

After his final escape sometime in 1943, he managed to find

some friendly Italians to stay with. He wore Italian civilian clothes and lived with a peasant friend, Giuseppe Vettorello. He kept in touch with other PoWs and gave advice to those seeking to escape from the camp and out of Italy. He is credited with helping forty-seven PoWs escape. Incredibly, this went on for two years, though it appears that eventually Russell became somewhat complacent about the dangers he faced. Because he was dressed in civilian clothes, he knew that if he was captured he would be treated as a spy not a soldier. One evening, Russell went to a local bar where some Germans were drinking and, unwisely, spoke English. An Italian, aware of the danger he faced, punched him in order to get him out of the bar and then tried to persuade him to find an underground shelter. However, Russell returned to Vettorello's home where he was arrested by a patrol of Italian Fascist and German troops on 22 February 1945. Vettorello was also arrested.

His captors, members of a mixed German–Italian police regiment, took him and Vettorello to the headquarters of Oberleutnant Haupt at Ponte di Piave. Vettorello was accused of sheltering Russell, but Russell convinced his captors that he had never set eyes on Vettorello before the day of their arrest and the Italian was eventually released. Another Italian later revealed how Haupt viciously beat up Russell, who he believed knew where other PoWs and Italian partisans were hiding. Russell revealed nothing and so eventually he was chained to a stable wall and told that if he did not give up information in three days he would be shot. Russell received no food or water for those three days and was mercilessly beaten. An Italian who was guarding him tried to persuade him to save his life, but Russell replied: 'Let them shoot me.' On the third day, 28 February 1945, he was placed against a stone wall, shot dead and hastily buried. Russell was thirty-three when he died.

The recommendation for the GC came from his adopted country, courtesy of the New Zealand Prime Minister. His decoration was announced on Christmas Eve 1948, in recognition of 'gallant and distinguished services whilst a prisoner of war in German hands (prior to September, 1945)'.

After the war, Russell's remains were exhumed and, treated as a New Zealander rather than British, he was given a handsome gravestone in Udine War Cemetery in Italy. At the Waiouru Army Museum in New Zealand there is an exhibition in his honour. A ward at Napier Hospital, Hawke's Bay, was also named after him. Perhaps the greatest tribute to Russell's courage came from the interpreter to Haupt, Russell's German tormentor, who said: 'The behaviour of the Englishman [sic] was splendid, and it won the admiration of Haupt himself.'

NOOR INAYAT KHAN

Rank/title: Assistant Section Officer
Unit/occupation: Women's Auxiliary Air Force, seconded to the Women's Transport Service ('FANY')
DATE OF BRAVERY: 16 JUNE 1943–12 SEPTEMBER 1944
GAZETTED: 5 APRIL 1949

Noor Inayat Khan, known to so many simply by her code name 'Madeleine', was the first woman operator to be infiltrated into enemy-occupied France in the Second World War. Born in Moscow on New Year's Day 1914, she was the eldest of four children. She came from a truly international family. Her father, who was Indian, had travelled to America in 1910. He had originally intended to stay only a short time but did not return to his homeland for another sixteen years. He met his American wife when she attended his talk on Indian mysticism and they married on 20 March 1913. Stays in London, Paris and Moscow followed, hence young Noor's birthplace. However, the couple returned to London with their six-month-old daughter in July 1914, as the international situation deteriorated and the likelihood of a war in Europe increased. When the First World War ended, the family moved to France. After Inayat Khan's father died in 1927 from pneumonia, aged forty-four, her mother remained grief-stricken for a long time and she, as the eldest child, became the unofficial head of the family despite being only thirteen. Inayat Khan was educated at the Lycée de St Cloud from 1925 to 1931. This was followed by the Sorbonne from 1932 and Ecole des Langues Orientales from 1937 to 1939. Inayat Khan was a talented author and she wrote children's books and plays. From 1939 to 1940 she, along with her younger sister, joined the nursing volunteers Union des Femmes de France. As the Germans invaded, she worked in hospitals but her family eventually escaped to England, where they were determined to play a role in the war effort.

Aged twenty-five, Inayat Khan joined the Women's Auxiliary Air Force (WAAF). She became a skilled wireless operator and on 1 December 1942 became a leading aircraftswoman. As a fluent French speaker – as well as a wireless operator – she was soon being considered for the secretive Special Operations Executive (SOE), which had been formed in the summer of 1940 after the fall of France. She eventually joined the SOE on 8 February 1943, and four days later was seconded from the WAAF to the Women's Transport Service ('FANY'). In the event, Assistant Section Officer Inayat Khan's training was rushed – there was work to be done in France – and she was dropped by Lysander aircraft into enemy territory on 16 June 1943. Her task would have been a desperately dangerous one even for an experienced agent, yet she was just twenty-nine and a novice spy. She was given the false identity of Jeanne-Marie Renier and was told that if she was captured she should say that her mother was an American who had been married to a Frenchman who was now dead. She was tasked with meeting up with the Prosper circuit – part of the French Resistance movement – in Paris. Inayat Khan had to appear to be an ordinary citizen, yet her role was to move from flat to flat with her codebooks and wireless. After meeting trusted agents and other contacts, she had to transmit the valuable information back to

Britain. Inayat Khan and her French comrades were caught up in a German ambush in Grignon in July 1943 but she and some others narrowly escaped capture.

The Gestapo were involved in a massive clampdown on Resistance activities and, one by one, the number of agents and contacts that Inayat Khan had once had gradually diminished. At one point, she was almost single-handedly responsible for contact between the entire Resistance movement and London. When her spy bosses in Britain became convinced her role had become too dangerous, she was given the opportunity to return home. However, she did not want to leave her French comrades without communication and she was convinced the Resistance group could be rebuilt.

By now, however, the Gestapo had an accurate description of her but they only knew her code name, Madeleine. With the Germans determined to capture her, Inayat Khan was eventually betrayed after three and a half months' work in France with the Resistance. She was arrested in October 1943 and taken to Gestapo headquarters at Avenue Foch, Paris. The Gestapo had found her codebooks and messages, and they wanted her to work with them. Inayat Khan refused to give them any information and was initially imprisoned in a cell on the fifth floor of the headquarters. She was held there for several weeks during which time she made two unsuccessful escape attempts. Inayat Khan was asked to sign a declaration saying she would not attempt to escape again, but she refused. The Chief of the Gestapo then asked for permission from Berlin for their prisoner to be sent to Germany for 'safe custody'. This was approved and Inayat Khan became the first agent to be sent to Germany.

She was transported to Karlsruhe and then on to Pforzheim prison, where her cell was located away from the main jail. Her captors considered her a particularly dangerous and uncooperative prisoner. She spent up to nine months in solitary confinement, much of it in chains. Inayat Khan could apparently often be heard sobbing in her cell but she remained defiant and ingenious to the end: she and a Frenchwoman in the main prison communicated by scratching messages on the bottom of their tin food bowls. Despite further brutal interrogation from the Gestapo, Inayat Khan still refused to give any information about her work or her comrades and was taken to Dachau concentration camp in Germany, along with three other women agents. They arrived at midnight and, early the next morning, they were all taken to the crematorium, made to kneel on the ground – in pairs next to each other, holding hands – and they were shot in the back of the head. They died on 12 September 1944. Inayat Khan was thirty years old.

After her death, some questioned whether the SOE had been foolish to send such an inexperienced young woman to take on so daunting a task. Yet this quietly determined, self-contained woman had been intent on risking her life for the causes of two countries she loved, Britain and France. Even while she was being held in captivity, Inayat Khan was being considered for the GM and the MBE. Neither was approved. After the war, on 16 January 1946, she was awarded a posthumous Croix de Guerre with Gold Star.

Her posthumous GC took much longer. It was eventually announced on 5 April 1949. The lengthy citation, which is believed to have been rewritten four times, ended: 'Assistant Section Officer Inayat Khan displayed the most conspicuous courage, both moral and physical, over a period of more then 12 months.' She is commemorated on the Runnymede Memorial in Surrey.

On 17 July 1967, a moving ceremony was also held in Suresnes, France, for 'Madeleine' of the Resistance. It took place at the old home from which her family had fled to England in 1940. A commemorative plaque was fixed near the entrance to the property and dignitaries from France, India and Britain attended. Brigadier Sir John 'Jackie' Smyth, the VC recipient and author, was asked to send a message for the unveiling in his capacity as President of the Victoria Cross and George

Cross Association. It was read out by the legendary Colonel Buckmaster, who had been head of the French section of the SOE during the war: 'I, and all the members of my association, both holders of the Victoria Cross and George Cross, will always revere Noor Inayat Khan GC and cherish her memory as one of the most splendid and gallant women in our history. In her life – and particularly in her incredibly valiant work for the Resistance – she was always utterly staunch and true to the cause of freedom and to the comrades who were working with her, and she faced her death with the same courage she had always shown in her life.'

It is impossible to know exactly what motivated this extraordinarily brave young woman. Her brother, Pir Vilayat, was convinced she had obtained great inspiration from the Buddhist Jataka Tales. He said that the stories of self-sacrifice and compassion left a deep impression on his sister. 'I think that the inner cultivation of these ideals prepared her for the heroic work she decided to do,' he said. It seems that Inayat Khan was also inspired by a remarkable comment made by her father to his children: 'When you enjoy the comfort and security of a country, then you must be ready to defend it.' Few people, men or women, have ever done more to defend their country than Noor Inayat Khan.

10

THE AWARDS OF 1950–3

ROBERT GEORGE TAYLOR
Rank/title: **Mr**
Unit/occupation: Newspaper advertising representative
DATE OF BRAVERY: 13 MARCH 1950
GAZETTED: 1 AUGUST 1950

Bob Taylor was born in Fishponds, Bristol, on 10 June 1920. The son of a mechanical engineer, he was the middle one of three children. He attended Dr Bell's School in the city and was a keen cyclist, swimmer and gymnast. Aged nineteen, Taylor joined the Territorial Army and was soon mobilised. As a sergeant in the 76th Royal Artillery, he saw action in North Africa, Sicily and Italy. He was the battery malaria expert and, although he contracted the disease himself, he gave instructions on preventative measures. As a soldier he was nicknamed 'Tiger', suggesting that he was fearless. After being demobbed in 1945, he, like many others of his generation, found himself in his mid-twenties without any training for a career. He applied for and got a job as an advertising representative on the *Bristol Evening World*. After leaving the Army, Taylor, who lived at home with his parents, also became accomplished at martial arts – judokwai – and he was treasurer of the Bristol Judokwai Club.

In an idle moment, many have probably pondered what they would do if they saw someone robbing a bank. That question became a reality for Taylor on a spring day in 1950, just three months before his thirtieth birthday. On 13 March 1950, he was working in the Henleaze area of Bristol when two men entered a sub-branch of Lloyds Bank and, after threatening the cashier and guard with a revolver, stole some cash and escaped. As the alarm was raised, the two men took off over open land and Taylor, who had heard the words 'Stop them, there's been a hold-up', led the pursuit. As he caught them up, the robber with the gun turned and fired at Taylor at point-blank range. Taylor died from his serious injuries aged twenty-nine. Others who had joined in the chase, aided by the police, eventually caught the two robbers.

A week after Taylor's death, the directors of Lloyds Bank sent Taylor's parents a cheque for £1,000. Lord Balfour of Burleigh, the chairman of the bank, wrote saying: 'Your son's gallant action and the sense of duty which led him to intervene are highly appreciated.' The two robbers, both Polish labourers, were caught and tried for the murder of Bristol's have-a-go hero. Even though only one had fired the gun, they were both hanged in Winchester, Hampshire, on 7 July 1950.

Taylor's posthumous GC was announced three weeks later on 1 August when the citation ended: 'Without any regard for the hazards, Taylor intervened out of a desire to help in the preservation of law and order and gave his life in a gallant attempt to apprehend an armed and desperate criminal.' Another member of the public was awarded the George Medal and yet another received the British Empire Medal (Civil Division). In January 2005, Taylor was further honoured when a blue plaque was placed outside his former home, just a year after the last blue plaque in the city had been placed outside the former home of Bob Hope, the comedy actor.

BENJAMIN GOWER HARDY

Rank/title: Private
Unit/occupation: 22nd Garrison Battalion, Australian Military Forces
DATE OF BRAVERY: 5 AUGUST 1944
GAZETTED: 1 SEPTEMBER 1950

RALPH JONES
Rank/title: Private
Unit/occupation: 22nd Garrison Battalion, Australian Military Forces
DATE OF BRAVERY: 5 AUGUST 1944
GAZETTED: 1 SEPTEMBER 1950

Ben Hardy and Ralph Jones played crucial roles in trying to thwart one of the largest prison breakouts of the Second World War, or indeed of any war. Yet it took fully six years for their bravery to be officially recognised with the award of the GC to each soldier.

Hardy was born in Marrickville, Sydney, Australia, on 28 August 1898. The youngest of three children, he attended Randwick Public School in Sydney before the First World War. From 1910, he served with the Cadets and, later, with the Australian Military Forces. Hardy was a good marksman and was a member of Chatswood Rifle Club, winning the club championship in 1926. During the inter-war years he worked as a driver. He re-enlisted on 25 September 1941 with the 7th Garrison Battalion and was recognised as 'an authority on the Vickers machine-gun'. On 12 February 1944, he was posted to the 22nd Garrison Battalion at Cowra Prisoner of War Camp in New South Wales.

Ralph Jones was born in Gorleston-on-Sea, near Great Yarmouth, Norfolk, on 26 September 1900. The son of a journeyman wheelwright, he was the youngest of fourteen children. Jones was educated at Church Road School in Gorleston-on-Sea before being apprenticed, aged fourteen, to a local motor engineer. He was called up in 1918 and spent time with the 53rd Battalion, Rifle Brigade, before being invalided out with tuberculosis in 1920. After struggling to find long-term work, he emigrated to Australia in around 1926. He worked as a labourer in Sydney but, during the Great Depression, he again struggled to find work. However, in 1930 he eventually found work — and lodgings — with a couple, Tom and Madelaine Cook, in Tuena. After Tom Cook died, he became engaged to his former boss's widow. On 15 January 1942, he joined the Citizen Military Forces at Crookwell, New South Wales. Within a month he was posted to the 22nd Garrison Battalion at Cowra Prisoner of War Camp.

On the night of 4/5 August 1944, Privates Hardy and Jones were on duty at No. 12 Prisoner of War Camp, Cowra, which held more than 1,100 Japanese prisoners. The PoWs already felt they had dishonoured themselves and their country by being captured and might never be allowed to return home. During the day, on 4 August, they had been informed that in three days' time the non commissioned officers (NCOs) would be split from the other ranks – which caused huge anger and resentment among the PoWs, who were guarded by 104 men.

Hardy and Jones were members of the Vickers machine-gun crew guarding the compound when there was a carefully planned mass breakout at about 2 a.m. Japanese PoWs raced from their prison huts and set fire to them. Armed with knives, baseball bats and other weapons, they then bore down on the machine-gun crew protecting the eastern perimeter wire. The PoWs wanted to take over the gun – one of two – and turn it on their guards before taking over the armoury.

Hardy and Jones were hugely outnumbered but they remained at their gun mowing down advancing PoWs and holding their position. Hardy was firing, while Jones fed the ammunition. Eventually, however, realising the hopelessness of their position, they disabled the gun, capable of firing 600 rounds a minute, so that it could not be used on their fellow guards. They were then immediately overrun by the fanatical horde before being beaten and stabbed to death. Hardy was forty-five, Jones forty-three.

The self-sacrifice of the two men had won precious time for the other guards, including those manning the other machine-gun post. The breakout was largely thwarted and the greatest number of surviving PoWs were eventually pinned down in a stormwater drain. From there, they were either recaptured or committed suicide. In all, 334 had escaped from the camp into the bush, but were rounded up over the next few days. In total, three prison guards and an Australian lieutenant based near the camp were killed, along with 234 Japanese PoWs. A further three Australians and 100 PoWs were wounded.

Lieutenant Colonel Monty Brown, the Commanding Officer of the camp, had urged that the two men should receive a gallantry award. However, nothing came of it and it was not until six years later that a new Australian Government formally recommended them for the GC. Their posthumous decorations were announced on 1 September 1950 when their citations ended: 'Privates Hardy and Jones stood their ground and continued to work the gun until bashed to death, displaying outstanding gallantry and devotion to duty in their fight against an overwhelming onslaught of fanatical Japanese. They met their deaths in the true British spirit of sacrifice for their country.' Hardy's elderly mother, Emily, had died just days before the announcement was made.

Jones's brother, Walter, received the GC on behalf of their mother, Eliza, from George VI at Buckingham Palace on 14 February 1951. Hardy's sister, Beatrice, received his GC on 21 January 1952 from Sir William McKell, the Governor-General of Australia. There is a memorial to both men at the Cowra War Cemetery in New South Wales.

IVOR JOHN GILLETT

Rank/title: Aircraftsman First Class
Unit/occupation: Royal Air Force, Far East Flying Boat Wing, Singapore
DATE OF BRAVERY: 26 MARCH 1950
GAZETTED: 3 OCTOBER 1950

Ivor Gillett was born in Marlborough, Wiltshire, on 16 September 1928. One of two children, he attended Marlborough Grammar School before joining the RAF.

On 26 March 1950, Aircraftsman First Class Gillett was a member of the ground crew working at Seletar, one of three RAF bases then in Singapore. The ground crew were on a Sunderland Flying Boat which was on its mooring being 'bombed up': loaded with bombs for the next day's mission. Without warning, the Sunderland suddenly blew up and survivors from the blast were thrown into the sea. Rescuers were quickly on the scene and a lifebelt was thrown to Gillett from a launch.

Gillett had only received superficial injuries in the blast and could easily have been lifted to safety. However, he saw a badly injured corporal in the water who was in danger of drowning. Gillett was a friend of the corporal and knew he was not a strong swimmer so he handed the lifebelt to his comrade. The lifebelt kept the corporal afloat until he was rescued unconscious from the sea minutes later. However, without a lifebelt for himself, Gillett drowned, aged twenty-one, and his body was washed ashore two days later.

Gillett's posthumous GC was announced on 3 October 1950. His citation ended: 'By his action of deliberately saving the life of his injured friend, whilst injured and in great danger himself, Aircraftsman Gillett displayed magnificent courage. His extreme unselfishness in his last living moments, which resulted in the sacrifice of his life to save another, was seen in this act of great heroism which was in accordance with the highest traditions of the Royal Air Force.'

On 3 December 1950, a memorial service was held for Gillett in Preshute Church in Wiltshire attended by the Mayor, RAF personnel, friends and family. Gillett is buried in Kranji Military Cemetery in Singapore. His gravestone is engraved with the words: 'Greater love hath no man than that he lay down his life for his friend.'

JOHN ALAN QUINTON

Rank/title: Flight Lieutenant
Unit/occupation: 228 *Operational Conversion Unit, Royal Air Force*
DATE OF BRAVERY: 13 AUGUST 1951
GAZETTED: 23 OCTOBER 1951

John Quinton, who was better known as Jack, was born in Brockley, south-east London, on 2 February 1921. One of three brothers, his father had served in the Royal Army Medical Corps during the First World War. Although a trained accountant, his father worked as a marketing and sales executive after the war. Quinton attended Christ's College in Finchley, north London, and was practical as well as sporty and good at mathematics. He was also a keen Scout and cyclist. After school, Quinton trained as an engineer. At the outbreak of the Second World War, he volunteered for the Royal Air Force Volunteer Reserve and, later in the war, he was commissioned as a pilot officer. He had a 'good' war, being promoted to flight lieutenant and being awarded the Distinguished Flying Cross (DFC) for his courageous actions over France. After the war, Quinton returned to his old engineering firm, Specialoid. He also married and the couple later had a son. After his employers relocated to the Midlands and he had another job that did not suit him, Quinton rejoined the RAF, being based at RAF Leeming in North Yorkshire.

On 13 August 1951, Flight Lieutenant Quinton was the navigator in a Wellington aircraft on a training flight. The plane was in a mid-air collision when Quinton and a young Air Training Corps cadet were in the rear compartment of the Wellington. As the plane started to break up, Quinton grabbed the only parachute in the rear compartment and clipped it on to the cadet's harness. He then pointed to the ripcord and a gaping hole in the aircraft, indicating that the cadet should jump to safety. At that moment, a further portion of the aircraft was torn off and the cadet was thrown out of the fuselage. He was clutching his ripcord which he then tugged and he landed safely. All eight RAF personnel left on the plane died when it crashed to the ground in the Yorkshire Dales.

Quinton, who was twenty-nine when he died, was awarded a posthumous GC as a result of the cadet, who was on his first flight, explaining what had happened. The award was announced on 23 October 1951 when Quinton's citation ended: 'Flight Lieutenant Quinton acted with superhuman speed, displaying the most commendable courage and self-sacrifice as he well knew that in giving up the only parachute within reach he was forfeiting any chance of saving his own life. Such an act of heroism and humanity ranks with the very highest traditions of the Royal Air Force, besides establishing him as a very gallant and courageous officer who, by his action, displayed the most conspicuous heroism.'

Quinton's widow, Margaret, received her late husband's decoration in an investiture at Buckingham Palace on 27 February 1952, less than a month after what should have been his thirtieth birthday. It was the first investiture of the new Queen's reign and Margaret Quinton was the first to receive a decoration that day. An annual prize used to be awarded in Quinton's name at the School of Technical Training, RAF Halton, near Wendover, Buckinghamshire, but, since the school closed in 1993, the Quinton Trophy has been held at RAF Cranwell, Lincolnshire.

GEORGE CAMPBELL HENDERSON

Rank/title: Mr
Unit/occupation: Sub-Officer, Gibraltar Dockyard Fire Service
DATE OF BRAVERY: 27 APRIL 1951
GAZETTED: 20 NOVEMBER 1951

George Henderson was born in Nigg, Aberdeen, Scotland, on 15 January 1910. One of two sons of a fisherman, he joined the Gordon Highlanders after leaving school and saw action with his battalion in India. While serving in Gibraltar, he met and married a local girl and they later had two daughters. In 1938, after returning from a difficult and bloody posting in India, when only four members of his unit survived, Henderson left the Army – he was, in fact, listed as a deserter on 9 December 1938. During the Second World War, Henderson worked as a fireman, attached to the police, in Gibraltar until subsequently employed by the Admiralty Fire Service.

On 27 April 1951, Sub-Officer Henderson was on duty at the Gibraltar dockyard when a lighter – a flat-bottomed barge used to transfer goods to and from moored ships – caught fire with a cargo of explosives on board. At the time, it was alongside the *Bedenham*, an ammunition ship. Henderson was in charge of the fire engine that was sent to tackle the fierce blaze. Despite the giant flames and intense heat, Henderson leapt on board *Bedenham*. Even though he knew the fire would eventually lead to an explosion, Henderson continued to direct the jet of water from his hose on to the burning lighter. He remained there alone until the inevitable happened – and he was engulfed and killed by a huge explosion. Seven others nearby were also killed.

Days later, more than 1,000 Spanish workers attended his funeral – a sign of his popularity. His widow, Passionara Brancato, was so grief-stricken that she barely left their house for a year after his death. Henderson's GC was announced on 20 November 1951 when his citation ended: 'Henderson remained at his place of duty alone doing what he could to prevent the explosion although he must have known that his chance of survival was slight. He was killed when the ammunition blew up. Sub-Officer Henderson displayed courage of the highest order in the face of almost certain death.' A number of other gallantry awards were announced at the same time for bravery during the fire.

Henderson's decoration was presented to his widow by the Governor of Gibraltar at the first public investiture ever held on the Crown Colony. There is a memorial for the victims of the explosion at North Front Cemetery and a service was held in 2001 to mark the fiftieth anniversary of their deaths.

AWANG ANAK RAWENG
Rank/title: Mr
Unit/occupation: Dyak tracker, Johore, Federation of Malaya
DATE OF BRAVERY: 27 MAY 1951
GAZETTED: 20 NOVEMBER 1951

Awang anak Raweng was born in Sarawak, Borneo, in about 1925 – his exact date of birth is not known and he did not go to school. Instead, his first job was with the 1st Malaysian Rangers before he worked with the British Army.

During operations against bandits in Malaya in May 1951, a section of a platoon of the Worcestershire Regiment was ambushed by a fifty-strong enemy unit near Johore. The leading scout was killed instantly and the section commander was fatally wounded. Under intense fire, Awang anak Raweng, a Dyak (native of Borneo) tracker, was shot through the thigh bone and a soldier, who was moving behind him, was hit below the knee, the bullet completely shattering the bone. Raweng was lying wounded in the open under intense heavy rifle and automatic fire. However, he somehow managed to collect his and the other soldier's weapons and dragged the injured service-man into the cover of the jungle. Disregarding his own wound, he then took up a position to defend the injured soldier. Every time the bandits tried to inch closer, he fired on them and he successfully repulsed several attacks. Raweng was eventually hit a second time and this time the bullet shattered his right arm, which meant he was now unable to use his rifle. Despite losing a significant amount of blood from his undressed wounds, Raweng dragged himself over to the wounded soldier and took a grenade from his pouch. With the weapon clutched in his left hand and ready to pull out the pin with his teeth, he defied the enemy to approach. The bandits, who had pursued their attack for forty minutes, eventually withdrew when they were threatened by other sections of the platoon.

Both Raweng and the other injured man, Private Hughes, survived their injuries. Raweng's GC, one of the last two awarded by George VI, was announced on 20 November 1951. The citation ended: 'The coolness, fortitude and offensive spirit displayed by Awang anak Rawang [sic] were of the highest order. Despite being twice severely wounded he showed the utmost courage and resolution to continue the fight and protect the injured soldier.' He received his decoration from Sir Anthony Abell, the Governor of Sarawak, in January 1952. Speaking at the presentation in Kuching, the capital of Sarawak, Sir Charles Keightley, Commander-in-Chief, Far Eastern Land Forces, said: 'Wherever I go among fighting regiments in Malaya, I find Dyaks taking part in the fighting with great skill and bravery.'

Sadly, on one of Raweng's regular visits to London, his GC was stolen. He remains the only Malaysian to have been awarded the decoration. Raweng, who married four times and had eight children, later retired from the military and went to live in a 'long-house' where he farmed his own *padi* field. He is now believed to be about eighty-five years old.

GEORGE ANTHONY MORGAN TAYLOR
Rank/title: Mr
Unit/occupation: Commonwealth Vulcanologist, Papua New Guinea
DATE OF BRAVERY: JANUARY–APRIL 1951
GAZETTED: 22 APRIL 1952

Tony Taylor, as he was known, was born in Moree, New South Wales, Australia, on 30 October 1917. One of three children, he attended Maitland High School near Newcastle, New South Wales, before going to Sydney Boys' High School. A lover of nature and a keen scientist, he became a trainee analytical chemist after leaving school. However, in 1942, three years into the Second World War, Taylor enlisted into the Australian Army. Based largely in North Queensland, he developed an interest in the volcanic rocks around him. Taylor was discharged from the Army as a warrant officer class 1 and enrolled at Sydney University. After obtaining a B.Sc. at the university, he began work for the Commonwealth Bureau of Mineral Resources, and in 1950 he set up the Volcanological Observatory in Rabual, Papua New Guinea.

At 10.40 a.m. on 21 January 1951, the Mount Lamington volcano in Papua New Guinea erupted. In one of the most violent eruptions ever recorded, a large part of the northern side of the mountain was blown away and smoke rose 50,000 feet into the air. Mount Lamington, some twenty-five miles inland from the north-eastern coast of Papua, had no previous volcanic history until three days before the eruption. Within twenty-four hours of the eruption, Taylor was on the scene and he soon began drawing up a major assessment of the situation. A total of some 4,000 people died in the initial eruption and subsequent lesser ones, while more than ninety square miles were covered by molten lava, wiping out many homes. Rescuers were hampered by a suffocating pumice dust and sulphurous fumes.

In the most dangerous of circumstances, Taylor visited the volcano daily, usually in an aircraft but sometimes on foot. On some occasions, he even spent the night at the base of the cone. These visits continued for months even though there were further tremors and explosions throughout February and a second major eruption on 5 March.

Taylor's GC was announced on 22 April 1952 when his lengthy citation ended: 'Without regard for his personal safety he entered the danger area again and again, each time at great risk, both in order to ensure the safety of the rescue and working parties and in order to obtain scientific information relating to this type of volcano, about which little was known. His work saved many lives for as a result of his investigations in the danger zone he was able, when necessary, to warn rehabilitation parties and ensure they were prevented from entering an area which he so fearlessly entered himself.' His GC – the first and, so far, the only to a vulcanologist – was presented to him on 24 November 1952.

Taylor returned to Australia where he continued to work with volcanoes, often in great danger, and he was promoted to Senior Resident Geologist at Port Moresby. He married in 1954 and the couple went on to have three children. The analysis from the data that Taylor obtained under such dangerous circumstances was eventually published in 1958 by the Minister of National Development in Australia along with maps, photographs and other documents. Taylor died on Manam Island on 20 August 1972, aged fifty-four.

JOHN BAMFORD
Rank/title: Mr
Unit/occupation: Colliery worker
DATE OF BRAVERY: 19 OCTOBER 1952
GAZETTED: 18 DECEMBER 1952

John Bamford, who was always known as Jack, became, at the age of fifteen, the youngest person to have been awarded the GC, an honour he retains to this day. Born on 7 March 1937 in Ilkeston, Derbyshire, he was the second of six children. His father was a horse and scrap metal dealer. Bamford left school at fifteen and went to work at the Moorgreen colliery in Eastwood, Nottinghamshire, as a conveyor-belt fitter.

On Sunday 19 October 1952, a fire broke out in the Bamfords' Nottinghamshire house occupied by both parents and their six children. It was the early hours of the morning and his parents had returned earlier from a Saturday night out at Ilkeston fair. The blaze was fierce and when Bamford and his father, John, went downstairs and opened the living-room door, the entire interior of the room burst into flames. The intense heat meant they could not return upstairs to get to the rest of the family so Bamford and his father ran out of the front door and climbed on top of a downstairs bay window to reach the window of one of the bedrooms. They opened the window and helped Bamford's mother, Rachel, and three of the children to escape. Bamford and his father then clambered through the window into the bedroom where they could hear the two remaining children, aged six and four, shouting from their back bedroom, which was above the seat of the fire. The bedroom door and its surrounding frame were in flames. Bamford's father draped a blanket around himself and tried to reach his two sons. However, the blanket caught fire and he was driven back. Bamford then told his father to go round to the back of the house while he got down on his hands and knees to crawl through the flames to the rear bedroom.

Bamford's shirt was burned from his back but he reached the bedroom and put an arm around his two younger brothers and got them to the window. He dropped the four-year-old, Roy, to his father below. However, the six-year-old, Brian, who was deaf and dumb, slipped from his grasp and ran back into the room, which was by now full of flames. Bamford chased after his brother, caught him and threw him from the window to safety below. By this time Bamford was in a shocking state: barely conscious, he had severe burns to his face, neck, chest, stomach, back, arms and hands. However, he managed to force one leg over the window sill and then plummeted to the ground where his father partially broke his fall. As the three boys lay unconscious on the ground, a fire engine – called by a neighbour – eventually got the blaze under control.

Bamford was fifteen years and five months old at the time. His two younger brothers were soon off the danger list at Nottingham General Hospital but Bamford had to fight for his life. Only expert nursing, several skin grafts and his own determination to live meant he pulled through. On 16 December 1952, nine days before Christmas Day, his GC was announced. The lengthy citation ended: 'John Bamford displayed courage of the highest order, and in spite of excruciating pain succeeded in rescuing his two brothers.'

But the best day of his life was still to come: his investiture at Buckingham Palace by the young Queen. On 9 March 1953, two days after his sixteenth birthday, Bamford, his mother Rachel, his elder sister Jean, Sister Marjorie Odey, who had nursed him back to health, barely leaving his bedside for an entire week, were all allowed to join him, along with his local vicar. They were driven to London in a Rolls-Royce belonging to Nottingham Funeral Directors and spent a week in the capital as the guests of the National Coal Board.

Bamford remained in hospital for five months until March 1953, even undergoing an unrelated operation to remove his appendix on Boxing Day 1952. He then had to learn to walk and talk again: the smoke had affected his throat while his legs had suffered badly from the removal of so much skin to use as grafts on other parts of his severely burned body. It was not until early 1954 that Bamford returned to work for the National Coal Board and, when he was eighteen, he moved to the coal face. However, he left the colliery in 1959 and went to work with his father and two brothers as scrap metal and vehicle dealers. He had already been spending weekends working for the family business and eventually he had to choose between his two jobs.

In an interview at his family home in Awsworth, Nottinghamshire, Bamford recalled the incident from fifty-eight years ago, in his own words, 'as if it was yesterday'. He told me:

When we opened the [living-room] door, we were hit by a huge blast of flame. We went outside because we couldn't get back upstairs. We climbed on to the flat roof on top of the bay window and we got my mother and what we first thought was all of them [his sister and five younger brothers] out through the bedroom window. But then we had a count up and there were two missing. So me and my dad went back again. We could hear Roy shouting from the back bedroom. My dad tried to get through the flames by wrapping a blanket round him but the blanket caught fire. I told him to go round the back and I would get into their room and chuck them out the window. But it was hot – very hot – and I couldn't see anything because of the smoke. I got down low on my hands and knees because it was the best place with the smoke rising.

When I found them in the bedroom, I had Roy between my knees and Brian was next to us by the window. I slammed the sash window up but the bloody thing came down again and slammed my fingers. So I banged it up again and this time it stayed there. I chucked Roy out to my dad who caught him below. But when I turned round Brian had gone – he was frightened so he had got back into bed. I knew where the bed was so I got him and chucked Brian out too. I remember then I somehow got out of the window too. But the next thing I can remember was lying on the hearth in front of our neighbour Mrs Hale's fire and our doctor, Dr Towle, kept saying to her: 'Give him weak tea. Give him weak tea.' Even though all I wanted was lots of water. It's daft what you can remember.

Bamford said he never thought for one moment of not going to rescue his brothers. 'I had to get them out. I couldn't leave them, could I? I never thought about what might happen to me – I didn't have time to think about it.' He said he received hundreds of letters from well-wishers all over the world as he lay in hospital and Enid Blyton, the children's author, sent him some signed copies of her books. He said he had expected 'nowt' for his actions and did not know what the GC was when he was told he had been awarded it. Bamford stayed in touch with the ward sister who nursed him back to health and, years later, after an accident at the scrapyard, he was treated by her in hospital for a broken right leg.

Bamford, who nearly six decades on still bears the scars from the fire, 'retired' from the scrap metal business in 1993 and moved to live near Land's End, Cornwall, for five years with his wife, Madge. However, the couple, who have four sons and four grandchildren, returned to live in Awsworth in 1998. Since then, a plaque has been put up in the village hall to commemorate his GC. Since then, too, as well as dabbling in the family scrap metal business, Bamford, who is seventy-three, has been involved in buying and restoring vintage cars and tractors. 'I have had a lifetime breaking them [vehicles] up but now I put them back together,' he said with a chuckle.

FREDERICK WILLIAM FAIRFAX

Rank/title: Detective Constable (later Detective Sergeant)
Unit/occupation: Metropolitan Police Force
DATE OF BRAVERY: 2 NOVEMBER 1952
GAZETTED: 6 JANUARY 1953

Policeman's son Fred Fairfax was born in Westminster, central London, on 17 June 1917. He attended St Mary's School, Westminster, where he first joined the 1st Westminster Wolf Cubs and later became a Boy Scout. He won a scholarship to Archbishop Temple School in Lambeth, south London. A talented sportsman, Fairfax had hoped to become a teacher. However, his family could not afford to send him to college and so he went to work for the then Westminster Bank before following his father into the Metropolitan Police in June 1936, around his nineteenth birthday. Three months after joining the force, he became PC 1571 based at Peckham. After volunteering for military service in 1940, Fairfax became an instructor in the Royal Corps of Signals. A year later, he married and the couple went on to have a son. Commissioned in 1942 and posted to the Royal Berkshire Regiment, Fairfax was demobilised in 1945 with the rank of captain. He then rejoined the Met, first as a uniformed officer in Brixton, then serving in the CID in Croydon.

On 2 November 1952, shortly after 9 p.m., two men were seen climbing over the side gate of a warehouse in Tamworth

Road, Croydon. They then climbed up a drainpipe on to the flat roof of the building some twenty-two feet above ground level. The alarm was raised and DC Fairfax, PC Norman Harrison and other officers arrived at the scene in a police van, while two other officers also arrived separately.

When told where the men had last been seen, Fairfax scaled the same drainpipe to reach the flat roof. He was followed by PC Jamie McDonald, but this officer failed to negotiate the last six feet of the pipe and dropped back to the ground. In the moonlight, Fairfax could see the two men some fifteen feet away behind a chimney. He walked towards them, challenged them and grabbed one of them. But the man struggled free and his companion fired at Fairfax, wounding him in the right shoulder. Fairfax fell to the ground but after they ran past him he got up, pursued them and knocked one to the ground. A second shot was fired but Fairfax kept hold of the man, dragged him behind a skylight and searched him. The officer found a knuckle-duster and a dagger, both of which he removed.

McDonald, his fellow officer, now made a second attempt to get to the roof and succeeded after being dragged up by Fairfax. Fairfax called on the gunman to drop his weapon, but the man refused and made further threats. Harrison, the other officer, had by now climbed on to a sloping roof nearby and was edging towards the gunman by slithering across the roof with his heels in the guttering. However, he was spotted by the gunman who fired at him and a bullet narrowly missed Harrison's head. Harrison ducked behind a chimney and dropped to the ground where he rejoined more officers. A group of officers then entered the warehouse building, ran up the fire escape and pushed open the door that led to the flat roof. Fairfax shouted a warning that the gunman was nearby but PC Sidney Miles ignored it and jumped from the doorway to the roof. As he did so, the gunman fired and the officer was shot between the eyes. When Fairfax left cover to tend to the casualty, another shot was fired at him but it missed.

McDonald now crept forward and he and Fairfax dragged their dying colleague behind the fire escape exit. Harrison then jumped out and, from his position in the doorway, threw his truncheon and other objects at the gunman, who fired at him. PC Robert Jaggs, who had climbed up the drainpipe, then reached the roof. He, too, was fired upon before joining the other officers. After briefly leaving the scene to be given a police pistol, Fairfax quickly returned to the roof and again called on the gunman to drop his weapon. The gunman responded by firing at the officer again. Fairfax now advanced on the gunman firing his own pistol as he went. The gunman then jumped over the side of the roof to the ground below where he was finally arrested.

Fairfax's GC was announced on 6 January 1953 when the lengthy citation ended: 'The Police Officers acted in the highest tradition of the Metropolitan Police and gave no thought to their own safety in their efforts to effect the arrest of armed and dangerous criminals. Detective Constable Fairfax repeatedly risked death or serious injury and although wounded did not give up until the criminals were safely in the charge of the Police.'

Harrison and McDonald were both awarded the George Medal. Jaggs was awarded the British Empire Medal (Civil Division) and Miles was awarded a posthumous Queen's Police Medal for Gallantry.

The two would-be burglars, Derek Bentley, aged nineteen, and Christopher Craig, aged sixteen, were found guilty of murder in December 1952. Bentley was hanged and Craig, because of his age, was imprisoned but later released, in 1963. Yet Bentley was being restrained by Fairfax when Craig fired the fatal shot. On 30 July 1998, the Court of Appeal overturned Bentley's conviction and his case used to be highlighted by those pressing for the abolition of capital punishment. The case also prompted books and numerous newspaper articles and the events of that evening were also depicted in a film, *Let Him Have It*, which came out in 1991.

Fairfax made a full recovery from his injuries and was promoted to sergeant on the day he was awarded the GC. He was transferred to Savile Row, then to Streatham, before ending his career back in Croydon. He retired in 1962 after twenty-six years' service and then he ran a tobacco/sweet shop before selling the business to set up his own private investigations agency. Fairfax Investigators Ltd, which proved a success, was sold in 1980. The Fairfaxes retired to Dorset, where he played a full part in local church life and was an active Freemason. A keen former boxer, Fairfax ultimately became a boxing judge. He died in Yeovil, Somerset, on 23 February 1998, aged eighty.

DAVID BROADFOOT
Rank/title: **Mr**
Unit/occupation: Radio Officer, Merchant Navy
DATE OF BRAVERY: 31 JANUARY 1953
GAZETTED: 6 OCTOBER 1953

David Broadfoot was born in Stranraer, Scotland, on 21 July 1899. At the end of the Great War, aged nineteen, he went to sea as a radio officer in the Merchant Navy. His employer was the Marconi Wireless Telegraph company. Broadfoot was married with at least one son.

Early in 1953, Broadfoot was working on board the *Princess Victoria*, a roll-on, roll-off ferry which left Stranraer on the morning of 31 January for Larne, Northern Ireland. After passing Loch Ryan, the ship encountered north-westerly gales and squalls of sleet and snow. A heavy sea struck the ship and burst open the stern doors. Seawater flooded the space on the car deck, causing a list to starboard of about ten degrees. Although attempts were made to secure the stern doors, they were unsuccessful. The master of the ship tried to turn the vessel around back towards Loch Ryan, but the rough conditions prevented him from doing so. Some of the ship's cargo shifted from port to starboard which meant the list on the stricken ship increased.

All this time, as the drama in the Irish Sea was unfolding, Radio Officer Broadfoot constantly sent out messages giving the ship's position and asking for assistance. He remained calm as the list worsened, sitting at his transmitter, time and again sending wireless signals to the coast radio station so that it had the *Princess Victoria*'s exact position. When the ship finally got within sight of the Irish coast, the list had increased to forty-five degrees. With the vessel virtually on her beam ends, the order was given to abandon ship. Thinking only of how to save the lives of passengers, Broadfoot remained at his post and continued to send and receive messages, knowing that by doing so he had no chance of surviving. The first distress call went out at 9.45 a.m. on 31 January 1953, while the last went out just over four hours later at 1.58 p.m. Eventually, the ship foundered and Broadfoot went down with her. He died aged fifty-three and the accident claimed the lives of 133 of the ship's complement of 179 passengers and crew.

Three senior Northern Ireland politicians were among the dead, the victims of some of the worst weather of the twentieth century. The survivors were rescued by ships and boats that Broadfoot had summoned to the scene. Broadfoot's posthumous GC was announced on 6 October 1953. The lengthy citation ended: 'He had deliberately sacrificed his own life in an attempt to save others.' The ship's commander, Captain James Ferguson, was among those awarded the George Medal for gallantry in the same incident, which was one of the worst peacetime maritime disasters in British waters. In the summer of 1999, Broadfoot's family donated his GC to the Stranraer Museum, where there is a memorial to the victims of the disaster.

11

THE AWARDS OF 1954–9

DEREK GODFREY KINNE

Rank/title: Fusilier
Unit/occupation: 1st Battalion, Royal Northumberland Fusiliers
DATE OF BRAVERY: 25 APRIL 1951–10 AUGUST 1953
GAZETTED: 13 APRIL 1954

Joiner's son Derek Kinne was born on 11 January 1931 in Nottingham. After growing up largely in Leeds, West Yorkshire, he did his National Service and then went to work in a hotel. From an early age, Derek was close to his older and younger brothers, Raymond and Valentine, and they had three rings inscribed Kinne I, II and III for themselves. In 1947, when they bought the rings in a shop in Leeds, the brothers made a pact, one that they regarded as a solemn pledge rather than something said in jest. The agreement was quite simply that if the eldest died, the middle brother would take his place and if the middle brother died the youngest would do the same. So when Raymond Kinne was killed serving with the Argyll and Sutherland Highlanders in 1950, Derek Kinne honoured the pact and put his name forward for the 'Korean Volunteers Scheme'. At the time, Kinne also hoped that he would find his elder brother's grave. The Korean War had broken out in June 1950 between the Chinese and Soviet-backed Democratic People's Republic of Korea and the Western and United Nations-backed Republic of Korea.

Fusilier Kinne, who was serving with the 1st Battalion, Royal Northumberland Fusiliers, was captured by Chinese communist forces in Korea on 25 April 1951 on the last day of the Battle of Imjin River. From the moment of his capture, he had two priorities: to escape so that he could continue to fight the enemy and, while he was in captivity, to raise the morale of his fellow prisoners through showing his contempt for his captors and their brutality. Kinne first escaped within twenty-four hours but was recaptured within days as he tried to rejoin British forces. He was then put in with a large group of prisoners being marched north to prison camps. During a harsh one-month march, Kinne emerged as a man of outstanding leadership, who inspired his fellow prisoners.

Kinne's treatment during his time as a prisoner of war was even worse than it might have been because of his determination to defy his cruel captors. At times, he taunted them so much that they beat him with such ferocity that he was left close to death. By the middle of 1951, three months after his capture, he was well known to his captors and he was accused of being non-cooperative. He was brutally interrogated about other PoWs who had similar 'uncooperative' views. For refusing to inform on his comrades – and also for striking a Chinese officer who had assaulted him – he was beaten and tied up for periods of twelve and twenty-four hours. During this time, he was made to stand on tiptoe with a noose around his neck so that, had he relaxed, he would have been throttled. In June 1952, Kinne escaped a second time but was recaptured two days later. He was again severely beaten and this time placed in handcuffs, which were often tightened to restrict his circulation and which were kept on him for eighty-one days.

During this time, he was accused of 'insincerity', a hostile attitude to the Chinese, the sabotage of compulsory political study, escape and of being a reactionary. From 1 July to 20 August, Kinne was kept in a tiny box cell, where he was made to sit to attention all day and denied any washing facilities. At intervals, Kinne was beaten, prodded with bayonets, kicked and spat upon by his guards. On 20 August, after complaining of being beaten by a Chinese guard, he was forced to stand to attention for nearly seven hours. When he complained, he was beaten by a Chinese guard commander with the butt of a sub-machine gun, which went off and killed his assailant. For this accident, he was beaten senseless with belts and bayonets, stripped of his clothes and thrown into a rat-infested hole until 19 September.

Next Kinne was tried – on 16 October – by a Chinese military court. His 'crimes' were trying to escape and of being a reactionary. Initially, he was sentenced to a year in solitary confinement but this was increased to eighteen months when he complained at his trial that he had been denied medical treatment for a severe double hernia that he had sustained in June 1952, while training for his second escape attempt. On 5 December 1952, Kinne was transferred to a special penal company. His final period of solitary confinement began on 2 June 1953, when he was sentenced for defying Chinese orders and for provocatively wearing a rosette in celebration of Coronation Day. After an armistice was signed between the two warring sides in July 1953, Kinne prepared for his release as part of a prisoner exchange due on 10 August. On both 8 and 9 August, his release was nearly called off after he demanded an interview with the International Red Cross representatives who were visiting PoW camps to check on conditions. However, on 10 August 1953, after twenty-eight months of brutal treatment in captivity, Kinne was freed. His defiance was now legendary and he became known as 'the man North Korea could not break'.

Kinne was awarded the GC on 9 April 1954. His lengthy citation ended:

> Fusilier Kinne was during the course of his periods of solitary confinement kept in no less than seven different places of imprisonment, including a security police gaol, under conditions of the most extreme degradation and increasing brutality. Every possible method both physical and mental was employed by his

captors to break his spirit, a task which proved utterly beyond their powers. Latterly he must have been fully aware that every time he flaunted his captors and showed openly his detestation of themselves and their methods he was risking his life. He was in fact several times threatened with death or non-repatriation. Nevertheless he was always determined to show that he was prepared neither to be intimidated nor cowed by brutal treatment at the hands of a barbarous enemy.

His powers of resistance and his determination to oppose and fight the enemy to the maximum were beyond praise. His example was an inspiration to all ranks who came into contact with him.

The GC was presented to Kinne by the Queen at Buckingham Palace on 6 July 1954. As well as his Korean War Medal, he received the United Nations' Service Medal for his actions in Korea. Kinne wrote his autobiography, *The Wooden Boxes*, which was published in 1955. In his book, he describes first being brutally beaten by four 'muscle-men' in jail after he had struck out – in self-defence – against his interrogator while a PoW. He wrote: 'I expected a beating and I got it. With my legs bound together, my hands tied behind my back, the muscle-men took their revenge on me. I was kicked round the room while one of them had a go at me with a leather belt.' Shortly afterwards, Kinne was given an even worse and longer beating for trying to escape. This was the start of a prolonged period of abuse, including him being bound and handcuffed and suspended from a ceiling by a rope. Time and again, Kinne was beaten, yet still he refused to confess to his 'crimes' against the Chinese. This led to him being kept in a wooden box five feet nine inches long by four feet six inches high and two feet six inches in width. His worst beating came after his guard had accidentally shot himself dead. Kinne wrote: 'On the 1st, 3rd, 13th and 16th September, I was beaten until I longed for death.'

After finally returning home to Britain at the end of the war, Kinne moved to North America in 1957 and married his wife,

Anne, also British, in Ottawa, Canada, on 10 July 1959. The couple arrived in Arizona in 1961, soon bought a house and set up a framing and laminating business in Tucson. Kinne, who has a grown-up son and a daughter, along with four grand-children, retired in 2005.

Today Kinne has vivid memories of his ordeal as a PoW. In an email to me from his home in the USA, he described harrowingly how, on 4 September 1952, after yet another beating, he woke up and decided to take his own life on what he knew was his sister's wedding anniversary. 'They had really given me their best shots. When I awoke, I was gagging: I was choking on my own blood. I could not scream. I was in one hell of a mess. It hurts me to say it but I could endure no more. I decided to finish it all. There was a bloody big nail in the post. I was banging my feet against the mud wall. I bent my head down and rammed it into the nail. All hell broke loose; it must have been one hell of a mess and the wall was knocked down. I had woken the officer who was sleeping next door. I was covered in blood. The doctor looked at me and told them I was dying. So they [his captors] figured out what I had done, that I'd had enough.' After that, he said, his treatment improved.

Kinne, who is seventy-nine, went back to Korea in the spring of 2010 with two of his grandchildren, although this was not the first time he had revisited the country.

TERENCE EDWARD WATERS

Rank/title: Lieutenant
Unit/occupation: West Yorkshire Regiment, attached 1st Battalion, Gloucestershire Regiment
DATE OF BRAVERY: APRIL–SEPTEMBER/OCTOBER 1951
GAZETTED: 13 APRIL 1954

Terry Waters was born in Salisbury, Wiltshire, on 1 June 1929. He was the elder son and, like his father, who had played county cricket for Gloucestershire, he was a talented sportsman. Like his father, too, Waters attended Bristol Grammar School, where he played for the first XI at hockey and was a sergeant in the Cadet Force. He then went to the Royal Military Academy, Sandhurst, in 1947 and was commissioned into the West Yorkshire Regiment, then based in Austria. Waters volunteered to serve in the Korean War, which had broken out in June 1950. He went out to the Far East with the Royal Northumberland Fusiliers, but later became attached to the Gloucestershire Regiment.

Lieutenant Waters was captured by Chinese communists after the Battle of Imjin River, which lasted from 22 to 25 April 1951. During the battle, he had received a serious head wound and another nasty injury to one of his arms. Despite being in severe pain, he set an example to his fellow prisoners of war, including other injured servicemen, during the enforced march to Pyongyang. After the three-week trek, during which the PoWs were brutally treated by their captors, they arrived at an area west of Pyongyang known as 'the Caves'. The prisoners were incarcerated in a tunnel built into the side of the hill which had a stream continuously flowing through it and which flooded much of the floor area. European and South Korean prisoners were kept in filthy rags and were crawling with lice. They had no medical care and just two small meals of boiled maize each day. Every day, prisoners were dying from their wounds, sickness or malnutrition and it soon became clear to Waters that few of the British PoWs would survive.

The PoWs received a visit from a North Korean 'political officer' who tried to persuade them that they should volunteer for a PoW unit known as 'Peace Fighters'. In reality, this was a propaganda group acting against the PoWs' own side. They were bribed with the offer of better food, medical treatment and other amenities, but the prisoners had no interest in going along with the proposal. However, such was the desperate plight of his men that Waters, who was determined to save lives, ordered the British PoWs to pretend to accede to the request.

However, Waters decided that he would not go along with it because he felt it necessary to maintain British prestige. 'As a British officer, it is my duty to remain here,' he told one sergeant, who had urged him to accompany his men to an improved PoW camp: number 12.

The North Koreans were angry that Waters had not gone along with their proposal and, despite several more efforts to persuade him to join the 'Peace Fighters', his health continued to decline. Waters died in 'the Caves' a short time later, in either September or October 1951, aged twenty-two. His GC was announced on 9 April 1954 when the lengthy citation ended: 'He was a young, inexperienced officer, comparatively recently commissioned from the Royal Military Academy, Sandhurst, yet he set an example of the highest gallantry.'

HORACE WILLIAM MADDEN

Rank/title: Private
Unit/occupation: 3rd Battalion, Royal Australian Regiment
DATE OF BRAVERY: 24 APRIL–NOVEMBER/DECEMBER 1951
GAZETTED: 30 DECEMBER 1955

Bill Madden was born in Cronulla, Sydney, New South Wales, Australia, on 14 February 1924. One of three children (one of whom died in infancy), he was working as a fruiterer's assistant when he was mobilised on 26 May 1942. However, he fell ill and it was not until 10 August 1943 that he was finally able to join the Australian Army. Known to comrades as 'Slim' because of his build, he was transferred to the 8th Field Ambulance in November. After taking part in operations in New Guinea, he contracted malaria which limited his participation in the remainder of the Second World War and he was discharged on 2 June 1947. After that he worked at a mental hospital, first as an orderly and later as a moulder. The Korean War broke out in June 1950 and two months later, on 19 August, Madden re-enlisted into the Australian Korea Special Force. He served with the 3rd Battalion, Royal Australian Regiment, initially as a driver, then as a signaller.

Private Madden was captured by Chinese communists on 24 April 1951 after apparently being twice concussed by grenades during fighting near Kapyong. Even by the brutal standards of the Chinese communists at this time, Madden's treatment was particularly cruel. All the enemy's attempts to get him to collaborate were met with defiance. His repeated courage meant his name soon became known to various groups of prisoners of war. Several officers and men later testified to Madden's quite outstanding bravery. Despite endless beatings and similar ill treatment, Madden remained outwardly cheerful and optimistic. One of his many punishments was to receive only tiny amounts of food yet, even then, he shared these meagre rations with other sick prisoners. It is believed that, like Lieutenant Terry Waters, Madden was held at the area west of Pyongyang known as 'the Caves'.

Madden died of malnutrition sometime between 6 November 1951 and 6 December 1951, almost certainly during the last twelve days of this period. He was aged twenty-seven and the only Australian to die in captivity during the conflict. His GC was announced on 30 December 1955 when his citation ended: 'It would have been apparent to Private Madden that to pursue this course [defiance] must eventually result in his death. This did not deter him, and for over six months, although becoming progressively weaker, he remained undaunted in his resistance. He would in no way co-operate with the enemy. The gallant soldier's outstanding heroism was an inspiration to all his fellow prisoners.'

Captain Anthony Farrar-Hockley, of the Gloucestershire Regiment, wrote an affectionate tribute to Madden's sister, Florence, after the Korean War ended. The officer, who had been with Madden when he died, said in his letter: 'Let me assure you that he did not die in pain; and was only semi-conscious throughout the last two days of his life, at the end of which, unable to withstand a final bout of enteritis, he passed away.'

JOHN AXON

Rank/title: Mr
Unit/occupation: Engine driver, British Rail
DATE OF BRAVERY: 11 FEBRUARY 1957
GAZETTED: 7 MAY 1957

John, or Jack, as he was better known, Axon was born in Stockport, Cheshire, on 4 December 1900. One of five children, he was from a long-standing Stockport family. After leaving school, he became an apprentice painter but, by the age of eighteen, he had changed to a career on the railways. He was first employed from 1919 with the London & North Western before switching to the London, Midland & Scottish Railway and, eventually, to British Rail. Axon, who worked as an engine driver, married in 1930 and the couple went on to have two sons.

On 11 February 1957, Axon was in charge of a train being driven from Buxton, Derbyshire, to nearby Chapel-en-le-Frith. The train was carrying more than 500 tons of freight and was travelling at some fifteen mph along the London, Midland region line. Axon was preparing to slow the train before descending a steep hill when there was a deafening noise in the driver's cab. The steam pipe feeding the brakes had fractured and, at the same time, blinding, scalding steam was being discharged at high pressure on to Axon's feet. Axon, despite his burned feet, had ample time to save his own life by abandoning the cab. However, realising the dangers caused by a runaway train, he chose to stay at his post and, with great courage, battled to get the train under control using the handbrake. As the train's speed increased, Axon urged the fireman to apply as many wagon brakes as possible and then to jump clear.

Conditions in the cab were now almost unbearable, with steam and boiling water still pouring into it, but Axon none the less waved a warning to a signalman that the train was running away and stayed with it as it overtook another freight train. Axon's train eventually collided with another goods train and he was killed. He was fifty-six. His GC was announced on 7 May 1957 when the citation ended: 'Driver Axon displayed devotion to duty, fortitude and outstanding courage in highly dangerous and alarming conditions. He gave his life in an attempt to prevent a collision.' John Creamer, the guard, also died.

An electric locomotive was later named in honour of Axon and a plaque was also erected in honour of him and his guard at Chapel-en-le-Frith railway station in 2007 – to mark the fiftieth anniversary of the incident. Earlier, the BBC had recorded a radio documentary about the story called *The Ballad of John Axon*.

MICHAEL PAUL BENNER
Rank/title: Second Lieutenant
Unit/occupation: Corps of Royal Engineers
DATE OF BRAVERY: 1 JULY 1957
GAZETTED: 17 JUNE 1958

Brigadier's son Paul Benner was born on 14 April 1935. A talented linguist and sportsman, he was educated at Canford School in Wimborne, Dorset. After leaving school in 1953, he attended the University of London and Merton College, Oxford. As a student, he enjoyed climbing, skiing, walking and rowing. After university, and still with surplus energy to expend, he waited to do his National Service by working as a steel erector's mate by day and a barman in the evenings. Once he was called up, Benner chose to serve, like his father, with the Corps of Royal Engineers. Ever resourceful and determined, he was selected for a National Service Commission and his squadron commander described him as the best junior officer ever to pass through his hands.

During the summer of 1957, Second Lieutenant Benner was taking part in a training exercise in Austria. He was in command of a group of non commissioned officers (NCOs) undergoing mountain training in the Alps. On 1 July, he led six of his men on a traverse up the 12,400-foot Grossglockner. By 6 p.m., the men had successfully reached the summit but a storm had delayed their long ascent and made conditions particularly difficult. In preparation for their descent, which should not have been difficult, the party unroped.

Benner led his men down the mountain, where the track was snowy, icy and slippery. At one point, Sapper Phillips, who was following Benner down, missed his footing and began to slide down a steep snow slope. Seeing his comrade in difficulty, Benner did not hesitate for a moment. Leaving his own safe position, he leapt on to the open slope where he caught the falling man. He now tried to hold Phillips with one hand and, at the same time to dig his ice axe into the snow. However, he was unable to get a grip and the two men started to slide down together. Eventually, they disappeared to their deaths over an even steeper area of the mountain. Benner was just twenty-two.

His GC was announced on 17 June 1958 when his citation ended: 'In making his attempt to intercept Sapper Phillips this gallant young officer took, as he well knew, a desperate risk. As the two gathered speed down the slope he must have realised that he could save himself only by releasing his grasp on Sapper Phillips' arm but he did not do so. He held on to the last, struggling to obtain a grip in the snow with his feet and axe. With supreme courage and devotion he sacrificed his life endeavouring to save his companion.'

There are memorials to Benner in the Austrian ski resort of Kals and at Merton College. Appropriately, the Benner family motto is 'Forti et fideli nihil difficile' (To the brave and faithful, nothing is difficult).

HENRY WILLIAM STEVENS

Rank/title: Police Constable (later Chief Inspector)
Unit/occupation: Metropolitan Police
DATE OF BRAVERY: 29 MARCH 1958
GAZETTED: 21 OCTOBER 1958

Henry Stevens was born in Upton Park, east London, on 24 January 1928. One of six children, his father died when he was six. Stevens went to school at Bow Central, but during the Second World War was evacuated to Worcestershire. In 1945, aged seventeen, Stevens joined the Fleet Air Arm, in which he served for seven years. In 1949, he married and the couple later had a son and a daughter. In January 1953, he joined the Metropolitan Police and Stevens thrived on the career switch.

On 29 March 1958, Stevens was on duty in plain clothes with two other officers in a police car in Bromley, Kent. They received a radio message shortly before 8 p.m. to go to a nearby house where the burglar alarm had been set off. Once they reached the house, two officers went to the front while Stevens went to the rear where he found a high fence between the road and the property. As he walked towards the back garden, a man appeared from behind the fence just five yards in front of him. Stevens shouted that he was a police officer and called for the man to stop. The man, however, ran off and Stevens pursued him. After some seventy-five yards, the man stopped, turned and pointed a gun at the unarmed officer. Even though he threatened to shoot, Stevens kept running at the man. When Stevens was almost level with him, the man fired and the bullet struck Stevens in the mouth, shattering his teeth and part of his jawbone. Despite his injuries, Stevens hurled himself at the man, wrenched the gun from him and pinned him against some railings. The criminal stopped struggling and intimated that he would yield, but then suddenly he ran off again along the road. Stevens picked himself up and once again pursued the man. After the man had run some forty yards he doubled back and tried to pass the officer in the road. Yet again, Stevens hurled himself at the man and threw his arms around him. However, the criminal struggled free, leaving his jacket and coat in the officer's hands. Stevens set off in pursuit once again, but this time collapsed, exhausted and injured. The jacket and coat were later traced to the man, who was also recognised by Stevens from photographs. Ronald Easterbrook, a known criminal, was arrested eleven days after the shooting.

Stevens, who was then aged thirty, made a good recovery from his injuries. He was awarded the GC on 21 October 1958 when his citation ended: 'Constable Stevens displayed courage of the highest order in disregarding a threat with a firearm, closing with a gunman after being shot in the mouth and, although seriously injured, continuing in his efforts to arrest the criminal.' Easterbrook later denied attempting to murder the officer but admitted intent to cause grievous bodily harm. At the Central Criminal Court in May 1958, he was jailed for ten years for the crime and for a further six years, to run concurrently, for other offences.

Stevens continued to serve in the Met with distinction and enjoyed two periods with the Flying Squad and one with the Serious Crime Squad. In 1971, he served in Northern Ireland for eight months at the height of the IRA's terrorist activities. His last job in the force was as a chief inspector investigating complaints against the police. Stevens retired from the police in January 1983 and became security manager of the Sainsbury's supermarket chain for a decade.

Nearly three decades after the shooting, Stevens wrote an article for *Police Review* which appeared in the January 1987 edition. He recalled:

On Saturday 29 March 1958 I was on duty as a PC Aide to CID and was posted in plainclothes to the 'P' Division 'Q' car. At about 8pm a radio call went out to the local Bromley R/T [road traffic] car regarding 'suspects on premises' at a house called

'Genden' in Bickley Park Road. Being in Bromley and knowing the location well, we decided to assist and attend.

We arrived at the scene first, a large house, set back from the road at the end of a gravel 'U shaped' drive, and situated on the corner of Bickley Park Road and St George's Road. Whilst both the other two members of my car's crew ran down the drive to the house, I decided to cover the rear of the premises and ran down St George's Road, which was a small, unmade gravel road, illuminated with the old-fashioned gas lamp posts.

As I ran down the road, I saw a man climbing over the wooden fence from 'Genden'. As he jumped down, I shouted: 'I am a police officer: stop.' The man took no notice and ran down St George's Road towards the railway bridge. I chased after him and was gaining on him. When I was about three or four yards from him, he half-turned, pointed a gun at me and shouted, 'Stop or you'll get this.' I ignored his threat, and edged to within three or four feet of him, when he raised his gun and fired. I remember clearly seeing a flash, hearing a report and, at the same time, my face seemed to explode. I momentarily saw stars and I recall tasting blood.

I recall saying to myself: get the gun, this man means business! So I threw myself at him and during a struggle managed to grab the muzzle of the gun in my right hand and held him with my left hand round his neck. During the struggle that ensued I was able to twist the gun out of his hand. He then eased off struggling and said, 'All right, I've had enough.' Believing him, I also eased off a bit. I welcomed it as I was beginning to feel a bit groggy. I was behind him at this stage, with my left arm still around his neck, when he suddenly put his right hand behind him and grabbed and squeezed my testicles. The surprise and the pain of this caused me to jump back and he slipped my grasp and ran back up the road towards Bickley Park Road.

Again I chased after him, by now bleeding extensively from my mouth, in which I could feel bits of broken teeth. To my surprise, when he had gone some 40 or 50 yards back up St

George's Road he suddenly stopped, turned around, started to come back towards me and tried to pass me, first on my left side and then on my right side, but each time I blocked his path.

As I blocked his path, we stood face to face about five to six feet apart, me with blood streaming from my face and covering my shirt and jacket. I said to him, 'You bastard, I'll know you again wherever you go. I'll get you.' Under the gas lamp, I must have looked a pretty sight, because he seemed to freeze for a few seconds. Then [he] appeared to compose himself and ran past me on my right hand side. I managed to grab him as he did this, but after a brief struggle he broke free and as he ran back towards the railway bridge I was able to grab him again. He pulled away from me – I was really feeling groggy and all at this stage – and I managed to grab the collar of his coat and jacket and held on for grim death. He kept going and dragged me along the road, but I was determined to hang on, which I did, and in sheer desperation in order to break free he slipped off his top coat and jacket, leaving them in my grasp, and he ran off over the railway bridge. I ran after him but was obliged to give up upon reaching the bridge where I was now joined by my other two crew members.

I was taken to Bromley Hospital, where I was examined and found I had had a clean bullet hole through my lower lip, part of my lower jaw was missing, and three or four of my lower teeth had been smashed. An examination and probe of my tongue led to an immediate operation and the removal of the spent bullet from my tongue . . .

Whilst in hospital I was able to pick the man, Ronald Easterbrook, out of a number of photographs shown to me. Further, the jacket I retained was part of a two-piece suit bearing the Bermondsey Tailors name therein. Records at the tailor's revealed that only two had been made, one for a local businessman, the other for a well-known villain, Ronald Easterbrook. On 9 April 1958 Easterbrook was arrested . . .

Summing up: that night I did what 95 per cent of my colleagues would have done in the circumstances. My first reaction when he pointed a gun at me was: arrest, one for the back of the book, so to speak, the thrill of nicking a villain.

Having been shot, fear and pain never really entered into it, it was temper. I was livid – he wasn't going to do that and get away with it. No way. I'm convinced it was temper and revenge that made me keep going the way I did.

Stevens is now eighty-two and lives in Ilford, Essex, with his second wife, Jenny. As well as their two grown-up sons, the couple have a granddaughter. Stevens also has four grandsons by the daughter from his first marriage.

12

THE AWARDS OF 1960–9

RAYMOND TASMAN DONOGHUE
Rank/title: Mr
Unit/occupation: Tram conductor
DATE OF BRAVERY: 29 APRIL 1960
GAZETTED: 11 OCTOBER 1960

Raymond Donoghue was the first – and so far only – Tasmanian recipient of the GC. He was born in Hobart, Tasmania, on 10 December 1919. After attending Albuera Street School in the city, he enlisted in the Australian Army on 14 March 1940 at Brighton, Tasmania. More than five years later, on 7 November 1945, Donoghue, a private, was discharged from the Army. After the Second World War, he had a succession of jobs including working as a cleaner with the Metropolitan Transport Trust in 1959. In early April 1969, when married with six children and with his wife once again pregnant, he switched to a job as a tram conductor in Hobart.

Donoghue, who was nicknamed Puddin, had only been doing the job for three weeks when he was the conductor on a tram which was involved in a major collision with another vehicle. The tram went out of control and ran backwards, rapidly gaining speed, on a steep hill. Realising the danger to passengers, he shepherded them to the front of the compartment, furthest from any likely impact. If he had leapt off the tram, or also gone to the front, his life too would have been saved.

However, Donoghue instead went into the driver's cab where he continuously rang the alarm bell to warn the busy traffic of the dangers from the out-of-control tram. He also tried in vain to apply the emergency brake in order to stop the tram racing down the hill. At the bottom of the hill, the runaway tram collided with a stationary tram. Donoghue, who was still at his 'post', was killed on impact. He was forty. However, although nobody else died, forty-three people were injured. The *Hobart Mercury* newspaper ran the story under the headline: 'The hero on tram No 131'.

Donoghue's posthumous GC was announced on 11 October 1960 when the citation ended: 'By sacrificing his life Donoghue was responsible for saving the lives of a number of other persons.' His widow, Eileen, went on to have their seventh child and, although a fund was set up for the family, times were hard for her as a single mother. She received his GC from the Governor of Tasmania, Lord Rowallan. He said of Donoghue: 'During those minutes of extraordinary selflessness and heroism . . . the light of Raymond Tasman Donoghue's life shone with more intensity than that of anyone else in Australia.' His GC is on display at the Tasmanian Museum and Art Gallery, Hobart.

JONATHAN ROGERS
Rank/title: Chief Petty Officer
Unit/occupation: Royal Australian Navy
DATE OF BRAVERY: 10 FEBRUARY 1964
GAZETTED: 19 MARCH 1965

Jonathan Rogers was born in Vroncysylite, near Llangollen, Denbighshire, Wales, on 16 September 1920. The son of a labourer and the fifth of seven children, he attended Acrefair Central School near his home village. After leaving school at fourteen, he worked in a local brickyard, while also boxing and playing football. On 22 November 1938, Rogers joined the Royal Navy. During the Second World War, he served on at least three types of motor boats – an anti-submarine boat, a torpedo boat and a launch. In 1943, he was promoted to chief petty officer. He had married on 4 April 1942 and the couple went on to have four children. Rogers was awarded the Distinguished Service Medal (DSM) on 19 September 1944 for bravery at sea in actions against enemy forces. After being discharged in 1946, Rogers worked at a colliery and also built pre-fabricated homes. However, he longed to return to sea and he hoped for a better life, too, in Australia. So in 1950, Rogers applied to join the Royal Australian Navy. He was accepted on 6 July 1950 and taken on initially as an able seaman after which he and his young family settled in New South Wales.

On 10 February 1964, Chief Petty Officer Rogers was serving in HMAS *Voyager* when she was involved in a collision with another ship, *Melbourne*, in Jervis Bay off the Australian coast. It was a major incident and *Voyager* was soon sinking. At the time of the collision, Rogers had been organising a game of tombola in the ship's cafeteria. Rogers helped some fifty to sixty men evacuate from the cafeteria. But it was impossible for many more to escape and they soon knew their fate. Rogers calmly led them in prayer and hymns until the ship went down. One of the eighty-two victims, Rogers died aged forty-three.

His posthumous GC was announced on 19 March 1965 when the citation read:

> In recognition of his outstanding gallantry and devotion to duty in saving lives at sea when HMAS *Voyager* was sunk after collision on 10th February 1964, for maintaining the morale of junior ratings in great adversity, for organising the escape of as many as possible, and for supporting the spirits of those who could not escape and encouraging them to meet death alongside himself with dignity and honour. He upheld the highest traditions of service at sea and of his rating of Chief Petty Officer (Coxswain).

Rogers' posthumous GC was later presented to his widow, Lorraine. On 10 February 1995 – thirty-one years to the day after the incident – Rogers' daughter, Rhonda Jones, presented her father's GC and other medals to the Australian nation, where his awards are now on display in the Hall of Valour in Canberra.

MICHAEL JOSEPH MUNNELLY
Rank/title: Mr
Unit/occupation: Journalist
DATE OF BRAVERY: 24–25 DECEMBER 1964
GAZETTED: 29 JUNE 1965

Michael Munnelly was born in St Helens, Merseyside, on 17 April 1941. He was the son of a contracting plasterer, who also worked as an auxiliary fireman. Munnelly was a journalist for the *People* newspaper and was based in Cardiff. However, in 1964, he had gone to London to spend Christmas with his brother, James.

On Christmas Eve, a gang of fourteen youths, mainly teenagers, went on a drinking spree in Kentish Town, north London. They then travelled in a van to nearby Regent's Park Road to a flat where two of them had been invited to a party. The youths were extremely rowdy and were swearing so they were refused entry to the flat en masse. While some responded by attacking the occupier, others went to a dairy opposite. There they took milk bottles from the crates and started bombarding the flat with them, resulting in many windows of the property being broken. The window of the shop next door was also smashed. Onlookers were too frightened to interfere when the youths went on a wild, violent rampage at about 12.30 a.m. on Christmas Day.

In an attempt to protect his property, William Griffiths, the dairyman, went into the street where he was immediately attacked: butted, kicked and knifed in the groin. Michael Munnelly, James Munnelly and a friend, Donald Smith, were in a third-floor flat and, hearing the commotion, looked out and saw the dairyman being kicked on the floor. All three men decided they must go and help the man so they ran down into the street. They initially detained two of the assailants but Michael Munnelly was hit on the head by another attacker and released the man he was holding. The gang's van, which had earlier left the scene, then returned and was followed into a turning by Smith. In an attempt to stop the van, Smith banged on the side of the vehicle and, when it stopped, he grabbed a youth who was sitting next to the driver.

The passenger shouted for help and suddenly the back door of the van sprang open and a group of youths, some armed with knives, attacked Smith and kicked him senseless. Michael Munnelly then went to his friend's rescue. Bottles were thrown at him, he was kicked and, finally, he received a fatal stab wound to the left abdomen. The journalist was twenty-three. The youths then fled, leaving a scene of carnage.

Munnelly's GC was posthumously announced on 29 June 1965 when the citation ended: 'Munnelly saw his friend being attacked with knives and immediately went to his rescue. Within a few minutes he was dead. He had given his life to save that of his friend.' Smith, the brothers' friend, was awarded the George Medal, and Griffiths, the dairyman, received the British Empire Medal.

After a major police investigation, several youths were charged with various offences. Fred Bishop, aged eighteen, was found guilty of murdering Munnelly and was sentenced to life imprisonment. Most youths arrested were charged with causing an affray, while others were charged with possession of an offensive weapon and wounding.

In a joint award, Munnelly and Smith also received the Binney Memorial Medal. This was awarded in memory of Captain Ralph Binney, who died in 1944, aged fifty-six, trying to thwart a getaway car after a robbery. The Binney Medal, designed in 1948, was awarded to 'the British Citizen, not being a member of the police force or any other force maintaining order, who performs the bravest act in each year in support of law and order within the Metropolitan and City police area.'

Munnelly is believed to be the only recipient of the GC also to be awarded the Binney Medal.

BRIAN SPILLETT
Rank/title: Mr
Unit/occupation: Fitter
DATE OF BRAVERY: 9 JANUARY 1965
GAZETTED: 29 JUNE 1965

Brian Spillett was born in Edmonton, north London, in the third quarter of 1937 (his exact date of birth is not known). He worked as a fitter, as well as being a member of the 298th Parachute Regiment, Royal Horse Artillery (Territorial Army). He married in 1963 and the couple went on to have a daughter.

On 9 January 1965, at around 5.30 a.m. and shortly before dawn, a fire broke out in a house in Waltham Cross, Hertfordshire. Living in the property were a couple, their child and the child's grandfather. The blaze was already fierce when the family were roused but, with great difficulty, the wife, child and grandfather were able to escape. By the time Spillett arrived, having being woken by the commotion, only the father was left in the house, apparently trapped on the first floor.

On being informed of the situation, Spillett, who was only partially dressed, raced straight into the flames, brushing aside every attempt to restrain him. By now flames were shooting from both floors. Spillett managed to reach the first floor but was unable to get to the father. With the house now an inferno, Spillett escaped by jumping from a first-floor window. He was only found some time later in the garden of an adjoining house; he had received extensive burns and other serious injuries. He died in hospital a week later, aged twenty-seven.

Spillett's posthumous GC was announced on 29 June 1965 when his citation ended: 'Mr Spillett sacrificed his life in an effort to save that of a neighbour.'

WALLACE ARNOLD OAKES

Rank/title: Mr
Unit/occupation: Engine driver, British Rail
DATE OF BRAVERY: 5 JUNE 1965
GAZETTED: 19 OCTOBER 1965

Wally Oakes was born in Nantwich, Cheshire, on 23 April 1932. The son of a labourer and one of two children, he was educated at Acton Church of England Primary School near Nantwich. In 1947, around his eighteenth birthday, he joined the London, Midland & Scottish Railway as a locomotive cleaner based in Crewe. Three years later, he was called up for National Service and served for two years with the Royal Electrical and Mechanical Engineers. On his return to the railways, he was promoted to fireman and, later, driver. Oakes married on 25 August 1956.

On 5 June 1965, Oakes was driving a relief passenger train from Crewe. The steam-hauled train consisted of ten carriages liberally filled with passengers. Seven miles after leaving Crewe, and with the train travelling at sixty mph, the engine cab suddenly became filled with smoke and flames which had blown back from the firebox. The fireman managed to climb through the cab window and on to the steps of the engine where he extinguished his burning clothes by rubbing himself against the plating. He was unable to see into the cab but he realised the brakes had been applied by the driver and so he waited for the train to stop.

Once the train stopped near Winsford, the fireman climbed back into the cab. Initially, he could not see Oakes but then he saw him lying on a slope in front of the cab. His clothing was severely burned and he had suffered eighty per cent burns to his body. Oakes was dazed but he was still conscious and able to speak. The first person to inspect the controls of the cab was the fireman from another train who had stopped to pick up the injured men. He discovered that the brakes were fully applied, the regulator partly open and the blower valve open. The fireman's assessment was that Oakes, rather than escape from the cab as soon as the blow-back had occurred, had been responsible for all three actions to prevent the train careering out of control. Oakes never recovered from his injuries and died in Wythenshawe Hospital, Manchester, on 12 June 1965, aged thirty-three.

His posthumous GC was announced on 15 October 1965 when the citation ended:

> The position in which he [Oakes] was found shows that he did not leave the engine until it had come to rest. Mr Oakes must have been aware that to remain at the controls of the locomotive was a grave risk to his own life. Nevertheless, he applied the brakes fully and took all the measures he could to reduce the effects of the blow-back. Mr Oakes' gallant action showed that his first thought was for the safety of his passengers, and he thereby sacrificed his life, for he died a week later. He set an outstanding example of devotion to duty and of public service.

Oakes was also awarded the Bronze Medal of the Carnegie Hero Trust for his bravery. Two locomotives were later named after him and there are memorial plaques for the courageous driver at Crewe railway station and his former primary school.

ANTHONY JOHN GLEDHILL

Rank/title: Police Constable (later Detective Sergeant)
Unit/occupation: Metropolitan Police Force
DATE OF BRAVERY: 25 AUGUST 1966
GAZETTED: 23 MAY 1967

Tony Gledhill was born in Holbury, Hampshire, on 10 March 1938. The eldest of three children, his father served in the RAF during and after the Second World War. When young Gledhill was just three, and staying at a cottage in Fawley, he remembers

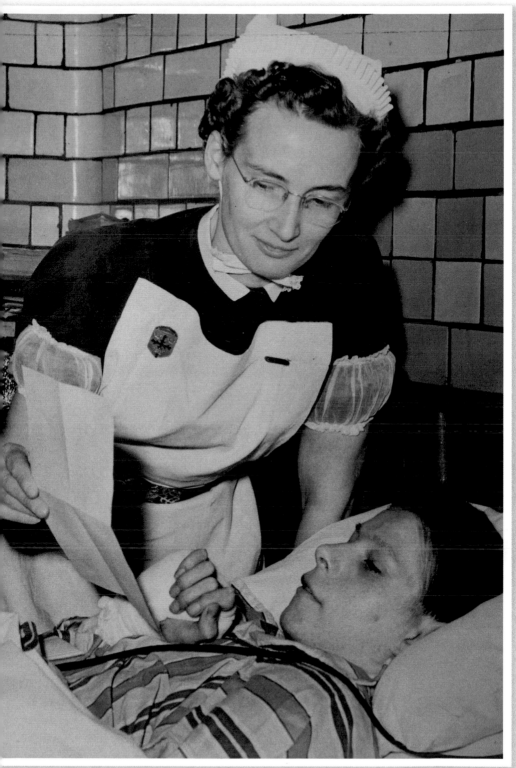

n Bamford is pictured in Nottingham General Hospital with Sister Marjorie Odey, who nursed him back
health after he nearly died from severe burns received in rescuing his two younger brothers from a fire at
home in October 1952. Then just fifteen, Bamford, who is known widely as Jack, remains the youngest
son to be awarded the GC. Bamford is now aged seventy-three.

Police Constable (later Chief Inspector) Henry Stevens was awarded the GC in October 1958. In March of that year, Stevens, who was unarmed, was shot in the mouth, after tackling a gunman following a burglary. Stevens survived the attack and is now aged eighty-two.

Policeman's son Detective Constable (later Detective Sergeant) Frederick Fairfax was awarded the GC in January 1953 after an incident two months earlier in south London in which he was wounded and another officer was killed by two armed burglars. One of the offenders, Derek Bentley, aged nineteen, was hanged after being convicted of murder.

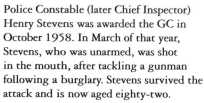

Tram conductor Raymond Donoghue, a keen sportsman, was awarded a posthumc GC in October 1960 after refusing to abandon his 'post' in a crisis in April that year. After the brakes failed on the tram i Tasmania, he sounded the alarm and herd passengers away from the point of impact Donoghue, aged forty, was the only one to be killed in the resulting crash, although forty-three passengers were injured.

This was the scene of the tram crash in April 1960 that saw Raymond Donoghue, the conductor, become the first – and so far only – Tasmanian recipient of the GC. A veteran of the Second World War, Donoghue was hailed as 'The hero on tram No 131' by his local paper, the *Hobart Mercury*.

Police Constable (later Detective Sergeant) Tony Gledhill was awarded the GC in May 1967 for his gallantry in pursuing and tackling, along with colleagues, five armed raiders in south London in August 1966. Gledhill, who was unarmed, survived his ordeal, despite needing hospital treatment for his injuries, and is now aged seventy-two.

Police Constable (later Inspector) Carl Walker was shot and injured after pursuing five raiders in his patrol car after an armed robbery in Blackpool in August 1971. He was awarded the GC in November 1972 along with the same posthumous award for Superintendent Gerald Richardson, who was killed during the same shoot-out. Walker recovered from his gunshot injuries and is now aged seventy-six.

Inspector (later Chief
Superintendent) Jim Beaton
(*centre*) is pictured with two
police colleagues who helped
him catch a gunman who was
trying to kidnap Princess Anne
in central London in March
1974. Beaton, who was her
protection officer, was awarded
his GC in September that year
after recovering from gunshot
wounds. He is now sixty-seven

Major (later Lieutenant
Colonel) George Styles (*centre*)
of the Royal Army Ordnance
Corps (RAOC), was awarded
the GC for defusing two
complex bombs planted by
terrorists in the Europa Hotel
in Belfast in October 1971.
He was awarded his GC in
January the following year. He
is pictured with two George
Medal recipients at an RAOC
dinner in October 1973.

The parents and sister of Captain Robert Nairac, of the Grenadier Guards, are pictured with his posthumous GC after receiving his award at Buckingham Palace in May 1979. The charismatic Nairac was working undercover in South Armagh when he was taken from a Republican pub, brutally tortured and shot dead in May 1977.

Warrant Officer Class 1 (Staff Sergeant Major) Barry Johnson, of the Royal Army Ordnance Corps, was awarded the GC for bravery after almost losing his life when a terrorist mortar weapon exploded in his face as he was handling it in October 1989. He recovered to receive his award in November the next year. He is now fifty-eight.

PRESS ASSOCIATION

Trooper (later Lance Corporal of Horse) Chris Finney is pictured in February 2004 with Lance Corporal Alan Tudball, whose life he saved in Iraq in March 2003. Finney was awarded his GC for braving 'friendly fire' and became, at nineteen, the youngest serviceman to receive the GC. He is now twenty-six.

Captain (later Major) Pete Norton is pictured with his Tom, then three, in November 2006 after his investitu at Buckingham Palace. Norton, a bomb disposal expert with the Royal Logistic Corps, received horrendous injuries in Iraq from an exploding Improvised Explosiv Device but his concerns were still for his men rather tha himself. He is now forty-seven.

The Queen met two GC recipients, Colonel Stuart Archer, then eighty-nine and the oldest living recipient of the award, and Trooper Chris Finney, who was just nineteen when he was awarded the decoration, at the opening of the Ministry of Defence's new main building in London in October 2004. Both GC holders are still alive, aged ninety-five and twenty-six respectively.

Staff Sergeant (later Warrant Officer Class 2) Kim Hughes is pictured with his citation after learning he had received the GC in March 2010. The bomb disposal expert with the Royal Logistic Corps received his award for incredible gallantry in Afghanistan in dealing with complex Improvised Explosive Devices in August 2009. He is now thirty-one and expects to tour Afghanistan again.

The Queen is pictured presenting the GC to Lance Corporal Matt Croucher, a Royal Marine, at Buckingham Palace in October 2008. He received his award for falling on a booby-trapped grenade that he had triggered while on a mission to a Taliban compound in Afghanistan in February 2008. He saved his comrades' lives by smothering the explosion with his day sack, and yet he received only minor injuries. He is now twenty-six.

Christina Schmid, the widow of Staff Sergeant Olaf 'Oz' Schmid, of the Royal Logistic Corps, is pictured with her husband's posthumous GC. She received the award from the Queen at Buckingham Palace in June 2010, when she spoke of her pride towards her husband.

Staff Sergeant Olaf 'Oz' Schmid, a bomb disposal expert with the Royal Logistic Corps, was described as 'the bravest and most courageous man I have ever met' by his Commanding Officer. He was awarded the GC in March 2010 for repeated gallantry in Afghanistan which cost him his life in October 2009.

GETTY IMAGES

repeatedly sheltering under a heavy kitchen table during air raids on Southampton. Gledhill attended schools in Southbourne and Westbourne, both in Hampshire, before attending Doncaster Technical High School in South Yorkshire because of his father's RAF posting. In April 1956, aged eighteen, Gledhill started at Hendon Training School in north London as a police cadet. The next year, the day after his nineteenth birthday, Gledhill was sworn in as a police constable in the Metropolitan Police. Later the same year, he attended the scene of the Lewisham train crash, when ninety people were killed and 173 injured. It was a sight of carnage and horror that he would never forget. Gledhill married in September 1958 and the couple went on to have two children. In late 1966, Gledhill successfully applied for entry to the Criminal Investigation Department (CID) and he started in January 1967 as a temporary detective constable in Lewisham.

On 25 August 1966 – just thirteen days after Harry Roberts, the notorious police killer, had murdered three officers in Shepherd's Bush – Gledhill, then aged twenty-nine, was on duty in south-east London, in a patrol car, call sign 'Papa One'. He and another constable, PC Terry McFall, were told over their police radio that five suspects in a car had been seen acting suspiciously in Creekside Street, Deptford. In fact, a schoolboy looking out of the window had seen them putting on balaclavas and then testing a firearm so, through his father, he raised the alarm. As the police car arrived at the scene moments later, the vehicle they were looking for drove past them on the opposite side of the road apparently en route for a wages' heist at a nearby factory. The police car gave chase and the vehicle drove recklessly at speed on the wrong side of the road and then the wrong way down a one-way street. The chase, at speeds of up to seventy mph, lasted for five miles and over nearly fifteen minutes. During this time, the occupants of the car fired fifteen shots from a sawn-off shotgun and two revolvers. At one point, three different gunmen were firing, two from the rear passenger windows, one from the front passenger seat. Three times pellets from the shotgun hit the windscreen of the police vehicle. Finally, at a junction, the escaping car careered into a lorry.

All five men fled from their car; one, with a pistol in his hand, ran into the yard of a transport contractor. As the police car came into the yard, the men ran towards it and the one with the pistol held it to Gledhill's head. The two officers, both unarmed, were ordered to get out of the vehicle or be shot. The gunman then got into the driving seat of the police car and prepared to make his getaway. However, as Gledhill was backing away, the man reversed away from the gates towards him, pointing his pistol at the officer as he did so. The gunman momentarily turned his head away from Gledhill as he struggled to put the automatic car into gear and, as he did so, Gledhill grasped the criminal's gun hand. As the vehicle started to drive off, Gledhill held on to the car window with his left hand, still holding the gun hand with his right. While this was happening, McFall ran along the road to try to get a group of men to block the road with a lorry.

By now, Gledhill was still hanging on to the window of the car but the vehicle had picked up speed, dragging the police officer along the road. However, the front tyre then burst and the police car veered across the road into parked cars. Gledhill was hurled to one side but regained his feet. McFall then arrived at the passenger door with his truncheon raised and started raining blows on the criminal. With the man distracted, Gledhill tried to get at him through the driver's door. However, just as he reached it, the driver's door was pushed open violently, knocking him to the ground. The criminal got out, and, as both officers approached him, he fired a shot that went between them and struck a wall behind them. Then he tried to fire another shot but the officers heard a 'click' as the gun jammed and they rushed towards him. McFall struck the criminal with his truncheon as Gledhill grabbed his right hand and took away the gun. A struggle ensued in which the two officers attempted to restrain the man as he tried to reach inside his overall for an automatic pistol. The two officers eventually succeeded in overpowering the man before Gledhill went by ambulance for hospital treatment.

Later, in February 1967, four of the criminals, including the notorious John McVicar, were tried and found not guilty of attempted murder. However, they were convicted of using a firearm with intent to endanger life, conspiracy to rob and other firearms offences. All received long jail sentences – and the boy who had originally alerted the police to their suspicious behaviour was awarded £15. At the end of the hearing, Mr Justice Hinchcliffe ordered the two officers to stand before the court and said: 'I think your conduct in dealing with these armed bandits is beyond praise. Both of you displayed courage of a high order and you carried out your difficult duties in a way that has earned you the respect and admiration of all right-thinking persons. I commend you both and I direct that this commendation be sent to the appropriate authority.'

On 23 May 1967, it was announced that Gledhill had been awarded the GC, while McFall was awarded the George Medal. Gledhill's citation ended: 'They [the two officers] had faced a sustained firearm attack and from the early stages knew the risks they ran of being killed or seriously injured.' Gledhill's investiture took place on 11 July 1967 at Buckingham Palace, which his wife and their two children attended to see him receive his GC from the Queen. Later that year, he was voted one of twelve 'Men of the Year' and attended a lunch in November at the Savoy Hotel in London hosted by the British Council for Rehabilitation of the Disabled.

In 1976, Gledhill transferred to Z Division in south London, and shortly afterwards was promoted to sergeant. Gledhill retired in March 1987, handing in his warrant card 'with a tear in my eye'. He later worked in security and auditing until 1997 when he retired completely.

In an interview at his home in West Sussex, Gledhill recalled the day he almost died forty-four years earlier. He told me:

> I just wasn't prepared to let them get away. I was determined they should be caught. I didn't have time to stop and think – I just went after them. I stayed about fifty yards behind their vehicle most of the time, hoping they would crash on the wet roads. I was hoping their driver would make a mistake or I would get help from other [police] units. But I think someone was looking after me that day. I had three particular pieces of good fortune. Just past Rotherhithe police station there was a sharp right-hand turn into Southwark Park. For some reason, I stopped and edged forward and they were waiting for me. They had stopped their car to ambush me: there were two leaning out with their guns but I stayed back. The second bit of good luck was when the bandit put a gun to my head. I instinctively put my hands across each other in the shape of a cross which somehow stopped him from shooting me. My third bit of good luck was when he drove off in the police car. For no apparent reason – because there were forensic tests done later – the front tyre of the police car blew just as he was driving off with me clinging on to the window.
>
> It was also fortunate that day that no member of the public was hurt either from a shot or being struck by one of the speeding cars. One guy of about nineteen was coming out of Surrey Docks tube station when the bandit fired from his car and he could feel the whoosh of air as the bullet narrowly missed his head. He was very lucky. It was only when I got home that night that perhaps it hit home how close I had come to being killed. Once I got back from Guy's Hospital, I talked all night to my wife about what had happened. But I still went to work the next morning.

Today, at seventy-two, Gledhill, is a keen DIY enthusiast and gardener, and he enjoys playing bowls and golf. He and his wife Marie have seven grandchildren. Gledhill is the Treasurer of the

Victoria Cross and George Cross Association and a member, and former President, of the Association of ex-CID Officers of the Metropolitan Police. He published his memoirs, *A Gun at My Head: The George Cross, East End Gunmen and Thirty Years in Blue*, four years ago. The final chapter opens: 'Even to this day, whenever I watch a film at the cinema, or on television, and see that a Police Officer has been killed, leaving a widow and family, I think "there but for the grace of God go I". It hits me even more when it happens in real life – and there have been a number over the past few years.'

BARBARA JANE HARRISON
Rank/title: Miss
Unit/occupation: Stewardess, British Overseas Airways Corporation
DATE OF BRAVERY: 8 APRIL 1968
GAZETTED: 8 AUGUST 1969

Jane Harrison, as she was always known, is one of only four women to have been awarded the GC and the only one to receive it for gallantry for actions other than during the Second World War. Harrison was born on 24 May 1945 in Bradford, Yorkshire. Her mother died while she and her older sister were still young. Harrison attended Newby County Primary School in Bradford and then Scarborough High School for Girls. Vivacious and full of fun, Harrison joined a bank in Doncaster after leaving school. She then worked as a nanny in San Francisco, California, and in Switzerland before joining the British Overseas Airways Corporation (BOAC) in June 1966. At the time, Harrison wanted to travel and liked meeting people.

On 8 April 1968, Harrison was a stewardess on a BOAC Boeing 707 passenger jet taking off from Heathrow airport with 126 passengers and crew on board. About a minute after take-off from Runway 28 Left, number two engine caught fire. Just two and a half minutes later, and shortly after the burning engine had fallen off, the aircraft made an emergency landing

271

on Runway 05 Right back at Heathrow. By the time the plane landed, the fire on the port wing had intensified.

In an emergency, Harrison's duties included helping the steward in the aft section to open the appropriate rear door and to inflate the escape chute. Then she was expected to assist passengers at the rear to leave in an orderly manner. When the aircraft landed and stopped, Harrison and the steward opened the rear galley door and inflated the chute. However, the chute became twisted on the way down and so the steward had to climb down and straighten it before it could be used. The steward could not then return to the burning aircraft.

Harrison was therefore left alone to carry out the task of shepherding passengers to the rear door and helping them out of the aircraft. She encouraged some to jump and, for their own wellbeing, pushed others out on to the chute. When huge flames eventually prevented further escapes from the tail of the aircraft, Harrison redirected passengers to another exit while she remained at her post. However, she then realised that an elderly disabled passenger was still seated in one of the last two rows. Harrison went to the woman's aid and was therefore unable to escape when both apparently became overcome by the smoke and flames. Harrison's body was found close to that of the elderly woman. She was just twenty-two when she died. Passengers praised her courage and calmness during the evacuation.

Her posthumous GC was announced on 8 August 1968 when her citation ended: 'Miss Harrison was a very brave young lady who gave her life in her utter devotion to duty.' The chief steward on the flight, Neville Davis-Gordon, received the British Empire Medal for Gallantry (Civil Division). An official inquiry into the accident, in which five people died and thirty-eight were injured, made three safety recommendations.

Later, in 1971, Harrison was also awarded the Flight Safety Foundation Heroism Award. Established in 1968, the award recognised the bravery of aircraft crew and ground personnel whose actions exceeded the requirements of their job. Memorial plaques were put up in Harrison's honour at Scarborough High School for Girls, St Laurence's Church in Scalby, near Scarborough, and in the chapel at Heathrow airport.

13

THE AWARDS OF 1970–89

MICHAEL WILLETTS

Rank/title: Sergeant
Unit/occupation: 3rd Battalion, Parachute Regiment
DATE OF BRAVERY: 25 MAY 1971
GAZETTED: 22 JUNE 1971

Michael Willetts was born in Sutton-in-Ashfield, Nottingham-shire, on 13 August 1943. After leaving school, he worked temporarily in Summit Colliery, near Nottingham. He then volunteered for the Parachute Regiment, joining on 20 March 1962. After passing the selection course and qualifying for the regiment, he joined 3 Para. He married on 9 October 1965 and the couple went on to have two children. In January 1967, Willetts was promoted to corporal and, in January 1970, raised to sergeant. He proved to be a talented radio operator who was particularly good at Morse code. He was chosen as the radio operator in the Battalion's Rover Group. After serving in Malta, Sergeant Willetts was sent with 3 Para to Northern Ireland in 1971. Two years into the Troubles, the regiment was based in Armagh and, later, West Belfast.

At 8.24 p.m. on 25 May 1971, a terrorist entered the reception hall of Springfield Road police station in Belfast. He was carrying a suitcase with a smoking fuse protruding from it. The man dumped the suitcase on the floor and quickly fled. In the reception area were Patrick Gray and his daughter, Colette, four, and Elizabeth Cummings and her son, Carl, also four, along with some Royal Ulster Constabulary police officers. One of the officers saw the smoking suitcase and raised the alarm while others started to organise the evacuation of the reception hall, with people eventually leaving through a door at the back of the building.

Willetts was on duty in the inner hall when he heard the alarm. He sent a non commissioned officer (NCO) upstairs to the first floor to warn those working there, while he went to the reception area where a police officer was ushering the four members of the public to safety. Willetts insisted on holding the door open while everyone passed through it and then stood in the doorway so that he could shield those rushing for cover. The suitcase bomb then exploded with a fearsome force, mortally wounding Willetts, who was twenty-seven.

Willetts' posthumous GC was announced less than a month later on 22 June 1971 when his citation ended:

> His duty did not require him to enter the threatened area: his post was elsewhere. He knew well, after 4 months' service in Belfast, the peril of going towards a terrorist bomb but he did not hesitate to do so. All those approaching the door from the far side agree that if they had had to check [stop] to open the door they would have perished. Even when they reached the rear passage, Sergeant Willetts waited, placing his body as a screen to shelter them. By this considered act of bravery, he risked – and lost – his life for those of the adults and children. His selflessness, his courage are beyond praise.

In a witness statement, Patrick Gray, one of those in the reception area, described Willetts' courage. 'We all rushed as fast as we could through the Enquiry Office towards the door at the other end of the room. I remember this young Sergeant standing in the door and holding it open for us all. He was very calm and stood there until we had all moved through. I am sure that he saved our lives. He could easily have saved his own life.' A man was later charged with Willetts' murder and he was acquitted in June 1972.

STEPHEN GEORGE STYLES

Rank/title: Major (later Lieutenant Colonel)
Unit/occupation: Royal Army Ordnance Corps
DATE OF BRAVERY: 20 OCTOBER 1971
GAZETTED: 11 JANUARY 1972

George Styles, as he was better known, was born in Crawley, West Sussex, on 16 March 1928. The younger of two children, he had a serious childhood accident which meant that he had to learn to walk again. Before the Second World War, the teenage Styles used to make a modest living trapping rabbits for food and their skins. He won a scholarship to Collyers Grammar School in Horsham, West Sussex, and then won a place at King's College London. Just four days before he was due to take up his place, he received his call-up papers and joined the Royal Sussex Regiment, based at Colchester, Essex, on 10 October 1946. The following year, he was commissioned into the Royal Army Ordnance Corps (RAOC). In 1949, he tried once again to take up his place at King's College but he was told there was a three-year waiting list. He decided to stay in the Army, joining the Light Infantry before subsequently rejoining the RAOC. He married on 1 March 1952 and the couple later had three children. Styles' talents led to a series of promotions as he became an experienced bomb disposal expert. From 1969 to 1972, the first three years of the Troubles, he worked as senior ammunition technical officer in Northern Ireland and he helped to develop new equipment to combat the terrorists.

On 20 October 1971, Major Styles was called to deal with an apparently new explosive device placed in a phone booth at the Europa Hotel in Belfast, which later became a frequent IRA target. Styles went to the scene and ensured that the military and police had secured the area. He then took charge of the operation to neutralise, remove and dismantle the bomb. An assessment of the bomb revealed it was a previously unknown and complicated construction, with anti-handling devices aimed at defeating attempts to disarm it. Those tackling it knew that until the electrical circuit had been neutralised, the slightest movement could set off the bomb, a substantial device which contained between ten and fifteen pounds of explosives. Styles placed himself at great personal risk to minimise the danger to his team. However, after seven hours of planning and execution, the operation was completed successfully.

Just two days later, Styles was called to the same hotel after a second bomb was planted by terrorists. With more than thirty pounds of explosives, this bomb was larger and even more complicated than the previous one. The aim was clearly to kill the bomb disposal expert chosen to try to neutralise it. Once again, Styles coolly took control of the situation. After nine hours of intense and highly dangerous work, he successfully disarmed, removed and dismantled the bomb.

Styles's GC was announced on 11 January 1972 when his citation ended:

> As a result of his courageous and dedicated resolution, two determined and ingenious attempts by terrorists against life and property were defeated, and technical information was obtained which will help to save the lives of operators faced with such devices in future. Throughout each operation Major Styles displayed a calm resolution in control, a degree of technical skill and personal bravery in circumstances of extreme danger far beyond that of the call of duty. His work was an outstanding inspiration and example, particularly to others engaged in this dangerous type of work.

Styles went on to enjoy a distinguished career in the Army, rising to the rank of lieutenant colonel. He retired from the Army in 1972 and worked for a security company. He died in Abingdon, Oxfordshire, on 2 August 2006, aged seventy-eight.

ERROL JOHN EMANUEL

Rank/title: **Mr**
Unit/occupation: District Commissioner, Papua New Guinea
DATE OF BRAVERY: MARCH–19 AUGUST 1971
GAZETTED: 1 FEBRUARY 1972

Jack Emanuel, as he was always known, was born in Enfield, New South Wales, Australia, on 13 December 1918. He went to school in Sydney, and later worked as, first, a police officer and, later, as a fireman. However, after the Second World War, he went to Papua New Guinea, off northern Australia, as a patrol officer.

In July 1969, he was given special duties as District Commissioner for the East New Britain area. There were some hostile indigenous groups there but Emanuel insisted on travelling alone to meet them, often at night, in order to build up their trust. For two years, he encouraged some 70,000 Tolai people to discuss their problems in a peaceful manner. However, he was often the target of death threats. On several occasions, Emanuel encountered public confrontation and scenes of imminent violence between police and protesters. He often placed himself in great danger by leaving the protection of the police ranks to try to pacify the dissidents and time and again his courage averted bloodshed.

On 19 August 1971, at a plantation on the Gazelle peninsula, Emanuel again took on the role of peacemaker in the presence of hostile locals. Some of the Tolai had donned warpaint to show their open hostility. At the invitation of some of the dissidents, Emanuel left the protection of the police and went alone down a bush track. His aim was to discuss the local grievances and negotiate a peaceful resolution. However, he was struck down and killed. He was fifty-two.

His posthumous GC was announced on 1 February 1972 when his citation ended: 'Mr Emanuel's continued acts of the most conspicuous courage over a long period of time in circumstances of extreme danger, and in complete disregard of threats against his life, were in the highest traditions of bravery and sacrifice carried out beyond the call of duty.' There is a memorial in Emanuel's honour in Canberra, Australia.

GERALD IRVING RICHARDSON
Rank/title: Superintendent
Unit/occupation: Lancashire Constabulary
DATE OF BRAVERY: 23 AUGUST 1971
GAZETTED: 13 NOVEMBER 1972

CARL WALKER
Rank/title: Police Constable (later Inspector)
Unit/occupation: Lancashire Constabulary
DATE OF BRAVERY: 23 AUGUST 1971
GAZETTED: 13 NOVEMBER 1972

Gerry Richardson was born on 2 November 1932 in Norbreck, Blackpool, Lancashire. One of two children and the son of a painter and decorator, he attended Blackpool Grammar School. He joined the Police Cadet Service, in the Blackpool Borough, in August 1949, aged sixteen, before doing two years' National Service from 1951 in the Royal Military Police. He joined Blackpool Borough Police in 1953 and was promoted rapidly so that he became a superintendent in 1958, two years after he got married. After the Blackpool force was amalgamated with the Lancashire Constabulary, Richardson took control of the Blackpool sub-district of the new force and was greatly involved with the entire community.

Carl Walker was born on 31 March 1933 in Kendal, Westmorland (now part of Cumbria). The son of a paper mill worker and the middle child of seven, he went to school in Burneside, near Blackpool, before attending Kendal Grammar ' School. He left school at fifteen and went to work as an apprentice joiner. Aged eighteen, he began his National Service, spending two years in the RAF Police. After completing his National Service, he joined the Lancashire Constabulary in 1953 as a 'bobby on the beat', aged twenty. He married two years later, and the couple went on to have a son. After just eighteen months, Walker left the police, disillusioned with the pay and conditions, and moved to Cumbria. After working again as a joiner for a wood-turning company, he spent time in an asbestos factory – long before the dangers of working in asbestos were known. In 1959, he joined the Blackpool Borough force. When, nine years later, his force amalgamated with the Lancashire Constabulary, he ended up working once again for his original employers.

At 9.40 a.m. on 23 August 1971, PC Walker, then aged thirty-eight, was on duty in Blackpool when he received a report on his radio that an alarm had gone off at Preston's jewellers in the town. When he arrived alone at the scene in his Panda car, he saw a robber running towards the getaway vehicle, a Triumph estate car. As Walker, who was unarmed, approached the vehicle with five robbers in it, one of the men pointed a shotgun at him through the rear window. The getaway car then sped off and Walker, who had remained in his Panda car, pursued it. A short but high-speed chase followed. At one point, Walker lost sight of the Triumph only to then come across it stationary down a blind alley. With all the occupants out of the car, Walker parked his Panda car at right-angles to the alleyway to block any getaway. Seeing their escape route blocked, the men jumped back into their car and reversed at high speed into the Panda car with Walker still in it. Another officer, Constable Ian Hampson, then arrived at the scene in his Panda car as the damaged getaway car made off. Hampson pursued the getaway car in a second high-speed chase through the streets of Blackpool, radioing his position as he went. When the Triumph screeched to a halt, Hampson pulled up just five or six yards behind it. One of the gunmen then ran up to the Panda car and shot Hampson through the passenger window, badly wounding him in the chest. The officer slumped to the ground but managed to reach for his radio and ring in his position to the control room. Walker, who had resumed the chase after recovering from the shock of having his car hit, then saw the Triumph again and for a second time blocked its escape road at the end of a street. By now, other police cars were arriving at the scene. As at least two police vehicles closed in on their target, Constable Pat Jackson deliberately crashed his Panda car into the getaway vehicle. All the gunmen climbed out of their car and, when Constable Andrew Hillis got out of his CID car, one of them fired at him from close range but all two, or possibly three, bullets missed the officer. Hillis then ran after one of the robbers, rugby-tackled him and overpowered him after a violent struggle.

Three senior officers, including Superintendent Richardson, arrived at the scene and pursued three of the robbers, one on foot, two in their car. By now Walker and Jackson were some way behind the main group of the remaining three robbers. When Walker got to within ten yards of them, the driver of the getaway car turned and fired but again missed his target. At the end of the alley, the gunman stopped a second time, and turned and fired twice more. The first shot missed but the second hit Walker in the groin. The gunman now ran over to a Ford Transit delivery van parked outside a butcher's shop. He jumped into the driver's seat and sped off with the two other robbers alongside him. Richardson and Inspector Gray now arrived on the scene in their car and their colleague Jackson joined them. The three officers now pursued the van which crashed into a garden wall as it tried to turn into another alley. The police car stopped behind the crashed vehicle and Gray jumped out and tried to keep the back doors of the van closed so that the robbers could not flee. Richardson and Jackson ran to the front of the van, but it was empty because the driver had already jumped out. As the superintendent and the constable ran to the back of the van, the doors burst open and the two robbers ran off. The superintendent and the inspector tried to persuade the driver to give up his gun but he refused, threatened them and also ran off. The two unarmed officers again gave chase and after only a few yards Richardson grabbed the gunman. The robber now turned, put the gun into Richardson's stomach and fired. As Jackson approached, the gunman fired a second shot into Richardson as he fell to the ground. The gunman then made off, commandeered yet another van as an escape vehicle and drove away.

Other officers were still in pursuit of the other two robbers. Two officers, Sergeant Ken Mackay and Constable Edward Hanley, drew alongside the bandits, who were now on foot, in a CID car. As they did so, one of the men turned his gun on Mackay, but the officer opened his driver's door and knocked the gunman off balance. Both gunmen now ran off once again. Mackay this time drove past them in his vehicle and turned it around. The gunman came round to within six feet of the car and pulled the trigger of his gun, but it jammed. The officer then drove his car straight at the two robbers, knocking them over. Once again, the robbers ran off. Remarkably, the two men, with officers in pursuit on foot, now ran back to the butcher's shop where Walker had been shot. Inspector Stephen Redpath, who had remained there, saw the two robbers emerge from an alleyway and run towards him with Sergeant Mackay closing on them. Redpath could see that one of the gunmen had a revolver but he stood his ground. Mackay rugby-tackled the robber as they reached the inspector and, as he did so, Redpath kicked the gun out of his hand. Constable Hanley knocked down the other man and arrested him.

Walker was taken by ambulance to hospital with Richardson, who died, aged thirty-eight, the next morning. Hampson required surgery for the gunshot wound to the chest, although he eventually made a full recovery from his injuries.

After his death, Richardson's body lay in an open coffin for a day as thousands paid their respects. On 26 August, a civic funeral was held for him at St John's Church in Blackpool. Almost the entire town lined the route, with 400 police officers from the local force. Another 300 followed the hearse and Richardson was buried at Layton Cemetery. His widow, Maureen, said of him: 'He filled the room. He was noisy and full of fun.' To date, Richardson is the most senior police officer to die in the line of duty.

Four robbers were detained on, or soon after, the day of the robbery when £106,000 of jewels were stolen as they were being put into the window when the shop opened for business after the weekend. But Joseph Sewell, who shot dead Richardson and who wounded Walker, remained at large for well over a month during which time he was described as 'Britain's most wanted man'. All five men were eventually charged, found guilty and received long jail sentences. Sewell said of Richardson at his trial: 'I shall see him every day of my life. He just kept coming. He was too brave.' He was found guilty of murder and jailed for life, with a recommendation that he serve a minimum of thirty years.

Richardson's posthumous GC and Walker's GC were announced on 13 November 1972, well over a year after the incident. In all, nine officers were decorated for their bravery during the attempt to arrest the robbers. The lengthy citation for the two GCs ended: 'Throughout the pursuit which ended the robbery, all the police officers concerned were aware that they faced the threat of death or serious injury, but gave no thought to their own safety in their efforts to effect the arrest of armed and dangerous criminals.' Among the other decorations were four George Medals. At Buckingham Palace, Walker received his GC and Maureen Richardson received her husband's posthumous decoration. Richardson received numerous other posthumous awards and memorials, including the Medal of the American Federation of Police.

After he was shot, Walker was in hospital for four days but he was determined to go home because he wanted, as he said, to 'sleep in my own bed'. Afterwards, he had two months off work but was unable to pursue his two favourite sports, rugby and wrestling, again. He was promoted to sergeant the month after the robbery and eventually reached the rank of inspector in 1976. However, he was medically discharged in 1982 as a result of his gunshot wound, which regularly caused him – and continues to cause him – great pain. For a time, Walker had a share in a taxi company, but driving in the cold weather aggravated his injury and he had to stop. In 2000, he was diagnosed with the 'asbestos plague' – an aggressive form of cancer resulting from his short stint nearly half a century earlier in the asbestos factory.

In an interview at his home near Blackpool, where he lived at the time of the shooting, Walker revealed to me how, when he was shot, his right foot had been forced back almost behind his right ear. However, he was so determined to get at the man who shot him that he forced it back on the ground, picked himself up and hobbled towards his attacker who, by then with his accomplices, had commandeered a butcher's van.

I thought: 'Sod him'. I hopped towards him and went for him. But when I got to the van, the gunman came at me holding his pistol and so I pretended I was badly hurt and went down on the floor again. But I cursed him. I told him: 'You have no chance of getting away. The whole town is sealed off.' But they drove off and that was me out of it. The others [fellow police officers] had to take over. But I went to the hospital in the same ambulance as [Superintendent] Gerald Richardson, who was lying on a stretcher. He said to me: 'I had him [the robber] by the throat but the bastard shot me.' They were his last words. I could see he was dying. The colour went from him completely. He was a real good boss. He addressed everyone as 'officer' and treated them as human beings. All I wanted in the ambulance was a drink of water because I remember I had a vile taste in my mouth. At the hospital, I saw one of the robbers come through on a trolley in handcuffs. I needed patching up. The bullet went straight through my groin and missed the main arteries, bones and nerves. But the hospital told me I couldn't have chosen a better path for the bullet. Looking back on it, I just wanted to get them [the robbers] – to do my job. In court, my attacker said he had to shoot me or I would have killed him. An animal instinct of preservation had kicked in. I would have been quite capable of picking him up in the air and slamming him down. I was exceptionally strong in those days.

Now aged seventy-six, Walker's fell-walking days are over. However, he lives with his wife, Kathleen, and he keeps active doing DIY and pursuing his hobby of photography. He is a committee member of the Victoria Cross and George Cross Association.

MURRAY KEN HUDSON
Rank/title: Sergeant
Unit/occupation: Royal New Zealand Infantry Regiment
DATE OF BRAVERY: 13 FEBRUARY 1974
GAZETTED: 11 OCTOBER 1974

Murray Hudson was the first recipient of the GC to be born in New Zealand. Born in Opotiki on 24 February 1938 and educated at Opotiki College, he joined the New Zealand Army on 24 May 1961, aged twenty-three. For the first two years of his career, he served in Malaya with 1st Battalion, New Zealand Regiment. In 1964, he was promoted to lance corporal while still based in his homeland. After a posting to Borneo, he again returned to New Zealand and was appointed acting sergeant in 1967. His position was confirmed in 1970, and postings to Singapore and Vietnam followed. He had married on 28 February 1969 and the couple later had two children.

On 13 February 1974, Sergeant Hudson, who was known to colleagues and friends as Kina or Huddy, was supervising live grenade practice at Waiouru Military Camp, in the town of the same name in New Zealand. He suddenly became aware that another non commissioned officer (NCO) in his grenade-throwing bay had accidentally and, apparently unknowingly, armed the grenade that he was about to throw. Hudson ordered the man to throw it, but he froze. He then grasped the man's throwing hand in both his own and attempted to hurl the grenade over the front parapet of the throwing bay. The valiant attempt came within inches of success, but the grenade then exploded, killing both men. Hudson was thirty-five when he died; the NCO who died with him was Sergeant Graham Fergusson.

His posthumous GC was announced on 11 October 1974 when the citation ended:

> As an experienced soldier, Sergeant Hudson would have realised immediately that once the grenade became armed there was less than four seconds to detonation. While he must have been aware of the great risk involved he took no action to safeguard himself, but instead attempted to dislodge the grenade from the NCO's hand and throw it over the parapet. Sergeant Hudson displayed devotion to duty and courage of a very high order when, with a complete disregard for his own safety, he attempted to save the life of a fellow soldier.

Hudson's widow, Shona, a nurse, was presented with his decoration on 11 December 1974. She later made unsuccessful attempts to discover the exact circumstances of her husband's death, after she had not been permitted to see his body following his death.

JAMES WALLACE BEATON

Rank/title: Inspector (later Chief Superintendent)
Unit/occupation: Royalty Protection branch, Metropolitan Police
DATE OF BRAVERY: 20 MARCH 1974
GAZETTED: 27 SEPTEMBER 1974

Jim Beaton was born in St Fergus, Aberdeenshire, Scotland, on 16 February 1943. The eldest of five children and the son of a farm worker, he went to his local school in St Fergus before attending Peterhead Academy in Aberdeenshire. Aged nineteen, he joined the Metropolitan Police in 1962 as a uniformed constable, a 'bobby on the beat'. Beaton married in 1965 and the couple went on to have two daughters. In 1971, he underwent basic training as a marksman and, two years later, he became the tenth member at A Division of a team of officers chosen to protect the Royal Family. In the summer of 1973, he was selected as Princess Anne's protection officer – in effect, her personal bodyguard.

By the spring of 1974, Beaton had been guarding Princess Anne, then aged twenty-three, for less than a year. Shortly before 8 p.m. on 20 March 1974, he was in the front seat of her black Daimler as the Princess was returning to Buckingham Palace from a royal engagement in the City. In the front, next to Inspector Beaton, was the driver, Alexander Callender. In the back, next to Princess Anne, was her then husband, Captain Mark Phillips. Also with her was a lady-in-waiting, Rowena Brassey, who was sitting in the fold-down, or 'dicky', seat facing the Princess and Captain Phillips.

As they reached the junction of the Mall and Marlborough Road, a white Ford Escort swerved in front of the royal car and forced the driver to stop suddenly. The driver of the Escort got out and went towards the royal vehicle so Beaton got out of the passenger seat to see what was wrong. As he approached, the man drew a revolver and shot the police officer from a distance of about six feet. The bullet struck Beaton in the right shoulder.

Despite his injuries, Beaton drew his handgun and fired at his assailant. However, because of his wounds, Beaton's shot missed. His gun then jammed, meaning that he was unable to fire again. As Beaton moved away to attempt to sort out the problem with his weapon, the gunman told him that if he did not drop his gun he would shoot Princess Anne. Knowing it was still defective and literally staring down the barrel of a gun, Beaton put his weapon on the ground. The gunman was now frantically trying to open the rear offside door while also demanding that Princess Anne come with him. Inside the car Princess Anne and her husband were struggling to keep the door closed. The lady-in-waiting now left by the rear nearside door and Beaton seized his chance and climbed into the back of the car next to the royal couple.

Beaton was fearless: he immediately leant right across the car to shield Princess Anne with his body. Captain Phillips kept the door closed and, as the man prepared to fire again, Beaton put his hand up to deflect the bullet away from the royal couple. As the gunman fired, shattering the window, Beaton's right hand was badly injured by the bullet and the glass. Even though Beaton now had two wounds, he urged Captain Phillips to release his grip on the door so that he (Beaton) could violently kick it open, hoping to knock the gunman off his balance. However, before he could do this, the gunman opened the door and fired at the officer a third time, this time hitting him in the stomach and pelvis. The inspector fell out of the offside door, but was still conscious.

Unsurprisingly, this ended Beaton's gallant involvement in the attempt to thwart the kidnap, but the drama still had a long way to go. Callender, the driver, now tried to get out of the car but the gunman put his revolver to his head and threatened to shoot him. Undeterred, Callender got out of the car and grabbed the assailant's arm in an attempt to grab the gun. In the ensuing tussle, the gunman fired again, this time shooting the driver in the chest.

A member of the public, John McConnell, was travelling in a taxi along the Mall when he heard the shots. Seeing that a royal car appeared to be involved, he told his taxi driver to stop and he ran back to the scene, where he could see the gunman shouting at the occupants of the car. The gunman told McConnell to get back, but when McConnell continued to advance, he fired and shot him in the chest. McConnell collapsed on the floor, the third victim of the shooting spree.

Another to hear the commotion was Constable Michael Hills, who was on duty at nearby St James's Palace at the time. He reported the incident – what he thought was an accident – on his personal radio and then quickly made his way to the scene. When he arrived, he saw a man trying to pull someone from the back of the car and he touched his arm. The gunman then spun around and pointed the gun at the uniformed officer. As the officer advanced to try to grab the revolver, the gunman shot him in the stomach, claiming his fourth victim. The gunman then returned to the back of the car. Despite his injuries, Hills radioed a clear and concise message to Cannon Row police station leaving nobody in any doubt as to the gravity of the situation. Hills then saw Beaton's discarded gun and he picked it up, intending to shoot the gunman. However, he felt so faint that he was not confident about his aim and so he refrained. Shortly afterwards, Hills collapsed at the side of the road.

Another member of the public, seeing what had happened, drove his car in front of the gunman's white car to prevent him escaping. The driver, Glenmore Martin, went to the royal car to offer assistance but the gunman pushed his pistol into his ribs. Yet another member of the public, Ronald Russell, who was also driving along the Mall, stopped when he heard shots. Arriving at the scene, he saw Martin helping Hills, the police constable, to the side of the road. Russell could see the gunman holding Princess Anne by her forearm and trying to wrestle her from the car. So Russell ran up and punched him on the back of the head. The gunman turned and fired, but this time he missed. Russell then tried to grab Hills's truncheon but when he returned to the car the gunman was still trying to drag Princess Anne from the vehicle while holding his gun in the other hand. Yet she had somehow delayed him by engaging him in conversation. As this was going on, Captain Phillips grabbed his wife firmly by the waist and was trying to pull her back into the car. Russell then ran to the other side of the car where Princess Anne was now situated having broken free of the gunman. She was about to leave by the nearside door when the gunman came behind Russell and again tried to reach Princess Anne. Russell now punched the gunman in the face and he ran off as police officers started to arrive at the scene.

One of the first to arrive was Constable Peter Edmonds who saw the gunman running off with his revolver still in his hand. Despite being unarmed, Edmonds did not hesitate: he chased after the gunman and shouted at him to stop. The gunman paused and pointed his revolver at the officer. Edmonds dipped his shoulder and charged at the gunman knocking him to the ground. Other officers then leapt on the gunman and disarmed him.

The four wounded men were all taken to hospital. Bullets were removed from Beaton, Callender and McConnell. However, no attempts were made to remove the bullet from Hills's liver. It later emerged that the gunman was armed with two weapons: a .22 revolver and a .38 revolver. After being taken to hospital by ambulance, Beaton underwent emergency surgery. Princess Anne went to see him in Westminster Hospital the next day to thank him and to check on his condition. Beaton spent the next two weeks in hospital recovering from his injuries before being off work for another five and a half months. In those days, he was not offered counselling. He heard rumours that he had been nominated for the GC over the summer and admits he was excited by the prospect of the decoration – and the £100 that came with it.

His GC was announced on 27 September 1974 when six others involved in the incident were also given awards. Michael Hills, the police constable, and Ronald Russell, an area manager of a cleaning company, were both awarded the George Medal. Alexander Callender, the royal driver, Peter Edmonds, the police constable and John McConnell, a freelance journalist, were each awarded the Queen's Gallantry Medal. Finally, Glenmore Martin, a chauffeur, received the Queen's Commendation for Brave Conduct.

The citation for their actions was lengthy and ended: 'All the individuals involved in the kidnap attempt on Princess Anne displayed outstanding courage and a complete disregard for their personal safety when they each faced this dangerous armed man who did not hesitate to use his weapons. It is entirely due to their actions – as well as to the calmness, bravery and presence of mind shown by Princess Anne and by Captain Mark Phillips in circumstances of great peril – that the attack was unsuccessful.' Weeks later, all seven attended an investiture at Buckingham Palace and received their respective awards from the grateful Queen.

After recovering from his injuries, Beaton returned to work as a royal protection officer, again for Princess Anne, for another five years. From 1979 to 1983, he went back to uniform work as a chief inspector in Notting Hill, west London. He returned to a senior role, as superintendent, in the Royalty Protection branch in 1983 in the wake of Michael Fagan breaking into the Queen's bedroom at Buckingham Palace. His final rank, before retiring from the Met in 1992, was chief superintendent. He then spent eight years as a security manager for a major oil company.

In an interview close to his home in Beverley, East Yorkshire, Beaton played down his role. He did, however, bring me a copy of the statement he had made from his hospital bed on 28 May 1974, just eight days after the shooting. It revealed that, initially, he had got out of the royal car expecting the driver of the car that had pulled in front of it to remonstrate with his driver 'over some imagined traffic incident'. He continued – and I quote from his own statement (which has never been published before):

I could not hear what he said, but I opened the front passenger door, got out of the car and went round the back of the royal car to its rear offside. As I walked towards him he pointed a pistol at me and shot me in the right shoulder. I was aware of a feeling in my shoulder as he fired; it was like a punch or a kick, but it did not register I had been wounded. I drew my Walther 9mm semi-automatic pistol which was loaded with a clip of bullets. I aimed at him and fired in his direction. When the gun lowered, I realised I had hit the back of the royal car. It was then I realised I was wounded in, and bleeding, from the shoulder, and I feel this must have distorted my aim. I then went a few feet north of the rear offside of the car, and took position to shoot at him again in a two-handed position. I did this, but the gun would not fire. I then returned to the nearside of the royal car at the rear, and crouched down to try and clear the gun. I saw the magazine slide was back. I put my finger in and nothing seemed to move. I then looked up and saw the nearside passenger door opening. Miss Brassey [the lady-in-waiting] came out in a crouch, very low, leaving the door open. I stood up and walked towards the door. I saw the man silhouetted in the offside doorway (passenger) opposite me.

That door was open. He looked at me and said something like, 'Put your gun down or I'll shoot her', as near as I can remember it. As the gun was jammed already, I laid it in the roadway. I then held my hands up towards him to show him I had done as he asked, and gradually began to move towards him, into and through the car in an effort to get between him and Princess Anne. I heard the man saying something like, 'Come with me', to Princess Anne, still pointing the gun towards her. I then moved further into the car and reached the 'dicky seat', which was down.

The man then pointed the gun at me and told me to keep back. Her Royal Highness said something to him to ask him why he wanted to take her and he said something like: 'I'll get a couple of million.' I managed to edge a little bit closer and I think I was now resting my elbow on her knees, trying to get between him and her. The man appeared to draw back for some reason and Captain Mark Phillips leaned past me and pulled the door shut. The man appeared at the offside passenger door window. I was partly on the floor and partly leaning against the Princess and could see him clearly. He shouted something to the effect, 'Open the door or I'll shoot.' I could see the muzzle of the gun pointed to the inside of the car. The window was shut. I immediately held my right hand up in its path, everything seemed to explode at once. I was shot in the hand but was not aware then of much pain. Captain Phillips was still holding the door shut, and I told him to release it as I intended knocking the man back into what I imagined was a crowd of people outside, thereby hoping they would capture him. He let the door go, and I kicked it. I think the fragmented glass then flew out of the window frame, leaving it clear. I don't think the door opened that much, if at all. I have a vague recollection then of him disappearing for a second, then coming back. It is very hazy indeed but he shot me again. I think he opened the door to do it. I am extremely hazy about the events of that period. Although I didn't feel anything I knew I'd been shot in the pelvis. I felt tired and very drunk, although I hadn't been drinking. I just wanted to lie down. It sounds silly now, but I remember being aware I had a new suit on, and I went out the offside door, and I walked round the front of the car. I was walking gently and went to lie down gingerly because of my new suit, by a tree. As I got to the tree, I was about to lie down when I heard a roar like a football match and saw a bunch of people jumping onto somebody. It is only an impression so I can't describe it any more than that, but I knew he had been captured. I then lay down by the tree and was later taken off by ambulance. I did not see anybody else being shot and I can't remember seeing Mr Callender after I left my original seat. I can't remember seeing anyone else lying about. I felt very faint. I was wearing a blue pinstripe suit, a red and white shirt and a dark tie.

With that final, precise description of his attire, Beaton had signed his statement in the presence of his friend and colleague, Detective Inspector George Piggott. Thirty-six years on, the GC holder said: 'I was extremely lucky. The first bullet went through my lung but missed my vital organs and bones. Months after the incident, I saw my suit jacket and it had a second bullet hole on the elbow – so he must have originally fired two shots and the second one narrowly missed me altogether.

'I was just doing my job. I was young and keen and I just wanted to do the job as best I could. I think the adrenaline kept me going. Looking back on it, there were only two directions for me to go – forwards or backwards. And I suppose backwards, to use modern parlance, wasn't in my vocabulary. So I just kept going and I suppose I was hoping to confuse the guy enough that he didn't do too much harm. In the end, we had a good result in that nobody was killed and we caught the fellow.' Perhaps the greatest tribute came from Ian Ball, the gunman, when he was asked by police officers why he had shot Beaton, their police comrade, three times. 'He kept coming forward' was the honest reply.

After the kidnap attempt, it emerged that Ball had hoped to hold Princess Anne hostage and a letter written to the Queen sought a £3 million ransom demand. Ball, aged twenty-six at the time, was prosecuted for the attempted murder of Beaton and other offences. He was sentenced to life imprisonment and confined to a mental hospital. The kidnap attempt led to a total overhaul of royal security.

I have written in the past about the difference between spur-of-the-moment – or 'hot' – courage and 'cold' courage. The former is perhaps displayed by someone who, with his blood up in the heat of battle, goes to save a wounded colleague. The latter is perhaps displayed by a Special Forces soldier who goes undercover for days or longer behind enemy lines, exposing himself to prolonged danger. Jim Beaton told me he had also considered the differences between the two forms of bravery and, in my view, he plays down the bravery involved in spur-of-the-moment courage – and his own gallantry – too much. However, with great modesty, he said:

> My so-called courage is very puny compared to the courage of bomb disposal officers. They are streets above me because they go about their business knowing there is a fair chance they will tackle a lot of bombs – and they could be killed. Their courage is truly amazing: especially as some of them who have been blown up even stayed on at the scene to give advice to those [fellow bomb disposal officers] who were following them. I can't put into words how brave these people are or how much I admire them. These people have an amazing discipline – or courage – that is bred into them.

Beaton, now sixty-seven, and his wife, Anne, have four grand-children as well as two grown-up daughters. He enjoys golf, walking and reading, and is currently the chairman of the Victoria Cross and George Cross Association.

JAMES STIRRATT TOPPING KENNEDY

Rank/title: Mr
Unit/occupation: Security Officer, British Rail Engineering Ltd
DATE OF BRAVERY: 21 DECEMBER 1973
GAZETTED: 15 AUGUST 1975

James Kennedy was born in Carmunnock, Glasgow, Scotland, on 11 September 1930. The son of a post office worker, he was one of six children. He spent part of his childhood on the Isle of Arran where he was home-schooled by his grandfather, a former headmaster. After completing his unconventional education,

Kennedy worked for the Forestry Commission before being called up to do his National Service in the RAF. Following a spell working in London, he returned to Glasgow and got a job as a security officer with British Rail Engineering. Kennedy married on 4 July 1964 and the couple went on to have three daughters.

In the early hours of 21 December 1973, six armed men attacked security guards who were moving the pre-Christmas payroll for British Rail Engineering from the administrative block to various pay-out points. During the robbery, two guards received slight wounds from a sawn-off shotgun. The robbers then moved off to the exit from the works.

That night Kennedy was the security officer on duty at the main gate. After hearing the shots, he stood in the gateway in an attempt to prevent the armed men from escaping. Kennedy tackled the first robber and initially stopped him from leaving the yard. However, the other robbers turned on Kennedy and they hit him with the barrels of their shotguns and succeeded in freeing their fellow criminal. The robbers then climbed into a van which had been driven into position. Kennedy, who already had two deep lacerations to his skull, ran towards the van and tried to reach its passenger door. The passenger in the vehicle, however, fired two shots at Kennedy and killed him. He was forty-three.

His posthumous GC was announced on 15 August 1975 and the citation ended: 'Mr Kennedy displayed exceptional gallantry and devotion to duty in circumstances of extreme danger. He showed no regard for his personal safety in the face of armed and ruthless criminals.' His GC was presented to his widow, Mary, and daughters by the Queen in November 1975.

The robbers made off with £20,000 from the raid in Charles Street, Springburn, Glasgow. Seven men – the six robbers and another who stayed with the getaway vehicle – were all caught and sentenced to life imprisonment after being convicted of murder. Kennedy also received a posthumous

Glasgow Corporation Medal for Bravery in April 1974. In addition, a locomotive – *James Kennedy GC* – was named in honour of the security guard.

ROGER PHILIP GOAD
Rank/title: Captain
Unit/occupation: Explosives Officer, Metropolitan Police
DATE OF BRAVERY: 29 AUGUST 1975
GAZETTED: 1 OCTOBER 1976

Roger Goad was born in Jutough, India, on 5 August 1935. At the time, his father was a staff sergeant in the 12th Light Battery, Royal Artillery, and was based at Ambala, India. On 2 September 1953, Goad enlisted as a private in the Royal Army Ordnance Corps (RAOC). He was awarded the British Empire Medal – for dealing with improvised explosive devices (IEDs) – while serving with the RAOC in Cyprus. Goad married and the couple went on to have two daughters. On 26 February 1968, Goad was promoted to staff sergeant and, later, to acting captain on 1 December 1968. He was then promoted to captain on 26 February 1970. In the early 1970s, Goad retired from the RAOC and became an explosives officer with the Metropolitan Police.

On 29 August 1975, a telephone call was made to the offices of a national newspaper saying that a bomb had been planted in a shop doorway in London. The information was immediately passed to the police who sent two patrol cars to the scene. A plastic bag was discovered by two officers in the shop doorway and closer examination revealed that there was a pocket watch fixed to the top of the contents of the bag by adhesive tape. Fearing a bomb with a timer device, the police sealed off the area and cleared it of people. The occupants of nearby buildings were urged to retreat away from the suspected bomb and to stay clear of windows.

Captain Goad had just returned to London after dealing with

another suspect package. He was called to the scene and on arrival was briefed by a senior police officer as they walked to the shop. Some distance from the shop, the officer stopped and allowed Goad to advance alone to the shop doorway. Eyewitnesses saw him bend over the package and start to defuse the bomb when it exploded. The force of the explosion instantly killed Goad, who was aged forty.

At Goad's funeral, Sir Robert Mark, the then Metropolitan Police Commissioner, said: 'We are here today, police, Army and civilians, to pay tribute not only to Roger Goad, richly though he deserves our respect and admiration, but to pay tribute also to the ideals which he personified and which we, as a nation, value above life itself: that man should live in a world which puts justice before force, logic before emotion, and humanity and compassion above all.'

Goad's posthumous GC was announced on 1 October 1976 when the citation ended: 'Captain Goad displayed exceptional gallantry and devotion to duty in circumstances of extreme danger. He showed no regard for his personal safety when without hesitation he attempted to defuse the bomb.' His widow, Maureen, received his decoration at Buckingham Palace.

Those who planted the bomb were members of the so-called Balcombe Street gang, a four-man terrorist cell operating in London during the mid-1970s. Their campaign came to an end when they embarked on another attempted bombing which ended in them taking a couple hostage during a siege which lasted for 138 hours. The four men were eventually convicted of up to fifty bombings and shootings. They were all given life sentences.

JOHN CLEMENTS
Rank/title: Mr
Unit/occupation: Schoolmaster
DATE OF BRAVERY: 12 APRIL 1976
GAZETTED: 7 DECEMBER 1976

John Clements was born in Codicote, Hertfordshire, on 25 August 1953. One of three children, he attended Codicote Primary School and nearby Hitchin Boys' Grammar School. Clements, a sports enthusiast, attended Loughborough College of Education where he trained to be a physical education teacher. In 1974, he started his first job at Prior Park College in Bath and also got married. In 1975, he moved to Sherrardswood School, Welwyn Garden City, Hertfordshire, where he was a PE teacher and games master at the independent, co-educational school.

Over the Easter holidays in 1975, Clements was one of six adults and thirty-seven children, aged from seven to eighteen, who were enjoying a school trip – an eight-day visit at a north Italian ski resort. At about 4 a.m. on 12 April, smoke was noticed at their hotel in the town of Sappada. The schoolmaster was one of those who raised the alarm and who ushered the children downstairs. A number of children were led through dense smoke to safety, while others were helped down from the first-floor balcony.

Clements had climbed down from a third-floor to a second-floor balcony before making his way to the first floor. There he organised the children into small groups and helped them escape down a rope he had made from knotted bedsheets. Even when the room was empty, the master refused to leave the burning hotel. Clements was seen on at least two separate occasions going back into the hotel after carrying or even dragging people to safety from inside the building. He was eventually overcome by fumes and he died in the fire. He was twenty-two. Two pupils, both boys, also died in the fire.

Clements' posthumous GC was announced on 7 December 1976 when his citation ended: 'Mr Clements displayed outstanding gallantry and devotion to duty in circumstances of extreme danger. He showed no regard for his personal safety when he remained in the fiercely burning hotel in his endeavours to save those still trapped by the fire.'

Anita Chaytor, one of the pupils saved by the PE teacher, said: 'Mr Clements was in complete command of the situation and was very composed. All the time he kept lowering children one after another, taking care to see that the youngest and those who were the most frightened went first.' Clements' widow, Wendy, received his GC from Queen Elizabeth the Queen Mother at Buckingham Palace on 10 February 1977. There is a memorial plaque dedicated to the courageous teacher at Sherrardswood School and other memorials at the former schools and college where he was educated.

MICHAEL KENNETH PRATT

Rank/title: Police Constable
Unit/occupation: Victoria Police Force, Melbourne, Australia
DATE OF BRAVERY: 4 JUNE 1976
GAZETTED: 4 JULY 1978

Michael Pratt was born in East Melbourne, Victoria, Australia, on 13 November 1954. One of six children, he was educated at the Christian Brothers Parade College in Bundoora, and Preston Technical School, both in Victoria. He joined the Victoria Police as Cadet No. 1465 on 5 February 1973, aged eighteen. He was sworn in as a constable on 26 September of the same year and began 'on the beat' at Russell Street station on 12 June 1974. He married on 28 February 1976 and the couple went on to have a son and three daughters.

On the morning of 4 June 1976, three masked men entered a bank and carried out an armed robbery. One of the men ordered the staff to lie on the floor while another jumped over the counter and removed cash from the tills. The third man remained in the public area and, at one point, one of the robbers fired a shot in the direction of the manager and a customer as they ran towards the back of the bank.

Constable Pratt, who was off duty and unarmed, had been driving past the bank – the Clifton Hill branch of ANZ (Australia and New Zealand banking group) – when he spotted the three masked and armed raiders about to enter the building. He immediately turned his car, switched on the lights and, sounding his horn, mounted the kerb to block the exit from the bank. He also instructed a passer-by to call the police and alert them to the robbery.

After carrying out the robbery, the three raiders found their exit blocked by Pratt's car. One robber threatened him with a gun and ordered him to move the vehicle, but the officer refused and instead armed himself with the handle of a car jack. The men then tried to leave the bank by kicking in the lower section of a glass door and climbing over the bonnet of the car. As the first robber tried to straddle the front of the car, Pratt grabbed him. There was then a violent struggle and the raider was briefly knocked unconscious. A second armed robber now climbed over the car. The gunman extended his arms at shoulder height and threatened to shoot Pratt. The first robber had now regained consciousness and Pratt grabbed him. His response was to shout to his fellow robber to shoot the officer. A single shot was fired and Pratt was seriously wounded. The robbers then fled the scene.

Pratt spent four weeks in hospital being treated for his injuries. His GC was announced on 4 July 1978 when his citation ended: 'Constable Pratt displayed outstanding bravery, devotion to duty and a complete disregard for his own safety when, unarmed and single-handed, he faced and attempted to arrest these dangerous armed criminals.' All three robbers were eventually arrested, charged and convicted. Their sentences varied from six to eighteen years.

In a telephone interview from his home in Australia, Pratt recalled the day when, aged twenty-one and off-duty, he was driving alone in his two-door Mazda coupe to get a haircut.

At one point, there is a merging of a number of roads. I looked to my right and suddenly saw three men run into the bank. As they did so, they were pulling scarves over their faces and were producing hand-guns. When I realised a bank robbery was taking place, I immediately switched on my hazard lights and drove my car across the door of the bank. I suppose I acted on a combination of instinct and training: I wanted to get the crooks.

I jumped out of the car and looked into the bank. I could see one man just inside the door who was standing guard. There was another man standing on the counter – he had a hand-gun and had made all the staff and the customers lie on the floor. The third man was in the tellers' 'cages' taking money from the drawers. When I crashed my car across the entrance, I had hit the door of the bank and given the man nearest the door a hell of a fright. So as I got out of the car, he was motioning with his gun for me to remove the car - and I took no notice of course. The men all had firearms and I only had myself. So I went to the boot of the car where I thought I had a long-handled shovel but it wasn't there. So I grabbed the jack-handle instead.

As I was taking the jack-handle out of the car, there was a bystander coming towards me and so I said for him to ring the police. He quickly shot into the store next door to the bank to make the call. I then went to the side of the car and the man who was standing on the counter was having some sort of disagreement with the man who was taking the money from the drawers. I could clearly hear the man who was taking the money from the drawers tell the man who was at the door of the bank: "Shoot him, shoot him. Get him out of the way." The man on top of the counter then jumped off it and ran out of the back door of the bank. But just before he jumped off, he fired a shot in the direction

303

of the manager and a customer who were coming out of the manager's office. The bullet landed in the door frame at about head height.

Then the other two men tried to get out of the front of the bank but my car had buckled the door and they had to kick the glass out so they could open the door. I hadn't decided exactly what I would do but I knew they would come out and I would worry about it then. After getting through the door, they came over the bonnet of the car. I grabbed the first one. We struggled a bit and then I gave him a belt right in the mouth – with my fist not the jack-handle – and down he went. He was semi-conscious down beside me and then I looked around to see where the other bloke had gone and he was standing about six or seven feet away with his hands outstretched. He then said: 'Don't move or I'll shoot.' Then the man at my feet was starting to get up so I grabbed him in a bear-hug hoping the other bloke wouldn't shoot. A bit of a struggle took place, we traded a few blows and then the guy with the gun got around behind me and shot me at close quarters: a single bullet in my back fired from about six feet. I went face down on to the pavement and it felt as if someone was standing on my back even though they weren't. I could hardly breathe because, although I didn't know it at the time of course, the bullet had punctured both lungs and brushed my aorta. The two men then got in their getaway car and drove off.

Pratt was taken to St Vincent's Hospital by ambulance still conscious. There, lying on a trolley in the emergency ward, he was given the last rites by priest in the presence of a nun who he described as 'about four and a half feet tall'. Pratt, who at that point had received no anaesthetic, added: 'Then a young doctor who realised I wasn't doing very well jumped on the trolley with a scalpel, kneeled over me and went slash, slash on my chest. There were big spurts of blood and they put tubes into both sides of my chest and pumped out three pints of blood. From there, my memory is a bit sketchy.' Pratt spent eight days in intensive care then a further three weeks in total in St Vincent's and a nearby police hospital.

Following the incident, Pratt was forced to retire from the Victoria Police Force on 21 July 1979, aged just twenty-four. After the shooting, he had been off work for two and a half years before briefly returning to his job as a police office. However, he later got a job with the Victoria Totalizator Board where he worked until 1986. Afterwards, he ran a delivery business, followed by a pizza restaurant, until 1992. After a further job with a fire protection company, he rejoined the Victoria Police Force as an administrator in December 1996. He is a keen bowls player and regularly attends reunions of the Victoria Cross and George Cross Association. Aged fifty-five, he and his wife, Dianne, continue to live in Victoria. The couple have three grandsons and three granddaughters.

ROBERT LAURENCE NAIRAC

Rank/title: Captain
Unit/occupation: Grenadier Guards
DATE OF BRAVERY: 14–15 MAY 1977
GAZETTED: 13 FEBRUARY 1979

Robert Nairac was born in Mauritius on 31 August 1948. The youngest of four children from an Irish family, he attended Ampleforth College in North Yorkshire. In October 1968, he went up to Lincoln College, Oxford, to read history. He attended an interview for the Grenadier Guards on 1 September 1971 and, as a result, he was offered a cadetship and granted a commission into the regiment on 3 January 1972. Between 1973 and 1977, he served four tours in Northern Ireland at the height of the Troubles. He had received SAS training but was not part of the unit; however, he did specialise in intelligence and surveillance work. On his final tour, he was a liaison officer at Headquarters 3 Infantry Brigade and, by then, he had already earned a reputation for his courage, physical stamina, resource-fulness, charisma and analytical thinking.

On the night of 14/15 May 1977, Captain Nairac was carrying out surveillance operations in south Armagh, so-called 'bandit country' because the IRA had rendered it lawless. Without any back-up, he ventured into the Three Steps Inn, a pub in the heart of the staunchly Republican border county. Locals became suspicious about his assumed identity and Nairac was abducted by at least seven men. Despite struggling fiercely with his captors, he was taken over the border into the Republic of Ireland. Nairac was savagely beaten and tortured in an attempt to force him to give information that would have endangered lives and future operations. However, he gave nothing away and even made repeated efforts to escape. After several hours in the hands of his captors, they realised they were going to get nothing of use so they summoned a gunman who shot Nairac dead. The gallant soldier was aged twenty-eight and his body was never recovered.

His posthumous GC was announced on 13 February 1979 when the citation ended: 'His assassin subsequently said, "He never told us anything." Captain Nairac's exceptional courage and acts of the greatest heroism in circumstances of extreme peril showed devotion to duty and personal courage second to none.' His GC was presented to his parents.

Liam Towson was convicted of Nairac's murder in November 1977 and sentenced to life imprisonment. The following year, five more men were arrested and all were convicted: two of murder, one of manslaughter and two of kidnapping. It was Towson who had said in a statement referred to in Nairac's citation: 'I shot the British captain. He never told us anything. He was a great soldier.'

Numerous articles and books have been written about Nairac and his death. There are also several memorials to him and even a slow march – 'Nairac GC' – dedicated to him. In November 2009, Patrick Mercer, the Conservative MP for Newark and a former infantry officer, wrote an affectionate tribute to Nairac in the *Mail on Sunday*. In it, he said that he always suspected that 'Robert's life was only ever going to end either in brilliant success or heroic death. The man was the very definition of charismatic.' The former Shadow Minister for Homeland Security, who had himself completed nine tours of duty in Northern Ireland, also revealed that he had been with Nairac the night before the young officer died. He wrote: 'Unfortunately, his bravery overreached itself.'

14

THE AWARDS OF 1990–9

BARRY JOHNSON
Rank/title: Warrant Officer Class 1 (Staff Sergeant Major)
Unit/occupation: Royal Army Ordnance Corps
DATE OF BRAVERY: 7 OCTOBER 1989
GAZETTED: 6 NOVEMBER 1990

Nobody had been awarded the GC for a more than a decade when Warrant Officer Class 1 (Staff Sergeant Major) Barry Johnson broke the trend after a terrifying incident in Northern Ireland during the Troubles. Indeed, few living people, if any, in the entire history of the award could have come any closer to receiving it posthumously.

Johnson was born in Wood Green, north London, on 25 January 1952. Until he was about forty, he believed his stepfather to be his natural father. However, he later found out that his true father, a worker in a stained-glass studio, had separated from his mother shortly after he was born. He was brought up and educated in Buckinghamshire, where he had a half-brother. Johnson left school at fifteen determined to embark on a 'uniformed career' in the military. He arrived at the Army Apprentices' College in Chepstow, South Wales, in April 1967 and embarked on three years' training as an ammunition technician. He married in 1971 and the couple went on to have two children. After postings to Germany, Canada and Belize, he did a tour of Northern Ireland, as a staff sergeant, and a second tour in 1989 as a warrant officer. Just months before the first Northern Ireland tour, he had undergone a specialist course in explosive ordnance disposal and, by his second tour, he was a veteran of dealing with all manner of suspect devices.

Both tours of the province – where no fewer than seventeen ammunition technicians lost their lives during the Troubles – were particularly busy and hazardous. Time and again, Johnson was faced with bombs and weapons finds, as well as the inevitable false alarms and hoaxes. During his two tours, he dealt with eighty disposal tasks, including the safe neutralisation of twelve live devices.

On 7 October 1989, Johnson was called to a van which had been abandoned in the middle of a housing estate in Londonderry. The driver and passenger of the vehicle were seen behaving suspiciously by an Army patrol. The van was then driven away at speed in the late afternoon but the two occupants soon abandoned it and fled, although they were later detained. By the time Johnson and his team arrived the security forces had already evacuated the area – including moving patients from a nearby hospital to a safe area. Someone had already looked through the window of the van and seen six barrels loaded with mortars and ready for Republican extremists to fire at their intended target, the security forces.

Johnson, then thirty-eight, knew he had to deal with the vehicle at the scene, rather than risk moving it. The close proximity of houses, a hospital and a barracks meant time was short. He knew he had to look for the 'firing mechanism' – a timer in a small wooden box – and disable it with a remote-controlled 'wheelbarrow' device on caterpillar tracks. The 'wheelbarrow' had a camera, disruptor and shotgun. Once the terrorist vehicle was made 'safe', the six barrels then had to be dismantled – but this was a manual not a mechanical task. With his assistant, he first lifted the device from the van and placed it on the ground. Then he placed the firing tubes so that they faced away from the threatened buildings lest they should detonate unexpectedly. Johnson made sure his colleagues were well away from the scene in case of an accident. In the dark and in a bitterly cold drizzle, Johnson had successfully tackled five of the mortars when the sixth detonated, without warning, with a huge blast.

At his Devon home, Johnson recalled that day, more than twenty years earlier, in astonishing detail. He told me:

You can't imagine the sound of an explosion when you are that close to it. It is a violent detonation. I saw a boiling cloud of flame engulf me with red-hot sand being blown past my face. That's a vivid memory that will stay with me for ever. I found myself on the ground in a ditch. I was in a world of silence and darkness. I was so disorientated I didn't know whether I was still alive or not. Eventually, trying to think logically, I realised I must still be alive and it was probably best if I exited the area pretty sharpish and got to safety. But before the sound [of the blast] had died away I knew I was in a situation that was life-changing – where I would never be quite the same again because of the gravity of it all. I went to stand up, but I toppled over. It was then that I realised I had some other injuries that I couldn't really identify. Everything was hurting: face, hands, legs, but what dawned on me was that I hadn't taken a breath since the explosion. The actual explosion had clasped my chest so I couldn't breathe and that was more worrying than anything else. I started to feel dizzy and it took a while to restart my breathing. It took real concentration: the only way I could do it was to breathe out slightly and then breathe back in slightly more. I gradually increased it through short breaths and managed to get my breathing going. I was on my own and I couldn't see a thing. But then I heard Army boots running towards me and so I knew someone was coming to assist. Two lads picked me up and took me back to the ICP [incident command post]. I was probably in a mess. I could hear my number two shouting over the radio for an ambulance, which turned up pretty promptly. Then we took a hectic drive to the hospital in Londonderry which was almost as frightening as everything else that had happened. I was on a stretcher in the back of the vehicle and we were screaming around corners. At that point, once I had arrived at the hospital, I started to drift in and out of consciousness.

After a night or two, he was transferred to Musgrave Park Hospital, Belfast. His worst injuries were to both eyes. Both his legs were in plaster because they were broken and he had forty-one stitches holding together a mass of facial wounds. Yet Johnson was largely oblivious to such injuries; instead, he repeatedly asked the doctors to make saving his eyesight their priority. He underwent several operations on his eyes and stayed in hospital in Belfast for more than two months. His eyes, which had been sealed shut for many days, remained his greatest problem. To start with it seemed his left eye was less badly damaged.

All the surgical effort went in to saving that eye but right at the end of the process – and after a number of operations – my retina detached and so I went blind [for good] in that eye. Then the emphasis switched to trying to save my right eye. I had operations on that and eventually I got partial vision back in that eye. Interspersed with operations on my leg – including bone grafts and muscle transplants – I had eight operations on my two eyes. That was ample because the anaesthetic wears you down after a while. But I was young and fit and so they used to wheel me down [to the operating theatre] from time to time to have another go [at saving his eyesight]. In Musgrave Park Hospital, I used to take phone calls from people in a small room. Sat there, I could see a pink sign on the wall which over the days was getting clearer and clearer. And after a few weeks I could read what it said: 'No smoking'. That was a marvellous moment. But mainly I had audio books or my wife would read books and newspapers to me. She did a marvellous job.

Johnson was cheered up by scores of cards and letters from well-wishers and his aim was always to be back in England for

Christmas. He made the deadline and was 'casevaced' (casualty evacuated) back to Woolwich Military Hospital in south-east London. He was soon on crutches and was discharged just days before Christmas to Didcot, Oxfordshire. His family had been based in Germany while he was in Northern Ireland, but they moved back to the UK after the blast. Johnson recalled: 'I had a great determination to get back to work. It was one of my guiding aims – to get fit enough to be able to work again. It was something I focused on. It was good: had I not had something to focus on I may have given up a bit. And I did get back that next year – 1990. It was an office job on research and development. I wasn't physically well enough to have tackled another device and it wouldn't have been fair on me to ask me to try. But I did a year's good work before I finally retired, aged forty. I officially retired in January 1992 but I started winding down a few months before that.'

He had found out on 5 November 1990, after he was back at work developing explosive ordnance disposal equipment, that he was to receive the GC and that it would be announced the next day. It never crossed his mind that he would receive a gallantry award and when he was asked to see his Commanding Officer, Brigadier Derek Baughan OBE, the Director of Land Service Ammunition, Johnson was convinced that he was in trouble. In his CO's ground-floor office at Didcot, the brigadier told Johnson he had 'great pleasure in informing him he had been awarded the George Cross'. He also said the previous GC for the 'trade' had been for George Styles in 1972. Johnson said the news left him 'stunned and overwhelmed' and he did not fully take in the significance of the award. He said: 'I went home and told the wife and she said: "That's nice. Have a cup of tea." The following day it was arranged for me to go to London and meet the press. It was quite big news for a couple of days. I remember travelling on the train down to London and this chap opposite me had a paper with a huge picture of me on the front page but he didn't recognise me. That amused me.'

The lengthy citation for his award ended with a tribute to his sense of duty and dedication as he lay there critically injured after the blast: 'Such was his courage and determination to ensure that the task was completed safely that, although in great pain, he refused to be evacuated until he had carefully briefed his assistant on the precise details of the device so that the operation could be safely completed by a replacement operator.'

Sir Martin Gilliat, the Queen Mother's private secretary, wrote to Johnson saying he had been asked 'to convey Her Majesty's warmest congratulations on your outstanding award for heroism'.

Neil Kinnock, then the leader of the Labour Party, also wrote a letter of congratulations saying: 'Your coolness, determination and extraordinary sense of duty – even when badly wounded – shows a very special sort of courage and the admiration I have for you is, I'm sure, shared by millions of other people. I hope that you will continue to make a complete recovery from your injuries and enjoy a long – and very peaceful – future.'

His investiture was held on 11 December 1990 at Buckingham Palace when he received his award from the Queen. He was given special permission to have not just the usual one guest but three: his wife, Maria, and their children, Bevan and Adele. Johnson also met Jim Beaton, who had been awarded the GC seventeen years earlier. For many months afterwards, Johnson says he felt 'overwhelmed' by the honour of receiving the decoration.

Johnson moved to Devon to enjoy his retirement in 1992. Despite having physical and mental scars from the day he nearly died, Johnson today looks remarkably fit and well, something he puts down partly to a 'special contact lens [for his injured right eye] at a special price!' He enjoys walking, cycling, fishing and photography, and he and his wife have four grandchildren. Now fifty-eight, Johnson is a committee member of the Victoria Cross and George Cross Association. In 2009,

Johnson quietly and anonymously attended the funeral of Staff Sergeant Olaf 'Oz' Schmid in Truro Cathedral, Cornwall, out of respect for the bomb disposal officer who gave his life carrying out his job. 'I felt duty-bound to attend. He received some astounding eulogies: young Schmid must have been a very special man,' said Johnson, not for one moment considering that he is undoubtedly 'a very special man' himself. At the time Johnson was interviewed for this book, early in 2010, he was unaware that, just weeks later, Schmid would also be awarded the GC.

STEWART GRAEME GUTHRIE
Rank/title: Sergeant
Unit/occupation: New Zealand Police
DATE OF BRAVERY: 13/14 NOVEMBER 1990
GAZETTED: 19 DECEMBER 1991

Stewart Guthrie, usually known as Stu, was born in Dunedin, New Zealand, on 22 December 1948. He was the youngest son of a waterside worker (a 'wharfie') and a nurse. The youthful Guthrie attended Port Chalmers Primary School, near Dunedin, before attending Otago Boys' High School. In January 1965, having recently turned sixteen, he joined the New Zealand Navy. After nine years in the navy, he joined the police and spent fifteen years in the Armed Offenders Squad (AOS). In August 1985, Guthrie, who was married with three children, was promoted to sergeant.

On 13 November 1990, a man ran amok with a gun, killing twelve people, including four children, and injuring three others at the resort of Aramoana. Sergeant Guthrie was the sole officer at Port Chalmers police station that day and he was able to identify the gunman as someone he knew and who lived in the village. Guthrie made his way to Aramoana unarmed and alone, although on arrival he was able to call on the assistance of a local constable. Guthrie took control of the situation and armed his fellow officer with a privately owned rifle. The pair then began to reconnoitre the village which was strewn with dead bodies. It was close to dusk and the situation could hardly have been more fraught with danger.

On nearing the gunman's house, Guthrie instructed the constable to cover the front of the building while he went to the rear, the more dangerous location, alone. A detective and two constables also arrived at the scene and, by now, the gunman had been seen inside the house. Guthrie gave clear and precise instructions to the police control room and indicated his intention to 'contain' the gunman. Guthrie, who was by now armed with a police revolver, could see the gunman inside the house but became concerned that he was about to move on after the criminal blacked up his face and grabbed a backpack. Guthrie reported the gunman breaking windows and throwing what appeared to be an incendiary device into the house. He lost sight of the gunman who moved in the direction of one of the constables who, in turn, issued a challenge. The gunman then retreated and went to the back of the house.

Due to poor communications, Guthrie was unaware of this movement. He remained in the sand dunes to the rear of the seaside cottage. Suddenly, to the surprise of both men, the gunman and the sergeant found themselves face to face. Guthrie challenged the man saying: 'Stop . . . stop or I shoot.' He then fired a warning shot from his .38 calibre revolver. The gunman immediately moved towards the officer and unleashed a volley of shots, as a result of which Guthrie, aged forty-one, became the killer's thirteenth fatality.

That night New Zealand's Special Tactics Group (STG), the specialist counter-terrorist unit, was dispatched to the village. The gunman, David Gray, thirty-three and unemployed, was killed in a shoot-out the next day. It emerged that he had started shooting people indiscriminately after a dispute with a next-door neighbour. Armed with a scoped semi-automatic rifle, he had been responsible for the deadliest shooting in New Zealand's history. Coincidentally, he had attended the same two schools as Guthrie.

Guthrie's posthumous GC was announced on 19 December 1991 when the citation ended: 'Throughout this ordeal Sergeant Guthrie displayed conspicuous courage. His actions in placing himself in danger to protect his staff and members of the public at the cost of his own life were selfless acts of heroism. His bravery and courage were in the highest traditions of the New Zealand Police.' There were also a series of other gallantry awards linked to the massacre.

THE ROYAL ULSTER CONSTABULARY
Rank/title: N/A
Unit/occupation: N/A
DATE OF BRAVERY: 1969–99
GAZETTED: 23 NOVEMBER 1999

The second, and to date final, collective award of the GC was made to the Royal Ulster Constabulary on 23 November 1999. The citation issued from Buckingham Palace read:

> For the past 30 years, the Royal Ulster Constabulary has been the bulwark against, and the main target of, a sustained and brutal terrorism campaign. The Force has suffered heavily in protecting both sides of the community from danger – 302 officers have been killed in the line of duty and thousands more have been injured, many seriously. Many officers have been ostracised by their own community and others have been forced to leave their homes in the face of threats to them and their families.
>
> As Northern Ireland reaches a turning point in its political development this award is made to recognise the collective courage and dedication to duty of all of those who have served in the Royal Ulster Constabulary and who have accepted the danger and stress this has brought to them and their families.

As with the collective award to the island of Malta, it is impossible in just a few pages to know where to begin and end in attempting to describe the bravery of the RUC and its members. The RUC was formed in 1922 and bore the brunt of its losses during the principal phase of the Troubles from 1969 to 1999. During this period some 8,300 officers were injured and there were some 3,300 attacks on RUC police stations.

The Queen presented the GC to the RUC on 12 April 2000. Addressing around 1,500 RUC officers, along with many more civilian support staff at Hillsborough Castle in Co. Down, she concluded that 'a terrible price' had been paid for the force's 'brave and resolute stand'. The Queen said: 'This award is an exceptional recognition of the outstanding contribution made by the RUC to peace in Northern Ireland. It is a singular acknowledgement of the gallantry and courage shown and, in all too many cases, the ultimate sacrifice paid by members of the Constabulary during the past 30 years of terrorism and civil unrest.'

The Queen presented the force's collective GC to an officer whose individual courage and suffering came to represent that of the RUC in general. His name was Constable Paul Slaine who, on 27 March 1992, lost both his legs when his patrol car was hit by a remote-controlled mortar. The device also killed his colleague, Constable Colleen McMurray, aged thirty-four. Sir Ronnie Flanagan, the Chief Constable of the RUC, said of the award: 'Each one of us recognises the signal honour that has been bestowed on our most proud organisation.'

Slaine said the award was 'a huge honour' and added: 'I know I suffered greatly and have had to learn to live my life again, but I'm here. My four children still have a father. My wife Allison still has a husband. We are lucky to be together as a family. There are 302 RUC families who cannot say that. Yes, I have suffered but I'm happy to be here and happy to still be serving.'

Yet even as Slaine was recovering in hospital from his injuries in 1992, his wife, Allison, and their children had to be rehoused after being subjected to intimidation. By November 1993, twenty months after the terrorist attack, Slaine returned to work specialising in the field of information technology. On 30 June 2000, just over two months after receiving the GC from the Queen, Slaine met Diana, Princess of Wales, at a garden party at Hillsborough Castle.

Few, if any, writers and journalists have written more knowledgeably on the Troubles and the RUC than Chris Ryder. In his book *RUC: A Force Under Fire*, he noted that, at one point during the Troubles, Interpol, the organisation facilitating international police cooperation, had assessed Northern Ireland as the most dangerous place in the world for a policeman to work. Yet such was the respect that the force enjoyed, it consistently attracted twenty times more applications than there were vacancies. Many fine men built their reputations as Chief Constable of the RUC, including my friend Sir Kenneth Newman, who led the force from 1976 to 1980. Sir Kenneth, who went on to become the Metropolitan Police Commissioner, introduced innovative changes that transformed the force from the 'poor cousin' of the British police to being a far more streamlined and effective organisation. In *RUC: A Force Under Fire*, first published in 1989, Ryder wrote:

> In writing this book I have been motivated by a limitless admiration for the valiant men and women of the modern RUC. They represent all that is best about the good people of Northern Ireland and they are truly the cement that holds the divided community together . . . In recent years I think the RUC has increasingly proved itself to be an impartial police force, tackling terrorists and criminals without fear or favour and, when necessary, plucking the bad apples from its own ranks. The lack of reprisals by the RUC, despite all it has suffered, is a remarkable testimony to its integrity.

Richard Doherty, the distinguished Irish military historian, wrote in his book *The Thin Green Line: A History of the Royal Ulster Constabulary GC 1922–2001*:

> When the force was awarded the George Cross in 1999 that decoration was seen as a reward for duty nobly done; for the tremendous courage that the men and women of the force had shown over three decades; and for the pain and suffering that they, and their families, had endured throughout those years. In the [then] sixty year history of the George Cross there is only one parallel to the award made to the Royal Ulster Constabulary – that made to the island of Malta during the Second World War. That parallel provides a perspective to the achievements and courage of Northern Ireland's police officers and is a sure indication of the respect in which the Royal Ulster Constabulary was held – and continues to be held.

Doherty noted that few officers who served between 1968 and 2001 escaped without sustaining some injury. However, he added:

> But there was another, almost invisible, price to pay for policing Northern Ireland that was measured in terms of stress on officers and their families. It has been estimated that about seventy officers committed suicide between the early 1970s and 2001. In addition, many others have suffered from the stress of being a police officer with all the risk involved in the profession in the decades since 1969. Officers have also had to live with memories that, as Winston Churchill once commented, no human being should have to endure. Those have included witnessing the murders of colleagues as well as those of innocent bystanders. Among the most horrific memories are those of trying to recover body parts after explosions, carrying the lifeless and shredded body of an infant from the scene of a bombing, and arriving at the scene of a murder to find the victim's body in the driving seat of his car but

with the top of his skull blown out and his brains lying in the pocket of the driver's door. All these, and more, have been experienced by many officers, some of whom have also become victims themselves.

On 4 November 2001, the RUC was controversially renamed and became the Police Service of Northern Ireland. Two years later, on 2 September 2003, the Prince of Wales opened the Royal Ulster Constabulary George Cross Garden in Belfast as a tribute to policing in Northern Ireland. The garden contains a roll of honour inscribed with the names of all those officers who died between 1922 and 2001.

15

THE AWARDS OF 2000–10

CHRISTOPHER FINNEY

Rank/title: Trooper (later Lance Corporal of Horse)
Unit/occupation: Household Cavalry Regiment
DATE OF BRAVERY: 28 MARCH 2003
GAZETTED: 31 OCTOBER 2003

Chris Finney is the youngest serviceman to receive the GC and he is also believed to be the only serviceman to receive the decoration as a result of a 'friendly fire' incident – what the military call a 'blue on blue' attack. The son of an IT worker and the second of three children, he was born in Brussels on 23 May 1984. However, he was brought up in, first, the Manchester area, and then, Dorset, where he attended Ferndown Upper School. While there, he joined the Dorset Army Cadet Force, aged thirteen, after he and his best friend decided on a military career. Aged sixteen, he joined the Army on 10 September 2000 at the Army Foundation College in Harrogate, North Yorkshire. He began the second phase of his training on 11 September 2001 – the day of the 9/11 terrorist attacks on the US – specialising as an armoured vehicle (AV) driver. On 6 January 2002, he was posted to the Household Cavalry – the Blues and Royals – stationed in Windsor.

As Britain prepared to join the Coalition invasion of Iraq – to topple Saddam Hussein – Trooper Finney was based in Kuwait as part of D Squadron. His squadron crossed the border on the morning of 21 March 2003. A week later, on 28 March, it was advancing along the Shatt-al-Arab waterway, north of Basra, Iraq's second city. The group was in an exposed area of desert some thirty kilometres ahead of the main force of 16 Air Assault Brigade. Their mission was to recce Iraq's 6th Armoured Brigade. Finney, still only eighteen with around eighteen months' experience as an AV driver, was in the lead Scimitar, a 'mini tank', which is fast and manoeuvrable over rough terrain.

In the early afternoon the two lead vehicles paused beside a levee to allow the troop leader to assess the situation. Without warning, they were fired on by two Coalition forces ground-attack aircraft which had mistaken them for the enemy. Both vehicles were hit and caught fire. In the ensuing chaos, ammunition began exploding inside the turrets of the Scimitars. Finney scrambled out of his driving position and started to run for cover when he noticed that his vehicle's gunner was trapped in the turret. Finney climbed back on to the fiercely burning vehicle, thereby putting himself at great risk from more incoming fire. Despite the flames, smoke and exploding ammunition, he managed to pull out the injured gunner and to get him off and away from the Scimitar. Once in a safer area, Finney began to bandage his comrade's wounds.

The troop leader in the second vehicle had also been injured in the attack and there was no senior rank to take control of the situation. Recognising the need to inform headquarters of the circumstances, Finney broke cover, returned to his burning vehicle and calmly radioed a report on what had happened. He then immediately returned to his injured gunner and helped him towards a Spartan vehicle from the Royal Engineers which had moved forward to help.

As Finney looked to the skies, he saw that the aircraft were lining up for a second attack. Yet still he helped his colleague towards the Spartan. When both aircraft fired their cannon, Finney was wounded in the lower back and legs while the already injured gunner was hit again. Despite his injuries, Finney completed his task of getting the gunner to the Spartan. Finney then saw that the driver of the second Scimitar was still in his burning vehicle and he attempted to rescue him as well.

Finney climbed up on to the burning Scimitar, but the combination of heat, smoke and exploding ammunition beat him back. He collapsed a short distance from the vehicle and had to be helped by the crew of the Spartan.

Four of those in the two Scimitars were injured and the gunner in the second vehicle, Lance Corporal of Horse Matty Hull, aged twenty-five, was killed. Lance Corporal Alan Tudball, the gunner in Finney's vehicle, was the most seriously wounded although, after a month in a coma, he survived. The injured were taken by Puma helicopter to a field hospital in Iraq and, later, by Chinook helicopter, for treatment on RFA (Royal Fleet Auxiliary) *Argus*, a hospital ship. Eventually they were flown back to Liverpool for hospital treatment and, although Finney was off duty for six weeks, he made a full recovery.

Finney's GC was announced on 31 October 2003 when the lengthy citation ended: 'During these attacks and their horrifying aftermath, Finney displayed clear-headed courage and devotion to his comrades which was out of all proportion to his age and experience. Acting with complete disregard for his own safety even when wounded, his bravery was of the highest order throughout.' Finney received his award from the Queen at an investiture at Buckingham Palace on 25 February 2004.

In February 2007, the official British board of inquiry report into the death of Lance Corporal Hull blamed American pilots for shooting at the soldiers' vehicle 'without authorisation' and after woefully inadequate checks. Weeks later a British coroner ruled that Hull's death had been unlawful and a criminal act by the American A10 pilots, a decision rejected by the US. By the summer of 2008, a year after he had been promoted to lance corporal of horse, Finney became disillusioned with military life and gave a year's notice that he was quitting the Army. He left in July 2009.

In an interview at his home in Bournemouth, Dorset, Finney recalled the few minutes that led to the award of the GC. He told me:

We were by a berm [a bank] with water to our left. All the villagers were coming out waving flags and we had pretty much stopped because my commander, who was the ears and eyes of the patrol, wanted to check they were friendly. I had the hatch closed and, as the driver, it's literally like looking through a letter box and you can't see much around you. The gunner was to my side and our commander was directly behind me. That's when we got hit – completely out of the blue. I assumed we had been hit by a RPG [rocket propelled grenade]. My commander started shouting: 'Reverse. Reverse. Reverse.' What I didn't know was that he said it as he was climbing out. Because then he was no longer in the vehicle and so I kept reversing until there was another massive bang, which I initially thought was us being hit again, but, in fact, I had reversed into the other vehicle. As I got up to get out [of the burning vehicle] I saw three people running, which I initially thought were enemy but in fact it was my commander and the commander and driver from the vehicle behind us. I then reached for my rifle behind me and it was then that I realised how bad the flames were because they stopped me from getting to it. Then I got out of the vehicle and stood on top of the vehicle. I didn't have my combat helmet or my rifle and my body armour was open so then I felt very vulnerable. I jumped off the front of the vehicle and came around between the front and the berm for cover. Then I saw Alan [Lance Corporal Tudball] was trying to pull himself out of his hatch but he couldn't get out and he was shouting for help. Everyone says I made a big, brave decision to go to help him, but it gave me something to do rather than stand there panicking. So I climbed back on to the vehicle and literally grabbed him. With the adrenalin flowing, I literally pulled him up with one hand. The vehicle was burning quite badly and the ammunition was starting to go off so it was a bit hairy. But there was no decision to be made. He was a friend of mine and so I wasn't going to walk off and say 'See you soon.'

We got off the vehicle – it wasn't the smoothest landing. He was stumbling around holding his head, but after a few steps he just went over – his left femur was smashed to pieces. A 30mm round from the plane had gone straight through his thigh bone. I went over to him and could see he had a horrific injury. I was trying to help him but I was struggling to reach his morphine from his right leg pocket when the planes came round again. That was the first I knew we had been hit by a plane and I could see the pilot [of one of the planes] and that was when I knew we had been hit by friendly fire.

Then the planes started firing again and, although it sounds clichéd, the whole thing went into proper slow motion. Apparently it's the result of your brain reacting quicker than your body can keep up. I thought, right: 'I have got to drag Alan round to the front of the vehicle, tuck him underneath and hopefully the rounds will come over us.' But, as I grabbed him, my whole arm shook, which I later realised was him being hit and the force going through me. I then got hit – I went down on my knees – but I got back up and I honestly didn't feel anything because of the adrenalin and things. Then I looked down and there was blood pouring from my backside and my right calf. But then I saw Alan and he was a mess: his head was smashed open, the muscle and tissue was hanging from one of his arms, his eyes were rolled back and there was blood coming from his head and chest – while his leg, from before, was still a mess. I thought he was dead. But I lay down next to him and put my arm round him because he was a really good friend. Then two Spartans from the Royal Engineers arrived to help.

Then I went back to my vehicle and, using Alan's headset, I rang through [to headquarters] what had happened. Then Staff Sergeant 'Syd' Sindall [who had arrived on the scene] and I heard the gunner in the second vehicle shouting for help. We both got back on the vehicle but it was burning horrifically and there was nothing we could do. So we jumped off the side and I tapped the side of it and said: 'Ta, ta, Matty'. The next thing I remember is one of the [Royal] Engineers coming over and throwing me over his shoulder. The next bit is hazy because I guess I must have passed out.

When Joe Calzaghe, to date Britain's only undefeated world boxing champion, read in November 2009 that Finney was working in a call centre, he offered him a year-long job as his corporate ambassador, spearheading his charity work for Help for Heroes. Now twenty-six, Finney has a baby daughter with his fiancée, Liz Scorse, a nurse. The couple plan to marry in 2011.

PETER ALLEN NORTON
Rank/title: Captain (later Major)
Unit/occupation: Ammunition Technical Officer, Royal Logistic Corps
DATE OF BRAVERY: 24 JULY 2005
GAZETTED: 24 MARCH 2006

Pete Norton was born in Edmonton, north London, on 10 December 1962. He never knew his natural parents and was adopted aged three months. Taking the surname of his adoptive parents, he grew up in the Kent village of Garlinge, near Margate. Here he went to the local infants' and junior school before attending Dane Court Technical High School in Broadstairs, Kent. After belonging to the Air Training Corps as a teenager, his dream of joining the RAF was thwarted because a doctor had – incorrectly as it turned out – diagnosed him with asthma as a boy. He left school at seventeen to work in a sports shop in Margate. However, by the end of 1982, shortly before his twentieth birthday, he decided to join the Army. Although he initially applied for a commission, he eventually decided that, rather than delay his admission, he would enlist in the Royal Army Ordnance Corps to train as an ammunition technician (AT). At the end of his basic training in 1983, he was selected as 'best recruit'. Norton then, in 1984, attended the Royal Military College of Science (RMCS), Shrivenham, Oxfordshire, and the Army School of Ammunition, Kineton,

Warwickshire, to undertake further AT training, again qualifying as the best student. Over the next two decades, he served in Germany, Oman, America, Kenya and Northern Ireland (five tours), as well as Britain. In 2001, while serving as the warrant officer class 1 (WO1) senior ammunition technician in Northern Ireland, he was appointed to Conductor Royal Logistics Corps (RLC), the most senior and prestigious warrant officer appointment in the British Army. In July 2002, he was commissioned into the RLC as an ammunition technical officer (ATO) with the rank of captain. He had married in 1994 and he and his wife later had two sons.

Three months after the birth of his younger son, Captain Norton was deployed on operations to Baghdad. He was serving in that war-torn country, two years after the overthrow of Saddam Hussein, as the second-in-command of a multi-national, US-led Combined Explosives Exploitation Cell (CEXC) based in Camp Victory on the outskirts of Baghdad. The unit was tasked with investigating improvised explosive device (IED) incidents, including gathering forensic post-blast evidence in order to build up intelligence on the enemy. Needless to say, this usually involved highly dangerous work.

On the afternoon of 24 July 2005, a three-vehicle US patrol from B Company, 2nd Battalion, 121st Regiment of the Georgia National Guard, was attacked by a massive IED in the al-Bayaa district south-west of Baghdad. The explosion completely destroyed one of the patrol vehicles, a Humvee, killing four US servicemen. Parts of the vehicle, military equipment and human remains were spread across a vast area. A CEXC team, commanded by Norton, was briefed on the incident and arrived at the scene shortly after 7 p.m. By the time his five-man team arrived, also in a Humvee, it was dark. Once there, Norton took charge of a scene of devastation and carnage – with the fatalities still lying on the ground. In an ideal situation, an explosive ordnance disposal (EOD) team would have gone to the scene first to check for other devices. However, there were so many IEDs going off in Iraq at the time that weapons' intelligence teams were regularly having to attend the scenes of explosions without an EOD team having gone there first. When Norton reached the scene, he knew that there were likely to be secondary devices hidden in the ground which could be triggered by command wires, remote control or pressure pads. He also knew that it was dangerous for the military to remain in one place, especially at night; it made them vulnerable to small-arms fire, rocket-propelled grenade (RPG) attack, indirect mortar fire or suicide bombers. After questioning those US soldiers who had been present at the time of the explosion and visually assessing the scene, Norton could see that the area was well trodden, which reduced the risk of a secondary IED. However, he was informed that a possible command wire had been spotted in the vicinity of the explosion site. Norton seized the initiative and ordered his team and the US forces to stay with their vehicles. Wearing only his body armour, helmet and standard kit, he decided to do a 'rapid clearance of the scene'. Alone, as a 'one-man risk', he searched the area using a combination of image-intensifying night-vision goggles, other night-time equipment and 'white light' to search for secondary devices.

Norton had examined the north side of the road and was about to cross to search the area to the other side when his left foot trod on a pressure pad, hidden beneath the surface, and triggered a huge blast. Norton remained conscious even though he had horrendous injuries and the explosion had ripped off his left leg just above the knee in what is called a 'traumatic amputation'. He also suffered serious blast and fragmentation injuries to his right leg, left arm, lower abdomen and back. Yet, when the medical team first came forward to treat him, he was lucid and even concerned for their safety. Norton had deduced correctly that he had stepped on a victim operated improvised explosive device (VOIED) and that it was highly likely that other, similar devices were present. As he lay severely wounded and before receiving any treatment, he directed the team on the areas which were safest.

The citation for his GC announced on 24 March 2006 concluded: 'Despite having sustained grievous injuries he remained in command and coolly directed the follow-up actions. It is typical of the man that he ignored his injuries and regarded the safety of his men as paramount as they administered life-saving first aid to him. It is of note that a further device was discovered less than ten metres away and rendered safe the following day. Norton's prescience and clear orders in the most difficult of circumstances undoubtedly prevented further serious injury or loss of life.'

Significantly, Norton's GC was also to honour him for no fewer than three other incidents of bravery earlier in his tour and which were also mentioned in the citation. On 30 April 2005, he and his team came under fire from RPGs as they analysed the aftermath of an IED. On 9 May 2005, Norton was examining a supposedly 'neutralised' suicide vest, packed with high explosives and ball bearings, when he noticed the detonators were still connected. He immediately, at great risk to himself, made the device safe by hand. On 23 June 2005, he was examining the aftermath of another IED explosion when he identified a secondary radio-controlled 'claymore' IED beside the road. He quickly evacuated the area and saw to it that a US explosive ordnance disposal team cleared the device, thereby ensuring no lives were lost. His citation ended: 'Norton has come under fire and has been exposed to significant danger on a number of occasions. He has consistently behaved in an exemplary fashion and his professionalism has been of the highest order. Norton displayed outstanding bravery at the incident in Al [al-] Bayaa and throughout his tour.'

In an interview at the Defence Academy's College of Management and Technology, in Shrivenham, where Norton now works, he recalled the moment his life changed five years earlier with the massive explosion beneath him. He told me:

There was a huge rush of hot air gases running past me and an immense pressure pushing me upwards. This was accompanied by a huge, instant deafening noise. Then I had a feeling of flying and tumbling through the air which was brought to an end by a crushing thud as I hit the deck. I was thrown a distance of about twenty-five feet. I couldn't feel pain but I knew straightaway that I had been hit and it wasn't good. First I had to get my breath back because it had been seriously knocked out of me. I couldn't really move much but I managed to roll on my back. At that moment, I could have relaxed and I would probably have died there and then. But as it was I said: 'I am not going. I am going to get back and see the kids.' I decided to fight it [death]. I remember calling out for a medic – I think the only reason I did this was to let them know I was still alive. After watching all those Vietnam war movies, it just seemed like the right thing to do. They [the medics] said later it had taken a long time to see where I was. There was a lot of smoke and it looked like I had just disappeared. As I was being treated, I was keen that nobody else moved around unnecessarily because I felt there were bound to be other devices around. I knew where I had been – and they needed to know where I had checked [for IEDs] and where I hadn't. They were applying tourniquets etc and, as soon as they were happy to move me, I was taken on a stretcher to the ICP [incident command post]. Then they stabilised me until the Black Hawk medical helicopter arrived, which they later said was about forty minutes.

Norton cannot remember anything from taking off in the Black Hawk helicopter to waking up in Selly Oak Military Hospital in Birmingham. However, he had been taken, still conscious, to the Combat Support Hospital in central Baghdad. In fact, he had been put into an enforced coma by surgeons in Baghdad and, in Norton's words, was given 'twenty-four hours to either stabilise or die'. He was kept there for twenty-four hours and was then moved to a hospital in Germany for three days, where he underwent further surgery, before being transferred to Selly Oak.

His injuries were horrendous. As well as losing his left leg, his left hand had been so badly damaged that the arm had to be amputated below the elbow. Norton also lost 80 per cent of his right buttock, most of his right hamstring and right calf, leaving him with no movement in his right leg below the knee. Furthermore, he fractured three ribs and was hit by a large fragment of artillery shell which caught the plate of his body armour along his spine, fracturing three vertebrae. In addition, he lost four inches of sciatic nerve and suffered blast damage to his lungs. 'That was about it,' he said with a shrug and a smile after listing all his injuries.

He was treated in Selly Oak for eleven months during which he learnt he was being awarded the GC: that news in March 2006 had left him 'gobsmacked' with a sense of pride and delight. He later, in November that year, received his award from the Princess Royal because the Queen was suffering from back pain on the day of his investiture. 'It was a superb day,' Norton recalled. Coincidentally, Princess Anne is the Colonel-in-Chief of the Royal Logistic Corps, adding to the enjoyment of the occasion. After Selly Oak, he was transferred to Headley Court rehabilitation centre, near Epsom in Surrey, where he spent a further thirteen months, and he admits there have been dark times recovering from his injuries.

Sadly, Norton's departure from Headley Court in July 2007, two years after he received his injuries, coincided with the break-up of his thirteen-year marriage. Norton and his wife, Sue, are now divorced but he remains close to his sons, Tom, seven, and Toby, five. After leaving Headley Court, he did a year-long master's course in explosive ordnance engineering, which he had been planning while he was serving in Iraq. After completing this in August 2008, he decided to remain at the Defence Academy's College of Management and Technology in Shrivenham and, on 8 July 2009, he was promoted to major. Aged forty-seven, he is now directing staff in explosive ordnance engineering and counter-IED technologies. He is contracted to work until the age of fifty but he enjoys his job and hopes to continue until he is fifty-five. Norton is a committee member of the Victoria Cross and George Cross Association, a trustee of the Victoria Cross and George Cross Benevolent Fund and a member of the Council for the Institute of Explosive Engineers. He also plans to write his autobiography when time allows.

Norton and Colonel Stuart Archer, aged ninety-five, were both present in March 2010 when the Ministry of Defence announced the GC for Staff Sergeant (now Warrant Officer Class 2) Kim Hughes and the posthumous GC for Staff Sergeant Olaf 'Oz' Schmid for their gallantry in Afghanistan.

MARK WILLIAM WRIGHT

Rank/title: Corporal
Unit/occupation: 3rd Battalion, Parachute Regiment
DATE OF BRAVERY: 6 SEPTEMBER 2006
GAZETTED: 15 DECEMBER 2006

Mark Wright was born in Edinburgh, Scotland, on 22 April 1979. An only child, his father was – and still is – a painter and decorator, his mother a nursery worker. The young Wright attended Prestonfield Primary School in Edinburgh and, later, St Serf's School in the city. Easy-going, sporty and a supporter of Heart of Midlothian FC, he left school at sixteen and worked with his father for a time before fulfilling his ambition of joining the Parachute Regiment. Wright passed out and became a member of 3 Para on 10 October 1999. He completed three tours of Northern Ireland before being promoted to corporal. In May 2006, he was deployed to Helmand Province, Afghanistan, as part of Operation Herrick IV. As well as being committed to his family, he loved his job: so much so that he had asked to do an additional tour attached to 2 Para in Iraq. Wright was a mortar fire controller and was so good at his job that his comrades joked he could land a mortar on a 50p piece. He and his fiancée, whom he had known since she was sixteen, had been due to get married in October 2006.

From July 2006, a fire support group (FSG) from 3 Para, consisting of mortars, snipers, heavy machine guns and anti-tank weapons, held a high ridge to the south of Kajaki Dam in northern Helmand Province. The group was there to defend the dam from Taliban attack. On 6 September, Lance Corporal Stuart Hale was ordered to lead a sniper patrol down the southern side of the ridge in an attempt to engage a group of Taliban fighters that had been reported to be operating on the main road to the east of the ridge. However, 300 metres from his 'main position', Hale stepped on a mine which blew off one of his legs. Wright saw and heard the mine explode from the top of the ridge and, after gathering some other servicemen together, rushed down the slope to help his badly wounded comrade.

Wright knew that it was highly dangerous to enter a probable minefield and that he could easily trigger a mine himself. When he reached Hale, Wright took command of the situation and directed two medics to treat the lance corporal. Because of the danger, Wright instructed the others to stay clear of the area while he arranged the evacuation of the patient. Wright assessed that his comrade was likely to bleed to death if he was moved back up the slope so, instead, he called for a helicopter and ordered a route to be cleared through the minefield to a possible landing site. This task was undertaken by Corporal Stuart Pearson, but he suffered a traumatic amputation of his left leg when he moved back across the area that he thought he had cleared, only to step on a mine. Despite the acute dangers, Wright now moved immediately to treat Pearson until one of the medics took over. Once again, Wright ordered all non-essential medical personnel to stay out of the area and he sent a second situation report to headquarters. Wright also ensured that further medical supplies, urgently required by the two wounded servicemen, were passed down the ridge.

A Chinook helicopter arrived soon afterwards and landed close to the scene. However, as Wright stood up to make his way to the helicopter, he initiated a third mine and sustained serious injuries to his face, chest and left shoulder. The mine also caused serious injuries to one of the two medics with him. The uninjured medic began treating Wright but then set off a fourth mine, injuring himself and another servicemen at the scene, and causing further wounds to Wright and Pearson. The blast also blew off the leg of the soldier treating Pearson. There were now numerous casualties, three of whom had lost limbs. Medical supplies were running out and the Chinook had to abort its mission because it was too dangerous for its staff to enter the minefield.

Wright suffered horrific injuries and the situation in the minefield was desperate, but still he tried to stay in control. He gave his identification details over the radio and directed other injured personnel to do so too in order that they could get urgent treatment once evacuated. Eventually, Wright was brought out by an American helicopter equipped with a winch. While he was waiting for help, he was conscious and repeatedly shouted encouragement to his injured comrades. Wright, who was twenty-seven, died on the helicopter during the flight to the field dressing station.

His posthumous GC was announced on 15 December 2006 when his citation ended:

There is absolutely no doubt that Corporal Wright entered the minefield to assist Lance Corporal Hale in the full knowledge of the dangerous situation. He had the option to wait for a mine clearance team to arrive, but decided to take action immediately, realising that conducting a full mine clearance to reach Lance Corporal Hale would take too long and he was likely to die before it was completed. When further casualties occurred he again ordered others to safety, but continued to move around the minefield to control the situation. In doing so he suffered mortal injury but still continued to demonstrate command presence that was so vital to eventually ensuring that all casualties and members of the rescue party were evacuated from the horrific situation. It is notable that from the time of responding to the first mine-strike, Corporal Wright spent three and a half hours in the minefield and for a significant amount of that time he himself was very seriously wounded and in great pain. His outstandingly courageous actions and leadership were an inspiration to all those around him during an extremely precarious situation. His complete disregard for his own safety while doing everything possible to retain control of the situation and to save lives constitutes an act of the greatest gallantry.

After the announcement of Wright's posthumous GC in December 2006, his father, Bobby, said:

It is with great honour and sadness that I am here today to acknowledge the award of the George Cross on behalf of my son Mark who was killed in Afghanistan on 6th September 2006. Both my wife Jem [Jemima] and Mark's fiancée Gillian [Urquhart] are very proud of Mark's achievements whilst serving with 3rd Battalion, Parachute Regiment. We do have some comfort in the knowledge that Mark died saving the lives of his fellow para-troopers that had become injured in a minefield. The selfless action was typical of Mark, as a commander he accepted full responsibility for the care of his soldiers. Mark was extremely proud to serve in the British Army and especially the Parachute Regiment. He had planned to have a long and full career in the Army but this aspiration was tragically cut short. Mark was killed while carrying out his duties as a paratrooper, a job that he loved and was immensely proud to serve in. Mark was a typical fun-loving young man, a caring son and devoted partner to Gillian. He will be sorely missed by all who knew him. I would like to thank the 3rd Battalion, The Parachute Regiment, for their conduct and support throughout this very sad and trying time in our lives.

At Wright's inquest in October 2008, Andrew Walker, the coroner, paid tribute to the soldier's bravery but also criticised the shortage of crucial military equipment: notably radio batteries, rechargers and a helicopter with a winch.

> Cpl Wright was an exceptional soldier amongst those rare breeds who can, and do, act with unhesitating courage in the most desperate circumstances that are faced by soldiers almost daily in Afghanistan. The loss of Cpl Wright will, I have no doubt, be keenly felt by his family, his friends, his unit and our armed forces. I have frequently encountered bravery and courage as I have sat here listening to the sad circumstances of many military inquests but it must not pass without comment that this exceptional soldier, who was rightly awarded the George Cross, not only organised a rescue party from the observation point at Athens following the first mine explosion but, despite being gravely injured and knowing that help was a long time away, joked and kept up the spirits of those trapped in the minefield. Cpl Wright's last act was to reach over to check the condition of the wounded soldier placed next to him on the aircraft, only relaxing when the medic told him the injured soldier would be all right. This selfless courage forms part of a tradition within our armed forces and Cpl Wright will continue to be an inspiration to those who follow. That a brave soldier is lost in battle is always a matter of deep sadness but, when that life is lost where it need not have been because of a lack of equipment and assets, those responsible should hang their heads in shame.

MATTHEW CROUCHER
Rank/title: Lance Corporal
Unit/occupation: Royal Marines' Reserve
DATE OF BRAVERY: 9 FEBRUARY 2008
GAZETTED: 24 JULY 2008

Matt Croucher was born in Solihull, near Birmingham, on 14 December 1983. The older of two children and the son of two teachers, he had wanted to be a Royal Marines Commando

– and pull on the famous green beret – since he was thirteen. As a sports-loving schoolboy growing up in Birmingham, he considered the Royal Marines Commandos to be invincible and that they were 'elite warriors born to fight'. After joining the 2030 (Elmdon and Yardley) Squadron Air Training Corps at thirteen, his first taste of the military meant he was 'hooked'. He was later 'ecstatic' when, in June 2000, he received a letter inviting him to report to the Commando Training Centre in Lympstone, Devon. There he passed a tough, four-day Potential Royal Marines Course (PRMC), thereby qualifying for the nine-month Royal Marine Basic Training. Croucher described the course as anything but basic and, more accurately, 'thirty weeks of sheer hell'. Despite the physical and mental demands of the course – and the high drop-out rate – Croucher passed with flying colours. When he received his green beret, in front of his proud parents, he regarded it as 'one of the best days of my young life'. In his book, *Bulletproof*, published in 2009, Croucher wrote: 'I was seventeen. Legally I wasn't even allowed on to the battlefield. But I knew my time would come.'

In March 2003, Croucher found himself on HMS *Ark Royal* bound for Iraq, with Delta Company Royal Marines. His unit was part of the British spearhead for the invasion of Iraq as part of the Second Gulf War. It was there that Croucher got his 'first taste of war, twenty-first-century style'. Alongside US Navy seals, he was one of the first 200 western troops into Iraq. It was here too, in battle, that the young Marine got his first 'kill' before seeing further action as the Allies quickly overthrew Saddam Hussein's brutal regime.

From August 2004 to February 2005, Croucher was back in Iraq, serving with 40 Commando as part of Operation Telic 4. In October 2004, he received a fractured skull when a roadside bomb went off during a routine patrol but, by the end of 2005, Croucher was back in Iraq for a third time, after transferring to the Royal Marines' Reserve. This allowed him to take up lucrative private security work. He was now part of 'The Circuit'

– a new world of professional bodyguards and security guards. However, after being seriously injured in a motorcycle accident back in Britain, Croucher decided to turn his back on 'The Circuit' to re-deploy as a lance corporal reservist in the Marines. 'I wanted to have that feeling again of being part of something special . . . I wanted to get out there [Afghanistan] and I wanted to do it for Queen and country,' he wrote in his book, *Bulletproof*. 'I really wanted a piece of the action. Everything about it appealed to me – the danger, the hostile environment, and making a difference. Down the pub my civvy mates thought I was crazy, and told me it was time to get a safer job. But being a Royal Marine Commando is a state of mind.'

Croucher had to undertake an OPTAG (Operational Training and Advisory Group) course with 40 Commando before deployment to Helmand province as part of Operation Herrick VII. By September 2007, Croucher found himself at FOB (Forward Operating Base) Inkerman in the Sangin Valley. Conditions were spartan and it was dangerous too – British servicemen had dubbed it 'FOB Incoming' because it attracted so much Taliban fire. The base would be hit by the enemy virtually every day and Croucher and his 200 comrades found themselves in firefights with the enemy for ten days in a row. It was physically and mentally demanding work – his first patrol had been due to last for four or five hours but, in fact, lasted for fifteen hours. Throughout November, there were numerous battles with the enemy, including a huge contact on 9 November 2007, which Croucher described as 'a date that will live long in the memories of everyone out there'.

By February 2008, Croucher was based in the Sangin Valley at Forward Operating Base Robinson – known as 'FOB Rob' to one and all. It was situated at the edge of Helmand's so-called Green Zone, where the Taliban hid out in large numbers on both sides of the River Helmand. Like FOB Inkerman, FOB Robinson was at the 'sharp end' and those based there knew they would see plenty of action. The area around FOB Robinson was fertile and used by many local Afghans to grow poppies for their illegal, but lucrative, heroin trade. By now, it was winter and night-time temperatures constantly plunged well below freezing. One day, Croucher was informed that he would be part of a mission involving forty men. He was to be a member of a four-man Commando Reconnaissance Force CTR (Close Target Reconnaissance) team tasked with searching a Taliban compound. It was intended to be a quick in and out job, gaining intelligence on a suspected bomb-making factory so that it could be targeted at a later date. The servicemen were briefed that they should not seek to engage the enemy and that they should 'let sleeping dogs lie'. The plan was that once they had completed the recce, they should then radio headquarters and get out of the area.

By 1 a.m. the next morning – 9 February 2008 – the men on the mission had received their final briefing. Captain Dan Venables, the troop commander, told his men not to take any unnecessary risks: 'If, for whatever reason, the mission is compromised, you know the drill. Make a fighting retreat back to the LUP [Lying Up Position] where we'll be supporting you. No heroics, lads, okay?' he said.

With full battle kit, including Night Vision Goggles (NVGs), the group then left the base, leaving some fifteen metres between each man so as not to present a group target to any hidden Taliban forces. As they ventured out into the night, they wanted to be close enough not to lose contact with those in front – but far enough apart to survive if the man in front stepped on a landmine or triggered a booby-trapped grenade. When they came to the enemy compound, the four-man team split in half. Croucher and his comrade checked out a stable block where they found some 200 kilos of bomb-making fertiliser, along with batteries, circuitry and wires. After gathering evidence of the bomb-making facilities during a forty-five-minute stay at the compound, the four men regrouped outside and prepared to return to FOB Robinson.

In an interview with me in London after returning from South Africa, where he had been carrying out security work for the 2010 World Cup, Croucher recalled the incident that came so close to claiming his life.

Our job that night had been reconnaissance. We wanted to get in and out with as little noise as possible but with as much evidence as we could gather. But after our stay in the compound, I went off at a slight tangent. I had NVGs but it was still relatively hard to see. Suddenly I felt a tension just below my knee. Then I heard the distinctive noise of a fly-off lever ejecting from a hand grenade. I looked down and saw the grenade on the floor. I realised that meant I probably had a three- to five-second delay before the grenade exploded. In the darkness, I had walked through a four-metre tripwire that led to an old pineapple-style Russian grenade. This had been attached around a stake and driven into the ground. I was, to say the least, a little bit worried and I had to decide, in a split second, what to do. There was nowhere to take cover. Everything seemed to go into slow motion.

Ads [his comrade] was now directly behind me, just feet away. He was followed by Scottie and Dave. I shouted 'Grenade! Take cover!' but I knew they didn't really have enough time to react. Ads hit the deck behind me while Dave, last in the patrol, darted back behind the building wall for cover. So I thought the best option was to throw my day sack on the grenade and lie on it with my back towards the grenade, hoping my day sack would provide some protection. I threw my day sack off one shoulder on to the grenade and at the same time dropped to the ground. Then, pulling my legs up, I tucked my head back so my body armour and helmet would make a shield against the inevitable blast. I counted to about six or seven seconds and I began to wonder whether the grenade would ever go bang or not. I gritted my teeth and thought about what might happen. Then it eventually did explode.

I saw a plume of orange sparks go shooting to the sky. The

next thing I knew I had been flung through the air – not far, only a metre or so. I was lying face down in the dirt. It was total confusion and I was covered in dust. My ears were ringing, my head was spinning, and I had blood coming out of my ears and nose. I checked that my arms and legs were all still attached and then worried about everything else after that.

I immediately smelt the cordite from the grenade – there was a distinctive burning smell. I wasn't sure who it was, but I could feel someone frantically patting me down. Later Scottie and Dave told me they had run their hands under my armour to check for injuries, searching for holes in my combats that would signify a shrapnel entry point. My eyes and face were caked in dust and I struggled to breathe. But they [Ads, Dave and Scottie] helped me up and I found my feet.

As he surveyed the scene in the near darkness, Croucher could see that his day sack had been blown fully ten metres away from him after the shoulder strap had been sliced away by shrapnel. Croucher was in no doubt that the badly damaged day sack had saved his life. Although his helmet and body armour were peppered with grenade fragments, his equipment had prevented potentially lethal shards of metal from penetrating his body and he had relatively minor injuries. His comrades, too, only had minor injuries. Suddenly, there was another bang and Croucher initially feared that a second explosive device had gone off. In fact, it was the lithium battery inside his sack exploding, but fortunately it was too far away from the group to injure anyone. Scottie could not believe that Croucher had so few injuries. 'You're in one piece,' he said, in disbelief.

Croucher told me: 'We needed to get out of there. We did a quick patrol back to our QRF [Quick Reaction Force] which was about two hundred metres away. I was able to walk, though I was still a bit dizzy and one of them [his comrades] had to support me.' Later on, the back-up team arrested seven suspected Taliban who turned up at the compound. They also retrieved his day sack which had been severely damaged in the explosion. As dawn broke, a single Taliban fighter was spotted down by the river. Dressed in a black dishdasha and carrying an AK-47 rifle, he was shot dead by Croucher – and others – when he raised his weapon against the British forces. Miraculously, a thorough check-up back at the base revealed that Croucher had nothing worse than mild concussion, perforated ear drums, and cuts and bruises.

I was deeply impressed by Croucher's unselfish actions. Indeed, I wrote an article for the *Sunday Telegraph* on 6 April 2008 calling for him to be awarded the Victoria Cross. Croucher refers to my article in his book. I wrote: 'It is widely accepted that to be awarded the Victoria Cross a serviceman needs to show such astonishing courage that nine times out of ten he would die carrying out the action. If that is the case, Lance Corporal Matthew Croucher is absolutely entitled to be awarded Britain's most prestigious bravery award.'

However, the authorities ruled that Croucher should instead be awarded the GC – on the grounds that he was not 'in the face of the enemy' when the bomb went off. His gallantry award was announced on 24 July 2008. At the time, Air Chief Marshal Sir Jock Stirrup, the Chief of the Defence Staff, said of Croucher's actions: 'His exemplary behaviour and supreme heroism are fully deserving of the highest recognition.' Admiral Sir Jonathan Band, the First Sea Lord and Chief of the Naval Staff, said: 'His action epitomises the ethos of selfless devotion to duty, courage and comradeship in the Marines.'

Croucher was presented with his award on 30 October 2008 by the Queen, when his citation was read out. He was accompanied by his parents, sister and his maternal grand-parents. The citation said he had been 'quite prepared to make the ultimate sacrifice for his fellow Marines' and ended with the words: 'Lance Corporal Croucher is an exceptional and inspira-tional individual. His magnificent displays of selflessness and gallantry are truly humbling and are the embodiment of the finest traditions of the service.' Croucher, who is single and aged twenty-six, transfered back to the Royal Marines' Reserve after the 2007–8 tour and set up a security company. He now co-owns the company Pinnacle Risk Management, and works all around the world. His GC and day sack are on display at the Imperial War Museum in London. Croucher, who lives just outside Birmingham, remains a member of the Royal Marines' Reserve. In his book *Bulletproof*, he writes: 'I'm still a Royal Marine . . . I'm still ready to serve Queen and country at a moment's notice. I wouldn't think twice.'

KIM SPENCER HUGHES

Rank/title: Staff Sergeant (later Warrant Officer Class 2)
Unit/occupation: Royal Logistic Corps
DATE OF BRAVERY: 16 AUGUST 2009
GAZETTED: 19 MARCH 2010

Kim Hughes was born in Munster, Germany, on 12 September 1979. He was the middle one of three children and the son of an Army serviceman who was a staff sergeant in the Royal Electrical and Mechanical Engineers (REME). As a boy, Hughes was brought up in Weston-super-Mare, Somerset, and, later, Telford, Shropshire. He attended William Reynolds Junior School and Thomas Telford School for his secondary education, both in the Shropshire town. He left school at sixteen to join the Royal Logistic Corps (RLC) but was initially unsettled in the Army and quit after less than a year. However, he quickly decided that Civvy Street was not for him and, after a year doing manual work, rejoined the Army at eighteen – and never looked back. He was a private working as an RLC driver for three years, before training to be a driver with a bomb disposal team. However, he then successfully applied to become an ammunition technician, training for three years and being promoted to lance corporal. He subsequently served three tours in Northern Ireland, two in Bosnia, one in Iraq and one in Afghanistan.

Hughes went to Helmand Province, Afghanistan, in April 2009 as a staff sergeant working as a high-threat improvised explosive device disposal (IEDD) operator. He took part in Operation Panther's Claw and worked closely with the Danish Battle Group. By August, Hughes was working alongside the Royal Engineers' Search Team (REST) and was tasked with providing close support to 2 Rifles Battle Group during an operation to clear a route south-west of Sangin.

As part of the preparations for the operation on 16 August 2009, a part of A Company was deployed early to secure an emergency helicopter landing site (HLS) and to isolate enemy compounds to the south of the route. During these preparations, a serviceman initiated a victim operated improvised explosive device (VOIED) and was seriously wounded. As the casualty was being recovered, one of the stretcher-bearers initiated a second VOIED which resulted in two people being killed outright and four others being very seriously injured (one of whom later died from his wounds). It thus became abundantly clear that the area was effectively an IED minefield being overwatched by the enemy.

Staff Sergeant Hughes and his team were called to what the Army described as a 'harrowing and chaotic situation'. Their task was to recover both casualties and bodies, and they knew speed was of the essence if further lives were not to be lost. To save time, Hughes did not wait to put on protective clothing. Instead, he immediately set about clearing a path to the injured servicemen, while providing constant reassurance that help was on its way. When Hughes reached the first injured soldier, he discovered another VOIED within a metre of the casualty. This threatened the lives of all the casualties and, of course, Hughes himself. Hughes did not know the power source of the IED but he knew full well that the servicemen needed urgent medical help so he carried out a 'manual neutralisation' of the device knowing that any error would be instantly fatal.

He had, in effect, carried out a 'Category A' action where not taking action is almost certain to result in further casualties and the emphasis is on saving other people's lives, if necessary, at the expense of the operator. Hughes had, by any standards, been responsible for an exceptional act of gallantry. With shots now keeping the enemy at bay, Hughes calmly turned his attention to the remaining casualties and to retrieving the dead: servicemen will never knowingly leave the bodies of comrades.

As he cleared a path, Hughes discovered two further VOIEDs. Twice more, he carried out exceptionally risky 'manual neutralisations'. By this selfless action, he enabled all the casualties to be extracted and the bodies recovered. Yet even this was not the end of Hughes' courage. The REST had detected a further four VOIEDs in the immediate vicinity. Hughes set about disposing of them too – just as he had done to more than eighty similar devices over the previous five months of his tour of duty.

His GC was announced on 18 March 2010 – one day ahead of when it was formally published in the *London Gazette* – when the citation ended: 'Dealing with any form of IED is dangerous; to deal with 7 VOIEDs linked in a single circuit, in a mass casualty scenario, using manual neutralisation techniques once, never mind 3 times, is the single most outstanding act of explosive ordnance disposal ever recorded in Afghanistan. That he did it without the security of specialist protective clothing serves even more to demonstrate his outstanding gallantry. Hughes is unequivocally deserving of the highest level of public recognition.'

After the news of his GC and his courage was made public, Hughes said that the thought of being killed had not entered his head. 'You are always thinking one step ahead. Thinking you are going to die doesn't cross your mind. You just crack on and get on with it.' Colonel Stuart Archer and Major Pete Norton, both awarded the GC for equally hazardous bomb disposal work, were present when the Ministry of Defence announced the award for Hughes and the posthumous award for Staff Sergeant Olaf 'Oz' Schmid. Hughes' father, Barry, and four comrades joined him for the 'awesome' day of the GC announcement.

Hughes received his decoration from the Queen at an investiture at Buckingham Palace in June. After the ceremony, he said of his GC: 'When you do your training, you don't think you'll get recognition like this. We're just out there doing our job: to get this is outstanding. I accept it on behalf of all the other operators in Afghanistan.' His mother, Frances, brother, Sergeant Lee Hughes, and sister-in-law, Emma Hughes, joined him at the investiture.

In an interview at Marlborough Barracks in Warwickshire, Hughes disclosed to me that on his last day 'on the ground', before the incident for which he was primarily awarded the GC, he had been injured in an explosion working with the Danish Battle Group. On that occasion, prior to his rest and recuperation (R&R) back in the UK, a VOIED had initiated directly under Hughes as he sat in an armoured personnel carrier. He was knocked unconscious, injured his leg, had a perforated eardrum and suffered concussion, the latter resulting in his R&R being brought forward after he was 'casevaced' in a US Black Hawk helicopter to Camp Bastion.

His first day back 'on the ground' after R&R was when his eleven-man team came across the terrible scenes of dead and injured servicemen on 16 August 2009 near Sangin.

We had gone out on patrol from FOB [Forward Operating Base] Jackson with 2 Rifles. It was just before first light and we had been briefed that we had to clear a route. Guys were patrolling forward when the first explosion took place. We were about 100 metres back at the time. My search team then got a request to clear an HLS [helicopter landing site] but once they had done that a second explosion took place within five to ten minutes. We heard there were casualties and we got called forward. As soon as we got there, I went forward with two [IED] searchers leaving the rest of the team behind. I just had my body armour and helmet on. Straight away I could see a fallen soldier who was dead. Then I could see the carnage – bodies and soldiers all over the place and a young female medic was screaming. The two searchers then started finding the devices [unexploded IEDs], initially three in close proximity to the injured soldiers. For me, it was just a case of cracking on and rendering the devices safe. When there is a 'Category A' situation – a grave and immediate threat to life – you just have to get on with it. There wasn't the time to get a bomb suit on or send a robot down the road. The priority was to get the casualties out.

I was faced with a device and I had to make an assessment of how it worked. I was able to uncover parts of the device to see the key components and then make them safe. I tackled them one by one: each had a main charge of about twenty kilos. To be brutally honest, if I had got something wrong I wouldn't have known about it [because he would have been dead], which in a sick sort of way is the beauty of it. The search team then found another two devices and I found another two, so I dealt with seven in all. The whole task was completed in about forty-five minutes. Eventually, we learnt that all seven devices were linked to one circuit, which we hadn't seen before.

Hughes said that the Taliban tactic of using IEDs is hard to combat.

We are fighting an enemy we can't see. When we move on from an area, they move back in and place IEDs but that is the nature of the beast over there. The part that keeps me going is that I am achieving something by helping the Battle Group and the troops out on the ground. To see the faces of the troops when you rock up is great – it's like the cavalry has arrived. They are very appreciative of what we do. But there are down days too – notably when we lost four of our [bomb disposal] guys in fifteen months.

We are all very, very close and so it's hard to lose mates – people who feel like family. It's horrendous really.

Hughes has a son Jack, aged four, from a previous relationship, while his girlfriend, Corporal Kelly O'Connor, also works for the RLC as a driver with a bomb disposal team. Hughes is currently training high-threat IEDD operators. Aged thirty-one, he expects to serve at least another two six-month tours in Afghanistan over the next four years. Hughes, who was promoted to warrant officer class 2 (WO2) in the summer of 2010, admitted that this prospect is a formidable challenge: 'It's tough out there – it's a war zone. But it's my job: that's what I am paid to do.'

OLAF SEAN GEORGE SCHMID
Rank/title: Staff Sergeant
Unit/occupation: Royal Logistic Corps
DATE OF BRAVERY: JUNE–OCTOBER 2009
GAZETTED: 19 MARCH 2010

Olaf Schmid was born in Truro, Cornwall, on 19 June 1979. The elder of two sons with an older stepbrother, he was the son of a German mother and a Swedish father who had moved to Cornwall to own and run a hotel. Young Schmid attended Polwhele School and Penair School, both in Truro, and became head chorister at Truro Cathedral in 1993. He left school at sixteen and first worked as a chef serving with the Royal Logistic Corps (RLC). However, he later took an interest in bomb disposal work and was posted to 11 Explosive Ordnance Disposal Regiment, RLC. He was deployed to Northern Ireland, Bosnia, Sierra Leone and the Falklands, working his way up from an ammunition technician. In addition, he became commando- and paratrooper-trained. Married in 2007 and with a young stepson, he passed his high-threat improvised explosive device disposal (IEDD) course in 2008, which qualified him to operate in Afghanistan. His second deployment to Afghanistan was as a staff sergeant with 821 Squadron Alpha Troop, which provides the bomb disposal capability for Special Forces.

Schmid, who was known to his comrades as 'Oz', went to Helmand Province in June 2009 at the time when Taliban activity against the British forces was at a peak. The threat of IEDs had increased by some 400 per cent compared with eighteen months earlier. Schmid deployed during Operation Panther's Claw and immediately went into the fray in what the Army described as one of 'the most physically draining, mentally intense and hazardous jobs in Helmand'. Schmid usually had to deploy on foot which meant he rarely had the luxury of using remote-controlled vehicles, while the intense heat meant he often decided against wearing specialist protective clothing. He spent long periods in close proximity to victim operated improvised explosive devices (VOIEDs), meaning he was constantly in great personal danger. During his five months in Helmand, Schmid responded to forty-two IED tasks (alerts) and personally dealt with seventy confirmed IEDs.

On numerous occasions, Schmid showed quite exceptional courage to help his comrades, but three incidents perhaps stand out from the rest. An infantry company based in Wishtan Province became isolated by a substantial minefield and the infamous Pharmacy Road, the only resupply route, was blocked by two vehicles that had been blown up by IEDs. Intelligence, first-hand experience and unexplained explosions indicated the whole area was laced with IEDs. Schmid started work at 8 a.m. on 9 August 2009 in temperatures of 45 degrees C. It took him just 100 metres to find and clear the first IED. When he was within 100 metres of the two vehicles, he decided to use remote controlled vehicles (RCVs) and remote explosive clearance devices. One RCV hit an IED and was destroyed yet Schmid pressed forward well inside the lethal arc of the device and manually placed explosive charges, clearing a route to within five metres of the abandoned vehicles. Schmid's team then moved to clear a compound adjacent to the two vehicles in order to drag them off the road. After a second IED was found, Schmid made a second manual approach and quickly disposed of the device. A fresh approach was made – using explosives – so that the two vehicles could be dragged clear. It was Schmid who painstakingly cleared the route up to both vehicles during a one-hour stint in which he used only his eyesight and his knowledge of enemy tactics. Schmid decided against explosive clearance and instead put heavy chains on the stricken vehicles, which were likely to be booby-trapped, to drag them clear. As the light faded, Schmid then led a high-risk clearance of the road where the vehicles had been, manually disposing of two further IEDs. The entire clearance took eleven physically, mentally and emotionally draining hours, but the road was finally reopened and the company resupplied. The success of the operation was largely due to one courageous, selfless man: Olaf Schmid.

On 8 October 2009, Schmid was dispatched to Sangin District Centre to deal with an unexploded artillery shell reported by Afghan National Army (ANA) troops. On arrival, Schmid was led directly to the device where he realised that he, the soldiers and civilians in the bustling bazaar were all in great danger. The danger intensified when Schmid assessed that it was a radio-controlled IED which meant there was a strong likelihood that the enemy was watching and a bomber was choosing when to detonate it. Schmid immediately decided to neutralise the bomb manually – a tactic only to be employed in the gravest circumstances and at huge risk to the operator. Schmid, whose action was a success, had put his own life on the line again to save the lives of numerous Afghan civilians.

By the end of October, Schmid was involved in an operation near Forward Operating Base (FOB) Jackson, which was in Battle Group North's area. On 31 October 2009, Schmid had already dealt with three IEDs when a searcher discovered a command wire running down the alleyway they were using.

Schmid and his team were trapped in the alleyway, not knowing in which direction the IED had been placed. Schmid seized the initiative and eventually traced the wire to a complex command-wire IED which incorporated three linked and buried main charges. As he dealt with the device, it exploded, killing him. He had sacrificed his life – aged thirty – for the sake of his comrades.

There are many outstanding tributes in this book to many worthy GC recipients. But the tributes to Staff Sergeant Olaf 'Oz' Schmid from his commanding officers and comrades are not only hard for anyone to match, but they also come from the heart. Perhaps the most moving of all came from Lieutenant Colonel Robert Thomson, the Commanding Officer of 2 Rifles Battle Group, who said:

> Staff Sergeant Oz Schmid was simply the bravest and most courageous man I have ever met. Under relentless IED and small-arms attacks he stood taller than the tallest. He opened the Pharmacy Road and, twenty-four hours later, found thirty-one IEDs in one go on route Sparta. Every single company in 2 Rifles adored working with him. I adored working with him. No matter how difficult or lethal the task which lay in front of us, he was the man who only saw solutions. He saved lives in 2 Rifles time after time and for that he will retain a very special place in every heart of every Rifleman in our extraordinary Battle Group. Superlatives do not do the man justice. Better than the best. Better than the best of the best.

Christina Schmid, the victim's widow and the mother of his five-year-old stepson Laird, said after her husband's death: 'Oz was a phenomenal husband and loving father who was cruelly murdered on his last day of a relentless five-month tour. He was my best friend and soulmate. The pain of losing him is overwhelming. I take comfort knowing he saved countless lives with his hard work. I am so proud of him.'

Mrs Schmid became hugely respected nationwide with her show of defiance when Schmid's remains were flown back to Britain and his coffin was paraded through Wootton Bassett, Wiltshire. She stood in the High Street and, as the hearse carrying his coffin passed the war memorial, mouthed: 'Love you, love you. You've been the best dad and you've done so, so well. I'm so proud of you.' She then applauded her late husband.

In an interview with the *Guardian* newspaper on 14 November 2009, Mrs Schmid revealed that shortly before her husband died she had had a dream – a nightmare. Her husband had appeared in her dream clearly in serious trouble. He was saying: 'I need some help, help me.' He had been killed on his last day in the field and had been due home a week later.

On 24 November 2009, more than 1,000 family, friends, comrades and admirers attended the funeral service for Schmid at Truro Cathedral. Mrs Schmid said her husband had believed in 'traditional warrior values' and had wanted to protect the country he loved. 'Olaf lived and stood for something he believed in. And in the end he paid the ultimate sacrifice for those beliefs. Please do not allow him to die in vain.'

Schmid's GC was announced on 18 March 2010 – one day ahead of it being formally published in the *London Gazette* – when the citation ended: 'His selfless gallantry, his devotion to duty, and his indefatigable courage displayed time and time again saved countless military and civilian lives and is worthy of the highest recognition.'

Mrs Schmid, from Winchester, Hampshire, received a framed copy of this citation at a presentation in London also attended by Staff Sergeant Kim Hughes, her late husband's fellow new GC. She described the decoration as 'a legendary award for my legendary husband'. She added: 'I am as proud of my husband as he was magnificent and I'm truly thrilled. The George Cross is a fitting tribute to decorate Oz for his outstanding bravery. It is a fantastic, positive reminder of what he achieved. Oz would be really, really proud . . .'

In May 2010, Mrs Schmid presented a *Panorama* television programme, *A Very British Hero*, which questioned whether the Army had failed in its duty of care to her late husband. She gave an insight into the desperation of her weary husband as he neared the end of his tour. She said he was 'flaking' and had suffered from the 'absolutely relentless' demands of his job in Afghanistan. In the programme, she revealed the contents of a letter from her husband written shortly before he died. It read: 'Staying alive is like a lottery and patrolling the Afghan badlands is playing Russian roulette with your feet.'

Mrs Schmid was not alone in her concern about the pressures put on high-threat IEDD operators. On the very day that *Panorama* was broadcast, Colonel Bob Seddon, the head of the Army's bomb disposal squad, revealed that he was resigning over his concerns that financial cutbacks had left his men overstretched to deal with some 250 IEDs a month in Helmand Province. Colonel Seddon, who was head of 11 EOS (Explosive Ordnance Disposal) Regiment, was worried his men would face long-term health risks. 'I'm very concerned that some of my people who have done phenomenally difficult and dangerous work in Afghanistan may pay a deeper psychological price.'

In June 2010, Mrs Schmid received her husband's GC from the Queen at Buckingham Palace. She was accompanied to the private ceremony by her now six-year-old son – formally recorded as Master Laird Schmid – and her parents. Afterwards, Mrs Schmid released a statement quoting Thucydides, the Greek historian: 'The bravest are surely those who have the clearest vision of what is before them, glory and danger alike, and yet notwithstanding, go out to meet it.'

She added: 'The George Cross serves as a reminder of all the endurance and sacrifice of all our servicemen and women out there on the ground now. In heralding and awarding Oz, one soldier, I hope it serves to raise the status of each and every one of them. To have seen him receive this award in person would have been a wonderful experience. The image of him pointing to it on his chest and grinning cheekily would have brought tears of pride.'

In an interview with me after she received her husband's posthumous award, Mrs Schmid described how she was so determined to show pride and defiance – rather than break down in tears – when her husband's body was repatriated to Britain. 'It was an absolute promise to Oz. He had told me numerous times during his last tour that the likelihood was he was not coming back. When we moved house during the tour, he even said: "Don't unpack my stuff. The likelihood is that I am not coming back." He also said: "Will you go to Wootton Bassett if I come in [dead]? I want you to stand there and be bloody proud that I am your husband and that you supported me in all the adversity. Even if I am blown up, I want you to show that our love has not been blown up." And I said: "Yes. I will be there." I was there [at Wootton Bassett] because I wanted to celebrate his life – and let him go with love. I didn't want to be put in a box of "grieving wife". Oz was not an "average operator" and I was not going to be an "average wife". So I stood there defiantly and showed Oz love beyond the grave. I felt it was my duty to Oz.'

Mrs Schmid said she was incredibly proud to read the tributes to her late husband from his comrades and officers. 'For [Lieutenant Colonel] Rob Thomson to say Oz was simply "the bravest man I have ever met" just beggared belief. But his comments hit the nail on the head: they were very touching. I knew my husband and if he was tasked with something, he was determined to succeed at it.'

She said the passing of time made it harder, not easier, to come to terms with her husband's death. The couple had been planning a new life in Schmid's home county of Cornwall before he was killed. 'I still feel this immense love for him. I am under no illusion that he is dead and gone – and I treated him as if he was almost dead when I dropped him off [for his last tour]. But I just feel so sad that he can't continue to be a father to Lairdy and that he can't be the husband that he enjoyed being. He had said to me: "Men walk away with medals but I just want to walk away with my life – and my legs – from this tour." But it was not to be. I will never take my wedding ring off. He was my soulmate and I will love him for ever.'

APPENDIX I

The George Cross was instituted by a Royal Warrant of 24 September 1940, and was published in the *London Gazette* on 31 January 1941:

GEORGE RI

GEORGE VI, by the Grace of God, of Great Britain, Ireland and the British Dominions beyond the Seas, King, Defender of the Faith, Emperor of India, to all to whom these Presents shall come.

GREETINGS!

Whereas by a Warrant under Our Sign Manual dated the twenty-fourth of September, one thousand nine hundred and forty, We, having taken into Our Royal consideration the many acts of heroism performed both by male and by female persons, especially during the present war and wishing to honour those who perform such deeds, did institute and create a new Decoration to be styled and designated 'The George Cross', which we desired should be highly prized and eagerly sought after:

And whereas We deem it expedient that the seventh clause of Our aforesaid Warrant should be amended:

Now therefore We do hereby declare that the rules and ordinances contained in Our said Warrant shall be abrogated, cancelled and annulled, and in substitution thereof We by these Presents of Us, Our Heirs and Successors are graciously pleased to make, or ordain and establish the following rules and ordinances for the governance of the same which shall from henceforth be inviolably observed and kept.

First: It is ordained that the Decoration shall be designated and styled 'The George Cross'.

Secondly: It is ordained that the Decoration shall consist of a plain cross with four equal limbs, the cross having in the centre a circular medallion bearing a design showing St George and the Dragon, that the inscription 'For Gallantry' shall appear round this medallion, and in the angle of each limb of the cross the Royal cypher 'G.VI' forming a circle concentric with the medallion, that the reverse of the Cross shall be plain and bear the name of the recipient and the date of the award, that the Cross shall be suspended by a ring from a bar adorned with laurel leaves, and that the whole shall be in silver.

Thirdly: It is ordained that the persons eligible for the Decoration of the Cross shall be

(1) Our faithful subjects and persons under Our protection in civil life, male and female, of Our United Kingdom of Great Britain and Northern Ireland, India, Burma, Our Colonies, and of Territories under Our Suzerainty, Protection or Jurisdiction,

(2) Persons of any rank in the Naval, Military or Air Forces of Our United Kingdom of Great Britain and Northern Ireland, of India, of Burma, or Our Colonies, and of Territories under Our Suzerainty, Protection or Jurisdiction, including the Home Guard and in India members of Frontier Corps and Military Police and members of Indian States' Forces and in Burma members of the Burma Frontier Force and Military Police, and including also the military Nursing Services and the Women's Auxiliary Services,

(3) Our faithful subjects and persons under Our protection in civil life, male and female, within, and members of the Naval, Military or Air Forces belonging to, any other part of Our Dominions, Our Government whereof has signified its desire that the Cross should be awarded under the provisions of this Our Warrant, and any Territory being administered by Us in such Government.

The Cross is intended primarily for civilians and award in Our military services is to be confined to actions for which purely military Honours are not normally granted.

Fourthly: It is ordained that awards shall be made only on a recommendation to Us, for civilians by Our Prime Minister and First Lord of the Treasury, and for Officers and members of Our Naval, Military or Air Forces, as described in the previous Clause of this Our Warrant, only on a recommendation by Our First Lord of the Admiralty, Our Secretary of State for War or Our Secretary of State for Air, as the case may be.

Fifthly: It is ordained that the Cross shall be awarded only for acts of the greatest heroism or of the most conspicuous courage in circumstances of extreme danger, and that the Cross may be awarded posthumously.

Sixthly: It is ordained that every recommendation for the award of the Cross shall be submitted with such description and conclusive proof as the circumstances of the case will allow, and attestation of the act as the Minister or Ministers concerned may think requisite.

Seventhly: It is ordained that the Cross shall be worn by recipients on the left breast suspended from a ribbon one and a quarter inches in width, of dark blue, that it shall be worn immediately after the Victoria Cross and in front of the Insignia of all British

361

Orders of Chivalry, and that on those occasions when only the ribbon is worn, a replica in silver of the Cross in miniature shall be affixed to the centre of the ribbon.

Provided that when the Cross is worn by a woman, it may be worn on the left shoulder, suspended from a ribbon of the same width and colour, fashioned into a bow.

Eighthly: It is ordained that the award of the George Cross shall entitle the recipient on all occasions when the use of such letters is customary, to have placed after his or her names the letters 'GC'.

Ninthly: It is ordained that an action which is worthy of recognition by the award of the Cross, but is performed by one upon whom the Decoration has been conferred, may be recorded by the award of a Bar to be attached to the ribbon by which the Cross is suspended, that for each such additional award an additional Bar shall be added, and that for each Bar awarded a replica in silver of the Cross in miniature, in addition to the emblem already worn, shall be added to the ribbon when worn alone.

Tenthly: It is ordained that the names of all those upon or on account of whom We may be pleased to confer or present the Cross, or a Bar to the Cross, shall be published in the *London Gazette*, and that a Register of such names shall be kept in the Central Chancery of the Orders of Knighthood.

Eleventhly: It is ordained that from the date of this Our Warrant, the grant of the Medal of the Order of the British Empire, for Gallantry, which was instituted and created by His late Majesty King George the Fifth, shall cease, and a recipient of that Medal, living at the date of this Our Warrant, shall return it to the Central Chancery of the Orders of Knighthood and become instead a holder of the George Cross: provided that there shall be a similar change in relation to any posthumous grant of the Medal of the Order of the British Empire, for Gallantry, made since the commencement of the present war.

Twelfthly: It is ordained that reproductions of the Cross, known as a Miniature Cross, which may be worn on certain occasions by those to whom the Decoration is awarded shall be half the size of the George Cross.

Thirteenthly: It is ordained that it shall be competent for Us, our Heirs and Successors by an Order under Our Sign Manual and on a recommendation to that effect by or through Our Prime Minister and First Lord of the Treasury, Our First Lord of the Admiralty, Our Secretary of State for War, or Our Secretary of State for Air, as the case may be, to cancel and annul the award to any person of the George Cross and that thereupon the name of such person in the Register shall be erased: provided that it shall be competent for Us, Our Heirs and Successors to restore the Decoration so forfeited when such recommendation has been withdrawn.

Lastly: We reserve to Ourself, our Heirs Successors, full power at annulling, altering, abrogating, augmenting, interpreting, or dispensing with these rules and ordinances, or any part thereof, by a notification under Our Sign Manual.

Given at Our Court at St. James's, the twenty-fourth of September, one thousand nine hundred and forty, in the fourth year of Our Reign.

By His Majesty's Command,
Winston S. Churchill.

APPENDIX II

Recipients of other awards who have been eligible to have their decorations converted to the George Cross.

Albert Medal (AM):

Abbott, Edmund Geoffrey
Abbott, George Fawcett Pitts
Allen, Florence Alice
Armytage, Reginald William
Ashburnham, Doreen Winifred

Bagot, Arthur Gerald
Bain Smith, George Stewart
Bastian, Gordon Love
Brown, Richard
Bryson, Oliver Campbell
Buckle, Henry
Butson, Arthur Richard Cecil

Cannon, Horace James
Chalmers, Jack
Cleall, Walter Charles
Cowley, John Guise (later Sir John)

Davis, Thomas Neil
Day, Harry Melville Arbuthnot

Ellis, Bernard George
Evans, David Hywel

Fairclough, John
Farrow, Kenneth
Feetham, Christopher
Ford, Albert
Fraser, Harriet Elizabeth (later Mrs Barry)

Gibbons, John Edward
Gibbs, Stanley Frederick
Goad, William
Gregson, John Sedgwick

Harwood, Harrie Stephen
Hawkins, Eynon
Hay, David George Montagu (later the Marquess of Tweeddale)
Howarth, Albert
Hutchison, Albert James

Kavanaugh, Robert Murray
Keogh, Michael Sullivan
Knowlton, Richard John

Lowe, Alfred Raymond
Lynch, Joseph

Maxwell-Hyslop, Alexander Henry
May, Phillip Robert Stephen
McAloney, William Simpson
McCarthy, William Henry Debonnaire
McCormack, Thomas William
Miles, Alfred
Mitchell, John Henry

Newman, Alfred William

Oliver, Dick

Rackham, Geoffrey
Reeves, James Arthur
Rhoades, William Ernest
Richards, Richard Walter
Ridling, Randolph Gordon
Riley, Geoffrey
Robertson, Paul Douglas

Spoors, Robert
Stanners, John George

Vaughan, Margaret (later Mrs Purves)

Walker, Charles Henry
Walton, Eric William Kevin
Watson, Victor Albert
Western, David Charles
Williams, Sidney
Wolsey, Hilda Elizabeth

Edward Medal (EM):

Allport, Ernest

Baker, John Thomas
Baldwin, Wilson Charles Geoffrey
Baster, Norman
Baxter, William Frederick
Beaman, George William
Blackburn, Sydney

Booker, David Noel
Booker, Samuel
Brown, David

Charlton, John Daniel
Clarke, Azariah
Craig, Bert
Crosby, Bertram Frederick

Darker, Richard Edward
Dixon, John

Edwards, Arthur Frederick

Fisher, Bernard
Fletcher, Donald
Flintoff, Henry Harwood

Gough, John Ingram

Haller, Fred
Harris, Charles Thomas
Havercroft, Percy Roberts
Heslop, George Christopher
Hulme, Thomas
Hutchinson, John

Jameson, Thomas
Johnston, James
Jones, Benjamin Littler

Kent, Ernest William
King, Richard Henry

Lee, Walter Holroyd
Little, Robert Stead
Lloyd, William
Locke, George

Manwaring, Thomas George
McCabe, John
Meadows, Albert John
Morris, Alfred Ernest

Nix, Frank Emery

Pearson, Robert
Pollitt, James
Purvis, James Sidney

Robinson, Harry

Saunders, Robert Benjamin
Schofield, Carl Mallinson
Shanley, Joseph
Shepherd, John William Hersey
Smith, Charles
Soulsby, Oliver
Sykes, Frank

Temperley, Samuel Jarrett
Thomas, Arthur Devere
Thomas, Thomas Derwydd
Thompson, Matthew
Tyler, Albert

Wastie, Granville Charles
Waterson, William
Weller, John

Weller, Percy Barnard
Whitehead, Thomas Atkinson
Wilcox, Charles
Williams, Osmond
Wilson, Harry

Yates, Philip William
Young, Archibald
Younger, William

Empire Gallantry Medal (EGM):

Adamson, George John
Alder, Thomas Edward
Ali Bey, Yusuf Hussein
Anderson, Frederick Christie
Anderson, Walter
Andrews, Wallace Lancelot
Arnold, Walter
Ashraf-un-Nisa
Atkinson, Thomas

Barnett, William
Barraclough, Arnold
Bayley, Clive Cyril Anthony
Beattie, John Gray
Bell, John Frederick
Blackburn, Richard
Blogg, Henry George
Bogdanovich, Theodore
Bonar, Eric Watt
Brett, Douglas Alexander
Brooks, Arthur
Burke, John Lewis Victor
Burton, Herbert Edgar

Button, William John

Campion, Michael Patrick
Chalmers, Robert Mills
Chant, Frederick
Charrington, Harold Francis
Child, Frederick William Henry Maurice
Clark, Joseph
Close, Gerald Charles Neil
Cobham, Anthony John
Crossley, Edwin

d'Souza, Baptista Joseph
Deedes, Richard
Douglas, Robert Ewing
Duffin, Charles Godfrey

Elston, Ernest Matthew

Farr, John Henry
Fattah, Rashid Abdul
Fleming, William George
Frost, Ernest Ralph Clyde

Golandaz, Abdus Samid Abdul Wahid
Graveley, Reginald Cubitt

Hand, William George
Harrison, George Willet
Hemeida, El Amin Effendi
Henderson, Herbert Reuben
Henshaw, George
Hodge, Alexander Mitchell
Humphreys, Patrick Noël

Idris, Taha

Jamieson, William
Jolly, Richard Frank

Kelly, Cecil Francis
Khalifa, Muhammad
Khan, Pir

Low, John Niven Angus
Lungley, Alfred Herbert

Mahoney, Herbert John
Maltby, Reginald Henry
March, Frederick Hamilton
Mata Din
McAvoy, Thomas
McCabe, John
McClymont, John McIntosh
McKechnie, William Neil
McTeague, Thomas Patrick
Miller, Henry James
Miller, Thomas Frank
Mirghany, Ahmed Muhammad
Mohi-ud-Din, Ghulam
Morteshed, Francis Austin
Mott, Joseph Edward
Muhammad, Muhammad Abdulla

Naughton, Frank
Negib, Ibrahim
Niven, George Paterson

O'Hagen, Leo Francis
Omara, Edwardo

Orr, Samuel
O'Shea, John Michael

Parker, Edward Donald
Pearson, Joan Daphne Mary

Reynolds, Edward Womersley
Rimmer, Reginald
Rodriques, George David

Sewell, Stanley William
Singh, Baldev
Singh, Barkat
Singh, Bhim Yadava
Singh, Bhupendra Narayan (Rajah of Barwari)
Singh, Rangit

Stewart, James Ernest
Stoves, John William
Sylvester, William George

Taha, El Jak Effendi
Talbot, Ellis Edward Arthur Chetwynd
Tandy-Green, Charles William
Taylor, Patrick Gordon (later Sir Gordon)
Thapa, Nandlal

Thomas, Dorothy Louise
Tollemache, Anthony Henry Hamilton
Townsend, Emma José
Troake, Frederick Henry
Turner, James Gordon Melville
Tutton, Cyril James

Waterfield, Albert

Wild, Robert
Wiltshire, Sidney Noel
Winter, Gerald

Yar, Ahmed
Yehia, El Imam

SELECT BIBLIOGRAPHY

Bisset, Ian, *The George Cross*, MacGibbon & Kee, London, 1961

Croucher, Matt, *Bulletproof*, Century, London, 2009

Doherty, Richard, *The Thin Green Line: A History of the Royal Ulster Constabulary GC 1922–2001*, Pen & Sword Military, Barnsley, 2004

Durrani, M. K., *The Sixth Column*, Cassell, London, 1955

Frayn Turner, John, *Awards of the George Cross 1940–2005*, Pen & Sword Military, Barnsley, 2006

Gledhill, Tony, *A Gun At My Head: The George Cross, East End Gunmen and Thirty Years in Blue*, Historic Military Press, Storrington, 2006

Hebblethwaite, Marion, *One Step Further: Those whose gallantry was rewarded with the George Cross*, Volumes 1–9, Chameleon HH Publishing Ltd, Witney, 2007

Kinne, Derek, *The Wooden Boxes*, Frederick Muller, London, 1955

Ottaway, Susan, *Violette Szabo: 'The Life That I Have . . .'*, Pen & Sword Military, Barnsley, 2004

Ryder, Chris, *The RUC: A Force Under Fire*, Methuen, London, 1989

Smyth, John, *The Story of the George Cross*, Arthur Barker, London, 1968

Spooner, Tony, *Faith, Hope and Malta GC*, Newton Publishers, Swindon, 1992

Stanistreet, Allan, *Gainst All Disaster: Gallant Deeds Above and Beyond the Call of Duty*, Picton Publishing, Chippenham, 1986

The Register of the George Cross, This England Books, Cheltenham, 1985

The Victoria Cross & George Cross, Imperial War Museum, London, 1970

INDEX

Note: Recipients of the George Cross are shown in bold. Page references in italics refer to appendix entries.

VICTORIA CROSS HEROES

MICHAEL ASHCROFT

The Victoria Cross is Britain's most prestigious military honour, awarded for valour in the presence of the enemy. It has been bestowed only 1356 times, proving the recipients' bravery beyond all doubt – always facing mortal danger, sometimes a certain death.

Since he was a boy Michael Ashcroft has been fascinated by the VC and by the daring circumstances in which each medal was won. He has assembled the single largest collection of VCs in the world, each bought specifically because of the holder's particular selfless action and incredible story.

Including a foreword by HRH The Prince of Wales, the President of the Victoria Cross and George Cross Association, this book is a moving testament to the many brave servicemen who have been awarded the Victoria Cross over the last 150 years. Their stories should not go unheard.

NON-FICTION / MILITARY HISTORY 978 0 7553 1633 5

SPECIAL FORCES HEROES

MICHAEL ASHCROFT

From the Cockleshell Heroes' daring 1942 raid deep into Nazi-occupied Europe, to the rescue of hostages from the clutches of terrorists at the Iranian Embassy in 1980, to the dangerous sorties into enemy territory during the Gulf wars, the actions of Britain's Special Forces truly epitomise heroism.

Fascinated by bravery ever since he was a boy, Michael Ashcroft set about assembling what is believed to be the largest private collection of British Special Forces medals in the world. Here he traces the origins of these elite fighting units, as well as detailing the action-packed accounts behind over forty medals, recognising the astonishing valour and ingenuity British servicemen have displayed time and time again.

Special Forces Heroes is a much-deserved tribute to the countless extraordinary feats performed by countless extraordinary men.

NON-FICTION / MILITARY HISTORY 978 0 7553 1808 7